ROME:
LIVING UNDER THE AXIS

A Look Back at a Turbulent Time in History
Through the Letters of a Young Seminarian
and Future Archbishop
1936-1940

Archbishop Philip M. Hannan

St. Andrew's Productions

THIS BOOK IS DEDICATED TO:

My parents, to whom I wrote the letters, and especially my mother for saving them.

Emily Kulchyski, my secretary, for her indefatigable efforts in compiling and organizing the letters.

ISBN: 1-891903-32-2
Copyright © 2003 by *St. Andrew's Productions*
All Rights Reserved

Published by:
St. Andrew's Productions
6091 Steubenville Pike
McKees Rocks, PA 15136

Phone: (412) 787-9735, (412) 787-9754
Fax: (412) 787-5204
Web: www.SaintAndrew.com

ABOUT THE AUTHOR

Archbishop Philip M. Hannan was born on May 20, 1913, in Washington, D.C., a member of St. Matthew's parish (later the Cathedral). He attended the Immaculate Conception Elementary School, St. John's College High School, St. Charles Seminary in Catonsville, and the Catholic University in Washington, D.C., receiving an M.S. in philosophy in 1936. He attended the North American College in Rome from 1936 to June 1940, receiving an S.T.L. in 1940. He was ordained a priest in Rome on December 8, 1939. Later, he attended the Catholic University and received a doctorate in Canon Law in 1949.

He became a Chaplain in the U. S. Army in 1942, appointed to the Army Air Corps, and later volunteered for the 82nd Airborne Division in Europe, 1942-1946.

He was appointed the Vice Chancellor of the Archdiocese of Washington, D.C., in 1948 and later was the Chancellor and founding Editor of The Catholic Standard, the official paper of the Archdiocese. He was consecrated Auxiliary Bishop of Washington, D.C., on August 28, 1956. He gave the sermon at the Funeral of President John F. Kennedy and conducted the interment services of Senator Robert Kennedy and Jacqueline Kennedy Onassis at the Arlington Cemetery.

He was appointed the Archbishop of New Orleans on September 29, 1965 and retired on February 12, 1989.

INTRODUCTION

The reader should bear in mind that these letters were written to my family and were never intended to be published. They reveal the daily living of one writing of events to his family and do not reflect the inward, spiritual progression of a soul to his God.

Because I never wished to worry my mother and my family, I did not always give a fully accurate account of events. For instance, on the ship going to Rome in 1936, we met with a huge hurricane. In my desire not to worry my parents, I only referred to it as rough seas. "The boat pitched and rolled," etc.

Later, when the war clouds were brewing over Europe, I made an optimistic account of it, never wishing to overly concern them. I wrote of the events as they happened without being unduly alarmed or nervous, as you will read. I merely reported what I knew without dwelling on the danger.

Still later, when I became ill in 1940, I never told my family about my extreme illness, calling it only a cold – it was Rheumatic Fever, and I had a very serious case of it. I prayed intensely especially during the night of crisis. God heard my prayers and I am deeply grateful. The doctor in Rome himself declared it (perhaps not critically) to be a miracle. But I remain uncertain of this. The illness was completely cured and I have had no trace of it since that time.

Many years later following the death of my beloved mother, the letters were discovered in her possession. Stacks of 15 or 20 were bundled and tied together with ribbon. Some were replaced in the wrong envelopes and occasionally a page is missing. I have put them in order as well as possible with the help of my secretary, Emily Kulchyski, and I offer them to you for whatever they are worth. They are the thoughts and feelings of a young seminarian who is often overly critical, sometimes willful, occasionally humorous and always sincere. And also, hopefully, trying to fulfill the will of God.

PREFACE

The years preceding World War II, from 1936 to 1940, were turbulent, wracked with sharply opposed factions in politics and philosophies. The situation in Europe, including Great Britain, was markedly different from that in the United States.

In Europe, an apt description of the situation was the great phrase later used by Sir Winston Churchill, "The Gathering Storm." Adolph Hitler had seized power in 1933 in a divided Germany and was ruthlessly consolidating the power of the Nazi regime, fanaticizing every generation from the *Hitler Jugend* to the retirees impoverished by the terms of the Versailles Treaty at the end of World War I. The chaotic economy suffered an inflation that finally produced a currency with one million Mark bills. For a long time I carried one of them in my slender pocket book to explain to fellow Americans in Europe the appeal of Hitler to a large part of the German nation.

At the other end of Europe, Communism had produced the Soviet Union, which under Josef Stalin had effectively enslaved Russia and was boasting that it would conquer the world. While Hitler was proclaiming the exaltation of the German *Volk*, Stalin was claiming the conquest by the Proletariat, the rule of the common man. Communism freed the people from the "shackles of religion" and converted the splendid churches into museums of atheism and warehouses of food and other supplies. Patriarchs, Bishops and clergy of the Orthodox Church and the Eastern Rites of the Catholic Church were killed or condemned to the "archipelago" of concentration camps throughout the Soviet Union.

These two opposite and aggressive ideologies were fiercely contending for support throughout Europe. They clashed fiercely in Spain where General Francisco Franco led the largely Catholic forces against the largely Communist Republican forces. The Lincoln Brigade, recruited in the United States, fought for the Republican forces with the moral support of a substantial section of the American people. Most of the Americans, influenced by the press, saw the Republican forces as fighters for "democracy" and opposed to the "anti-democratic" forces of Franco.

Despite the interest in the Spanish War, most Americans were concerned only with issues in the U.S. The U.S. had suffered from a disastrous drought with ghastly pictures of balls of tumbleweeds blowing across the scorched fields of Arkansas and Oklahoma. Ford jalopies, filled with poverty-stricken and despairing farm families, fled the drought en route to California. Concomitantly, the financial crash of 1929 imposed a serious challenge to the Presidency of Franklin D. Roosevelt to bring the U.S. out of the Depression.

Many Washingtonians nurtured bitter memories of the plight of the Bonus Marchers — unemployed veterans of World War I who came, in 1932, to demand early payment of their promised grants. They erected a shantytown in the flats of Anacostia, the section across the Anacostia River, and were rudely evicted by the Army under the direction of General Douglas MacArthur whose aide was Major Dwight Eisenhower. The Army burned down the shantytown, unfortunately with the loss of some lives. The neighbors did not blame the Army, acting under orders, but the Government of President Herbert Hoover.

Roosevelt responded vigorously, imposing a moratorium on the banks and stimulating the economy by a variegated series of measures. The Volstead Act, imposing Prohibition, was reduced by legalizing 3-percent beer which ended by a repeal of the "noble experiment". The famous New Deal of initiatives, including the NRLA (National Labor Relations Act) and the WPA (Works Progress Administration), gave varied jobs, such as building the Skyline Drive in Virginia, building of parks and community projects including artwork in public buildings by impecunious artists, and many jobs for the crowds of unemployed and restless youth.

International trade, as well as domestic business, was jacked up by devaluing the dollar and going off the gold standard. This caused some major rifts in the Democratic Party including the condemnation by Governor Alfred Smith, New York, of the "baloney dollar". A number of the new laws were declared unconstitutional by the conservative Supreme Court. Roosevelt retaliated by securing legislation to increase the membership of the Court (his famous "packing the Court") and with the aid of the new members created a new Court. The new Court regularly upheld the "Roosevelt" legislation.

The social legislation of Roosevelt included the Social Security Act to provide a "help" for the sustenance of the impoverished elderly and the laboring forces. The wife of the President, Eleanor, was a very efficient gadfly for support of the new legislation, publishing a daily press piece, My Day, which often produced ambivalent reactions. Even those who railed at it helped the publicity.

Meanwhile, news of the horrendous atrocities of the Nazis (culminating later in the Holocaust) began to circulate in the U.S. The insular foreign policy of our country began to be questioned and even condemned. The feelings of the extensive immigrant groups in our country gradually developed factions favoring or condemning the Nazis, Communists and Fascists in Europe. Senator Warren Nye became the stalwart champion of the isolationists who strongly opposed any participation "in a foreign war". The cry was that Hitler would never menace the U.S., and we "had no business meddling in Europe."

The isolationist sentiment was so strong that Roosevelt won re-election by a platform which pledged that the U.S. would not go to war. This did not stop the growing anxiety and alarm about the growth of Nazi power, which was substantially increased by the visit to Germany of Lindberg, who firmly stated the awesome strength of German military might, especially the air power, the Luftwaffe.

Naturally, the discussion led to a concern about the military strength of the U.S. The strength of the Army was ludicrous, having only about 50,000 troops early in the thirties; the Navy was much stronger, having a two-ocean Navy. Our air strength comprised only planes and pilots in the Army and Navy trained for their special needs. Of course, Roosevelt, despite his pledge, realized that the U.S. must eventually support England and its allies and sought to do this by the clever Lend-Lease program. This enabled the U.S. to lend finances and resources to England as well as to lease elements of our military to the Allies.

The manner in which the Lend-Lease program was realized was described by a cousin, in the Navy, who said while on leave, "I don't know what we mean by neutrality. We have been shooting at German submarines for a long time." It was a policy "more honored in the breach than in the observance" to quote Shakespeare.

These events had a pronounced effect on Americans according to their national and ethnic descent. The Jewish people were highly alarmed by the dreadful news they received from Germany. The Irish, English, German, Italian and Polish (Slavic) groups were very largely solidly against the Nazis and Communists. Of course, there were notable exceptions. Ambassador Joseph Kennedy was an outspoken isolationist, openly condemning any participation by the U.S. in the war and expressing that opinion to the Government and King of England. Roosevelt eventually replaced him.

The American Catholics, loyal to the teaching of the Holy Father, Pius XI, were strongly against Nazism and Fascism, and outstandingly against Communism. They were supportive of the condemnations by the Pope of Nazism, Fascism and Communism in three separate and penetrating documents. The most notable battlefield was the labor unions. Catholic priests on the staff of the National Catholic Welfare Conference, 1312 Massachusetts Avenue, N.W., Washington, D.C., and the Catholic universities, principally The Catholic University in Brookland, Washington, led a national struggle against the Communist infiltration of the labor unions.

Monsignor John A. Ryan was the leader in the field of social action, which not only condemned Communism but proclaimed the doctrine of the Church in social welfare. His dissertation for his doctorate at the University, "A Living Wage: Its Ethical and Economic Aspects", was the groundwork for later monumental documents as "Distributive Justice" and "Socialism: Promise or Menace?"

He was an enthusiastic New Dealer, becoming a member of the Industrial Appeals Board of the National Labor Relations Act. He considered the Fair Labor Standards Act the culmination of his life's work, and the National Labor Relations Act as the most important law for social relations and rights of workers in the history of the U.S.

Some of the actions of the Government in implementing the provisions of some of these laws were hotly contested by outstanding Catholic teachers. Monsignor Fulton Sheen, the legendary speaker, condemned the decision of the Government to slaughter pigs to maintain the economic balance of the nation. "Any decision to slaughter pigs at a time of poverty and hunger in our country and in the world is wrong." I was present at a subsequent lecture at The Catholic University when Monsignor John Ryan replied to "those who were friends of the little pigs."

Of course, Monsignor Ryan had many opponents to his "radical ideas" but was very successful in communicating them to every level of society. He gave an invocation at two of the Presidential Inaugurations of President Roosevelt. His teaching also won a wide audience among the Protestant workers who, with their Catholic counterparts, were poor or unemployed. He had a wide effect in the field of politics. His writings combined with government programs, as the electrification of the rural South, enhanced the Democratic Party and hurt the Republican Party. I remember an African-American friend, a political activist, saying, "I can't understand any fellow worker going to the polling booth with a loaf of bread in his hand and voting against Roosevelt."

Despite these concerns about the menace of Communism, the prevailing interest of the public was about economic recovery. My father, a plumbing contractor, tried desperately to secure enough work to keep his plumbers and laborers employed. The situation in Washington, D.C., was not so dire as in the industrial parts of the country because the Government was the largest employer and was engaged in establishing additional offices for the New Deal program. We lived near the "big houses"— the Duponts, Belmonts, etc. — on Massachusetts Avenue, which provided considerable work for maintaining the plumbing and other maintenance jobs. Nevertheless, my father would often talk about the demand for help made to the St. Vincent de Paul Society of our parish, St. Matthew's. Their charge was to provide help for every appeal; and they tried valiantly to redeem that pledge, my father frequently muttering, "I remember how much I needed help when I was a greenhorn (the name for Irish immigrants)."

Despite this prevalent concern about the Depression, the increasing war clouds over Europe received increasing attention. The Church in the U.S. was more concerned than the rest of the population because Hitler was bent on subjecting the nearby Catholic countries of Austria, Poland, and Czechoslovakia (because of the Sudeten section) and because of the heroic anti-Nazi stand of Catholic leaders in Germany like Cardinal Faulhaber of Munich. Cardinal Mundelein of Chicago supported his stand with the remark, "I understand that Hitler was a paper hanger, and I'm told a poor one." His stand was typical of the reaction of the American Catholic hierarchy.

Nevertheless, there was no great fear of an imminent war, and there was no hesitation on the part of Bishops to send seminarians to the North

American College in Rome. Consequently, when Archbishop Michael Curley of Baltimore (Washington was in the Archdiocese of Baltimore) stated matter-of-factly in 1936 that he would send some seminarians to Rome to join the other Archdiocesan seminarians there, it did not cause any surprise.

When the academic year of 1935-1936 ended in June at the Catholic University's Theological College, always called the Sulpician Seminary, we expected a couple of the Baltimore Archdiocesan seminarians to be sent to Rome. Later in the summer, I was delighted to receive the news that I was to be sent to the North American College for my theology courses. The other seminarian was Johnny Linn from Baltimore, a popular and very friendly student.

The news electrified my sister and older brothers (the two youngest brothers were pleased but confused), but my parents were subdued in their reaction. My father had gone to Ireland a few years previously; many of my cousins had fought in World War I, one eventually dying from the infamous gas attack of the Germans. Nevertheless, they were thrilled by the opportunity and joined in the preparations for my departure.

My parents loaned me and three of my brothers the family car, an old touring car Cadillac, to travel to New York to "see me off." During the trip to New York, we had an accident near Baltimore, the car swerving off the road and hitting an electric pole. My younger brother, Tom, and I hitchhiked to Baltimore and took a bus to New York, staying at a hotel owned by our cousins, the McDonalds. That night we were joined by my other brothers.

The next day we found our way to Hoboken and my ship, the S.S. Exochorda, a 9,000-ton combination freighter and passenger ship. My brothers were startled by the size of the ship, dwarfed by the nearby liners. Undaunted, I was absolutely thrilled by the prospect of the trip to Rome and Europe with four years of study at the North American College.

TABLE OF CONTENTS

1936

AMERICAN EXPORT LINES

ON BOARD

S.S. EXOCHORDA

Dear Everybody, or Anybody to Whom it May Concern,

Whereas, the duly appointed and designated Philip Hannan, after being deposited on board ship in New York and remaining thereon for some days, it has occurred to the same person to set forth his ideas on things in general.

The sea has been, for the most part, rough (thank God, because it is certainly dull when everything is as calm as the water in an aquarium). This palatial 9,000-ton tub at times does everything but bend over backwards. The captain insists — as all captains should — that the boat pitches but does not roll. But dammit, when the coffee runs over the sides of the cup and in every direction, I refuse to believe that it is only an optical illusion. Some few have become seasick, but not "yours truly"; the wriggling of the boat seems to help my appetite. We have not sighted a boat, sail, barge, bird or even a stray log. This absolute solitude reminds me of a line of poetry, "We were the first that ever burst into that silent sea."

Last night there was a movie, and everything about it was appropriate. There had been a very heavy sea during the day so for consolation there was the scene of an awful storm and shipwreck in the movie. It was all such a comfort.

The passengers are as different and odd as the display at a 5¢ and 10¢ store. Among the notabilities aboard are: Professor Baldwin whom nobody has been able to corner long enough to discover what he professes (he's a rare looking bird); a gentleman by the name of Slyman, the confidential type, who is forever drawing one aside to whisper some inside stuff on the situation in Spain or the politics in

New York; a Greek with an endless name who runs all the gambling joints in Egypt.

The captain told a few of us about the last trip during which they watched the bombarding of Palma at a distance of only half a mile; they took on ninety-five refugees. He also spoke of the situation in Palestine with the British and Arabs. The reports in the newspapers are very inadequate, says he. The British have a nice little method of cleaning up bands of Arabs. When an attack is made by the Arabs, the British send out mechanized units to surround the Arabs. Then the bombers come out and blow them all up. No runs, no errors, but plenty of hits.

Comments: Letter of September 22, 1936

The ticket for the boat, sent by the Chancery in Baltimore, was puzzling. The boat was unknown and the pier unknown — the S.S. Exochorda and Hoboken, New Jersey. My father had gone to Ireland several times and the boat was always well known as well as the pier — a Cunard liner as the Mauretania and a New York pier.

Three of my brothers, John, Bill and Tom, rode in our old Cadillac car towards New York. Just outside of Baltimore, we ran into a telephone pole, which damaged the car badly but left us unhurt. Tom and I hitched a ride to Baltimore and took a bus to Hoboken. John and Bill joined us that night at our hotel after getting the car put into a repair shop. Next day, we found the pier of the Exochorda, of the American Export Line, amid a jumble of docks and small boats. The sight of the Exochorda was startling, a small combination freighter and passenger boat certainly no bigger than 9,000 tons compared with the regular passenger liners of 40,000 to 60,000 tons.

With some head-shaking my brothers left me. Despite the surprise, I was delighted to be on my way. I found Johnny Linn, my companion seminarian from Baltimore, already aboard. Johnny was laughing at the size of the boat — which assured me that we would make very good traveling companions.

September 24, 1936

AMERICAN EXPORT LINES
ON BOARD
S.S. EXOCHORDA

The storm is steadily growing worse. Sunday morning at 5 a.m. it almost tossed us out of bed. Sleeping in the stateroom is practically impossible. We went down to breakfast, had been served when a sudden lurch of the ship sent everything on the floor. I made a grab at everything as it fell but ended up almost on the floor with only the napkin in my hands. Many are seasick, some have been slightly injured, and one woman has a real "shiner" — received when she was tossed into a door. This stuff has long since ceased to be funny. I recently discovered that this ship is only 4,000 tons net, but 9,000 tons when completely loaded with freight. There is no danger, but life isn't worth living on this desolate tug. "I know you'll be comfortable," was Father Nelligan's parting consolation to Johnny Linn as he gave him the tickets. Johnny and I decided last night that if we ever become bishops, we'll make Father Nelligan take a trip on this boat. Thank God that so far neither of us has been sick at all. The stern of the ship is being constantly swept by waves, but by a continuous miracle always keeps coming up. At meals now, they throw water on the tablecloth to keep the dishes from slipping so easily; everything is fastened down as tightly as possible. To drink soup you must hold the dish steady with one hand and gulp like a man dying of thirst to beat the waves. Everything in the stateroom is on the floor, even the glass cover on the bureau, and it all must be left there. Someone gave Linn a basket of fancy fruit, jam, etc. You should have seen that stuff splatter.

I neglected to mention some of the distinguished passengers aboard: two feminine missionaries, the most puritanical spinsters I have ever seen, (Someone asked them to join in the deck sports, and they refused on the grounds that it was gambling!); two parsons; a professor in the Biblical Institute at Chicago U.; an archeologist from Yale, who is going to excavate in Egypt; an old woman who constantly reads such books as "Moby Dick," "Hurricane," "Typhoon," during the storm.

September 25, 1936

AMERICAN EXPORT LINES
ON BOARD
S.S. EXOCHORDA

We stopped at the Azores, Ponta Delgada, contrary to what was expected. What a rout and rabble awaited us at Ponta Delgada! Half the town was there to sell things and the other half came to stare. We not only visited Ponta Delgada, they visited us. The mayor, aldermen, half a dozen policemen dressed in musical comedy outfits, and almost every man who could muster a suit and a hat, were all brought out to inspect the ship. There was a Mexican "warship" (a smelly old can that boasted of only one gun) in the harbor that was taking 250 refugees from Spain. To realize what the warship looked like, you must imagine the excursion boat "Steamer of Washington" on a hot August night with passengers as thick as flies around honey, make all the people chatter like monkeys and be purposelessly active and restless as if they had ants in their pants, cover the boat with mud and plant it in the middle of the ocean.

Ponta Delgada is a very picturesque town: the sidewalks are narrow and made of mosaic; all the houses are painted white, pink or yellow and all have iron grill balconies (a paradise for Romeos); the streets are clean but infested with cops and small cars (just a little larger than our Austins), horse-drawn carts, wagons, etc. They make everything that has four legs draw wagons or carts; I saw a sheep hitched to a small wagon. The doctors on the island have magnificent residences with patios or gardens in the rear. We met a little fellow who had lived in Boston so we let him pilot us around. He showed us the old churches (one was 450 years old) and carefully explained that they used to be Jesuit churches, but now the Catholics have them. One church has been made into a fort by simply filling in the window space; they overlooked the trivial detail of placing any guns in it. The people are very decent and polite; I realized that civilization is possible without movies, trucks, buses, etc. A young policeman with whom I spoke apologized for not having any education — he only spoke four languages!

Soon after we left the Azores, the storm passed, *Deo gratias*.

Then we sighted the coast of Portugal — a beacon flashing from Cape St.Vincent through the boundless black of the night. That light which seemed only to indicate the limitless darkness without expelling it, gave me a heartwarming thrill. So here is Europe. The following morning we steamed past Gibraltar, a mighty mass that seems to frown across the Mediterranean at Africa. But really, Gibraltar is not so imposing or impregnable as you would imagine (despite the ads of the Prudential Life Insurance Co.); on the eastern side they have a concrete watershed to prevent erosion and catch rainwater. It reminded me of an old apple tree cemented for preservation. The embattlements on Gibraltar are half hidden but very extensive and impressive. Only one warship was near — disappointment.

The Mediterranean is magnificent. As calm as a mountain lake, we glided over it like a skater across a frozen pond. At night the moon swells up from the oily bottom of the sea and then a fishing craft steals by like a ghostly ship on a magical errand. What a place! I am just beginning to enjoy the trip.

Did I tell you that I won the quoits tournament (known as horseshoes in Maryland)? I was a popular champ because I beat three people.

I'll end this letter so that all this dirty linen can be stuffed into one envelope without breaking it.

Sorry for the bad penmanship.

Love,
Phil

P.S. Johnny Linn is an excellent traveling companion, much quiet humor and popular on board ship.

September 27, 1936

AMERICAN EXPORT LINES
ON BOARD
S.S. Exochorda

Dear Mom and Dad,

We landed at Marseilles on Saturday and promptly saw why it is politely and affectionately called the hell-hole of the Mediterranean; it is dirty, rough, and tough. But there is a magnificent church, Notre Dame de la Garde, on a hill overlooking the city. Like churches in Quebec, it has lamps made of ships, which were saved from storms at sea.

We took the 10 o'clock train to Cannes and Nice. The trip takes four hours; apparently they make the journey that long simply from habit because it can be done in a little over two hours. At the railway station in Marseilles we saw all kinds of troops — sailors in their colorful red, white, and blue uniforms, soldiers in every imaginable and unimaginable outfit, and French colonial troops, Negroes from the Sudan, Arabs from Morocco (some are very handsome), and dark tribesmen from the northern part of Africa beyond Morocco. It is colorful and enchanting but sinister; the whole male population seems capable of going to war immediately. The Frenchmen seem far more handsome than the women.

Johnny Linn was dressed in white and must have looked official. An Arab soldier insisted on presenting him with his ticket and visa; finally Johnny took them, carefully looked them over and presented them back to him. He couldn't understand French, and we couldn't get his Arabic but the interview seemed to leave everybody contented and happy. We traveled third class on the train, and it isn't bad if you can stand the smell of garlic and are capable of tussling through a crowd. The coaches are arranged in compartments capable of seating eight persons; there is an aisle on the side of the car. The game is to grab a seat despite the whole excitable French nation; it's a case of free competition. Many of the seats are reserved, and no one comes to occupy them. But after you have gotten a seat, perhaps at the price of bursting a blood vessel, you jump up and stare out of the window as soon as the train has started. But honestly, the common people are very courteous to strangers. The amazing thing is how the women over here get into the fight as much as the men. I saw one young girl bring a hatbox, three bags each as large as my gladstone, and a canvas contraption about a yard long and two feet thick into the train. Then she went back and got her Singer sewing machine. *Gott in Himmel,* what people. The only appreciable difference (excepting the question of morality) between the French and us is their language; we express ourselves by a certain series of grunts, and they express themselves in a different series of grunts.

The language problem is easy; I can speak to them in French but they spit it back with machine gun rapidity, and it gets past me.

Directly outside of Marseilles the land is very hilly and desolate. It is mostly limestone. Occasionally beautiful old castles appear on the very tops of rocky crests. They were intended to withstand long sieges. Most of them are in at least a state of partial ruin, but the ruins are almost inexpressibly romantic looking. The whole landscape seems exhausted, old, and worn out. They grade and terrace and grasp at every inch of useful land. We don't appreciate our spacious America until we see this carefully rationed land.

And then like a dream come Cannes and Nice. A beautiful plain lies between Cannes and Nice. Suddenly, around Cannes, beautiful villas and chateaux (the storybook-type) spring out of the desolate surroundings like lilies blooming in sand. The villas and chateaux, each with a formal garden of stately palms, poplars and gorgeous flowers, are usually situated on the side of a hill. Cannes is a collection of villas, but it doesn't enjoy the marvelous site that has made Nice's reputation. Nice is set along a bay of the famous Côte d'Azur (blue coast) of the Riviera; everything is done in colors that somehow seem to blend with the deep, moving blue of the sea and the calm, lighter blue of the sky. Stony hills as high as the Blue Ridge Mountains lie just around Nice. Colorful villas clamber for a short distance up the hills and piles of soft white clouds forever cling to the crests of the hills. It presents almost a magical appearance. Clouds seem always to hang above the hills but are firmly anchored there and never spoil the expanse of blue sky. The promenade along the sea at Nice is magnificent. A solid row of stately hotels lies along the promenade; they have not the proportions of the hotels at Atlantic City but are more dignified. We saw new Auburns, Buicks, and even Lincoln "Zippers" in Nice. (Pardon these blurbs on the paper — a storm is rocking the Mediterranean now.) The Gardens in Nice are almost unbelievable.

We ate at a sidewalk café in Nice. The Germans may be the political enemies of the French, but they certainly use good German beer. I ordered a ham sandwich, which measured a foot in length.

Linn and I were both thrilled — Johnny especially since he had never been in an English-speaking country. I did almost all of the speaking in French. Johnny is a perfect traveling companion.

Enjoying great health so far. I hope to tour in southern Italy if it can be done cheaply.

Love,

Phil

October 1, 1936

NORTH AMERICAN COLLEGE
Via Dell' Umilta 30

Dear Everybody,

It seems to me that the last time I sent a lengthy, if not sensible, letter to you was just before I reached Naples. Well, I have seen some country since then. Two fellows met us at the boat and rescued us from the clutches of these greasy tourist agencies at Naples. Incidentally, Naples is the dirtiest place in spots that I have ever had the misfortune of seeing. Around the docks it is terrific. We went to some place to hire a car and ship our trunks to Rome. In that neighborhood they leave the garbage in the streets, and vendors make a continual bedlam. At the intersection of streets, women would set up dirty stoves for cooking and selling corn (cooked with the husks on) and chestnuts. When a lull in business occurred, they would feed their infants. In Naples, we stayed at a German convent — food and beds were fine. By the way, this myth about the water in Italy being no good is sheer nonsense; the water is as good as our water in Washington. I wish they would use more of it on themselves and the streets.

On Monday, we took a drive to Amalfi, Pompeii, and Sorrento. Pompeii is magnificent. Some of the market places and public buildings almost create the illusion that the hum and murmur of talk and business still lingers there. I bought two coral bracelets for Mom and Mary — I'll send them when I think of a way of getting them into the country. Everybody is willing to exchange almost anything for a package of American cigarettes; I could have gotten as much as 75¢ a package for cigarettes. At the new city of Pompeii, we visited a gorgeous new church that has a famous painting in it. A wedding was just being finished as we arrived. Italians of all kinds — old, young, fat, thin, thick, lean, dark, light — were swarming like locusts through the church. Never think that these people are not vigorous, good-looking, and noble. Some of them are incurably dirty, but some are as distinguished and cultured as anything I have ever seen.

Amalfi is a gorgeous spot on the Tyrrhenian Sea. It is situated on the side of a mountain — mountains are all along this coast — and was formerly a great city. Our driver explained that God, while resting after the work of creation, decided to amuse Himself by creating a little spot of Paradise and so He made the section around Amalfi. There are numerous little bays and caves all along the coast here where the Algerian pirates used to come and use as harbors. Some of their old mosques, now Catholic churches, are still standing. What a thrill it produces. All along the road are phrases from Mussolini's speeches printed and painted on every available spot; they read something like this, "Long live Mussolini," "Long live the King," "Mussolini is always right," "Mussolini and the King for us," "The Fascist will bends only before God, men or circumstances will never affect it." Almost every shop and hotel has some patriotic sign and pledge to Mussolini on it. You get as accustomed to seeing these signs as you do of seeing the sky. It is amazing the way he has pulled this country together. The amount of work he has done and is doing to clean up Italy is remarkable; only a complete dictator could accomplish it all.

We went to Capri on Tuesday. Our guide from the North American College got seasick on the boat ride over to the island. Capri is a very pretty and romantic spot. There are remains of villas built there two thousand years ago by the Roman emperors and we traveled on an old Greco-Roman road in a little carriage. The turns are so sharp that a fellow in the front seat could shake hands with someone in the back seat without turning around. There are a number of famous villas on the island — the Queen of Sweden, Maxim Gorky (the famous Russian writer, just deceased), Krupp (the German arms manufacturer) all have large villas here. Almost all nations are represented here.

On Wednesday, we went to Rome. The trains here are even more crowded with troops and men in the service than in France. It seems as if a uniform manufacturer had gone berserk, made as many different uniforms as his fevered imagination could invent and then threw them all out free for the public to wear. Actually there must be more military organizations in Italy than there are religious orders of nuns in the Church. The officers always look very trim and gallant in their brilliant uniforms.

We arrived in Rome at eleven o'clock. St. Peter's is dingy and disappointing from the exterior (except that the huge proportions are overwhelming), but the interior is a dream. The place is tremendous but one never realizes how large it is because the proportions are perfectly worked out. For instance, there are two holy water fonts supported by cherubs that seem quite small; actually they are about six feet high. There is a mosaic of St. Jerome near the dome and the pen he is holding is seven feet long, but it appears to be small. One really must see St. Peter's before he can appreciate it.

We snatched only glances at other important spots in Rome then went to the North American College, the worst disappointment I have ever had. It is very old and very medieval, but the spirit of the fellows is magnificent, even better than that at the Sulp Seminary, if I am allowed to make comparisons. I was promptly fitted out in a cassock, queer black, short pants, stockings as strong as gunnysacks and a shirt made from canvas. Besides that, you get a sleeveless coat called a soprana and a long overcoat with mantle called a zamara. I forgot to mention the hat — one of those inverted dishpan affairs. Feeling as if I had just been dressed for a musical comedy or something that the Marx brothers had thought up, I went to the villa near Castelgandolfo, the Pope's summer residence.

The villa is magnificent. Situated on a large hill that rises high above the plain in which Rome is built it commands a tremendous view of Rome, the surrounding country and the sea in the distance, and when at evening the plain is a purple glow and the sun is shattering itself into long crimson waves on the deep blue sea, it feels good to be alive. The villa was bought from the noble Orsini family for a very small sum. The grounds are very inviting. More of that later.

Friday afternoon during siesta time there was a very slight earthquake that shook the villa. I responded to this cosmic event in my usual way — sleeping right on. I am afraid that I'll miss the last judgment. There is too much to write about; I shall have to dish out the stuff in small doses. The food is simple, but unusually good. I have never felt better physically, at least within the past few years. It must be the wine, which is really quite good. Two and a half glasses of that is a perfect preparation for a nice siesta.

I am afraid that I left home my certificate of confirmation, parents' marriage certificate, and credit slip (a letter). They are in a large envelope on the mantle in the hall of the house in the city or in my bureau drawer in the country, or in the guest room in the country. I have my baptismal certificate and some of the others may be in my trunk, which has not yet arrived from Naples. Please send them as quickly as convenience will permit.

Sorry to put you to the trouble. I did not know that I would need them all so soon. I do not need them immediately (need them for registration at the Gregorian University).

Love,
Phil

P.S. Received Mom and Dad's letter with all the letters. Pardon the very poor typing; these tables are as bad as the Roman streets.

Comments: Letter of October 1, 1936

It was a laudable custom for an older seminarian of the Archdiocese to greet newly arrived seminarians at the boat in Naples and to guide them to Rome. Charlie Gorman was the older, third year seminarian, a very devout and accommodating fellow from Baltimore who was a good linguist. He was extremely hospitable and courteous. He took us to the famous shrine of Our Lady of Pompeii. As soon as we walked into the beautiful interior I was distracted by a lady seated on the floor near the wall, calmly feeding her infant at her breast. No attention was paid from the people streaming into the shrine, and no attention or remark from Charlie. "A different culture," I thought and hurried on. The people were devout and voluble, kissing statues and praying loudly to the Lord in the Blessed Sacrament. A wedding was in progress, a production of beauty, love and faith, very openly expressed. Their explanation of their devotion, "The northern people respect God so much that they don't really love Him. We love Him so much that we don't respect Him."

"It's new. But I certainly can understand them and like them."

Then Charlie took us on the famous Amalfi drive, traveling along the breath-taking road to Sorrento and Salerno. I was especially interested in Salerno because the relics of St. Matthew, the apostle and Evangelist are buried in the Cathedral. I sent postcards from there to the pastor of our parish, Monsignor Edward L. Buckey, pastor of St. Matthew's Parish, later the Cathedral.

I was intrigued with the omnipresence of Mussolini and Fascism on billboards of every description. Mrs. Capps, a very good family friend had always spoken very laudatorily about Mussolini, and this disposed me to think well of Fascism, a view which I grew to correct.

We went to Rome by train and then directly to St. Peter's. Charlie was chock-full of dates, places and people about everything we saw, and it was his reward to see us gape-jawed at the sight of St. Peter's.

The old North American College, about 450 years old, fronted on a very narrow street, (Via dell'Umilta 30) so narrow one could easily carry on a conversation with a neighbor across the street. The entrance opened into a cortile with a palm tree in the middle. The building was three stories of flat ochre-colored walls that seemed to have grown out of the earth. The small chapel on the ground floor was like a breath of heaven — beautifully covered marble walls, a gorgeous altar with the beautiful picture of the Blessed Mother by Guido Reni, which gave its name to the street, Madonna dell'Umilta (Madonna of Humility).

Charlie introduced us to the "house uniform", a cassock of midnight blue with a border of light blue and a red sash, and topped with a circular "Roman" hat. We felt as if we had really arrived and become a part of the College, a "bag", (a diminutive of "bagarrozzi", a roach, a name given by the anti-Catholic Italians.)

We drove to the Villa Santa Caterina near Castel Gandolfo and were deeply impressed by the beauty of the building and setting. As soon as we arrived, we were taken into a room full of students. The general hubbub of introductions was sharply shattered by an official looking person who staged a raid — examined our luggage and charged all with smuggling. I couldn't believe it. I looked around, all seemed serious, especially a former classmate from the Sulpician Seminary Marty Kileen who looked very worried. The official demoted the subdeacons and everyone was very subdued.

Newly arrived seminarians underwent a clever "hazing", a fake examination for acceptance. It was preceded by a well-done "raid" by the Seminary "authorities" who arrested several "sems". The colloquial word for fooling or deceiving the newly arrived was to "suck them in."

Next morning an exam was announced, and we all flunked. My examiner, Ed Collins, was not very impressive but mean. My fake exam was on Schleiermacher, a German philosopher whose works I knew by sheer accident. As soon as we were thoroughly distraught, the "official" laughed; and we shook hands all around. We were now officially students of the College. We had undergone the "suck in" or "hazing" staged for all newcomers.

Then I was too tired to care, ate dinner and went to bed after seeing a gorgeous sunset across the *campagna*.

The next day the new first theologian seminarians went on a short side trip, a "bum run" to nearby Fascati, famous for its wine. First and delightful experience with a wine cellar. A "bum run" is a trip or excursion to a nearby Shrine or tourist attraction.

Shortly thereafter, the "slate" of the College was read out. This was the listing of all the students in their respective "camerata", or group. I and Johnny Linn, as well as Marty Killeen, were in Camerata 12. Bob Arthur, a third year theology Baltimore seminarian was our "prefect", and a second year theologian, Jim Clark, was the "beadle", assistant to the prefect. The camerata lived in the same section of the building, took daily walks together, was a community within the larger community. The cam consisted of Bob Arthur, Jim Clark, George Spehar (a huge Croatian from Crested Butte, Denver Archdiocese), Johnny Linn and I from the Archdiocese of Baltimore, Charlie Noll from Cincinnati, and Jim Woulfe from Binghampton.

We discovered almost immediately that we were rebels, caustic about the constant use of several words to describe everything, "prosit" (good) and "augurri" (good luck) and the constant praise about the "spirit" of the College. Naturally, we also thought that we should be allowed more personal freedom than granted by the pervasive cam. We liked the individuals but disliked the corporate personality of the "del Nord", short for Collegio American del Nord (the North American College).

Our cam was assigned to the third floor, near the room of the Vice Rector. The bedding for each room was selected in a novel manner. All the mattresses in the Villa were carried by the students and dumped into a truck, which deposited all of them in a grand heap just inside the back entrance of the College. Each seminarian scrambled with all the others to grab a mattress which he then hauled up to his room. He then put on the sheets and the blanket. Very efficient system.

We devised our lampoon of the system at the New Men's Mix, an entertainment in which the members of each new camerata were to give an "act." Our act was "The March of Time", a three act, ten scene play, advertised in a printed program which we distributed before the act. Each one of us simply carried across the stage an alarm clock — no words. It worked. It baffled, then enraged the upper classmen. We became the Blue

Ribbon Camerata.

The "bum run" to Aquila, a ski resort, was unique. Encouraged by my first attempt at skiing, on the third day I attempted a difficult slope whose snowy surface was covered by a thin layer of ice (from a bit of thawing during the previous day). I sailed down the slope at a terrific clip, hit a hidden stone, somersaulted violently, tearing off one of my shoes and breaking both skis. One of the shoes is still out there, somewhere in the snow. End of my career in skiing.

October 3, 1936

NORTH AMERICAN COLLEGE
Via Dell' Umilta 30

Dear Rob and Mary, [1]

This typewriter has become practically indispensable; all furniture in the building is hereditary (each diocese controls a certain portion) and apparently it has been handed down since the time of the Apostles. It is practically impossible to write on the desks.

I won't bore you with an account of our rough sea trip except to say that this myth about the calm southern crossing is only sales talk — as far as our experience extends. But it did make us appreciate landing at the Azores and Marseilles. By the way, were you on the Mediterranean when the moon was up? Mon Dieu, what a glorious sight, — the moon gilding the crest of the furrows as we glided along that magically calm sea — a horrible preparation for the study of theology. Don't get excited; that moon was completely wasted because the passenger list was . . . . well, Mary, you saw it. Furthermore, I discussed the problem of realism and mysticism in Catholicism with a very shrewd Jew for almost the whole trip or as often as I failed to elude him.

Anyway, I started to talk about landing at Marseilles, the roughest, toughest town on the Mediterranean. We didn't fool around the town very long; in fact, we saw the two marvelous churches that are as out of place in that town as a peacock in a pig sty and then proceeded to Cannes and Nice. There are some gloriously fascinating ruins of castles and chateaux in the southern part of France. The romance of the past hangs like the odor of old roses in a Wedgwood jar. But all that is dispelled by the modern beauty of Cannes (which is far more beautiful than Nice) and the Cote d'Azur. Of course, we were not there in time for the season, but the villas remain even though the crowds have left. Although Nice and Cannes are very attractive and stately in their beauty, they do not have the marvelous beaches we have at Atlantic City, etc. The beaches are not sandy, have pebbles; but these people take sunbaths on the pebbles. They sell even the Saturday Evening Post at Nice — for only 38 francs! We traveled third class on the train. Traveling third class on a French or Italian crack train is equivalent to spending the fourth of July on Coney Island and trying to get a front seat at an inaugural address, but it is much fun.

At Naples we lodged in a German convent where the service and cuisine was excellent but a warm bath cost nine lira. [2] Water is plentiful but plumbing is certainly scarce. I wrote to the family about my trips around Naples, so if you are interested you'll probably see the letter. The ride to Rome was very interesting, as you know. St. Peter's exceeded my greatest expectations; the symmetry and proportions are exquisite. No use exulting to you people about something you are acquainted with, but I don't think you saw the medieval monstrosity that parades under the formidable title of the North American College. The Via dell' Umilta is noisy, narrow and dirty. There is nothing at all about the street that even faintly suggests anything about humility (Umilta means humility). As in all seminaries, one needs a sense of humor and a magnificent contempt for the American necessities of life. The *esprit de corps* of the fellows is magnificent; just what one might expect to find in a number of fellows 4000 miles from home and in a foreign land. In fact, this place reminds me forcibly of the Sulpician Seminary in respect to the general morale.

The summer villa is incomparably superior to the college in Rome. [3] It was formerly the property of the Orsini family, is next to the villa of another princely family and a stone's throw from the papal summer residence at Castelgandolfo. We arrived at the villa just a few hours after the Pope had left for the Vatican in Rome. The photographers have a clever trick of getting wildly enthusiastic Italians cheering the Pope. They take no pictures of the crowd while the Pope is speaking or even after he has finished. But when the Pope has departed, they call the attention of the crowd to the fact that they are to be photographed and ask for a demonstration. And do they get it!!! The Italians are camera crazy anyway, and they go mad for the photographers. The summer villa is situated in the foothills of the mountains and enjoys, or suffers, extremely cool weather. At the present time it is too cold to even play tennis. This balderdash about semi-tropical weather is sheer drivel. Actually, everybody is sleeping in his bathrobe under three blankets and yelling for more. These old villas with innumerable corridors that brew everlasting drafts and are chilled by the marble floors were not meant for this modern era. There is positively no heating apparatus; we have hot water on only one day a week — sometimes two days a week. It depends entirely upon one's attitude to determine his estimate of the food. It is very simple and served in old, large tin platters. About one-half of the cups have no handles. But honestly, I enjoy the whole set-up; I haven't enjoyed such good health in a long time — the long wait between meals makes me so hungry that everything is forced to click correctly. I make breakfast of very hard bread, atrocious coffee and jam; and I like it!! The wine is exceptionally good; not strong, but with a rather delicate flavor. I am beginning to suspect that Italians have their siesta because of the wine and not because of the heat. Lord knows we have no heat but still maintain the siesta — which makes me go sleepless at night. Many fellows don't indulge in the siesta.

Incidentally, Mussolini is doing wonders for Italy and the Italians. And I'll undertake his cause for beatification and canonization if he ever succeeds in cleaning up some of the dirty holes I saw in Naples. Speaking of Naples makes me think how much Dad would enjoy bickering for prices in Italy. We made contract with a fellow in Naples to see us around for a certain price; he tried to charge us twice as much. We left him shouting and gesticulating wildly that we were robbers and would disgrace the priesthood if we were ever ordained. Now I don't bicker at all — just pay them half of what they demand as the rock bottom price and walk off. If they care to indulge in voice culture that's their business.

Pardon this rambling and incoherent babbling. I suggest that Rob give his pupils this thing to straighten out and re-arrange as a problem in his English exams.

Love,

Phil

Comments: Letter of October 3, 1936

(1)   Mary was my only sister, and she was married to Rob (Mahoney) who taught English in the public schools of Hartford and later was the Superintendent of Education there.

(2)   In 1936 the value of the Italian lira was nineteen to a dollar. After World War II, it was about 2000 lira to a dollar.

(3)   It was customary for the seminaries in Rome to have villas near Rome as summer residences for the students. The Roman summers are very hot, and the Pontine Marshes near Rome had malaria-bearing mosquitoes until Mussolini succeeded in draining them. The danger of malaria and the hot weather were the reasons why the academic year for the seminaries began early in November.

October 8, 1936

VILLA DI SANTA CATERINA

(JUST A BIG NAME FOR A COUNTRY HOME)

Dear Mom and Dad,

Well, I have just completed my first week at the villa; what a life. On Sunday, I went with two fellows to a wine fest at a little village about two or three miles from here. The world and his wife with all their children and relations were there. Everybody, even the clergy, goes and participates or watches the fun. We created a particular attraction for there was one fellow in our party who is six feet six inches tall and weighs 260 pounds. Wherever he goes around here he creates a parade of admiring and wondering Italians. The big attraction of the program was the flowing of wine through the large fountain in the public square and the distribution of grapes to the grasping populace. The town was mobbed, but we pushed our way to a very advantageous position and watched the battle for the wine. If you can imagine twenty thousand kids scrambling for baseballs autographed by all the stars in baseball, you have some idea of these Italians pushing for the wine. Soldiers stood on the fountain and gave it out in paper cups, but whoever was lucky enough to grab a cup had to squeeze it. The result was that there was more wine on the square than in Italian gullets. Then they started to throw out the grapes; I never saw so many grapes splattered in all my life. I would have given a dollar to have been in civilian dress and gotten into that mess. A further attraction, for me anyway, was the sight of whole baked pigs on tables being sliced and sold for half a lira a slice. I was hungry but those pigs had been cooked without being cleaned well, so I stayed hungry. The whole afternoon I was thinking what pictures I could have gotten with a movie camera. [1]

No doubt you have heard that the lira has fallen until now they are nineteen for a dollar. Everything is working out magnificently. My travelers' checks can be re-cashed then changed into the present rate and thus give me three more to the dollar. I am taking care of that now. Next year it will be marvelous, if anyone comes over — almost all the countries in Europe have gone off the gold standard. The fellows here certainly know how to juggle currency (I'll tell you about that when you come).

A few days ago I went into Rome for the day. It's a city that slowly unfolds itself and like all great works it will return as much as one brings to the study of it. I was particularly impressed by the Pantheon, a great dome-like building with an opening in the top through which light comes to illuminate the interior. It has been used as a temple, church, museum and fort and is still standing. The interior used to be covered with bronze; but when Michelangelo was planning St. Peter's, he said that he would rebuild the Parthenon (a tremendous building in Greece) and put the Pantheon on top of it — and literally, that's just about what he did do. They used the bronze from the Pantheon to make the dome of St. Peter's. But before you come to Rome, you must realize that these buildings are centuries old and the exteriors are weather-beaten. The interiors are more gorgeous than ever. There are so many things that they defy description. I saw the palace in which Mrs. Chanler — who wrote <u>Roman Spring</u> — lived, saw the American Embassy (viva America!), and saw the Gregorian University where we take our classes. It is a new building and was presented by the republic of Argentina. Some of the lecture halls hold 750 or 1000 students. It is tremendously impressive and not at all frightening. I have discovered that I can make out remarkably well with this Italian language, so I have every reason to believe that in a year the Latin will be easy. [2]

Living in a Roman villa is a very good education. In the first place it has taught me to shave and wash in ice-cold water, to read and write comfortably in an overcoat, to make a filling breakfast on simply bread and coffee, etc. I am going to write a book entitled The Education of Phil Hannan or School Begins at Twenty-Three. Why, one even has to furnish his own toilet paper. But, compared to Basselin, or the Sulp Sem, it is a real treat; discipline, if there is any, is left to the discretion of the students. Everything is left to the individual, thank God, instead of being reserved to the faculty acting like a police force. It is no good if you do not know how to respond to it, but great if you have an ounce of sense. There is one great mistake that almost all Italians and persons living in Italy seem to make continually — they think, apparently, that an endless amount of tile or marble floors can, in some mysterious way, compensate for the lack of plumbing. Did I tell you that a warm bath at our hotel in Naples costs nine lira or about seventy-five cents? Wooden floors are a rarity and nobody could afford a frame house. [3]

It is very interesting to listen to the fellows returning from their trips. The talk is about Paris, London, Ireland, Munich, Vienna, Budapest, etc. Some of the stories are amazing; for instance, one fellow, recently ordained, went to Scotland for parish work during the summer. In that section every priest is serenaded each Saturday night by anti-Catholic, anti-papal songs (the words are unprintable), and the priests get a sock in the jaw on the average of once a week. Of course, that happens only in the remote country districts.

I'll tell you later about the faculty. They are all well liked — except the present Rector who had the misfortune of succeeding a very popular man. The Rector won't be here until December. (That bolsters my contention that the janitor of a Seminary is far more important than the president. I recall the time at the Sulp Sem when the President, Vice President and treasurer were either sick or absent and still the Sem went on well.)

Love,

Phil

Comments: Letter of October 8, 1936

(1)   The village we visited for the wine fiesta was probably Albano, a village near Castel Gandolfo. A wine fiesta, held in the fall, is a very

popular event. The wine actually pours from the fountain in the square, the piazza. The police help in the distribution; but nevertheless, the crowd jams towards the fountain, and everyone is in good spirits, despite the jamming. There is a common sense of discipline in these events that make it possible here in Italy, but which would be impossible elsewhere, especially in the U. S. Literally, the people know how much they can push without being offensive, and they do it while laughing and enjoying the whole affair. It was very enjoyable and a revelation of the character of the Italian villagers.

(2)   My optimism about being able to understand Latin, the language of the classes at the Gregorian University in Rome was well founded. I enjoyed the challenge and understood the lectures in a few weeks.

(3)   Life in the Villa was delightful despite the small inconveniences. The sunset was a great delight every evening, and many seminarians watched it as a kind of meditation, including myself.

October 15, 1936

NORTH AMERICAN COLLEGE
Via Dell' Umilta 30

Dear Mom and Dad,
    Yesterday the fellows from our diocese went on a "bum run" (the polite term for an outing or picnic) to a little village nearby and had a little meal. The "little" meal consisted of a soup dish full of spaghetti, bread, then steak and potatoes, and, of course, wine. The servings are enormous. The Italians consider it sheer gluttony to eat a large breakfast – even to eat eggs at breakfast; but it is apparently good manners to almost kill yourself with food later on in the day. The restaurant in which we ate was formerly a part of a church; those who remodeled the church didn't bother to tear down the bell tower with its old mosaics, so a shoemaker, barber and butcher

conduct business in the front part of the building, and the café proprietor conducts business in the rear — and the whole shebang has this big bell tower in the center as a sort of public ornament. There are about ten fellows from the Baltimore diocese over here; only two are from Washington, Winston and myself, but at present Winston is in Ireland. A couple of them are really outstanding. Like all seminaries, this place has its share of notabilities but it can't compare (so far as I have noticed) with the general level of intelligence and fellowship at the Sulp Sem. Maybe that is a rash judgment — we'll see. [1]

The outstanding characteristic of this Seminary is the government "for the people, by the people, and of the people." It is a complete democracy; the fellows conduct all the exercises in the house. Mass, benediction, etc., are conducted by men who were ordained the past year and are staying here to continue studies. I have seen only one member of the faculty, and he keeps himself well hidden. I haven't the faintest idea why they even bother with a Rector; and apparently no one else does — not even the Vice Rector. The present Rector, Bishop Hayes, is in the U.S. and will be there until after the Bishops' meeting at C.U. The most important thing he has done for the community was to get movies for the fellows once a week. But, he has also made a very silly (I think so, at least) ruling that ordinations in December are to depend upon marks instead of general conduct and standing; it used to be the custom for fellows to be ordained in December as a reward for their conduct, etc. The Rector has made himself needlessly unpopular by this decision. Again, I say that a Rector is useless, at least for the present time, around here.

Owing to so much counterfeit money in Italy, every shopkeeper's cashier has a marble top on which he clinks the money to determine whether it is genuine. A few days ago a couple of the fellows had quite a discussion with a restaurant owner about their money; at last he accepted it as good and brought back the change. They were a bit peeved, too, so in the crowded restaurant they dropped their change, coin by coin, on the tiled floor to see if it was genuine. It will be a long time before that proprietor haggles with Americans about their money. It is surprising how easy it is to distinguish the American fellows from other nationalities; the saying in Rome is that the English act as if they own the place, but the Americans act as if they don't give a d - - n who owns the place. It gives me a distinct pain to see the way Seminarians of other nationalities are herded around like six-year-old orphans. Of course, my sympathy is wasted — they are used to such treatment, don't mind it a bit. For example, at Propaganda (a large international college here — Tur and Archbishop Curley both attended there) the fellows are not allowed out at all, summer or winter. When they go out on walks they are marched two by two. Great stuff for those who can take it. I certainly admire the Americans who are there. Archbishop Curley, by the way, was given permission while a student there to take long trips — he had stomach trouble. [2]

Another thing to which I must accustom myself is the sight of begging monks. One comes to the villa once a week; though he is very dirty, he looks intelligent and alert. That life is certainly the height of holiness. The consoling feature is that they have produced some great saints. All the same, I prefer my saints well shaved and neat. But, of course, one has to understand the Italian temperament; they are simple and childlike. They are not the least bit ashamed of begging; in fact, they consider it as just accepting Christian charity and not at all degrading. Even old men who have a comfortable home will beg if there is nothing else to do or occupy their time. And the kids, in the villages, will ask you for anything from holy cards to bread. But, there is none of that stuff in the cities or where the government has surveillance. On the other hand one must admit that there is a problem of hunger in Italy (at least to our way of thinking.) Many of the country people live on bread and a little wine. Men going out to work in the fields carry out a hunk of bread for their lunch. Italian beer, by the way, is no good; tastes something like dish water with alcohol in it.

Our Hungarian cook has just learned to make apple pie. One of the fellows taught him but he insists on making them about four inches thick. The meals continue to be very satisfying and even the weather has gotten a bit warmer but the rainy season has set in.

The general sport at present is greeting and sizing up the new fellows. There are two new men from Buffalo just entering philosophy. They need a good bit of toughening, which they'll get. It is almost impossible to imagine the thin, scrawny fellows (like myself) developing into fat, well-padded pastors. The big wigs in the Church in Rome have enough mechanical sense to buy American-made cars; it reminds one of the U.S.A. to see a cardinal driving in his Packard.

Love,

Phil

24

Comments: Letter of October 15, 1936

(1)   The Seminarians of a diocese developed a keen sense of unity and fellowship. We of the Baltimore Archdiocese (Washington was a part of the Archdiocese of Baltimore) had only eight seminarians; two had been ordained and had left. Our group, according to their year of ordination, consisted of: Charlie Gorman, Bob Arthur and Joe Bradley; Tom Winston and Kailer Dunn; Johnny Linn and myself. Later during that first year Tom Winston and Kailer Dunn left the College.

(2)   The system of organizing a seminary according to "cameratas", a group of about ten students headed by a prefect and beadle was universal in Rome. The discipline at the Propaganda College, for seminarians for "foreign" countries, was very strict. Cameratas from different nations never joined in the daily "walks" and merely nodded to each other as they passed. The whole camerata system grated on the sensibilities of the Americans. The system was later discontinued.

October 17, 1936

NORTH AMERICAN COLLEGE
VIA DELL' UMILTA 30

Dear Mom and Dad,

    A few days ago I got my first glimpse of the papal gardens at Castelgandolfo. A whole mess of us went up there to inspect them; incidentally, when you hear it said that the Pope takes a little walk through his garden, you can be sure that the Holy Father is a real globe-trotter — the gardens must be about a mile and a quarter in length; but, of course, there are all kinds of paths through them. It is a formal garden with a vista of magnificently plotted shrubs always ending with a marble statue. There is statuary all over the place. In the center of the garden there is an imposing ruin of some ancient royal villa with broken pieces of columns and marble work scattered about the garden. At the far end of the garden is the Pope's dairy and poultry farm. The dairy barn is lined with blue tile and is probably the only clean dairy in all Italy; even the chicken houses have mosaics of the Blessed Mother at the top. The milk from the dairy is distributed to the poor and to the orphan asylums, etc. in Rome. Father Fenlon, the boss of the Sulps, remarked this summer (after he had seen the gardens), "It's very pagan." I don't know whether he expected to find a set of stations and hear the people singing "Holy God we praise thy name" but if the Pope is satisfied with it, I see no necessity for being more Catholic than the Pope. By the way, the apples and grapes in the garden are very good — think I'll go back some time. There's no use in giving a detailed description, you'll have to see it sometime yourself.

We had a track meet some days ago and half a dozen little Italians skipped school and came over to see everything. I had a great time with them. They tried to imitate everything they saw, whether it made sense to them or not. They didn't know what the fellows were cheering for, but they cheered right on. They met their downfall when the three-legged race came off, and they tried to have one of their own. The last I saw of them they were all tangled up so badly that you couldn't tell which bald head belonged to which pair of dirty legs. The track meet was a great success from our standpoint; we beat the Deacon class in the tug-of-war. Our success was due wholly to a little 260-pound boy from Denver who was anchorman. When things started to go badly for our class, he simply sat down, pulled in the rope and that was that. The Deacons should have been allowed one horse to offset our elephant.

As you have noticed, all this balderdash is just about things in the country; we are not in Rome and won't be there until about October 28. The king of Italy is to be made emperor on the 28th so I hope to be there and see it.

Our class went on a "bum run" today to Frascati, a very beautiful little town in the hills. There are some magnificent villas there. The purpose of the outing was to get us acquainted by giving us a big feed with wine to work us into a mellow mood. The idea worked; we have a real class now. At Frascati we were shown through a wine cellar. I can't describe it in an orderly way, but this was my impression of it: down a pair of long, winding stone steps for about three days — around corners until you can't tell whether you are standing on your feet or head — bump your head on the wall so often that you think the wall is reaching out and hitting you — more steps — more corners — more walls in the way — then rooms, rooms, rooms with wine bottles, wine casks, wine jars. I saw very little; I felt very much. The trolley on which we rode to Frascati was a double-decker that sways enough to give an ordinary person seasickness.

Believe it or not, I am in the semi-finals of the tennis tournament. The boat ride or the climate must have been very good for my tennis. In fact, I couldn't be in better shape for tennis than if I had been drinking goat's milk. The ridiculous part is that my partner only started playing tennis this year (and looks like it too), and we have been meeting really good players. Must be the spaghetti.

Once a week we have movies. Wouldn't the Sulpicians go crazy if they took a look at this institution? We have had "Rose Marie" and "If You Could Only Cook". There is a sound apparatus with the movie outfit, but the fellows supply most of the sound accompaniment — only it usually doesn't fit. The one member of the faculty here at present comes and usually makes more than his share of noise. By the way, he is being spoken of as a probable successor to Tur at Buffalo; his name is Breslin, Monsignor Breslin.

Archbishop Hanna of San Francisco is here now; this is his alma mater, and he comes back to make the retreat with the fellows. The old man is very likeable, and there is growing up a real tradition around here about him. Whenever he is near Rome, he comes over to throw out the first ball of the baseball season — then actually forgets that he is not the pitcher and continues to pitch until somebody goes out to bring him off the field. He has lost his memory for things of the present but can recall events of long ago perfectly. He often gets completely lost around here. This morning he was supposed to say Mass for the community; he went to take a shower before dressing (he always sings the Te Deum while taking a shower) and couldn't find his way back to his room. The master of ceremonies had to go out looking for him; he found him wandering around the building. Then after Mass he couldn't find the refectory, which is just twenty feet from the chapel. Whenever the choir sings during a ceremony he lifts himself out of his pew, goes back and sings with the bass section in the choir. Of course, he can hardly make a sound, but the fellows would rather have the old man there than the best bass in the country. He and Monsignor Pace were classmates around here and are considered the brightest men ever to have gone through the North American. They were selected, when students, to engage in a public disputation in philosophy in the presence of Pope Leo XIII. He is the type of person that gives an institution a real tradition, a background and spirit that makes one accustomed to great ideas. [1]

By the time you have received this, the yearly rustic frolic at the farm on Halloween will be over. Well I'll probably celebrate it in Rome in a slightly different way — we'll help the country cheer for the king's coronation as Emperor but also dedicate it to the holiday in the U.S.

I am seated at a table next to a French fellow who saw the Spanish war from Hendaye, France. He says that the southern part of France is in a sorry state from Communism, etc. One of my future profs at the Gregorian University was a chaplain in the army of General Mola in the Spanish War. I should hear some interesting stories.

Well, I must go down and start the retreat.

How is Cardinal Pacelli's visit to the U.S. being received? Incidentally, everybody over here says that it is simply a pleasure trip. All these Italians are eager to see the U.S. Cardinal Pacelli is the guest of Mrs. Brady, Msgr. Sheen's patroness.

Love,
Phil

Comments: Letter of October 17, 1936

(1)   The old Archbishop was Archbishop Edward J. Hanna of San Francisco, retired in 1935, famous for having mediated the settlement of a huge strike on the waterfront. He was considered one of the leading scholars at the College and always considered the College as a second home. His absent-mindedness may have been Alzheimer's disease, but it made no difference to the College. Everyone is glad to be of assistance to him.

October 19, 1936

NORTH AMERICAN COLLEGE
Via Dell' Umilta 30

Dear Mom and Dad,

Retreat closed today. Conversation was limited to grunts, head shaking, and clearing of throats; complete silence for a week is difficult — for some people. An old Paulist was the retreat master; he had gone to Georgetown University and asked me about a number of people whom he had known there. But the old Archbishop provided the comedy. He sat in the back of the chapel and made comments on the speaker's remarks. If the retreat master said, "I remember when —", the Archbishop would chime in, "Sure, I remember that too" and then give his version of the event. The only difficulty was that the old man would laugh at the wrong time and upset the morale for a time. And, of course, it took the whole community to keep him straight; he always has to ask someone what day it is to find out what part of his office to say, and then he says his office by heart! I didn't see him with a breviary once. The old man certainly got fooled one day; he asked a fellow where his room was (he never could find his own room), and the fellow replied, "I don't know, your excellency, I am a new man around here too." This Archbishop would make a prize heckler; in fact, I think he must have gone to some revival meetings on the coast and learned the technique of dropping remarks at the right time.

I received the credits, etc. this morning. Many thanks. These things won't be used for quite awhile (except the credits), but I am supposed to submit them to the office.

There is positively no news around here at present; but Wednesday is the King's coronation as emperor, and we'll be in Rome to see it. Anyone in Italy can get a round trip ticket to Rome for only <u>ten</u> lira, so Rome will look like Coney Island on a hot day. We'll see what these militarist states can stage in the way of parades. But to be more local, we are having a ball tomorrow night in honor of the end of the season at the villa, in honor of the fellows to receive subdiaconate, in honor of the end of the retreat, and in honor of anything anybody wishes to honor. Of course, the whole affair is a grand mess with a prize given to the genius who can write the most ridiculous song for the occasion. Then there was another celebration in the way of movies. On one night we had two shows — Mutiny on the Bounty and The Music Goes Round and Round. It doesn't seem to make much difference about the value of the movie; everything is enjoyed so long as it is on the screen and moves.

We must pack to send our stuff into the city, so I'll have to let this letter go, apologizing for spending money to send this, and promising something worth reading when I see something in Rome.

Love,

Phil

October 28, 1936

NORTH AMERICAN COLLEGE
Via Dell' Umilta 30

Dear Everybody,

This morning, the day of the coronation of the king as emperor of Ethiopia and also the fourteenth anniversary of Fascist rule, I saw and heard Mussolini for the first time. To say that the ceremony was interesting is a great under-estimation — like saying that Niagara is just a lot of water. At about eight-thirty in the morning we knew that things had started to happen. There were buses of soldiers, soldiers in company formation, soldiers straggling along, soldiers everywhere in all kinds of uniforms. The parade was to be at ten-thirty, followed by the personal appearance and address of Mussolini.

We scrambled down to the palace in which Mussolini has his offices and home; there is a tremendous square in front of it and on one side is a great, gleaming monument to Victor Emmanuel, first king of Italy. By the time we had elbowed, squeezed, puffed and pushed our way to a point in front of the Duce's palace, troops from every organization had covered Victor Emmanuel's monument and planted their brilliant standards all over the marble stone.

There was a stand covered with red plush carpet in front of Mussolini's palace; flags were grouped on either side with the golden standards of imperial Rome all around (these people know how to flash the color). There were half a dozen soldiers with silver trumpets on each side of the stand. When all the troops had filed into their positions, everyone got excited and started to cheer; then the trumpeters flashed out their instruments and blared out a salute — and out strode the Duce. The generals, ministers, etc. all stay in the background, he strides out alone to the front of the platform; everybody else is but a part of the scenery with him the only actor. The only person around him who is permitted to show that he is really a human being and part of the affair is an officer who reads an announcement proclaiming the occasion.

Mussolini presents a splendid appearance — arms akimbo, booted legs planted firmly and apart, chest thrust out, head and chin defiantly set; he stands there sweeping the cheering mass of people and when the ovation sweeps ever louder, he suddenly flings his hand up in the Fascist salute. Then all Italy responds — every pair of lungs roars out its allegiance and hands shoot up in salute.

When things have grown a little quiet, the officer who does the reading stills the crowd and starts to read the list of those who are to be presented with medals. A great number received medals or citations for almost every kind of achievement; medals were even presented to Italian athletes who had been winners in the recent Olympics. Any citizen who has performed his office with distinction, whether he be aviator or dishwasher, gets some recognition; even the children's organizations had members receiving rewards. After the presentation ceremony, Mussolini left the stand and went into his palace. He always speaks from a balcony high up in the palace so that everyone can see and hear him. There is a radio system for broadcasting his voice across the square, but we were so near that we could hear his voice without the loud speakers.

When he came out on the balcony, the crowd gave another roar — more salutes, then everything grew still. When he speaks, he takes a grip on the balcony railing and starts to throw his whole body into the effort of speaking. He uses powerful, sweeping gestures. After his speech he goes almost immediately inside — but he'd be furious if the people didn't recall him with their cheers. He gets about ten encores. Ordinarily, before each speech, the people yell in quick, staccato fashion, "Duce, duce, duce, duce . . . . ." Duce means leader. Then he shouts, "Duce a chi?" (Leader for whom?) and the crowd thunders back, "A noi" (for us!). The effect is tremendous, even the religious cheer and salute him. But something really startling and significant happened today. After the sixth encore (about that time, anyway) he brought back two Germans dressed in uniform with the Nazi swastika on their arms and the crowd gave them a tremendous hand. That was to cement that recent pact between Italy and Germany, and also to impress the Germans. [1]

Believe it or not, Mussolini is a rather short man, but he is so clever in posing and exhibiting his really magnificent proportions that he appears much taller. Besides, he is always careful to be photographed from angles that increase the impression of his height.

Today was the celebration of the King's coronation. The King was nowhere even to be seen — he only wears the crown.

But things more important than the coronation of the King have happened for "yours truly". We moved into the college in Rome. What a place this college is! Merely to remark that the building is over 400 years old gives you some idea of what it might look like. But further historical details are needed to form the background: it was formerly a convent for an order of nuns that was suppressed and has been used for everything from housing nuns to stabling horses. There is a tradition that Napoleon stabled some of his horses here; I believe the tradition — also believe that he stabled them here for a long time — further believe that it killed the horses.

But to describe the building, the outside looks like the rear of a very poor burlesque theater. There are two courtyards; the first is rather pretty, the second looks like a backyard. That gives you only a very rough idea of the place, but if you get a rough idea, you get a correct idea of it. I can't describe accurately the interior. It was apparently planned by one who had a creative frenzy for narrow halls, many stairs, high ceilings; he also had an extreme aversion for building in a straight line, even when such a plan seemed necessary, and was apparently dedicated to the idea of putting each room on a different level. The corridors wander away in all levels and all directions.

The system they have of managing the college rivals the awkwardness of the building. The student body is divided into "cameratas" (groups) and each group is assigned to a certain part of the building. The prefect of the camerata lets the fellows choose the room they wish in the section allotted them. The rooms have four walls and one bed — you are supposed to supply the rest. The first item on the program is to hustle down and grab a mattress, lug it up to your room (and I live on the fifth floor), then scatter around to find a lamp for the bulb the college supplies, and so on far into the night. Tradition decrees that a fellow's diocesan brethren help to furnish his room with furniture, so now I am very comfortably fixed. [2]

Candidly, I like the whole system very much. The necessity of creating a livable room from only four battered walls makes for a spirit that is not found in the ordinary Sem. Besides, the rules are "interpreted" in such a way that the interpretation almost swallows the rule. The first impression of the place is that of a madhouse; then very quickly you begin to like it (or maybe you start to go mad yourself and can't tell the difference.)

Next time I'll report on some of the activities around here.

Love,

Phil

Comments: Letter of October 28, 1936

(1)   The headquarters of Mussolini, always called "Il Duce" (the Leader), was in the Palazzo Venezia (Palace of Venice) which had been built in 1455 as the embassy of the Republic of Venice. The Palazzo was very close to the College and, therefore, very accessible for us.

(2)   The furniture for the rooms of the students was the property of the diocese to which they belonged, and were assigned to the new students by the older students. Of course, they were a curious set of hand-me-downs; and if a new student bought new furniture, it eventually became the property of the diocese. The result was that each student's room had different furniture that generally looked like a section of a store for used furniture. Painting the room was also an option.

During World War II the building was used as an asylum for war orphans. I visited it very briefly during a visit to Rome after the war. I was given a "leave" for a few days and engineered a ride in one of our military planes to Rome, had a semi-private audience with Pope Pius XII who asked me, "What part of the Army?" When I replied, "The paratroopers." He said, "Very dangerous. I will give you a special blessing," and blessed the rosaries I had. The rosaries were my "pay off" to the Catholic pilot of the plane. Incidentally, when I returned to my unit, my Colonel bawled me out for going into another "theater" of war without proper permission.

November 1, 1936
All Saints Day

NORTH AMERICAN COLLEGE
Via Dell' Umilta 30

Dear Mom and Dad,

One of the Baltimore fellows over here, formerly one of the brethren at the Sulp Sem, suffered a nervous breakdown and is returning to the States. He has very kindly offered to take back the crockery I bought in Rome (I am writing this letter before I do the purchasing so I can't comment on them). I bought the bracelets at Pompeii; American cigarettes are prized so highly that I could have bought a bracelet with a pack of cigarettes. A pack of cigarettes is worth seventy-five cents in such trades. Kailer Dunn, the fellow returning, will be in Washington shortly after his arrival. [1]

Since I wrote last, I have done a bit of gallivanting about Rome. Yesterday we went to St. Mary Major and saw a picture supposed to have been painted by St. Luke. Well, if St. Luke really painted it, he should have confined his genius to writing Gospels. St. Mary Major is a very colorful and beautiful church. [2] We came in when vespers were being sung and saw the canons in all their glory. There is a Baltimorean priest in the canons of St. Mary Major; I can only recall his nickname — "Eau de Cologne." He deserves the name. Some of the fellows met him yesterday, (I meant smelled him). There are any number of relics in St. Mary Major: the cradle in which Our Lord was carried when a child when the Holy Family fled to

Egypt; a part of the manger at Bethlehem; the table used at the Last Supper; many relics and bodies of popes and saints, the most curious of which are two little bags containing the brains of St. Thomas a Becket. [3] Then, of course, there are any number of interesting stories, as this: The tomb of Pope Sylvester II is in the church and is supposed to foretell the death of the popes. According to the Italians, Sylvester was a magician and had sold his soul to the devil; the devil, in return, helped Sylvester in his ambition to become Pope. Well, the devil did right by him, and Sylvester was eventually elected Pope. Then the Pope asked him how long he would be allowed to reign, to which the devil responded, "As long as you do not pass a certain threshold in a church." The Pope passed the spot one day and began to die. Then he became repentant, confessed to the world his crime and urged everybody to keep away from the devil. As a punishment he commanded his body, when dead, to be cut into four parts, loaded onto a wagon and dumped wherever the horses stopped. But God, to show that any sinner can be forgiven, moved the horses to proceed directly to St. Mary's; and there they buried him. And now, just before the death of any pope, the tomb becomes moist and the bones of Pope Sylvester are heard to rattle. [4] Well, it's a good story anyway. I just remembered that I muddled the story a bit — the tomb is in St. John Lateran, not St. Mary Major. The paintings in these churches are magnificent. A very curious chapel is built in St. Mary Major, which was planned to glorify the Blessed Mother in her title of Mother of God. Consequently, the church has paintings and mosaics to the saints and popes who had a special devotion to the Blessed Mother; and there is one chapel there with statues of two popes who did not have a special devotion to the Blessed Mother. Their statues depict them knocked down; they are prostrate. I forgot to mention that St. Mary Major was built after the Blessed Mother had pointed out the location by a miraculous fall of snow on the fifth of August; snow fell only on this spot. St. John Lateran is a great church, bewilderingly large, and very much harmed by the "improvements" in the nave that look like a sore thumb.

We had a real experience this afternoon. We went to the Santo Campo (Holy Field — just another name for cemetery) and found that half of Rome had already arrived; and the other half was on its way. This was All Saints Day and the vigil of All Souls Day; almost everybody in Rome comes to decorate the graves of their dead, and the rest come to watch others decorate. It is amazingly interesting; the Italians are even better mourners than the Irish. Everyone buys flowers and throws at least one or two flowers at the foot of a great statue to Our Lord that is just within the gates. By nightfall there is a pile of flowers (six feet high when I left) all around the statue. And as the people leave the cemetery, they salute this statue in farewell. It is very edifying to see Fascist captains, generals, and soldiers give the military salute while mumbling a prayer; most of the women throw a kiss to the statue. The Italians have an amazing amount of ornamentation on their graves or vaults (all the wealthy have large vaults) and most of them have colored mosaics or paintings of the deceased on the tombstone or vault; some have busts or statues of the dead over their graves. (5) There are enough works of art there to merit a visit even if the rest were not so interesting.

There is a good deal of ceremony attached to an Italian funeral. The hearse is drawn by horses, and the family (unless they are wealthy) marches behind the hearse. As the funeral passes, everyone stops and takes off his hat or salutes. This is a rigid law. During the late war with Ethiopia an Englishman failed to take off his hat; he landed in the hospital. (6)

Well, three fellows on our "camerata" became separated and lost. After waiting over an hour and a half to show up at the appointed place, we started back, arrived very late and had to sneak in — not that we would be blamed but because of the embarrassing explanations that would be asked of the three fellows missing. To get in the college without being seen is as difficult as getting in a World Series game with no ticket. But we worked it.

On Halloween night we had a "scald" (the technical term for a bull session and party). If anyone was waiting for the eats, he would have died of starvation. All of us were newcomers at the racket and had to pay for our inexperience. After searching the house for stuff with which to percolate coffee, etc., we assembled a collection that would have shamed a junk dealer. But as soon as we got the coffee pot set up over some sort of an alcohol stove, the electricity went off; and someone bumped the coffee, spilled it on the flame, and we were just where we had started two hours earlier — only much more hungry and with no lights. By eleven-thirty we had the coffee bubbling. The flame was so thin that we had to stuff handkerchiefs into the mouth of the pot to keep the steam in. The fellows around here are recompensed for the inconveniences by the laxity of the rule. These inconveniences are enough to put hair on your chest: washing in water so cold that it's a wonder it can flow (and shaving is a major operation); living in a room with no heat — they say that sometimes they turn on the heat in December to impress the visitors that come for ordinations around Christmas (here's hoping for visitors); supplying you with an electric bulb and expecting you to build a room around it, etc. But it is a very likeable madhouse. These "scalds" are a rather regular occurrence to celebrate special events or holidays.

This morning we went to a Capuchin Church in the basement of a cemetery. All the good old monks wanted to die in the Holy Land so the order sent for some earth from the Holy Land, placed it in the basement of the church and buried the monks there. And so everybody died happily. The earth and graves are there now. But that's only half the story. After the monks had been buried for a long time, the living brethren dug them up (maybe to make room for more) and decorated chapels in the basement with the bones. [7] Some pious monk must have gone berserk and then drawn plans for the decorations. Everything in the chapels (as you can see from the postcards) is made from bones; there is a particularly striking lamp and centerpiece made of jawbones; and if you think these old boys couldn't arrange the shoulder blades in chic patterns, you are all wrong. At the head of the stairs leading to the basement is an old Capuchin begging for money who looks as if he had been dug up from his grave.

Father Kelly from Hartford is taking me out to dinner with some fellows from that diocese. If you hear of any other people from the U.S. coming through, tell them to drop in.

Love,

Phil

Comments: Letter of November 1, 1936

(1)   Kailer Dunn had a room on the "Archetto" side of the building, an extremely noisy side. Being sensitive, he found it very difficult to sleep and eventually suffered a mild nervous breakdown. In my second year, my room was on the Archetto side; and during the first night there I awoke twice thinking that people were in my room, so loud was the talk from the apartment on the other side of the street.

(2)   St. Mary Major was the second most popular church in Rome because of its history and presence of the relics of the Infant Jesus. The church was built in its grand proportions in 432, as a result of the decision at the Council of Ephesus, which declared the Blessed Mother to be the Mother of God. Its history includes the famous defense of the Pope at Midnight Mass by the Countess Matilda of Tuscany who grabbed a candlestick and helped to protect the Pope who was seized by the Cenci Faction but was later rescued by the Roman people. The decorations on the ceiling of the church are gilded by the gold first brought from the New World and presented to the King, Ferdinand and Queen Isabella of Spain, who in turn gave it to the Pope for the decoration of the ceiling of St. Mary Major.

(3)   Some of these relics were later declared to be not authentic.

(4)   The sleazy legend about Pope Sylvester is no longer in current use. These legends are the fiction of guides pandering to the anti-Catholic visitors or resurrected stories to please the gullible. I heard a guide in St. Peter's Basilica explain to an American group that the beautiful memorial to the Countess Matilda who left her lands in Tuscany to the Pope was the "female Pope." Of course, the visitors cannot read the inscriptions in Latin and learn the truth. These stories are no longer used in Rome.

(5)   November 1 is the Feast of All Saints and the vigil of November 2, the Feast of All Souls. Campo Santo (Holy Ground) is the vast cemetery where practically every believing Catholic family visits to show respect for the deceased relatives — bearing flowers, reciting prayers while kneeling at the grave, kissing the pictures of the deceased on the grave stones. Many graves are decorated with large and exquisite statues, a veritable art gallery.

(6)   Respect for the dead is rigidly maintained. Priests are allowed to celebrate three Masses on the Feast of All Souls, a privilege granted by Pope Benedict XV who was horrified at the battlefield losses during World War I. The Pope wished to provide enough Masses for the repose of the souls of all the war dead.

(7)   The Capuchin Church on the Via Veneto has an astonishing collection of human bones in the basement of the church. The reason for the bones is the promise made to the Franciscans that they would be buried in the Holy Land. The promise could not be fulfilled, so the superiors brought land from the Holy Land, placed it in the basement and buried the deceased in it. The bones were exhumed to make a place for other deceased Franciscans, and the displaced bones were used to decorate chapels in the basement. The sight is a shocker for most visitors. The custom no longer perdures.

November 2, 1936

NORTH AMERICAN COLLEGE
Via Dell' Umilta 30

Dear Mary,

Your enthusiastic letters about this city make me interested in it. Though we get around the city very well, we can't "explore at our leisure" because of the camerata system here. The whole school is organized into cameratas (groups of about ten) that go around together, and there are always some who would rather sleep than see Mussolini do cartwheels across the coliseum; Nero fiddled while Rome burned, but I know some who would merely blink a weary eyelash and turn over while Rome blew up and bust. Then there is the extremely stupid type, who get lost if they merely turn around. While visiting the Santo Campo, the large cemetery in Rome, three of our brethren got lost, couldn't even find the front gate though both of them could speak Italian! ! ! ! ! & ! We waited for about two hours at the front entrance, where we had agreed to meet; after wandering around like lost children for an hour and a half, they left by a side gate, boarded a street car (which goes right by the front entrance) and left us there waiting. I had a great time watching the crowd — nothing half so colorful as a Roman crowd on a feast day like that of All Saints — but the rest of the fellows were ready to commit murder.

Today classes began. [1] As one approaches the Gregorian University (a magnificent new building) he encounters myriads of students pouring out of all the streets and piling into the Greg as though taking it by storm. There are the Germans in flaming scarlet cassocks, the Scotch in blue cassock and red sash, the Irish with the inevitable green sash, monks with bald pates, mission orders with mops of hair, etc. The first class was with Father Lopez, young, keen, tremendous personality, ranked already as one of the four greatest moral theologians in the Church. Mary, to hear his Latin is a treat; it rolls off in long periods without hesitation, without a break or pause as though it had all been memorized. [2] His pronunciation is very distinct — even I could get almost everything the first day. Then we had Father Zappolini, another Spanish prof, reminds one of the grandee type, speaks very rapidly. Some have gone through his course without ever understanding him. There is no kitchen Latin spoken here at the Greg, none of that Americanized, pig Latin.

The students are grouped in class according to nations. [3] The Germans are given the position of honor, first rows in front, because the German College is the oldest in Rome. But first I have to describe the classrooms: the prof has his throne in front and all the benches are arranged in tiers with the last row up near the ceiling. Classes are generally large; classrooms have capacities of from 500 to 1000. The Argentineans have a rather honored post since the Republic of Argentina donated the building — "Built by the South Americans, supported by the North Americans" is the slogan. We are in about the center. The Irish have the reputation, in some classes, of being the hell raisers; some of them used to get thrown out of class in Hebrew almost every day. Well, from the looks of faces and general demeanor it looks as though I am in fast company for a few years.

By the way, of all the typewriters brought over by fellows this year, the Underwood you gave me is the only one not to have needed any adjustments. I'll sign ads — for a consideration.

After class (cut short purposely) the student body went to the Church of St. Ignatius for a solemn High Mass. I have no aversion to these foreign nations or to their customs, but O Lord how I hope the garlic crop in Europe will be blighted for the next four years. Outside of that they are excellent.

Father Kelly was around, sent for me, was very pleasant, promised to take me and the Hartford fellows out on a "bum run". Tomorrow is the date set for that. If you know any more people like him coming to Rome, send them around. I haven't seen the others you mentioned in your letter. By the way, you asked about opportunity for reading magazines. They have a regular reading room with all the leading

Catholic American magazines, but I would appreciate it very much if after reading the New York Times, you would send over only the book review and editorial sections. They do not pay attention to the rule forbidding reading of papers; the rule isn't even mentioned. Almost every fellow here has a crystal radio set; helps in picking up the language. Nobody on the faculty objects.

Love,

Phil

P.S. Marty sends his regards. I sent a picture of myself in "bags" (the term for our uniform) to 1501.

Comments: Letter of November 2, 1936

(1)   Classes at the Gregorian University, attended by the College seminarians, began in early November because the nearby Pontine Marshes had malaria-bearing mosquitoes during the warm months. Mussolini gained a great reputation for cleaning up the Pontine Marshes.

The first day of classes is the great test for the new seminarians to test their knowledge of Latin. Everything was taught in Latin, even the Hebrew language. A favorite ruse was to get permission for a visiting professor of Latin from the U.S. to attend a class — and see his discomfiture. Knowledge of Latin was a great benefit to me during the War because half our officers in the paratroopers were West Pointers and had to take Latin, which they royally detested. A casual word from me that we spoke Latin in the seminary classes elevated my prestige immediately.

(2)   My sister, Mary (Mrs. Robert Mahoney), had earned a Ph.D. in Latin, Greek and a minor in mathematics at The Catholic University in Washington, D.C. and, therefore, was very interested in Latin being used at the Gregorian University.

She and her husband, Superintendent of Education for Hartford, Connecticut, had spent their honeymoon in Italy and were very interested in all the events there. They were particularly

41

interested in the organization of the Gregorian with its vast international student body.

(3)   Very often, American students who wished to learn colloquial Italian would make an agreement with an Italian student to spend the recreation time together, both learning the language of the other. It was a common sight to see these pairs walking and talking. I tried the arrangement for a few months but our agreement was finally discarded.

The reason for the distinctive dress for each nation was to cultivate a sense of unity as well as to satisfy (according to the prevailing rumor) the demands of the local police. The story prevailed that the Germans wore a red cassock not only because of their seniority as a student body but also because they were quarrelsome and the police wished to have an easily distinguished target in case of trouble.

November 21, 1936

NORTH AMERICAN COLLEGE
VIA DELL' UMILTA 30

Dear Everybody,

A few days ago we got into an old palace in Rome, one belonging to a powerful family that has ruled things in this section for about eight hundred years. Visitors are allowed in the picture gallery (mostly portraits of members of the family) and the great ballroom. Just off the ballroom is the throne room, once occupied by two Popes. (The family was strong enough to have one of its family elected pope, and instead of going to the Vatican he decided that he could protect his life better by staying in his home — no little consideration in those days.) The throne chair was turned towards the wall. [1] We asked the attendant why it was turned like that, and he told us that it was a custom in Rome for all cardinals to turn their chairs towards the wall ever since 1870 as a protest against the taking of the papal possessions by the Italian nation. And, of course, this throne chair was turned towards the wall for the same reason. However, they are all supposed to be turned around again now that the accord was signed between the Vatican and the Italian government. In the great ballroom they have left a cannonball on the steps just where it fell after being fired by French troops who took Rome in 1849.

This old palace, the Colonna, has a number of odd things connected with it. [2] They have a large church built in one section of the palace (what used to be the private chapel of the family) and that church used to be the scene of a really queer event. On certain feast days all the poor people were allowed to jam into the church and jump for live pigs and geese that were either thrown to them from the balcony or hung on ropes and lowered to about eight feet above the ground; whoever could grab them could keep them. Some fun.

I told you about the St. Vincent de Paul Society that was formed here. It seems to be developing a real business. The latest news has it that a Countess comes around for food; she has six dependents — only one of which is capable of landing a job. The situation would be really tough if living conditions over here were not so cheap; the society had to pay for the rent of a family of five — the rent was four dollars and a half a month.

The Vice Rector has decided to take some courses at the Greg University this year. He is studying dogma — I suppose simply to keep up interest in something or to keep from getting in a rut. The rub will come at the end of the year; he will, of course, be obliged to take a public exam just like the rest of the students. That examination room will certainly be crowded by students from our college the day of the exam. It will be just too bad for him if he fubs the exam, he will never be able to lay the law down to anyone for not studying. I think that he's a brave man for trying to improve himself at such a price — everything to lose if he flunks and nothing to win if he doesn't. All that reminds me of our first year at Basselin. A priest who had taught us at St. Charles was a student in one of our classes (German class). All during the year he kept repeating that Behrendt was going at just the right pace for him; the rest of us were squawking a bit because Behrendt was actually going at a terrific clip. At the end of the year everybody except the priest passed the exam; he flunked that year and the next year too.

Thanksgiving Day will be something unusual this year in Rome. We always go up to the American Church for the High Mass, but this year there will be an added attraction. The vice rector is scheduled to give the sermon, and he is billed as <u>Dr.</u> Allen Babcock — as a matter of fact, he doesn't have any degrees.

Love,

Phil

Comments: Letter of November 21, 1936

(1)   The custom of the cardinals in Rome turning their throne towards the wall as a protest against the Government's seizure of the Papal States in 1870 continued until the Lateran Pact or treaty in 1928, when the Church was ceded the territory of the Vatican State and certain buildings in Rome which had offices of the Church in them. There is no longer any tension between the government of Italy and the Church.

(2)   The Colonna Palace was very close to the college. The Colonna, the word means column or pillar, was one of the ancient and great families of Rome extending back to imperial Rome days, stronger from 1100 onwards. The family had two Popes, the more famous was Martin V, who ended the stay of the Popes in Avignon, for seventy years. The palace in Rome was a fort; their stronghold was in Palestrina, a small town outside of Rome.

The Colonna family opposed papal ownership of property. In times of crisis, a Colonna was chosen for crucial offices, for instance, as Mayor after World War II. After 1562, two Popes, Sixtus V and Gregory XVI, agreed to give to the Colonna and Orsini families the exclusive right to attend the papal ceremonies as an honorary guard. This ended the enmity of the Colonna towards the Church and cemented a friendship between the Orsini and Colonna families. TodaY, one may see them standing near the papal throne at important ceremonies in St. Peter's Basilica.

November 26, 1936
Thanksgiving Day

NORTH AMERICAN COLLEGE
VIA DELL' UMILTA 30

Dear Mom and Dad,

Every week (at least as long as I have been here) they have a parade or celebration in Rome. And yesterday they had a tremendous shebang in honor of the Regent of Hungary and his wife who are visiting the king — and incidentally patching up some sort of an agreement between the two countries. They had real pageantry: the royalty rode in the famous state coaches with footmen, horse guards and lackeys all loaded down with ornaments as if they were Christmas trees. I think it's a very good idea. It gives the people something to think about, something to cheer for; maybe F.D.R. ought to go in for that stuff. And speaking about royalty, it is the opinion of the English fellows at the Greg that the King of England is going to marry this Mrs. Simpson (a native of Baltimore) who is suing her husband for a divorce. But to get back to the parade. Everybody was dressed up like Generals, especially the King's lancers who have so many plumes that it looks as though a feather bed was poured over them. But they have some divisions that mean business; there were some units in which almost every man carried a machine gun, and there was plenty of artillery bumping along the street. But the blacks stole the show again; they are really the stuff in their long robes.

Unlike our parades, hardly anyone without a ticket can get within a good distance of the royal coaches or officials as they march past. To attempt an assassination one would need a long-range gun. One does not know what American liberty means until he comes over here. The newspapers amount only to a diary or propaganda sheet for the government in power. [1] There are no such things as "Letters to the Editor" about things in general or especially about the government. In fact, the newspapers are so strictly nationalistic in tone that one nation has almost no idea of what the next nation is really like. The only way these people secure information about the Americans is through the movies. To show you how strictly all European papers are guarded: the

English people know nothing about the King's affair with Mrs. Simpson, hardly know that she even exists. When the King sent her name with the list of those who were to assist at court for this season, it caused a huddle among the editors to see if they would even print her name! The English students knew about her only through the American magazine, "Time".

There are a number of Spanish refugees in Rome now. The Spanish College at the Greg is much depleted. Many of the Sems went home in July and were caught in the revolution; some escaped, but many of them were shot or were forced to serve in the ranks with the Reds. An unusual incident occurred the other day: one Spaniard has not been able to locate and has not heard from his family since the beginning of the war, but an Englishman was showing him the London "Times" when suddenly he pointed to a picture of the battle around Madrid and said, "That fellow in the front rank is my brother."

Well, our Thanksgiving entertainment came off beautifully. We, the supposed suckers, made the others the suckers. Then, for reprisal, they tried to ruin our finale by booing it under. The joke was on them — we didn't have an ending. It took some of them about ten minutes to realize that we were making them suckers. But these fellows are excellent; they can appreciate a joke on themselves. After the show we had a "scald" that was more enjoyed in preparing than in eating. The attitude around here seems to be that almost anything is permitted (at least until the rector gets back) if you do not disturb anyone — and don't get caught. Dragging a quart of milk into the house in one's pocket is a real job.

Happy Thanksgiving; we're having turkey too.

Love,

Phil

Comments: Letter of November 26, 1936

(1)   Freedom of the press was not a reality in Italy, especially in Rome. Every newspaper was owned by a political party and was totally subject to it. The paper was used to nurture and foster the progress of the party. This was especially true in regard to the Fascist Party and the government of Italy, which opposed in many instances the position of the Church. The Church had its own newspaper, <u>Osservatore Romano</u>.

From their viewpoint, the Italians did not believe there was any "freedom of the press." The attitude perdured even during the II Vatican Council; and because they do not believe in the freedom of the press, they were very strong in supporting the right of the government to suppress the press in time of a national crisis.

December 1, 1936

NORTH AMERICAN COLLEGE
Via Dell' Umilta 30

Dear Mom and Dad,

There is a bit of professional advice I want to hand on to Frank. If he ever forgets his instruments when going out on a sick call, don't let that faze him at all. In Rome it seems to be a sign of excellence in a doctor to hold instruments in contempt. The fellow rooming next to me developed a cold with a bit of fever. The doctor was called in. Along came the doctor with no instruments at all, just as free and easy as if he were making a social call. First of all he wanted to know how much of a fever the patient had, so he simply asked him how high his temperature was. So, of course, the patient told him that he had no way of satisfying his curiosity. His curiosity wasn't satisfied. Then he decided to take a look down his throat. So he told the fellow to open his mouth, lit a match and had his look. Prescription: two aspirin tablets. I don't know why they make you go to med school so long. [1]

The poor Italians have some quaint ways. On very chilly days they light a fire — but not inside the house. [2] They drag a large iron bowl outside the door, make the fire in it, and then the family comes outdoors to get warm. And to get warm quicker the little boys take off their shirts and undershirts and get up close to the fire. No one ever thinks, apparently, of trying to heat the house. There are, of course, no lawns in front of houses. There isn't one lawn in all Rome.

And as long as I am making this a social history of the modern Romans, I might as well tell you about some of the unusual dishes we get here. The all time record, so far, is the sardine soup we had a few days ago. Yes sir, try it some time when you feel plenty strong, are not hungry, and have plenty else besides to eat. Then they have unusual combinations, for instance, scrambled eggs and sauerkraut for Friday evening meal. But no matter how badly the cards are going, they always rely on their everlasting trump card to straighten everything out — wine. It seems to make no difference what the meal is, the magical wine perfects everything.

I haven't seen any American newspapers, so I don't know much about the condition of world politics; but according to the Italian newspapers, there seems to be a war impending. There is a rumor that three thousand Italian troops left Rome on their way to Spain on Sunday morning. It's a fact that 3000 left Rome but I don't know if they left for Spain. Furthermore, there is a rumor that some Italian official was killed in Spain. A crowd gathered in front of the Duce's palace on the Piazza Venezia — which is a sign that it was of real importance to the people. Anytime something rather important happens a crowd rushes to the Piazza Venezia to see what's going to be done about it. As I said once before, one can't tell from the Italian newspapers what is the true condition of things since the editors suit themselves and change to suit the governmental policy. For instance: right after the pact with Germany was signed anything that Germany or a German did was news. Schmeling made some very trifling remark that he was the number one candidate for the world heavyweight title (which everybody knows and admits), and it rated a whole column of space in the paper. And now I notice an extraordinary amount of space dedicated to condemning the Reds in Spain and Russia to the lowest position in hell. When the regent of Hungary came here recently, the report of his arrival took up the entire front page and most of the second. [3] The only extraneous material on the front page was the weather report. Maybe I'll get early ordination — there's bound to be a war.

Did I tell you that our Vice Rector is going to be pastor at White Plains, New York. He was given a farewell party and waxed sentimental, so everybody went up to his office the next day to get permission for something or other. The boss and the new Vice Rector arrive tonight. We are much interested; the new vice rector will have his room about ten feet from mine. The days of sweet freedom are over.

I hope that Kailer Dunn gets those two bracelets over to you.

I'll send Christmas Cards on the next boat. There is no Christmas shopping in Rome; they don't celebrate it like we do at all.

Love,

Phil

Comments: Letter of December 1, 1936

(1)   The description of the doctor's examination relates to an actual case. The "house doctor" for the College was a very pleasant doctor who had a very minimal command of English. He generally began every examination with the words, "Do you have pain (pronounced 'pine')?" I learned later, from experience, that the level of medical care in Rome was much lower than in the U.S.

(2)   The poor Italian families lit fires outside the home to prevent smoking up the home. Furthermore, fuel for heating was extremely expensive because Italy has no hard coal deposits; all the fuel was imported.

(3)   The support of the Fascist dictatorship depended upon constant excitement generally directed towards the national foes, the Communists. Mussolini was anti-Communist and helped the foes of Communism, especially Germany, as a means of gaining favor with Germany, bitterly opposed to Communism. There was a strong support of General Franco's forces in Spain and voluntary demonstrations favoring him in front of the Spanish Embassy. Hungary was a national ally because of its opposition to Russian Communism.

December 10, 1936

NORTH AMERICAN COLLEGE
VIA DELL' UMILTA 30

Dear Everybody,

Before I launch into my letter, let me say a "Very Merry Christmas and Happy New Year". And I had better tell you (in case the mail is held up) that I am sending my Christmas message by a record made here in Rome. It's much better than sending a cablegram — so I thought. The record should arrive before Christmas.

As you can imagine, the English are like old ladies caught doing something vulgar. They take an awful beating because of their King and complain of "that blasted American woman." It's really funny the ideas these Europeans have of the American women. Of course, the papers here capitalize on the fact that this Simpson gal has been divorced twice — and divorce is hardly heard of in most places in Europe. But the Scotch are getting a big kick out of the whole affair; "we knew he was a rat, anyway" is their general opinion. [1]

All the new men met the new Rector, Bishop Hayes, in his room. He did his best to be amiable and cordial, and pretty well succeeded. But the thing that rankles is that none of these former Roman students were ever at a first class university and think that the Seminary in Rome is the only good school in the world. They are so shortsighted that they can't see as far as their noses. For instance, they try to impress one with the standards, work needed, etc. But the cold fact is that it is easier over here in scholastic matters than it is in the U.S., at least at the Sulp Sem. But, notwithstanding his unpopularity, the Bishop is O.K. He does make some extraordinarily stupid blunders. For instance: the highest office in the house is that of first prefect and is appointed by the rector. A few days ago the new first prefect (the first one appointed by this rector) went in to see him about something. After the interview the Rector asked someone who his visitor was, complaining that he seemed too forward. He was told that it was the first prefect he had appointed. "Oh it was," says he, "I thought I appointed a tall, dark-haired boy." That's inexcusable. [2]

There is a very odd practice at the Greg University in regard to fellows who come late for class. By common consent, the whole class is free to hiss them although this reception interrupts the class and discomfits the prof. I don't mind any display of good old rowdyism, but this stuff is simply childish — they have been doing it for years (and probably will until the crack of doom) and still they laugh and carry on as if it were the most original thing since Noah's Ark. The Americans don't go in for it, rather resent it. I'd love to see somebody come in late and give them a great big hand salute from the nose. I just can't understand Italian humor. They say that their movies are (judged from our viewpoint) just about the dumbest thing that ever happened. Ed Latimer, whom you might remember, told me of going to see a vaudeville show during the past summer; the thing that knocked them out of their seats and rolled them in the aisles from laughing was the sight of a fellow kicking a girl — slapstick stuff. Not all of the Italians are like that. The Northerners are very refined. [3]

We still get a big kick out of making all the guards at monuments, etc. give us the salute when we tip our hats or give them a salute. They are the most obliging people in the world for posing that I have ever heard of. Even the officers will stand in the street and pose for a camera, and a private will salute until he gets muscle bound if he thinks you are taking a movie picture of him. They don't ask for a development — just enjoy being taken.

I am just getting accustomed to dodging automatically trucks, buses, horse carriages, etc. As you may have heard, it is against the law to blow a horn in the streets of Rome. And there are no sidewalks. Consequently, one never knows when a nice little bus is creeping up on him. The drivers flush the motor or bang on the side of the door to warn the pedestrians — if they warn them at all. As practice for walking the streets of Rome, try walking on F Street during the Christmas rush. [4]

What kind of a Christmas tree this year? Could you take a picture of it and send it over, an exposure?

Love,

Phil

Comments: Letter of December 10, 1936

(1)   To understand the embarrassment of the English about the affair of Wally Simpson with King Edward VIII, we must remember that the British Empire was at its peak at that time. It had great prestige in continental Europe and elsewhere and their King was the symbol of their eminence. It was a wrenching crisis for the nation, and the night that the King announced his intention of renouncing the throne, the whole world listened. The speech of the King was repeated on radio in succeeding days.

(2)   Bishop Ralph Hayes, the former Bishop of Helena, Montana, was the new Rector, and the rumor mill asserted that he was chosen "to restore order" in the College. Bishop Hayes had been, it was said, the first prefect in his senior year at the College. My petulant remarks about the scholastic rank of the College compared with the Sulpician Seminary which I attended neglects the fact that a major part of

our education in Rome was the presence of the Holy See and the historic nature of all Christian Rome.

(3)   The Gregorian University, as every institution, had its own unofficial code of conduct. Most of the faculty permitted the hissing of latecomers to class because the principal classes (of dogmatic and moral theology) had about 700 students. If late-coming was tolerated, the discipline would be destroyed. The professors had no public address system in those days.

(4)   The blowing of horns was abolished by Mussolini because the traffic noise was unbearable. As a substitute the drivers, especially the taxi drivers, banged with their hands on the door of their cars and yelled at the other drivers. The government employed some experts from Detroit to suggest a method of traffic handling (installing more traffic lights, etc.) but the report was disregarded. I asked a taxi driver (who was frantically beating on his door and screaming at another driver) why they didn't accept the report. He replied, "This way it's more poetic."

December 16, 1936

NORTH AMERICAN COLLEGE
Via Dell' Umilta 30

Dear Everybody,

The past week has been the most eventful of the year. Friday night we had a small fire in the roof, just enough to cause plenty of excitement and no danger. The center of attention was the faculty. All three, Rector, Vice Rector and Spiritual Director, rushed up to the top floor where about three of us were throwing water at the very small fire. The Vice Rector was like a schoolboy; I was generous enough to give him the basins of water that I lugged down the hall so that he could have the pleasure of throwing some. The whole student body was gathered below yelling and making cracks at the faculty (it happened about eight o'clock at night so no one could be blamed for any remark). The Vice Rector would lean out of the window and throw a basin of water, saying as he did, "I'll bet the fellows below get it this time." The Rector was poking his head all over the place, doing nothing but getting himself worried and in the way.

The cracks at the faculty were the most enjoyable part of the program. As the Rector, all dressed in his episcopal red and with a red birettum on, leaned out of the window to take a look some unholy scoundrel greeted him with, "Make way for the fire chief", and everyone who could manage it imitated fire sirens. He soon ducked in. As the first basin of water was thrown on the fire, someone shouted, "Wait until we find out whether it's insured" and, of course, there was all sorts of advice to throw gasoline instead of water on it. As the Vice Rector reached the scene and poked his head out of the window, a voice below suggested that he jump. As the faculty ran up the stairs to get a look at the fire, half a dozen fellows yelled the "bersaglieri march" (the bersaglieri are the crack emergency troops who always run). The fire started in the chimney and was not dangerous at all; one of the servants went up on the roof and started tearing away the tiles around the chimney so that he could kick the fire out. As he tore a hole into the roof, he was encouraged plenty; and there was many a fellow who would have volunteered to go up and do a real job on the roof. All in all I have never seen a more weird performance, one hundred and fifty fellows gathered below yelling at the faculty, and those trying to do something about the fire and no one lifting a hand to help. No one even suggested getting one of the two fire departments in Rome — not that they would have accomplished anything anyway. Incidentally, the fire company charges for its services.

But besides having a fire, we also had a flood scare. The Tiber rose very high and everyone was hoping that the rain would continue. No traffic was allowed to cross a couple of the bridges, especially the Milvian Bridge, the most famous one. I saw the Tiber, but there was no reason to either fear or to hope. It's close to Christmas, and since we are supposed to go on "bum runs" after Christmas a flood would be a very good opportunity for getting a longer vacation. Furthermore, the Rector decided to cut down the vacation limit to three days, so there was all the more reason for welcoming a convenient flood; and from his determined attitude at present, it seems as though it would take a large flood to allow us out longer. Three days for a Christmas vacation seems an absurdly short time to me; it takes almost half a day on an Italian train to get out of the railroad station, so two days of our three-day vacation will be spent on the train — if we go anywhere. No reason has been given for the new rule; maybe he thinks that we are all farmers and get a thrill out of riding on a train. I am still undecided on where to go.

The Sacred Congregation of Sacraments has decided that the students here should get tonsure (the first minor orders) during their second year of theology, instead of allowing them to get it in their third year. [1] That means that I will get a free hair cut sometime this year, probably in February. In America, getting tonsure means almost nothing, but over here one is supposed to wear his tonsure when in Rome — that is, he is supposed to have a little bald spot made on the back of his head. You can be sure that the Americans see to having a very small tonsure.

In my short stay in Italy we have undergone the dangers of fire, flood, earthquake, famine, and disease (if one counts epidemics of the "runs" as a disease). I can't boast of having been born in a log cabin or having had to fight Indians, but all that is like child's play compared to living in Italy. Come to think of it, it seems to me that the brave people were not the Europeans who came to America but those who stayed home to put up with Europe.

A few days ago we visited a very ancient and extensive catacombs, the catacombs of Saint Laurence. [2] They are about fifteen miles long, so we were told — we did not walk the whole distance. And it is just the sort of catacombs you imagine; everything is very narrow and tortuous; the level constantly changes; the corridors lead in all directions. It was formerly used as a pagan burial place and has an old pagan chapel in it; two frescoes of pagan gods are still visible on the walls. Then the Christians got control of it. How they ever kept track of all the passages and corridors is beyond me. Everything is pitch black. One must carry a candle with him because they have not illumined it with electricity. They have left a few of the old oil lamps on the walls where they were put two thousand years ago, but all of the bodies and bones have been moved. (A few bones are still to be seen in the burial niches.) A catacombs would be a terrible place for a man afflicted with rheumatism; water drips down in many places, and the whole thing is about as damp as a bathroom after a hot shower. I think a Christian deserved the palm of martyrdom for even living in one of those places. I would like to grab a couple of souvenirs from one of the catacombs, but I think there is a punishment of excommunication for disturbing any of the things there.

Happy New Year to everybody.

Love,

Phil

Comments: Letter of December 16, 1936

(1)   The ceremony of tonsure was the introduction to the clerical state. A bishop generally performed the ceremony, and it consisted of cutting a few locks of hair with an accompanying prayer. The candidate would complete the cutting of the tonsure after the ceremony. Some candidates for religious orders wore a "full tonsure", the cutting of all the hair except a rim of hair to denote the size of the tonsure. The Americans and other candidates for the diocesan or secular priesthood wore a small tonsure, a round section no larger than a half-dollar coin.

The whole tonsure ceremony was abolished by the II Vatican Council.

(2)   The catacombs deeply impressed me. I gradually developed a great love and deep respect for them and studied intensely about them. They are very impressive proofs of the faith of the early Christians, the hierarchical character of the Church, the devotional practices of the early Christians including their frequenting of the sacraments especially the Holy Eucharist. I celebrated one of my first Masses in the Catacombs of Priscilla in the "Greek Chapel" which contains the oldest picture of the Mass. I had the good fortune to know Father Joseph Wilpert, an Austrian priest who spent forty years excavating and studying the catacombs. Our **FOCUS** news team made a three-part documentary on the catacombs in 1990 emphasizing their catechetical value.

There are about 100 miles (about 150 kilometers) of excavated catacombs in Rome, the most well known are the Catacombs of Saint Callistus, Domitilla, Priscilla and Sebastian. Saint Callistus contains the famous burial chamber of the early Popes and other priceless tombs. The

Church has not pursued the further excavation of the catacombs because of the huge expenditure required and also the cost of maintenance.

December 18, 1936

NORTH AMERICAN COLLEGE
Via Dell' Umilta 30

Dear Mom and Dad,

Perhaps you will recall the frantic search made for my gold watch shortly before I sailed. The search is ended. I had looked in every imaginable and possible place, except the place that an ordinary person would look first, my watch box. And for the first time in my life I must have accidentally put it in the ordinary place, since I found it there yesterday. Furthermore, I distinctly recall that the last time I looked at it — three years ago — it was not running; and that wasn't simply my impression for I took it down to Mr. Paul's and he told me it would cost $3.50 to fix it. Well, it must have been suffering from a nervous breakdown and only needed rest for it runs perfectly now. Maybe it needed a change in climate. I found the watch wrapped in a shroud of tattered watch fob ribbons, which were also missing for a long time.

Two days ago I saw my first automobile accident in Rome. Even the way in which they have accidents is different and has its own peculiar Italian flavor. Two trucks smashed; the driver of one was apparently knocked cold and blood flowed from his mouth. About one hundred and fifty clerics of all forms, shapes and misshapes were there (the Greg had just finished classes for the day) besides the usual crowd. Although the driver seemed dead no one thought of getting a priest or administering the last Sacraments or even suggesting such a thing. Someone did ask a taxi driver to take him to the hospital — which suggestion the taxi driver positively and emphatically turned down unless somebody would pay for the bill. Then the usual argument ensued about the determination of the guilty party, so the injured driver was forgotten about as completely as if he had been in the tomb for a year. About five minutes later the driver came to, got up, and pitched into the argument too. [1]

You mentioned in your last letter your decision to see about accommodations for a trip over. Give me half an idea where you want to go (outside of Italy), and I'll fix up the whole itinerary and will find out from the fellows the cheapest and best hotels. Everybody says to go through Bavaria in Germany so don't forget that. [2]

And don't expect to get cloth, etc., too cheaply here. Things are going up since Italy went off the gold standard.

They have some Christmas trees in Rome, very small things. But they go in for dolls and almost all of them are little African dolls — Ethiopians. Furthermore, they believe that Santa Claus was a witch so he is dressed up in a witch's outfit. It looks more like our Halloween than Christmas.

Happy New Year,

Love,

Phil

Comments: Letter of December 18, 1936

(1)   Traffic arguments, as other arguments, in Rome never end in physical fighting. They simply shout at each other, a much more civilized behavior than fighting. The police, at such times, are admirable in their patience and restraint. On one occasion, my taxi drove so close to a sidewalk that the handle of the door speared a woman's bag from her arm. She screamed, I yelled, "Stop" at the driver, jumped out and apologized to the woman. The taxi driver simply yelled at her and blamed her for the accident.

(2)   Our family, especially my mother, was very avid travelers. I was in Rome only a few months when she began to question how to visit me in Rome and where to travel in Europe.

December 31, 1936

NORTH AMERICAN COLLEGE
Via Dell' Umilta 30

Dear Everybody,

I think I was telling you about our Christmas when I had to leave for Aquila. After the all-night session and Mass at St. Mary Major the next day, I was ready for the Christmas meal and went to bed after dinner. [1] The third year class presented a mystery show that night in which all but two members of the cast were shot — very appropriate for a Christmas show. Ed Latimer, whom you may remember, played the part of a society woman and committed suicide. It was an amazingly interesting play, but the acting was less than second rate. Anything may happen here on Christmas, anything but the usual manner of celebrating Christmas.

The day after Christmas seven of us pulled out for Aquila, a town in the mountains about one hundred miles from Rome. [2] The train left at about twelve, we arrived in Aquila about six thirty. On some of these side routes in Italy one must change trains about every time the engineer finishes a cigarette. Although the coaches are extremely crowded, the Italians insist on keeping the windows shut; but we had our giant along so we pulled the windows down and let the *Italians* squawk, and they squawked plenty. The ride to Aquila is amazingly interesting — walled towns, old castles and then the sight of snow-capped mountains. We spent Saturday night in a hotel in Aquila and went up to the crest of the mountain range on Sunday morning and stayed at a modern hotel, Albergo Campo Imperatore, which is right on top of the mountains. But I am getting ahead of my story.

We got up at five-thirty on Sunday morning, went to Mass at the cathedral in the town (they don't heat their churches at all so we did everything but roll up in a blanket while hearing Mass) and just gaped at the way these old Italian women can read their prayer books by candle light and keep praying while they are freezing. Grabbed the bus going to the mountaintop at seven o'clock; as usual it was crowded but everybody was in a great mood. The Italians would rip off a couple of songs, we'd give them a big hand and then sing a couple of American songs — they would give us a big hand and start singing again, etc. The Italians are amazingly friendly and splendid companions. After we had traveled about forty minutes or more on the bus, we came to the end of the road. What a ride then! We clambered into a cable car that "floats through the air with the greatest of ease" over a couple of minor mountain peaks and lands you in a valley on the top of the range. This car doesn't travel on a track, it is suspended from an overhead cable and as one floats over crags and valleys he either gets a distinct thrill or an awful feeling in the pit of his stomach. That's the time you are glad Mussolini is in power. All this sort of stuff is guaranteed by the

Fascist inspectors and is modern in equipment. The mountains are sublime in their rugged beauty; there is not a tree or anything living (except a bit of moss) on the whole range. The only things that I saw cross the mountains were two giant airplanes.

We arrived at the hotel about nine in the morning and found that they had three Masses every Sunday morning up there — and we had gotten up at five-thirty to hear Mass! We were dressed in "bags" (our uniforms) so the manager asked us if we wanted to say Mass. We politely refused. We couldn't get any skis immediately so Marty, Frank Latourette (a member of our party) and myself got ourselves climbing sticks and started up a mountain. Latourette comes from Denver and has done quite a bit of mountain climbing, good for us. Things went well for half an hour, then we lost the trail. For the next fifteen minutes we really went to work on that mountain side — no danger because the mountain was not too steep and had no cliffs, but we just had to crawl up fighting and digging for every inch. Johnny Linn, a diocesan, was along with us too, and his stocky build caused him no end of trouble; if anyone were listening, they could hear his puffing in Rome. About three-quarters up we met an Italian and his German wife coming down carrying skis; he had been to Florida so we had a nice talk — there's nothing half so sociable as a mountain climber. What surprised us was the manner in which the women are left to themselves when they go out to ski; no matter how tough the grade is or how much trouble they are having, their husbands don't pay the slightest attention to them. This Italian we met was a splendid fellow but never offered to carry his wife's skis and didn't even help her down the mountain. When we met him he was about one hundred and fifty yards ahead of his wife who was having what one might call a "heluva" time trying to balance herself and carry her skis, but hubby didn't even bother to look at her. Coming down the mountain, we offered to carry the skis of a girl who was falling on an average of every five feet; but she insisted on lugging the skis herself. Maybe she didn't trust us, maybe she didn't like us, or maybe she was stubborn, but at any rate, they all insist on carrying their own skis even though it half kills them. The last fifty feet up the slope were the hardest; the snow had melted on top and frozen. When we arrived there, a man about forty or fifty years old was in a mess. He couldn't make the grade, and he didn't want to turn around and go down (mainly because there is a hut on the top where one can get coffee with rum in it); so he started to bellow for help. A young woman came out, walked down that ice as though she were walking on a velvet rug, grabbed him by the arm and pulled him up. The view from the crest of that mountain is magnificent; I never felt so much like a pee wee in all my life. The card I sent gives you an idea of the view — it's useless to attempt a description. The hut has a very interesting sign with this friendly warning against any attempt at robbery on the top of the mountain, "Anyone who steals anything here not only commits a theft but prepares for an assassination; whoever takes anything not only commits a crime but a sacrilege . . . ." While up on the mountain we had an opportunity to watch three fellows scale a solid rock peak about a mile away, and I'll tell anyone that a mountain climber is no sissy. It is extremely windy up on top but not cold; the sun was bright and we got a sunburn. In fact, some of the veterans wore only woolen shirts with sleeves rolled up. When we went skiing, we wore plenty of sweaters — not so much for protection against the cold, but for protection against the ground, which continually hopped up and bumped us.

We went skiing for the first time that afternoon. We were prepared for a rather tough time because the old timers up there all declared that the snow was too frosted for good skiing. We started out bravely after making the mistake of trying to put on skis when out on the snow instead of on cleared ground. There's no doubt about it, a fellow can really slip along with those skis. In fact, he can't help from slipping at least in some direction. I put on the things, took a brave resolution, swallowed hard, and let go. For the first fifty feet or so I thought a miracle had happened; I was skidding along marvelously keeping my knees slightly bent and relaxed. But soon I got into a bumpy stretch and found myself still skidding along but with the skis in the air and my back on the ground. Getting up is not so much trouble if one is not too clumsy; but if one is clumsy, he had better take off the skis and then get on his feet. It is an amazingly thrilling sport as long as you are not afraid of taking spills and have not bruised your body too much; but when you have taken half a dozen bad spills, it's time to take off the skis, sit down on a very soft cushion and read a book or play cards — anything to take your mind off a few parts of your anatomy. [3]

The ability of some of these fellows at skiing is breathtaking. They can tear down a hill much steeper than that on 13 Street, turn in any direction coming down (they come down zigzagging) and come to a stop by making a very sudden and swift turn. Many of them can use their skis like skates, ride on one ski with the other off the ground. And all this happens on ground that is not smooth.

I had a strange experience one afternoon. I came out after dinner, put on skis and had a terrific time. I began to think that the wine had been too strong, when down the hill came a girl with mother, father, brother and boyfriend. She had put her skis in the wrong rack and I had taken them. It's a good thing I don't blush; I didn't mind being publicly dispossessed of a pair of skis, but I hated to think that I couldn't even navigate on girls' skis. I found later that she was really good at skiing and, like all regular skiers, waxed her skis. Waxed skis would be hard to walk on in dry ground, and on icy snow. . . . . . .

We could ski only on Sunday and Monday, because we had to start back on Tuesday. It was sufficiently long to learn a few things and especially to learn how to fall gracefully. Theoretically, we know how to turn and to stop, but the only practical way to stop is to fall. The remarkable thing was that no one was hurt in the least. The funniest thing I saw was one of our fellows, the first time he had put on skis, accidentally turn around on skis and slip down the slope backwards, and every time he tried to stop himself by digging his supporting sticks into the ground he'd push himself faster.

One of the greatest attractions was the heated hotel with good meals. The head waiter liked us (they like anybody who appreciates meals that don't have spaghetti as the chief dish) and piled the food on. They like the Americans simply because they are different and don't demand the regular, heavy meals of the Italians. We learned that if you compliment them on their meals or service they'll fall over you trying to help you. They had a French chef so we were really in the money. The whole trip — including train fare — cost only about two hundred lire, about ten dollars. That included all our expenses for the four days, even the rent for the skis, and we stayed at the best hotel they had. Our last night at the hotel we had a bottle of champagne that they reduced to twenty-four lire for us (about a dollar and a quarter) that was the climax to the farewell dinner. The fellow at the bar spoke English and has an English wife so he was delighted to meet us, drank a toast to us and smashed the glass. Where did that custom come from? They have a jazz orchestra up there so they welcomed us by playing American songs (which are as popular over there as in America). Our kind reception was due to the contrast between our appreciation of the service and that of a few big shot Italians there. There were a couple of families there that griped at everything (Italian service is usually rotten). Instead of griping, we praised them and got all the service. (I forgot to tell you that our bottle of champagne contained a liter, a little more than a quart.)

I got back and had a great time opening the mail that had come in. Jean sent me a fruitcake. Your fruitcake has not yet arrived — which is usual since the mail here is sometimes very slow.

Love,
Phil

Comments: Letter of December 31, 1936

(1)   The celebration of Christmas in Rome centered on the Midnight Mass in St. Mary Major at the high altar just above the relics of the crib for the Infant Jesus. It was always celebrated by the Pope. The splendor of the ancient Church erected as a tribute to the Mother of God, the presence of the Vicar of Christ, the awesome choir and the historical events in the Basilica made it the essence of Christmas. Nothing else was comparable and anything else was useless. Since then, every Christmas renews the thrill of the first Christmas Mass in the Basilica of St. Mary Major. Every time I return to that grand church I recall that Midnight Mass.

After the Mass, nothing else in the celebration of Christmas had any appeal for me and thus the reason for my nondescript description of Christmas in my letter to my folks.

(2)   Aquila was the nearest ski resort to Rome and had very comfortable facilities at a very low price, both in the little town and in the hotel at the top of the mountain where the ski runs were located.

(3)   I did not relate the climax of my ski lesson at the resort. I was relatively successful in my efforts for the first days. Emboldened by this success on the last day I tried the "big run" not realizing that slight thaw of the day before with consequent freezing at night made an icy but thin cover on the snow. I raced down the run, hit a hidden rock in the snow, catapulted head over heels and slid down the rest of the run on my buttocks. I shattered the skis, lost a shoe and limped unhurt to the ski lodge. I have never tried to ski again, and I have never regretted leaving that shoe in the snow.

Our camerata, 1936. The Prefect, Bob Aurthur in middle of back row.

Archdiocese of Baltimore group, 1936. Front row (left to right): Charlie Gorman, Jack Albert.

Front door of North American College on Via Dell' Umilta, 1936.

Patio inside the College, Statue of the Blessed Mother.

Chapel at North American College.

At Aquila on Christmas Vacation, 1936.

Prank, decorating a statue with uniform of College.

Charlie Gorman, Johnie Linn and Phil Hannan at Pompeii after landing in Naples in 1936.

"Bum Run" to Aquila, Christmas 1936.

1937

January 4, 1937

NORTH AMERICAN COLLEGE
Via Dell' Umilta 30

Dear Mary,

Happy Birthday – I can't tell whether or not this will arrive in time. I know age is a touchy point with some people, but I should like to show you the birthday card I received last year entitled, "We may be old birds but they ain't got us yet."

I have been learning a few things about the international situation through my job as editor. [1] For instance, we wrote to the old Herder Co. book firm for an ad. Their main office is in Germany. They were very willing to give as an ad but couldn't send any money out of Germany, not even for such a purpose. They have a large store in Rome so we naturally thought that the store could pay us from their cash register; not at all. Germany will not even allow them to pay for advertising with the money they collect in Rome – everything must go back to Germany. So then we began to barter. They will give us an amazing reduction on some very good sets of books if we will give them an ad, but they must receive something in the trade, some money; this is the way the situation stands now – we can get a very excellent <u>Lexikon Für Theologie</u> priced at 295 Marks for only 88 marks, a huge reduction. Now I must find someone who will pay us the price of the ad, and we can give him the set of books at the reduction. A labyrinthine way of doing business. I can't see how both Germany and Italy can hold out much longer; the taxes in Italy have gone up again because of the increased armament program. [2]

It is certainly *gauche* to ask for a favor on a birthday card, but . . . Could you get me a picture (a good postcard, a snapshot or anything) of St. Justin's Church in Hartford. I am getting up an article on modern church architecture in Europe, and I want to bring out a point at the end to the effect that one of our former alumni was capable of developing a very sincere and devout modern church. To me, the unrest in Europe is certainly evidence in the amazing confusion of "styles" for churches. Unfortunately, we hope to go to press during the first week of February; I don't know whether it is asking too much of you (and the postal service) to get the picture here by that time, but I'll hold up the works until it comes along.

As ever,

Phil

P.S. Any pictures of the interior would be very useful.

Comments: Letter of January 4, 1937

(1)   I became the editor of the house publication, Roman Echoes, through the efforts of Ed Latimer, a seminarian from Erie. I was eager to do it, and nobody else wanted the job. Our courses in English at the Sulpician Seminary were extensive and enabled me to produce a few magazine articles. A word of explanation about the various names of the Sulpician Seminary. It was so-called because the Sulpician Fathers conducted it; it was also called the Theological College because of its affiliation with The Catholic University in Washington, and also the Basselin Foundation (so named for the donor of the funds), because the grant establishing funds to pay for the costs of seminarians had a three year course, majoring in philosophy with a minor in English which eventually conferred on them an A.B. degree and M.S. in philosophy.

(2)   The reference to the taxes in Italy was a constant source of extreme irritation to the taxpayers. They paid not only excessive taxes for the current year but also in advance for the next year. Mussolini was determined to have a first-rate army, navy and air force. It was commonly said that he would grant funds easily for the construction of a new battleship but couldn't pay for the maintenance of it.

   Almost every male was in uniform – either in the armed forces or performing the required year of military training. Mussolini would shout at the end of one of his orations, "Italy is guarded with fifty million bayonets." I always thought, "You'll never win a battle with just bayonets."

January 8, 1937

NORTH AMERICAN COLLEGE
VIA DELL' UMILTA 30

Dear Everybody,

"Little Christmas" over here, the Epiphany, is really their big Christmas. [1] In front of the Pantheon they have what amounts to a country fair – everything except the sideshows with the snake charmer act. They have booths and stalls where one can buy anything from a doll to a car. It is also customary to give gifts to the police on Epiphany; one can see cars stop, especially on the principal boulevards, and give bottles of wine to the traffic cop. When we passed a traffic cop in the afternoon we had a couple of bottles of wine around his feet on the stand. Another quaint and very charming custom is to build platforms in the large churches on which little kids deliver speeches or recite pieces to the Infant in the crib. [2] Every year the fellows from the College go to Ara Coeli – an old temple converted into a church — and watch the performance. Each performer is presented with holy cards by the audience after the act and the number of holy cards received determines the performers popularity. To give the kids a real break the fellows take over their Christmas cards and hand them out; the children are the least interested group in collecting the cards — you ought to see the parents gather in the spoils. The kids are great; there was one little girl who clamored like a spoiled prima donna to give her piece and when they finally pushed her to the front she wouldn't do anything but smile, roll her eyes, and look cute. To get rid of her and get on with the act we gave her the usual presents but she refused to give up her place; that kid certainly wanted attention, she'll probably be a Mrs. Simpson when she grows up. The darling of the afternoon was a little dark-eyed kid dressed in a little fur coat who was quite a mess at reciting, but how she could gather the cards! At the back of the stand were all the fond parents pushing and coaching their kids as though they were breaking into grand opera. It reminded me very much of Madolin's May ball.

Just after we had watched the kids, we came back to find a real surprise for the new man at the College. Everybody was herded into the refectory; then the "befana" (witch) came in to give out prizes and read a little poem to each new man. [3] Don't think that it was a Sunday school affair; the poems were composed to insult the new fellows who, after the poem was read, went up to get the poem and a present. Some of the stuff written would disgrace a mule driver; this place has the most perverted idea of wit that I have ever met. [4] If Walter Winchell and Mencken were to pool their genius at making shabby cracks and insinuations, they couldn't have equaled some of the stuff poured out here in the name of fun. Strange to say I didn't get a particularly bad deal, but I certainly boiled at cracks made at some fellows I knew and liked. I rather enjoy hazing, get a big kick out of it; but these people haze you and then expect you to burst into a frenzy of praise for them and the college for their "cleverness." They kick you and then expect congratulations. Strange place, and strange occasion (Epiphany) on which to pull such a crude joke. No wonder some of the products of this place are not noted for their tact; they certainly won't learn it in Rome. I still think Rome is a marvelous place, but some of the people living there . . . . well, maybe I shall change my opinion in four years. The third year runs all this stuff; wait until we get in the third year, then we shall see.

But a great surprise and enjoyment was ready on the next day, Thursday. About twenty went to the catacombs of Saint Callistus where we sang a Mass (celebrated by one of the newly ordained priests). [5] It was dark, damp and very uncomfortable but amazingly appealing. We heard Mass in a chamber where eleven of the early Popes had been buried. There are not many inscriptions left on the walls, but they are very interesting. The most interesting to me was the inscription of a *swastika* (the same as that used by the Nazis in Germany today) on the wall; the swastika was used as a camouflaged cross by the early Christians. During the persecutions it was not safe to make use of the crucifix, so they painted things that looked like crosses – *swastikas*, anchors in the shape of a cross, tridents. The length of the catacombs in Rome is amazing; there are about three hundred miles of them in and around Rome. But, of course, not all are excavated.

Love,

Phil

Comments: Letter of January 8, 1937

(1)   The feast of the Epiphany was more popular than the feast of Christmas because the feast celebrated the inclusion of the gentiles among those to be saved — the three Magi represented the whole human race. Rome has some special celebrations for Epiphany — a day of thanks to the police and a day for children to salute the Infant by appropriate poems for which they then received a gift. The College is near the busiest intersection in Rome – in front of the Monument to Victor Emmanuel and the Palazzo Venezia (the headquarters of Mussolini). The avalanche of traffic is supposedly regulated by a policeman on a small pediment located in the middle of the square. On an ordinary day his job is impossible, and on the Epiphany his station is surrounded by piles of bottles of wine dropped off by the grateful drivers. Occasionally, a police van stops by to pick up the gifts. It's a very gracious custom.

(2)   The station for the children to perform is erected in many churches, notably in the Ara Coeli atop the Capitoline Hill, the spot where Rome began. We went there to see the children perform. They were from about seven years of age to ten, and they acted as if they were all slated for Broadway – gesticulating, voice modulating, and body language in action for every moment. The piece finished, they promptly made the rounds of the adults attending, collecting a holy card or a present from each.

        There are also some street performers, shepherds from the nearby regions who come in their distinctive dress and play bagpipes. Bagpipes were the invention of the ancient shepherds in Italy and they, possibly by the Roman Army, brought their instruments to England and Scotland. The pedestrians give offerings to the horn blowers who fare very well.

(3)   The custom of the "befana" (witch) giving presents is a secular invention, curiously so contradictory to the Catholic celebration.

(4)   The rude entertainment produced by the third year theologians, in

retrospect, was not so vulgar as I depicted; but it was in sharp contrast to the religious celebrations in the churches.

(5)   The trip to the catacombs of Saint Callistus was really inspiring. The glory and life of the early Church becomes tangible and amazing. The main section of the catacombs is about seventy feet underground; the different levels for the burials made necessary by the immense number of conversions. The levels were ventilated by airways that led up to the surface and are still in place, the product of excellent engineering. I cannot describe how fascinating were the catacombs and how instructive about the life of the early Christians. I could never understand how a visitor could remain unmoved by a visit there and how a Catholic could not have his faith invigorated by a visit.

It is estimated that at least 500,000 burials were made in the catacombs, and each burial was made to last forever. The reverence for the remains of a Christian inspired the authorities to seal every tomb so that the bones would remain until judgement day when they would be resurrected by our Savior. Unfortunately, the raids by the barbarians who overthrew the Roman Empire resulted in the looting of the catacombs. The barbarians, some of whom were heretical Christians, believed that every tomb contained a saint; and, therefore, they collected the remains as holy relics. Today it is forbidden under pain of excommunication to take anything of value from the catacombs.

January 13, 1937

NORTH AMERICAN COLLEGE
Via Dell' Umilta 30

Dear Everybody,

New Year celebrations are nearly the same the world over, it seems. Rome has the usual celebration — with a few variations. Due to the influence of the Pope, Rome has no nightclubs or "night life"; but, of course, there is no law against private parties. Just opposite the college is a large apartment house in which there was a real knockdown, carry-out party celebrating New Year. Consequently, there was a cordial spirit of cooperation between some of the fellows in the house and the party guests in doing the "hoo-ray" act. Some fellows had collected suitable cans, pipes and bottles for the occasion. So when the bells rang at twelve, the cannonade started and sounded like something between an earthquake and an explosion. It seems to be an old Roman custom to throw bottles down into the street below and, worse yet, throw water at any poor devil that comes along. The prize sport is to bombard open carriages as they come through; if you can't hit the passengers, you might hit the horse. There is also a sort of gentleman's agreement between the people in the houses and the people in the street. The pedestrians show their good will by kicking along the street the cans tossed from the houses. The particular target in our neighborhood was the Jesuit Biblical Institute across the street from us. Most of the inhabitants of that place are, of necessity, intellectuals and have occasionally been nuisances; so the only thing to do was bounce cans, bottles and pipes off the building. The climax (and end) of the celebration came when some sociable person at the party across the street decided to throw some fellow an orange. Of course, the only way they could give it to him was by throwing it through the window. As for myself, I slept through almost all of it — sign of a good conscience. [1]

Monsignor Corrigan, the rector at C.U., is in Rome spending his time in a hospital! Just out of sympathy for the Pope, I suppose. I think he has diabetes.

The fellows coming back from their Christmas vacations have some interesting stories. Some were down at Gaeta, a seaport, and saw a troop ship pulling out. After much wheedling and coaxing, they found out that 3,000 Italians were leaving for Spain to join the army and that 3,000 others had left a few days before. But, of course, there is no mention of such stuff in the Italian papers. Italy is not interfering, certainly not.

The big fruitcake arrived, very safe and very sound. There's nothing like fruitcake for Christmas, especially when it's made the way that cake was. You can imagine how my popularity increased around here. The cake actually tasted as though it had just come out of the oven, even the chocolate icing was soft. A thousand thanks. By the way, from what I have seen of

Italian service, do not be surprised if my package (which was mailed before Thanksgiving) does not arrive quickly. The Italians just can't understand anyone being in a hurry.

As soon as I can get them, I shall send a few pictures I had taken in the mountains. There was one thing of which a picture could not be taken, and it was the most beautiful sight of all — the moonlight on the snowy mountains. The moon seemed as though it were just a few feet above the mountain peaks and flooded the whole land with a soft light.

I speak Italian (or try to) with a couple of Italians from the Capranica College, the college for the rather well-to-do Italians. They are very sociable and shake hands every time they see you. They are much impressed by the fact that I am twenty-three years old — they are only twenty or twenty-one. The best feature about them is that they don't care to learn English (as most Italians do) and consequently are not pests. Every Italian, as far as I have had experience, wants to see the U.S. (2)

Love,

Phil

Comments: Letter of January 13, 1937

(1)   The New Year's celebration described here occurred only in the sections of Rome where the old apartment buildings are on narrow streets and the apartment dwellers are not very refined. The celebration of Capo d'Anno (New Year) differed according to the neighborhood.

Although the news was controlled in Fascist Italy, the wide-ranging travel of the students in the summer brought us news of every important event. There was widespread support of General Franco's forces in Spain and great indignation and sorrow at the thousands of priests and religious who were killed by the Communist members of the "Republican" Government. The doorkeeper of the College was a Spaniard whose relatives were in great peril.

(2)   Pope Pius XII attended the Capranica College (seminary) as a seminarian. He was in frail health and was allowed to live at his

home in Rome. The Capranica College had an interesting sign in its foyer, "Visitors are not allowed to wear their swords." I cultivated a friendship with one of their seminarians to develop my knowledge of Italian. My friend was a loyal follower of Mussolini because he was so anti-Communist.

January 20, 1937

NORTH AMERICAN COLLEGE
Via Dell' Umilta 30

Dear Everybody,

A few days ago they had a very scholarly event at the Greg, that is calculated, I presume, to knock us yokels speechless. They have a "disputation" about some point in theology; it is carried on by students and is public. [1] I should have said it is prodded on. Without a doubt it is the deadest, dullest, most wooden performance I have ever seen. Everybody collects in the main hall, expecting (if they are new men) a couple of shrewd scholars to stand up and throw very pointed objections and clever arguments at each other. But here's what we get: some dull fossil gets up and mumbles an introduction in Latin (everything is in Latin) about the purpose of this futile gathering until he has either bored the audience, or put them to sleep, or made them start to read the book they have brought along. Then some gallant champion of the TRUTH gets up to defend his thesis (all this stuff has been rehearsed until they could go through it in their sleep — in fact, from what I saw they could go through it better if asleep because they wouldn't get nervous from the crowd) and goes through the proofs for his statement; then a stooge in the audience reads objections to him which he must answer. It has all the pep, vigor, and freshness of a schoolboy recitation that has been rehearsed for six months. The only time the audience pays any attention is when the nervous speaker commits some full-sized heresy, and the crowd licks its chops, as they get ready to witness the execution. The persons for whom I really feel sorry are the members of the faculty who must come and put up with this stuff year after year. The Rector, an American Jesuit, does his best to put on a plaster smile, but the going is rather tough; one prof was interested enough to want to make an objection, but he was politely but firmly slapped down. The one impressive thing about the whole Punch and Judy show is the mastery of Latin; these Italians and Spaniards let it flow as easily as a Protestant quotes the Bible.

I passed by the American Embassy today and saw the flag flying in honor of Inauguration Day. It looked good.

Thursday was the feast of St. Agnes so we went out to the Church of St. Agnes (where there is also a catacombs) to watch them bless a couple of lambs from whom they get the wool to make cloaks (the pallium) for the Archbishops to be appointed in the next year. [2] We got there just as they were bringing the two lambs in a Lincoln; the things seemed as though they were wrapped in cellophane, were tied in baskets and had a few roses tossed on them. But despite all the finery, the little shavers were baa-ing their heads off. But before they can get themselves worked into the right mood, they must have a High Mass — during which, of course, everybody talks and shuffles about as though it were a country fair. After the Mass the two lambs are carried in a procession of girls up to the high altar and blessed by the bishop. I don't know when or how the custom of blessing things started, but whoever began it did a real job; they bless bells, palms, cows, etc., everything.

The catacombs at St. Agnes are almost unbelievably long. They reach for miles; if one gets lost, he may end up on the other side of town.

There was a further rumor around that the dollar is to go down a bit, so I invested fifty dollars in lira; I used one of the checks. If you come over this year, it will be used this summer; if you don't, well I have four years to spend here. The dollar has never been so high within the past six years (or rather the lira has never been so low).

I went to the store that shipped those plaques, and they insist that by the time you get this letter the stuff will be there. Great service.

Love,

Phil

Comments: Letter of January 20, 1937

(1)   Despite my objections, the "disputation" was an academic feature with a centuries-long history and promoted a fluency in Latin and

proficiency in presenting arguments in support of the doctrines of the faith. There were rumors that one of our American students was the principal in a disputation in the presence of Pope Leo XIII in the nineteenth century and in our day one of our students, Josiah Chataham of Mississippi was a participant in a disputation.

(2)   The lambs brought from the Church of St. Agnes (a famous young martyr, thirteen years of age and famed for her purity) were sheared to produce the wool for the pallium — the pallium is a white, circular vestment worn around the shoulders given by the Holy Father to Archbishops as a sign of their rank and their jurisdiction. Pope John Paul II makes the presentation of the pallium a very solemn event and a means of furthering the bond between the Pope and the Archbishops.

January 23, 1937

NORTH AMERICAN COLLEGE
VIA DELL' UMILTA 30

Dear Everybody,

To settle a few questions in Mom's letter: I received the fruitcake and the duty on it amounted to eleven and a half lira (about sixty cents); I didn't receive a cablegram from you – I received one from Bill and one from Tom; I have done all I could about hurrying the package I sent about two months ago; Father Stricker's books have been shipped (but when they will get there is a different matter). I would advise you not to send over cookies; packages are so long in coming that food often becomes very moldy. Fruitcake and candy are the only articles that come over in good shape, but don't bother about sending me anything now – save it for Easter. Much obliged. (1)

Despite all your newspaper clippings and remarks, there is no news over here about the Pope's hopeless condition. News here is rigidly censored, but – and this is the way we get all the dope – a fellow across the hall has a radio and gets the news broadcast from the U.S. (at five o'clock it comes in.) I know all about the floods. Is there any danger of the Potomac rising? Many thanks for the New York Times sections; they usually arrive on Sunday morning. [2]

On Friday, I enjoyed my first visit to the Vatican Museum, the greatest in the world. The first impression is that there is too much to see, too much to even think about. They have an art gallery (the collection of sculpture is the greatest of its kind in the world), a famous library that contains so many gifts to Popes from kings, etc. that one completely forgets that somewhere in there are books, the Sistine Chapel (which we didn't see), an Egyptian room, private apartments, etc. The most curious room was that devoted to Egyptian objects. They had about six genuine mummies with the cloth cut off the faces to show the state of preservation; even the hair was almost fully preserved on one woman — she was a red head. The great masterpieces in painting — those of Raphael, etc. — just sweep you off your feet. A curious fact about many of Raphael's works is that they contain portraits of him; he has painted himself (of course, as one of the characters in the picture) a number of times. But there is entirely too much stuff in a comparatively small space. I got a headache from simply looking. There are so many masterpieces of sculpture that they become cheap; and after about three hours of staring and gaping, everything begins to look the same. The only change to be had is to listen to some of the "art critics" show off before the uninitiated. The Pope's apartments occupy only a very small section of the building. [3]

The body of Saint John Baptist de la Salle, the founder of the Christian Brothers, was brought to Rome and placed temporarily in the Church of the Gesu (a famous Jesuit place). There was more confusion and bustle than at a country fair. The event was scheduled for four o'clock, the hour at which the train was to arrive at the depot. The body was to be carried in a procession of auto cars to the church. We were outside the church — where they had soldiers and cops of eleven different divisions arranging and directing the rabble — waiting for something to happen. At five thirty a motorcycle cop came tearing along announcing that the procession was then at St. Peter's (which is about a mile and a half away). Finally at about six o'clock the body arrived, carried on a Ford truck that was elaborately decorated. The bones were on view in the church. Personally, I don't go for that sort of thing very much; it's too hard on the feet. If ever you wish to get in at such an event, you simply have to tote a flag and park yourself near the door. They mass flags on every occasion.

Very soon it will be our turn to do some receiving at the college. A new Vice Rector is slated to arrive any day – in fact, has been slated to arrive every week since Christmas. He was appointed about the first of December. His name is Babcock. We are a bit interested since he will live on our corridor. It has taken Italian workers about three weeks to clean up his set of rooms. They do one thing at a time; wire the room one day, come back the next day and sweep it, then scrape the walls the next day. The prize performance was the painting of the two tooms – an Italian came dressed in a suit and felt hat to daub paint. [4]

There will be a big time here on the occasion of the Pope's death and re-election of a successor. Did you know that Cardinal O'Connell caused a terrific stir during the last election because they had selected the present Pope before he arrived? According to all accounts, he cut loose and raised a real dogfight.

Did you know that Bishop Duffy of Syracuse is the Bishop of Buffalo now? A couple of fellows here knew him and say that he is a "smoothy" and not yet fifty years old. [5]

Love,

Phil

Comments: Letter of January 23, 1937

(1)   The duty on fruitcakes was less than that on cakes, which had a higher sugar content.

(2)   Getting news, especially the "forbidden" news, was a daily pre-occupation and the only means of knowing what was happening in the world outside Italy. Every family had a radio for getting such news.

(3)   The vast and invaluable Vatican Museum demands more than one visit. The Vatican, as a residence for the Popes, goes back to St. Symmachus about 498. Additions were made to it by almost every succeeding Pope as it developed into a library, art museum, chapels and halls as well as reception rooms, etc. Today, it is the

greatest library and museum, with a residence of the Pope, in the world. Today, its greatest attraction is the famous Sistine Chapel with its stupendous painting by Michaelangelo and other famous artists.

(4)   The new Vice Rector was Monsignor Allen Babcock from Bad Axe in Michigan. His birthplace led to many uncomplimentary remarks. He was appointed to instill more discipline, a task of superhuman proportions given the circumstances of the time.

(5)   Our family's interest in Buffalo derived from my mother's relationship to Bishop William Turner of Buffalo, formerly a professor of philosophy at The Catholic University and a frequent visitor at our home.

January 28, 1937

NORTH AMERICAN COLLEGE
Via Dell' Umilta 30

Dear Everybody,

Already the graduating class is beginning to pull out. One priest (one of those whom we met at the papal audience last year at Castelgandolfo) pulled out very unexpectedly. His father was taken seriously ill; and even though he lives in Arizona, he is trying to get home in time. I think he flew to Paris to catch the Normandie and may fly from New York. Altogether he must have to travel about 7,000 miles. And another of the graduating class is leaving because of ill health. It always makes the year feel as though it were closing to watch fellows leave.

A few days ago there was an international game in soccer — our college played the South American College, and we lost rather badly. Of course, we have no real soccer players in the school, so they usually select the toughest or tallest fellows and let them go out to either kick the ball or kick the opposition. They usually kick the opposition; and although the opposition always ends the game in tough shape, they always win. The

South Americans and Europeans always play in their cassocks! Of course, they wear an abbreviated cassock that doesn't come much below the knees, but our fellows have a real difficulty in kicking the ball anywhere but in the cassock. The only thing that relieves a dull game like soccer is to have the other team dressed in some impossible outfit like that and watch them struggle. The idea is that Seminarians in Rome should always be in cassocks no matter what they are doing (of course, the cassocks always look and smell like that too). It looks unbelievably ridiculous to see the Americans dressed, or undressed, in regular sport outfits playing these fellows dressed in cassocks. Often the Spaniards or South Americans come up to watch a baseball game and just marvel why we don't get killed by the ball. Whenever anybody smashes a ball, they have a great deal of sympathy for the fellow who has to catch it. And unlike the kids in America, the little Italians run away from a baseball game instead of staying to see it. *"Periculoso"* (Dangerous) they yell and tear out of there. [1]

Almost every sort of impossible situation has arisen this year at the college. The latest is the case of a fellow who threw a cigarette out his window, and it landed in a car — with the usual result, the car caught fire. No one knew anything about it until the Rector started making the rounds of the house to find out who was in the habit of throwing cigarettes out the window. It's a serious offense in Italy to throw anything out the window because it either hits someone or dirties the street. Yesterday we had a real show just opposite my window; a housewife had hung her laundry out the window and somebody in the apartment above her swept her rooms, dirtying all her clothes. She did so much carrying on that a crowd gathered below to cheer the fight on. They take it out in talking; they never fight with fists for the simple reason that very few Italians know how to use their fists. [2]

Rome is a bit excited about the latest flight of Bruno Mussolini to Brazil. They had a big broadcast and held up everything so that young Bruno could tell the old man what a great son he had. They even held up the operas that were scheduled to go on the air. They say in Rome that this Bruno is more worry and trouble to the Duce than the whole country; he is very vigorous and headstrong. After he came back from fighting in Ethiopia, he wrote a book glorifying war that set the rest of the world on its ear with indignation; then he skipped off to fight in Spain, came back to get in the international air race and won second place in it, and now ended up with this last hop. I feel sorry for Mrs. Mussolini if her whole family is like that son. The successor to Mussolini is going to have a time dealing with all these little Mussolinis. [3]

They have opened a new exhibition in Rome to show how they can make substitute products in time of war. [4] They have one big machine into which a gallon of milk is poured and comes out cloth! In another part of the exhibit they make milk into wool. Good idea, but what happens if you can't get the milk? The whole business doesn't interest me much; I'd hate to order a milkshake and get a pound of wool.

Love,

Phil

Comments: Letter of January 28, 1937

(1)   The athletic or playing field of the College was the present site of the present College in Vatican City. The soccer game with the Pio Latino Seminary (for all Latin Americans) was a popular event for those interested in athletics. One Latino team brought as its referee one of the professors in their seminary. He gave our team a rough time and we tried to reciprocate.

(2)   The Rector has a deep and understandable interest in anything that happened outside the College in our immediate neighborhood. We, Americans, were guests of the country; and therefore, any misbehavior by our students was a serious matter.

(3)   Every dictator exploits any achievement to bolster his prestige with the people. Bruno Mussolini was an exceptional pilot, and his father exploited his prowess to the last degree.

(4)   Long before the war erupted, Italy was making substitutes for every staple of the diet. These substitutes were fervently described by the Italians whom no dictator could ever completely silence. The Fascists made many kinds of signs to regulate the thinking of the people. I remember a sign in a restaurant "High politics are not discussed here." (*Alta politica non discute qui*) to which the proprietor

pointed to stop a noisy political argument at a table. One of the guests replied, "We're not discussing high politics here. We're talking about low politics." The Italians were irrepressible in remarks about the government.

January 29, 1937

NORTH AMERICAN COLLEGE
VIA DELL' UMILTA 30

Dear Everybody,

These storms on the Atlantic have long ceased to be a matter of trivial interest; our new Vice Rector is on the sea and probably getting tossed about like a pair of dice. We are not concerned about the gentleman's comfort or welfare; but if he isn't a good sailor, he will be in a terrific mood when he gets here and he will be a very close neighbor of mine.

I would appreciate it if you sent some pictures of the flood. About five of the fellows here have probably lost their homes in that gigantic mess.

A few days ago, I heard some news about intended reductions in rates for transatlantic liners this summer. There is to be a world's fair at Paris this summer, and the steamship companies (or some of them, anyway) are going to reduce rates tremendously. Furthermore, the railroad tickets to Paris from Italy are to be cut in half. This seems to be the summer for travel. Of course, they will probably try to cheat like the devil in Paris to squeeze every cent they can out of the visitors. Don't make any reservations until there is something definite about special rates, and when there is something definite you had better make reservations promptly.

Last week, we went into Cardinal O'Connell's titular church in Rome, Saint Clement's. [1] I think it is the most interesting spot in Rome. There are three churches built on each other; as the level of the street changed during the course of the centuries, they built different churches. The lowest church was formerly the private home of Pope Clement, the third Pope. He converted it into a chapel and had his residence there, but when he was exiled by the Romans the property was confiscated and given to Persian soldiers to use as a barracks. They changed the former Christian chapel into a temple to their sun-god, and today one can still see their altar and statues down there. It is a tremendously interesting little place. Until recently, the whole lower part had been under water from the "mysterious Waters" of Rome. There are streams of water flowing (one can hear them) under the church, and no one has been able to find their origin or outlet. Marion Crawford has quite a bit to say about them in one of his novels. Cardinal O'Connell gave the money to drain and fix the place so they did the right thing by the cardinal and put a bust of him in the church. Furthermore, in one part of that underground passage there is the remains of a very substantial wall that was built by the Etruscans (the race that owned the land in Italy before the Romans came) and must be about 2700 years old. The second church (built over the home of Saint Clement) was quite large, but almost nothing is left in it; what was valuable was taken out and put in the third church where it is today. No one knew anything about these two lower churches until recently. They had buried a bishop or cardinal in the floor of the top church thinking that below the floor was the earth. But later they found that they had buried him in the rubbish that filled and covered the second church. [2]

There is an old custom around here (in Rome) to help yourself to anything in a person's room if he leaves permanently. For instance, immediately after a cardinal has been made Pope anybody and everybody descends upon his home and proceeds to take it apart for souvenirs, etc. Well after the Vice Rector left, the same thing occurred to his room. A few days ago the Spiritual Director came up to see whether there was enough furniture for the incoming man and found that he didn't even have a lamp left. So the Spiritual Director had to appoint himself detective and go around to almost every room in search of the former Vice Rector's stuff. These people believe in communism.

Another request. The weather here is becoming mild already, and the baseball season will start. (The college has a baseball field.) I have positively no shoes for playing baseball, never dreamt that there would be opportunity for it here. [3] I would appreciate it very much if you would get me a pair of spiked shoes at the Vim store. Many thanks.

Love,

Phil

Comments: Letter of January 29, 1937

(1)   Every Cardinal was assigned a titular church for which he was responsible. St. Clement was the titular church of Cardinal O'Connell, former Rector of the College and later the Archbishop of Boston. Titular meant a church owned by a person or family; it referred to churches in early Christian times.

Saint Clement's Church is a good example of the making of important discoveries in fairly recent years. The pastor of the Church, a Dominican priest, discovered in digging for a burial in the upper church that there was another church directly beneath it. Further excavations unearthed the two lower levels of the church. The second level of the church has the grave of the famous St. Cyril, who with his brother, St Methodius, were the apostles to the Slavs.

The upper church is the perfect example of an early medieval church – separate ambos for the reading of the epistle and gospel, space allocated for the choir, a place back of the altar in the apse for the throne of the Bishop (or abbot). Visiting the church is a thrilling excursion into the past.

(2)   Father Wilpert, a great authority on the catacombs has always contended that many more important discoveries can be made by Church archeologists.

(3)   Sports were an important part of life in the College. I was the left fielder on our baseball team, and I got the nickname "No hits" on the day that I managed to get three hits. What's in a name?

February 5, 1937

NORTH AMERICAN COLLEGE
Via Dell' Umilta 30

Dear Everybody,

A few days ago, I went with a couple of fellows to see an Italian soccer game. Rome was playing Turin, the champs. The stadium (which only holds about fifteen thousand) was crowded to the point where even the Italians admitted that no one else could get in. As we got to the stadium, we had our first experience of Italian secret service men — they must have at least ten thousand of them in Rome. The cab driver wanted to charge us extra for the extra passengers. Up came the secret service man, and the argument ended there. These secret service men are too officious and open to fool the people, though. But despite all their regimentation and military rule over here, they haven't learned how to line up at the ticket offices to buy tickets. Getting a ticket is a terrific fight; there isn't even a semblance of order, everybody fights and mauls to get to the window. It really is worth the trouble, at least for once, to watch the crowd. The players come in, got to the center of the field, stand and salute the crowd with the Fascist salute. There is as much enthusiasm and interest manifested as at one of our baseball games. They give the raspberry to the umpire or any of the players with real gusto and at the slightest thing that displeases them. [1]

We have a vacation next week due to the beginning of Lent. The "Carnival Days" are a national tradition over here. All business is suspended for a couple of days before Ash Wednesday, and everybody mills around the streets and parks. Already the kids are beginning to wear their outfits. The interesting feature for us is permission to take "bum runs" for a couple of days. [2] Our diocese is going to Siena, about one hundred and fifty miles from Rome. Every year, former students of the American College in Baltimore and Washington take up a collection and send the money to the fellows for a "bum run". We have enough to take us to Siena and to stay there a couple of days. I am told that Siena is a very nice place. We shall see.

Today I found out how the Italian troops are sent to Spain. They send them to Naples dressed in the African uniforms and apparently bound for Ethiopia or Libia. They sail from Naples but go to Genoa, then are sent from Genoa to Spain. The attraction that draws them to Spain is higher wages. In Spain they are paid about forty lira a day (about two dollars), whereas a common soldier in Italy gets paid fifty centesimi (about 2½ cents a day). A man may win glory in Italy's army, but he will certainly never win money. They say that the Italian troops in Spain are used only to occupy and hold the territory already captured by Franco's men. Maybe Franco is afraid to let them try to hold the front trenches.

I saw Mussolini for the second time on Friday. He reviewed troops just back from the Italian colonies in Africa. The really ridiculous feature of the program was the behavior of the troops. Their army hasn't the discipline that we are accustomed to see. For instance, when Mussolini went up to speak, one contingent insisted on yelling and trying to sing even when the speech had begun; the officers started yelling, "*Attentione, attentione*" but it didn't make a bit of difference. So the officers started in thumping the fellows on the chest to make them shut up. Then after the speech everybody started to wave hats, arms, guns; the orchestra and bands got in the spirit of the thing and began to wave their instruments — even the fellows with the big horns hoisted them up. Lot of fun if your feet and toes can stand the treatment.

The new Vice Rector was properly welcomed by the community. He is a very nice fellow but a little too active and intelligent to be really ideal. From the student's viewpoint, the ideal Vice Rector should be dreamy, absent-minded, a little cloudy in the brain. This fellow is young and wide-awake. He is the only disciplinarian in the house, quite a job for one man.

A week ago we had a Jesuit lecturer on Communism give us a very brilliant and incisive talk. He was scheduled to give a series of lectures, but after delivering the first, he promptly disappeared. Now the rumor is that he has been sent by the Vatican, or by his order, to Russia to get first-hand information. [3] He was the editor of a newly established magazine exposing the propaganda and method of communism and can speak eight languages. He is a Frenchman but delivered his lecture to us in English. What made everybody think that he did go to Russia was the absence of his tonsure — every cleric and priest is supposed to wear his tonsure, bald spot, in Rome. But this fellow had allowed his hair to grow out; that usually means only one thing – that the fellow is leaving this vicinity. Every day I grow more convinced that the men who really look after the church are the men in the black, not the big shots dressed in the red. At the present time our moral teacher, a Spaniard, has been gone for almost two weeks on some mission somewhere. He is supposed to be in Spain trying to straighten out something. [4] The Vatican knows how to send men to the critical spots.

End of reel.

Love,

Phil

Comments: Letter of February 5, 1937

(1)   No fisticuffs at soccer games.

(2)   There is no record of the derivation of the phrase "bum run", a trip of two or three days length by a group of students. Often the "bum run" was to a famous shrine or notable city. Siena is a gorgeous city with a world-class cathedral and a great attraction. The college uniform was often worn during a short "bum run", but for a longer "bum run" the college uniform (cassock) was deposited in a safety locker in the railroad terminal and claimed on return. But "bum run" always included the practice of attendance at daily Mass and visits to the Blessed Sacrament — even if done in illegal civilian clothing.

Siena is also the locale of the world-famous summer horse race in which there are no rules. Kicking, whipping and sideswiping of the mounts are perfectly legal.

(3)   The Vatican carried on a very rigorous, but hidden, strategy to infiltrate communist Russia while the communists reciprocated. After the demise of communism, the Catholic priests (Jesuits and others) surfaced, and at least one communist agent was found among the Jesuits, a teacher at the Gregorian University so the rumor said.

(4)   Father Lopez was the professor sent from the faculty to Spain.

February 7, 1937

NORTH AMERICAN COLLEGE
Via Dell' Umilta 30

Dear Everybody,

I have been receiving some very unusual letters from old alumni of the college to whom I had written to help me out on a proposed article for our college publication. Of course, as I had expected, they didn't limit themselves to the topic I wanted discussed; in fact, they didn't even mention it. But they did furnish some corking good stories about the college in the early days. Maybe they have a magnificent contempt for the truth; but at any rate, they are good storytellers. One old retired priest in New York wrote me an eight-page letter telling me that he knew nothing about the thing on which I had asked information but willingly spilled off a reel of happenings that would make a good story anywhere. For instance, he told me of the time he was selected by his Archbishop to present a purse of money to Pope Leo XIII. His Bishop had come over with the money but was taken sick and had to leave Rome. So this fellow went over accompanied by the rector to give the money to the Pope. As usual they knelt while the Pope came in to see them. The conversation and presentation was in French. Pope Leo XIII came in with a box of snuff in his hand — he was a notorious snuff user. So the fellow decided that as a souvenir he would like to carry home a bit of the snuff. As His Holiness turned to speak to the rector, the fellow grabbed a pinch of the snuff and put it into his pocket. The Pope turned around and told him that it was, "*Buon tobacco*" (Good tobacco) and let him keep the snuff he had taken. Mom and Dad can appreciate the story since they know how solemn a function is a reception by the Pope.

Another story the priest had was that of the brother of the rector in his day. The rector's brother was a big beer and lager brewer in New York; the rector was taken seriously ill and so the brother came over to see him. Of course, when he arrived, and during his whole stay, he had to drink wine. Apparently he didn't like it at all and felt rather sorry for the poor students who had to drink the stuff all the time. So on his return to New York, he sent over some cases of beer, enough to give every student a bottle – the only time in the history of the college when they had beer for meals.

After the old priest had given me all this dope, he ended his letter by saying that he was sorry he couldn't help me in the information I wanted, but there was another priest he knew who could give me all that dope (the priest he mentioned has been dead for about twenty years). After reading a few of these letters, I know what it must be like to attend a convention of the alumni of the college.

The Rector has been taking French lessons for the past few years. I went down to see him this morning, and as soon as I neared the door, I heard him grunting his French – no time to bother him then. If I didn't know any more French than he knows, I think I'd sue the teacher to get my money back.

The big shifts in the German cabinet caused quite a stir in Rome. [1] Blomberg, the German minister of war, was having his honeymoon in Italy and getting quite a big "blow" from the government – until news came that he has been given the gate. Now Italy doesn't know how to greet its guest, a tough wedding present.

Love,

Phil

Comments: Letter of February 7, 1937

(1)   Events in Germany were always of great interest in Italy, its close ally. Even when a surprising event occurred, as the dismissal of General Blomberg, there was always an avowal that the two allies still agreed "*cento per cento*" (One hundred percent). It was also firmly believed in Italy that the Nazis had sent enough agents into Italy to exert a good deal of control. In preparation for his visit to Rome, Hitler had insisted that he send enough "security men" into Italy to guarantee his personal security and the horde of Nazi agents never left Italy.

February 21, 1937

NORTH AMERICAN COLLEGE
Via Dell' Umilta 30

Dear Everybody,

I just returned from Siena yesterday. [1] Strange to say, it is a very clean little town, perched on the tops of two or three hills and surrounded by a wall. It still preserves a very distinctive spirit. We arrived there just before and during carnival time when everybody was whooping it up in their quaint way. The children are all dressed up in weird outfits as they are in America on Halloween – except that this is done far more seriously and the parents themselves apply the lipstick, rouge, etc. On Monday before Ash Wednesday they have a parade around the town; a number of the kids are dressed up and put in carriages and driven around the town. At night the old folks start to cut up. But the carnival spirit is dwindling very much – compared to what it used to be. In former times there was carousing and celebrating to a scandalous degree, so the Church went to work against it by having special devotions during the carnival days. In some places they have exposition of the Blessed Sacrament all day and a mass at Midnight – that put a real clamp on the hell-raisers.

There are a number of outstanding things in Siena that made it very much worth a trip there. They have a tremendous cathedral that took one hundred and fifty years to build, a very interesting town hall with tower about three hundred and fifty feet high, and a couple of very interesting picture galleries. But, the highlight of the whole place is the everlasting miracle that occurs in one of the churches there; they have three hundred and fifty hosts that have been miraculously preserved for two hundred years. During some solemn feast two hundred years ago a ciborium was stolen containing three hundred and fifty hosts. The next morning the hosts were discovered in a poor box in a nearby church. They were put on a linen corporal and put back in the tabernacle but instead of decaying, they stayed exactly as they were. After fifty years, they were put in a sealed container that has glass sides. Recently chemists made tests (by order of the church) to find out how long a host would stay without decomposing; they found that even if they were hermetically sealed, they would turn to powder in seven months. We saw the Sacred Hosts; they are a trifle yellow because the flour made two hundred years ago was not so thoroughly sifted, etc. as it is today and consequently was a bit colored, but otherwise they are in perfect shape. A very moving and thrilling sight. Personally, I think they shouldn't have put them in a special container, should have just allowed them to rest on the linen corporal to make the miracle even more impressive. If they remained preserved for fifty years in that way, they could certainly last any amount of time the Lord wished.

Recently, I invested in a very beautiful picture of the Blessed Mother, a copy of an original done by an Italian professor of art. It is a real beauty, splendidly framed. For months, I had noticed this very sweet Madonna in an art gallery on one of the main streets here and continually wondered why they couldn't sell it. [2]

Another one of my fellow diocesans is leaving the college, Thomas Winston, a Washingtonian who had had very poor health since he arrived. He is leaving the Seminary entirely and consequently wanted to sell his books; since I will need them next year I bought them from him (he needs money to get back to the U.S.). This was his tenth year in the seminary (he went to St. Charles for six years), but I know that he doesn't regret the time he spent there.

The weather is becoming delightful in Rome. Once it begins to get sunny, it stays that way for months until in the full summertime there is too much sun.

Love,

Phil

Comments: Letter of February 21, 1937

(1)   Siena was the medieval rival of Florence and is a very attractive city. The old church that contains the "miracle of the Hosts" provides a perfect setting.

Siena is also the site for the most unusual horse race in the world. Amid very impressive medieval pageantry, the race is held on the paved surface and without any rules – shoving, fouling, whipping a rival horse, etc. are allowed.

(2)   Shopping in Italy during this war scare time was unbelievably cheap. There were almost no visitors, and the shopkeepers were forced to sell at almost any price. The price was low and the quality was high.

February 23, 1937

NORTH AMERICAN COLLEGE
Via Dell' Umilta 30

Dear Everybody,

The package from Velati's landed today. [1] All the candy, even the caramels, was in excellent shape. The package was so large that I thought they had included one of their show cases in it; the amount of the "box of candy" was a tremendous surprise. Furthermore, it was very fortunate that it came during Lent, and not before, since it offers a very welcome relief from the variety of Tiber trout that is served during this holy, but not too healthy season of dieting. Many, many thanks. There is no celebration of St. Valentine's Day in Italy, chiefly because there are not enough good Jewish merchants to stimulate the practice. [2]

After much plastering of posters and notices, the practice air raids came off. What a dismal result! The sirens sound as though they had an incurable case of asthma — they would never awaken anybody, and not even the threat of an air raid would make the Italians follow orders promptly and neatly. Everyone was supposed to clear off the streets as soon as the siren sounded; the result was that everybody threw up their windows and looked out, while those who were on the street simply hastened their pace, but didn't stop from going to wherever they were headed. The prize bit of foolishness was awarded to those who didn't even put out their lights but simply closed the shutters and let the light stream out between the laths. Our Jesuit friends, the bookworms, either didn't know that anything was going on or didn't care; they kept their noses glued to the Hebrew books despite all of Mussolini's warning. [3] In fact, the air raid went over so badly that they decided to try it all over again. After bawling out the people over the radio for not cooperating, they had another air raid the next evening; it was a bit better, but in our section a few men celebrated it by smashing bottles against the buildings while everybody yelled "Bravo" to them. The only thing we had to fear was the Rector. All the lights went off in the building, but somebody had a flashlight which was confiscated by the rector and donated by him to the Vice Rector. While I am typing this another air raid is scheduled to be pulled off any minute.

When we were at St. Peter's a few days ago, we happened upon a procession to some service there. The Seminarians from the Lateran College were in charge of the affair. The kids ranged from about six or eight to about fourteen years of age, all dressed in the curious shade of violet that is their house uniform color. To anyone accustomed to the American way of doing things, it was a bit scandalous. I still am opposed to sending kids from the cradle to the seminary; they exchange their diapers for a cassock. And necessarily the whole affair is carried out with great sloppiness. At the head of the procession were two fellows carrying maces to make way for the procession and look after order, but they selected the shakiest old derelicts they could dig up and put them in front. All this stuff is, I suppose, a hangover from the Middle Ages and once had a real purpose, but now it is just a tradition that has a stranglehold. (4) All the functions here have the possibility of great dignity, but they never turn out that way. The Italians don't seem to mind. They pray and sing aloud regardless of everything.

By the time you get to Rome there should be a better approach to St. Peter's. All the old buildings and tenements approaching St. Peter's are being torn down to make a larger "piazza" (square). (5) Mussolini is gradually moving the people from crowded, dirty districts in the center of Rome to the outskirts, and everything new is being built in strictly modernistic fashion. It is a real surprise to see apartment houses built like cheese boxes with snaky, winding steps just beside old villas that may be four or five hundred years old. The building that is being done is characteristic of the Italian temperament — everything is extreme. They either build something very artistically or very ugly, so it seems to me. And the Fascists (as well as the Romans) have a real mania for size. Their treasury building was built to accommodate all the money they would like to have, not what they actually have.

This morning we were at Castel Saint Angelo, an old emperor's tomb that was turned into a fort and used later by the Popes as a defense for St. Peter's. (6) These old Popes knew more than theology; the fort had even a well in it to supply water and was practically a little city in itself — and a very strong city. To show you the ignorance of some visitors, an English lady (pointing to St. Peter's only half a mile away) said, "And what large building is that?" Somebody told her what it was, and she came back with the prize crack of all time, "Oh, a church; well, of what denomination?"

Love,

Phil

Comments: Letter of February 23, 1937

(1)   Velati's Store was our favorite candy store located on F Street N.W. I worked there during the Christmas holidays and remember well that we packaged and posted about two tons of candy per day; the

White House normally ordered four hundred pounds at Christmas time to be delivered to the White House.

(2) The Jews were very popular in Rome and very congenial with the Italians. During the War, through the efforts and orders of Pope Pius XII eighty percent of the Jews were saved from the Nazis (at least 600,000 other Jews were saved throughout Italy by the Church) whereas eighty percent of the Jews in other countries were deported and killed.

(3) The Jesuit friends referred to were the scholars in the world-famous Biblicum Institute near the College.

(4) In retrospect, I was too harsh in condemning the Roman system in the seminaries for youngsters. They ultimately produced an excellent group of priests. After the II Vatican Council, the whole Roman system of seminaries was changed.

(5) The destruction of the old Borgo section in front of St. Peter's was part of the program to build the present approach to St. Peter's with the broad *Via della Conciliazione* (Avenue of Conciliation) as the principal thoroughfare. The name of the avenue memorializes the Lateran Treaty of 1928, which settled the claim of the Church for reparations stemming from the seizure of the Church's territory in the unification of Italy in 1870 by the forces of the House of Savoy. Mussolini had a central role in the implementation of the plan to construct the new approach to St. Peter's.

(6) Castel St. Angelo was the funeral monument of the Emperor Hadrian, built in 130 A.D. Many succeeding emperors were also buried there. The present name is derived from the apparition of an angel at the top of the building sheathing a sword and surrounded by singing angels during a procession led by St. Gregory the Great in 590 while praying for deliverance from a raging plague in Rome. Rome was delivered immediately from the plague. Later it was frequently used as a fort and refuge for the Pope as in 1525 when

the army of Charles V sacked Rome with the Pope unharmed in the fort.

February 24, 1937

NORTH AMERICAN COLLEGE
VIA DELL' UMILTA 30

Dear Everybody,

Washington's Birthday was just another day at the college. The Rector didn't even make it a holiday — in fact didn't even change the ordinary meals. And then to completely bury poor old George from all remembrance, they didn't even put up our flag that is so old that it only has forty-five stars. So passed Washington's Birthday.

We have been having some rather distinguished visitors at the college. Cardinal Marchetti came one day for a meal and to see Archbishop Mooney and Bishop Duffy. [1] Of course, the visitors got a big hand from the students. Of course, they all knew that someone was supposed to give a little talk for the applause; such squirming and buck-passing you never saw. The Archbishop motioned to the Cardinal, who motioned right back, and then they both motioned to the Rector. But the Rector knew that we didn't want to hear from him; we get enough of him as it is. So they all sat like ninnies pointing at each other, and not one has pulled himself out of his seat yet. Of course, the Rector could have settled the whole matter by asking Archbishop Mooney to say a few words because he couldn't possibly refuse, but the Rector bungled again. Cardinal Marchetti likes the Americans very much. [2] He speaks a little English, what they call "small English" over here; this is a sample of his English, "Hello boys. Like it here? Lonesome? Want to go home?" It doesn't make any difference what you say to his questions or how you feel, because he can't understand what you are saying. He is a very popular Cardinal around the college and in certain sections of Rome because he has a reputation for never being late for an engagement — a great rarity for any Italian. But he caused quite a stir in Rome when he was first appointed; he insisted that a number of churches in Rome lock up most of the relics they were showing because they had no proof of their truth. Well, you can imagine how some of these people liked that. So the Archbishop made his last appearance at the college and left in a blaze of unpopularity. The normal thing in any seminary is for a visiting Bishop to give a talk, and ordinary politeness seems to demand that he at least acknowledge the applause. Furthermore, he was a student here for six years and then came back later as Spiritual Director. So his silence remains unforgivable. But the greatest mystery to me is how the Rector lets all these people get away without ever giving a talk to the students. Any number of very famous people come to Rome who are capable of giving very interesting and valuable talks (besides it is a distinct compliment to be asked to speak to this college because of its reputation), but we have never had anyone to address the community. [3] Any time someone has gotten up and spilled off a few words, it was because the students gave them such a hand that they were cornered; and last year Monsignor Sheen was backed into a corner by the whole student body and gave a very interesting little talk — but the Rector did nothing to help matters.

A Cardinal died a few days ago, and we went over to see how they exhibit the body. We were prepared to see a big layout with candles and black cloth and carpets everywhere. But death seems to be the one thing in Italy that is treated with the utmost simplicity. [4] First of all, they use very simple caskets, nothing more than a poor wooden affair; the casket was so small for this Cardinal that they actually had to press the corpse a bit to get it in. He was laid out in a room with the casket laid directly on the floor and two or three candles in front of it. Of course, the body was not embalmed. I don't know whether the attitude of the people is to allow the corpse to decay naturally because of a religious motive, or because their poverty prevents embalming. At any rate, they say that only a very great personage, as the Pope or King, is embalmed; the rest are just buried.

Another thing that stumped us was the fact that the corpse had no arms, or at least no hands. He was clothed in the Cardinal's vestments and with the usual Cardinal's gloves with his ring placed on the finger of the glove. That ghastly practice of amputating part of the body and sending it to different cities is supposed to be forbidden by the Church. But the mystery of his arms and hands still remains. Although a great deal of curiosity is shown in viewing a body over here, the people that came to look certainly prayed. In fact, they pray continually as they carry the body to the cemetery. Unless the family is very wealthy, they all walk behind the carriage carrying the casket and recite prayers. Wealthy people are not buried in the morning (unless the custom is now being disregarded); late afternoon is the accepted time for the funerals of well-to-do people. And it used to be that if you were very high up in the social scale, you were buried just at dusk or a little after nightfall; and a number of men were hired who carried candles and recited the penitential psalms as they walked behind the carriage to the cemetery. Strangely, they don't have many Masses said for the deceased as we do in the States; an Italian monsignor was telling us how surprised he was when he went on a trip to the U.S. and saw all the requiem Masses being said.

The Church in the United States was given a big blow the other day in history class. A German is our prof, and he said that the condition of the Church in the States today is the miracle of the century. [5] Further, he took a real rap at the European idea that the Church and State must be united or joined in some way, because he pointed out how well the Bishops in the States got along with the government and how the government never meddles in Church affairs. He certainly gave the American section a real glow. He also pointed out that the American people pay more to support their churches and the Holy See than any other nation in the world. This prof was run out of Germany for his plain speaking, and I can well understand it now; he never praises the Italian system in the handling of the Church and is very outspoken in his opinions. The tribute he paid the Irish one day was a knockout — said that their clergy had been the greatest the world has ever seen. [6] But he knows human nature; for instance, he gave as one reason for the preservation of Catholicism in Ireland the fact that England was against the Church and the opposition of the Irish to any opinion of the English.

Love,

Phil

P.S. Father John S. Kennedy of Hartford wrote an article in the <u>Columbia</u>, entitled "As Others See Us — And How", that is a very interesting account of the reception the English gave him. Reminded me of the Englishman in Paris telling Mom how surprised he was that she didn't talk with a harsh voice. You ought to read the article — he beats the h — l out of the English.

Comments: *Letter of February 24, 1937*

(1)   Archbishop (later Cardinal) Edward Mooney of Detroit was a very distinguished alumnus of the College and in our day there still were rumors about his brilliance as a student. He was born in Mt. Savage in western Maryland and made a sensation when he went on a nostalgic homecoming there a few years before he died.

(2)   Cardinal Marchetti was a jovial and very beloved figure who openly admired Americans. He was famous for his campaign to get rid of false relics in the churches in Rome, especially the nearby famous church of the Holy Apostles (Santi Apostoli). Naturally, many of the lay people, and some clerics, thought he was too highhanded but his campaign was necessary.

(3)   My complaint against the Rector for not getting more "talks" by the famous visitors was widespread among the students. Separated from everything in the U.S., we appreciated greatly a talk by a prominent American, clerical or lay. There was also a bit of self-serving from the fact that we generally gave such a noisy appreciation of their presence that sometimes they gave us a special dinner.

(4)   The funerals in Rome were admirably simple and spiritual. Respect for the horse-drawn hearse was universal, and an unknowing Englishman who failed to take off his hat for the funeral cortege years ago was beaten and sent to the hospital.

(5)   The accolade in the classroom was by Father Leiber, S.J., who was a refugee from Germany, driven out by the Nazis. He said that the greatest miracle for the Church in our century was the support and growth of the Church in the U.S. because of the generosity of the laity and the zeal of the clergy and religious. He emphasized the size and efficiency of the Catholic school system, the product of the generosity of the laity and the efforts of the clergy without any financial aid of the government.

(6)   He also paid a great compliment to the Irish clergy in the U.S. saying that they were the best in the world.

February 25, 1937

NORTH AMERICAN COLLEGE
Via Dell' Umilta 30

Dear Everybody,

The Italian government has published notice of an air raid this week. A siren is the warning signal; and they say the siren is loud enough to drown out the horn of Gabriel. Whenever the siren sounds, everyone is supposed to rush indoors regardless of the neighborhood in which you are. Anyone caught out on the street is fined ten lira (a fellow from our college was fined during the last raid). All traffic is to stop immediately, and the drivers and passengers are to run for cover. If the siren sounds at night, all lights are to go out and all noises to stop. Everybody is hoping that the siren rings when we are out on walks and near a nice restaurant or beer hall; in that event, we shall prolong the air raid.

During Lent it is an old custom in Rome to make the "stations"; the "station" is held at a different church every day. [1] The various churches take this occasion to show off everything they have; the relics are put on exhibition, the doors of the church draped, candles lighted at every shrine or every place capable of holding a candlestick. They usually have so many candles around the church that it would take a Senate investigating committee to find the altar in which the Blessed Sacrament is reserved. If the station is held at a church under the direction of some order, the order invariably has all the relics of saints from their order placed around the church. At St. Mary Major they had on exhibition the crib in which Christ is supposed to have been carried to Egypt during the flight of the Holy Family.

Last year the examinations at the Greg were finished on the eighteenth of July. Unfortunately, they begin with some letter of the alphabet and take the fellows in that order; this year they begin with 'M' so I will be among the last on the list. However, if you get over here by the eighteenth or thereabouts, I shall be finished then certainly.

Love,

Phil

Comments: Letter of February 25, 1937

(1)   Making the "stations" during Lent was a custom begun centuries ago of having a procession, led by the Pope or another prominent cleric, to the popular churches in Rome. Prayers, hymns and the rosary were recited during the procession and then prayers of penance and a Mass were said at the church. During Lent a cross or crucifix with a relic of the Cross was carried at the head of the procession. In the early years of his pontificate the Holy Father, Pope John Paul II, participated in several of the Stations but because of traffic and other obstacles, the procession is greatly reduced or omitted entirely.

      We, as a camerata, would visit the church of the station, and this was a widespread custom among the seminaries of Rome.

March 7, 1937

NORTH AMERICAN COLLEGE
Via Dell' Umilta 30

Dear Everybody,

      A fellow from Turin, Italy, who met Rob and Mary three years ago when they were on their honeymoon, stopped in to see me. He is studying to be a Salesian and, of course, finds things "different." For instance, he was for three years a prefect in a dormitory up there and found it difficult to keep the kids from jumping into bed at night with their pants on. One night he saw a fellow getting into bed with what looked like black pants on, so he made him get out to take them off. But the fellow had foxed him – he was wearing black underwear. It seems that all of them have quite a horror of taking showers. They are supposed to take two a year, but they fight like steers to get out of it. Even the professors don't fully approve of all this cleanliness business; one boasted that he hadn't changed his shirt in seven years and couldn't see why others had to be different. As long as one keeps on the beaten path and in the big cities in Italy things are rather clean, but get into the country and you see some real back-to-nature stuff. But what is more surprising than their lack of washing is the way they hang meat up in the stores; the customers get what the flies have left. [1] They never bother to put a cloth over the meat, just hang it up on the outside of the shop. They sell quite a bit of horsemeat in Rome. And they have a sparrow sandwich that would chase an American right out of the restaurant; they skin the sparrow but leave everything in it and don't even bother to cut its head off. These people can take it.

There is quite a bit of grippe and slight doses of the flu going the rounds in Rome. [2] It has all passed now, but there was hope at one time of the Greg stopping classes for a few days. It hit our "camerata" rather badly. There are eleven fellows in our can and at one time eight were in bed. But though I did my best, I couldn't muster a sniffle or cough to give me an excuse for going to bed. Living on the farm was good practice for Rome. The fact is that we, on the top floor here, are almost living in the open. It doesn't get cold in Rome, it only gets chilly; and on the top floor it gets a bit miserable if a fellow is subject to colds. The change of climate treats some fellows rather badly, but I find that it is much easier on one than the Washington climate. If you can live in Washington, you can live anywhere, I think.

This General Goering, the German, went to visit St. Peter's while in Rome. [3] What a hypocrite! It's amazing the way these people can do an about-face when it's for their benefit. This Goering leaves off punching at Catholics in Germany to come down and make a visit to St. Peter's. The Italians are like that to some extent. Ten years ago they were all against the church. In the streets they used to call priests and seminarians "Roaches", but today they are all for the Church. Quite a few of the Americans used to get in fights on the streets. A crowd of young Italians would form and block the sidewalk. The Americans would insist on pushing through; and if anybody wanted trouble, they didn't disappoint them. There is one story that a Scotch fellow got in a brawl in a small town with some anti-Catholics and killed one. There is none of that stuff any more, Il Duce stepped on that.

Love,

Phil

Comments: Letter of March 7, 1937

(1) The custom of hanging the meat on hooks in the butcher shops had curious effects. I knew one Italian who was so revolted by the sight of the bloody meat that he became a total vegetarian. A friend tried to cure him by offering him a hundred dollars if he would eat a piece of chicken and put the hundred dollar bill next to the cooked piece of chicken — but the lure failed.

Of course, the butcher shops have changed and now have the usual refrigeration, but Italians rightly prefer to have meat that has not been frozen.

(2) There was no flu vaccine available nor penicillin, and generally the only medicine was aspirin — but some doctors also ordered "warm wine" to be drunk, which generally succeeded in almost pickling one's tongue with no further benefit.

(3) We never knew why the Germans sent General Goering to Rome. As commander of the Luftwaffe (Air Force) he was considered to be merciless, and his ample firth made him look like a German butcher. His visit to St. Peter's was a public relations disaster. The Nazis never realized the basic difference between the utterly militaristic character of their regime and the easy-going but spiritual character of the Italians. A story about a German officer in Florence illustrates that point: The officer was watching an Italian band marching along a street, and one member dropped out of formation to tie his shoe. A nearby American asked the German officer, "What would you do as an officer if you saw that happen in Germany?" The officer answered, "I wouldn't do anything. I'd drop dead from surprise."

March 15, 1937

NORTH AMERICAN COLLEGE
VIA DELL' UMILTA 30

Dear Everybody,

The North American College these days is quite an interesting place in which to live. As I told you before, the new regime here has tried to install a "New Deal" in the way of discipline. There are a number of obstacles to such a policy. The rules are absurd, the faculty is completely inadequate to enforce any rules, and the whole place is in such abominable condition that a sort of good-natured anarchy is the only possible state of affairs. The food is, judged by ordinary Sems, below par; the toilets are almost Medieval; hot showers are available only for parts of two days of the week and only two showers are in working condition; all of which doesn't make any sort of hardship if the rules are not strictly enforced. But that is where they are making their mistake. In the first place, the building here is about three times larger than the Sem in Washington and there are only two men, the Rector and Vice Rector, to look after them. The climax of something or other was reached two nights ago when the Vice Rector went into the showers about ten minutes after ten (lights are supposed to be off at ten) and bawled the fellows out for not being in bed, even though the only time to get a steady stream of hot water is about ten o'clock. Now they actually have started, so it is said, a Master of Showers to whom one applies for a time in which to take a shower; and if one is caught taking a shower any other time, he is to be considered out of order. Our entire Camerata, except for three fellows, of whom I was one, took quite a dressing a few days ago; we are supposed to walk two by two whenever we go out. Well the cam was divided into two sections and the Rector met both parts. He worked himself into quite a lather about it, called in the Prefect and the fellows who were in the second group, told them that "this was anarchy, anarchy" and that he'd send them home if they didn't obey the rule better. [1] Wouldn't that brand him if he sent somebody home "because he was caught not walking two by two with his Prefect." It is all very amusing for me because I am simply on the outside looking in; this is my lucky year in dealings with the faculty. The ridiculous part of that episode was that the fellows who were caught were the most innocent in the house. Then to make himself even more popular, the Vice Rector stood outside the entrance to the chapel after High Mass and "caught" the fellows who hadn't shined their shoes just before High Mass. This is much more interesting than having a sensible faculty, but I sometimes wonder (since I am very near twenty-four now) whether I am getting soft-brained and silly, or whether the rest of the world is screwy. I haven't decided yet.

And as long as this is my fighting mood, I must tell you about the letter I sent to the editor of the <u>Baltimore Catholic Review</u> about the editorial they had in one issue about Monsignor Ryan of Catholic University. [2] It was a fright — even for the Review. Personally, I am not in favor of repressing the Review; I think that, like most European countries, we should have a Catholic Daily in the Archdiocese. When we need newspaper space we never get it from the other secular papers, and the present affair is practically no good. If anything does come up, it is only handled (and then very poorly) a week later when everyone has forgotten about it. And then if they reply, there is no answer to the reply for another week. Besides, Washington is just the place for the Catholics to have their little fling, if they want to have any effect. I wouldn't make the paper one of these blaring, loud-mouthed things that is usually associated with the Catholic Press. I'd make it simply a regular, dignified newspaper, carrying the national as well as church news and giving our attitude towards crimes, etc., especially movies. I am convinced that many non-Catholics would back it too. Such dreaming.

The Irish College is getting ready for St. Patrick's Day, big public ceremony. We won't celebrate that much because just two days afterwards, feast of St. Joseph, the rest of the Deacon class will be ordained. About twenty-five fellows this time. Two Baltimoreans will be ordained. Big day.

Love,

Phil

Comments: Letter of March 15, 1937

(1)   The reprimand of our camerata by the Rector for being "separated" remains a fond memory of the few remaining members of the

camerata. The Rector and Vice Rector while walking saw some members of the camerata (looking at bibles in a bookstore window) separated from the other members of the camerata.

On our return to the college our prefect was summarily instructed to assemble the camerata in the office of the Rector, and the prefect obediently rapped the door of each member yelling, "Hellza popping. Get down to the Rector's office." When duly assembled, we were told that we were "anarchists and communists" with no regard for law and order. We tried to look a bit penitent, but we realized that we would never be dismissed for "separating during a cam walk."

Years later, Monsignor Ed O'Connor said laughingly that the incident was the outstanding event of his life in the camerata.

(2)   The big fight about the Baltimore Catholic Review was the difference in opinion about the "packing of the Supreme Court" by President Roosevelt. Nobody doubted that his action was necessary for him to establish legally the New Deal, but many disagreed about his method; and the Baltimore Catholic Review, in its ham-handed editorial manner, blamed the famous Monsignor John Ryan of the NCCB for supporting Roosevelt.

March 19, 1937
Feast of St. Joseph

NORTH AMERICAN COLLEGE
Via Dell' Umilta 30

Dear Everybody,

They had ordinations today, the feast of St. Joseph. Everything was more impressive than usual. [1] There is a special little piece they sing, "*Tu es sacerdos in aeternum*" (Thou art a priest forever), written by Cardinal O'Connell when he was a student here, that is very expressive. I don't think Cardinal O'Connell wrote the music himself; he simply adapted it. Everything went off splendidly even though a very queer thing had happened among the visiting parents and friends. Somehow or other a couple of disagreements took place on board ship coming over. A priest from the house went down to meet them at Naples to show them around for a few days before bringing them to Rome. But the day he arrived in Naples he sent a call to Rome saying that they were coming up the next day and to make arrangements for them in different hotels (they had previously made arrangements for staying in the same hotel). And one family group kept so much to themselves, that the others didn't know who they were until they got off the boat at Naples. Just one great big family! It seems that they just couldn't agree on anything among themselves. But despite all that everything at the college was perfect, even the "abbess" was in fine spirits. Of all the queer and distorted pieces of humanity the "Abbess" is the most unusual I have ever seen. She is a woman of about twenty-seven with the mentality of a girl about thirteen and dresses with the taste of a kid of three. She is a Virginian who entered a convent but had to give up the life owing to ill health. She came to Rome because of the churches and all the pious fuss that is forever here, and hasn't left. She comes to all the ordinations and donates flowers in lavish style to the chapel. What makes her distinctive is the way she dresses; this morning she came all done up in a flowing purple velvet creation that swept to the floor. You have no idea how badly purple velvet can look at seven o'clock in the morning. Some generous soul volunteered to show her around the house so that she could get the blessings of the newly ordained priests, and when last seen he was having a terrific time getting her out of the door.

Ordination time is a good opportunity for a study in heredity. "Like father like son" is quite true. I had the job, for a time, of introducing the fellows to the mother of one of my diocesans, Mrs. Albert; and it was a real pleasure. She is a very charming woman, enjoyed the informal reception in the room of her newly ordained son and made everyone feel perfectly at home. What a relief from the Seminary life and its Puritanic faculty. I can understand why Father Plimmer used to run into 1501 occasionally. Through there is a general family trait, occasionally one meets a tremendous contrast between parents and son. A very mild and soft-spoken fellow was ordained last year, and before ordination he used to keep speaking about his mother (who was coming over for ordination) in an almost babyish way. The fellow who went down to Naples to meet his mother was all set to encounter some retiring, shy person. But when "Momsie" came down the gangplank, it was a loud, big, cheery Western woman with a cigarette stuck in her mouth and calling everybody "Honey" or "Dearie". When she came to Rome she used to put her son to bed at night then go out to see Rome by herself. She took her son to more beer halls than he thought had every existed in Rome.

Love,

Phil

Comments: Letter of March 19, 1937

(1)   There was a special aura and indescribable sense of spiritual bonding in the priestly ordinations in the beautiful College chapel. The intimacy of the chapel, its history, the threat of war and the clash of the pagan philosophy of Nazism and the singing at the end of the ceremony of the traditional hymn "Tu es sacerdos in aeternam" (You are a priest forever) made it an unforgettable experience. There was a feeling of timelessness, literally a "new creation," another Christ for the salvation of the world.

(2)   The variety of the relatives of the newly ordained priests and their human disagreements was a good statement of the pastoral challenge facing the priests. The experience of one mother, a widow, typified the anxiety and enthusiasm of the visitors. She was so afraid of oversleeping, despite her alarm clock and the promise of the concierge to call her by the house telephone, that she stayed awake all night. Strangely, she seemed to be in good shape and wide-awake during and after the ordination.

March 22, 1937

Holy Week

NORTH AMERICAN COLLEGE
Via Dell' Umilta 30

Dear Everybody,

The last time I wrote I think I was telling you about the Feast of St.

Joseph. On the afternoon of the feast day we went over to the church of St. Joseph to watch the celebration. [1] During the day they have a big public fair at which one can do everything from eating to shooting – they have whole pigs cooked without being cleaned, and doughnuts (the Italian version) that are made completely in public (the reason why I wouldn't eat them even if I were starving). About five o'clock the procession starts from the church; everybody is in it – men dressed in peculiar outfits, then children dressed in white, and women of all descriptions. One of the special attractions is a little fellow dressed in a Franciscan outfit led by a little girl; it looks as though she were running away with the holy monk. About twelve husky men carry a great statue of St. Joseph on their shoulders through the streets. A cardinal and bishop are also in the procession, which lasts for about three hours. They usually have a delegation of students from the American College in it, and they always sing "Holy God We Praise Thy Name" in English; the crowd always seems to like it.

On Sunday morning, I went out to the second Mass of one of the newly ordained priests and served his Mass in the catacombs of St. Priscilla. [2] It took us about ten minutes to get to the chapel where Mass was to be said; the corridors in the catacombs are very long because the rock here was ideal for excavation. There is a peculiar sort of rock here called "tuffa" that is about as soft as clay when in the earth, but when cut out, and exposed to the sun and heat, gets hard. It is very easy to dig it out and thus make catacombs. The chapel where Mass was said had only the bare earth. For all practical purposes it was like hearing Mass two thousand years ago. The next day I served Mass at the altar on the tomb of St. Peter in St. Peter's . Quite a thrill. Afterwards we went to breakfast at the American Convent and got a good American breakfast. Two events in one day.

I noticed that market is open on Sunday morning here for half a day. It seems strange to see them haggling and carrying on even on Sunday morning.

I just met General Lenihan at St. Mary Major's where he was listening to Tenebrae services (which were very poorly done). [3] He is going back to the U.S. very shortly to celebrate at West Point his fiftieth anniversary of graduation. The old man is very loyal to West Point and still is an army man to the core. His grandson just took a competitive examination in the District for an appointment to the Point; I hope he makes it for the old man's sake. At Christmas time he went to Palestine, came back and gave a lecture about it at St. Susanna's, the American Church in Rome. He knows quite a bit about the political situation there, says the Arabs are being cheated.

Holy Week in Rome is nothing compared to Holy Week at St. Matthew's or a first class Seminary in the U.S. On Palm Sunday they don't have palms, they have olive branches but the general public doesn't get in the spirit as in the U.S. But even if they did try to carry out the ceremonies with dignity, the canons would be sure to spoil it. Their conception of singing very nearly approaches that country custom called hog-calling; they are dressed magnificently — purple robes with ermine mantles — but the first requisite seems to be some sort of infirmity and either a very loud voice or a very hoarse one. Some of them have the technique of freight agents. This is a general description of Tenebrae services at any of the great basilicas in Rome; first of all Tenebrae is held in the afternoon, beginning about five o'clock; everybody strolls in, including beggars, and begins to pay attention to everything but the main service. There are no pews, so everybody stamps around until they get tired and then squat on the bases of pillars or on kneeling benches. [4] But there was an added attraction yesterday. It is an old custom for the cardinal in charge of the Sacred Penitentiary to go to St. Mary Major's on Wednesday and St. Peter's on Holy Thursday, sit in a chair and place the penitent's rod (a long stick) upon anyone's head who kneels before him. One gets three hundred days indulgence for that act of humility. [5] I didn't get around to it, too large a crowd. General Lenihan told me that "he had taken the rap on the head with the billiard stick."

Love,

Phil

Comments: Letter of March 22, 1937

(1)   St. Joseph is one of the patrons of Italy; and therefore, the Feast of St. Joseph in the church dedicated to St. Joseph is carried out with gusto — this means a very elaborate procession in addition to the Mass. Church processions go back to the early years of Christianity. Every generation is represented in the procession and the bambini (children) always steal the show.

The custom of the College permitted the newly ordained

priests to celebrate Mass in churches of their choice on the three days following their ordination. The priests also were allowed to invite their fellow seminarians or other friends to attend their Mass and to enjoy a breakfast with them. The breakfast finished, the newly ordained were expected to attend the remaining classes of the day!!!

(2)   Priscilla was a close relative of Senator Pudens who gave hospitality to St. Peter and St. Paul and was converted by St. Paul. It is one of the oldest and most famous of the catacombs.

(3)   General Lenihan was a commanding officer of the famous 69th Regiment in World War I and was a member of the St. Vincent de Paul Society of St. Matthew's Parish in Washington, D.C., our home parish. My father was a very devoted member of the St. Vincent de Paul Society and was a great admirer and friend of the General.

(4)   The major basilicas of Rome have a group of canons who have a role in the administration of the basilica and who also have the duty of chanting the daily "liturgy of the hours" (formerly called the "office"). The Tenebrae services (literally dusk or evening) were celebrated in the evening of the three first evenings of the Holy Week. These services were dropped by the changes of the liturgy during the II Vatican Council. Often dignitaries of the church were appointed as canons of the basilicas.

The Italians, with their seemingly casual conduct in a church, point out that there are far more Italian saints than those of other countries — a good point. I certainly gradually came to love God more, profiting from their example. I still prefer our system of having pews with kneelers in a church and admit freely that their absence is no norm of sanctity.

(5)   "Going to confession" during Holy Week was a well-observed custom in Italy as in the United States. The Holy Father encourages this custom by hearing confessions in St. Peter's. The remark of General Lenihan referred to the custom of having the head of the Sacred Penitentiary, during the last days of Holy Week, give a tap

on the head of penitents who knelt before him with a long, tapering rod. This act of humiliation was rewarded with an indulgence.

March 27, 1937
Holy Saturday

NORTH AMERICAN COLLEGE
VIA DELL' UMILTA 30

Dear Everybody,

Just arrived home after attending a concert given by Tito Schipa and Gianna Pederzini, opera stars, at the Angelicum College. [1] Very delightful affair – especially since we bought five lire tickets and got into the ten lire seats. The Italian princess, Princess Maria of Savoy, was there; the Queen of Spain and the Princess of Spain, Princess Borghese and two cardinals. After seeing the Spanish and Italian princesses, I cannot understand why Edward VIII gave up his throne to marry a commoner; the Spanish Princess is the blond, lofty type, the Italian Princess is the typical Italian type —large (tremendously large) brown eyes, olive complexion and very regular features. She is very gracious. The hall was small, adding to the intimacy of the occasion. Since royalty was present, both stars were very generous with their encores. I know Mom and Mary will be interested to know what the princesses and queen wore. Well, the audience was very smartly dressed; and thus, they didn't seem the least bit extraordinary. The Spanish princess, being blond, wore a light blue outfit with blue and white hat (very effective — rather regal looking); the Italian princess wore a dark blue outfit with a very small hat. She looks very much like just a pretty little girl and acts that way too, often looking around to see who is in the audience. After seeing two of the "eligibles", I just can't understand the present Duke of Windsor.

Before I forget; of course, we will have an opportunity to go to Ireland during the summer. I am trying to find the date of the famous Dublin horse show, supposed to be the best in the world, to see if it would fit in with any plans. I know it would be worth seeing.

Holy Week in Rome would be very impressive if one attended all the big ceremonies at St. Peter's; but at the college we try to do our own then get out to see the others, and it rather messes things. On Thursday and Friday of Holy Week the great relics of St. Peter's are brought out, and the crowd is blessed with them — the spear of Longinus, the soldier who opened the side of Our Lord when on the Cross, the veil of Veronica, and part of the True Cross. [2] The relics are left in their cases, and one can't distinguish one from the other. But the whole affair is impressive. Even more interesting is the washing of the altars, done by Cardinal Pacelli assisted by the canons of St. Peter's. [3] First they are sprinkled with, I believe, holy water and then wiped off with great big bushy wipers made of wood or paper that are thrown out to the crowd as souvenirs. This washing of the altars is carried out in all the churches, at least the large ones, with much singing and general commotion.

Many of the fellows here go out to assist at churches for the ceremonies of Holy Week. I went to Saint Susanna's, the church for Americans, for Holy Thursday. The four man choir gasped rather bravely, and the ceremony went off well; the British ambassador to Italy, Sir Eric Drummond, helped to carry the canopy over the Blessed Sacrament – reminded me of services at St. Matthew's with the prominent men of the parish doing the work. A peculiar coincidence is that the British ambassador to Italy is a Catholic, but the British ambassador to the Vatican State is not a Catholic. Probably, it is not a coincidence — afraid of the church influencing the diplomats. No one at the American Embassy in Rome is a Catholic. After the service we had a good breakfast at the parish rectory; the assistant, a Paulist, studied his theology at C.U. and was rather interesting, except that he laughed before and after telling a joke, and laughed far too long each time.

I celebrated Holy Saturday by sending a cablegram home, after which I solemnly swore never to do that again – costs too much money. These Italians don't have special rates for the holiday seasons, even if I were willing to write the cable in Italian. No wonder the government has to control industry here; they'd never get anything done. I also discovered, much to my disgust, that the picture I bought has not left Italy yet; the store sent me an application that must be signed by a bank, and the bank officials don't seem to know anything about it. A recent regulation must have been passed concerning exporting anything like that. Italian service is horrible.

Easter was a tremendous day. We all had special tickets to get in St. Peter's to see the Pope carried in and assist at the Mass said by the dean of the College of Cardinals. [4] We got there at eight o'clock in the morning, and there was a large crowd already in the church. I never saw such a crowd, such uniforms, and such an impressive ceremony. We scrambled up to the end of the section in which we were allowed to enter, jumped over the barrier (with the connivance of an American from San Francisco when the guards weren't looking) and got up to the section reserved for diplomats and special guests. I was standing with the Military Attaché to the American Embassy, who is not a Catholic but was very much impressed. His wife, who despite her painted face and all the technique of the beautifier threatens to dissolve into a corpse any minute, was very nice, gave me their card, wanted to know where I was staying, etc. I shall keep them on the string — never know when you can use people like that. Everything was working beautifully that day. After working myself way up, I showed two English women where they could get a view of the Pope on his throne (what a sight!) and explained a few things; after which they decided they had seen everything — they were not Catholic — and left, leaving me with their seats. I could see everything. The most impressive thing of the whole affair is the way uniforms of different centuries, and people of every race and creed, are all equally welcome and at home. The Swiss guards come in with their steel helmets, topped with a red plume, carrying weapons three centuries old, and they don't seem out of place. Then there are the official ushers, the Noble Guards who wear outfits of the seventeenth century and nobody stares at them. But the group that gave me the biggest thrill was the detachment of American sailors who came swinging up the main aisle and were given excellent seats (it seems that Americans really count over here now that Cardinal Pacelli has seen the U.S.). They had just arrived from Naples and acted like diplomats. The Pope is carried in, announced by a blare of trumpets and the sounding of the Papal March; then the fifty thousand or so in St. Peter's cut loose. He wears the famous triple-tiara and doesn't seem to be half dead, only vary tired. I would go through the whole scene if I had not already written it as an article for a magazine; I think I shall send it to Columbia (they pay best) and let you read it there. If it is rejected, it at least will make a nice, big letter. The Pope seems almost lost on the great throne, even though he wears a very large mitre.

I received the baseball shoes. Many thanks. Apparently the Italian customs inspector couldn't make anything out of such a stupid looking pair of shoes, so he charged only twelve cents import duty; I suppose the twelve cents was really for the socks. They go through everything sent in, because the package is always completely disturbed and the seals broken.

Hitherto, the students have been allowed to go out on short trips after Easter, but this year we are allowed only to take one-day trips. The reasoning seems to be a bit mysterious and cloudy; but I heard that some fellows had not paid for their last trip, and the bishop was holding up this one until accounts were settled. Anyway, there are a number of interesting places to see around Rome.

I forgot to mention that at the big functions in St. Peter's everybody, regardless of religion or race, is admitted. Around me there were mostly Protestants, and most of the people in the basilica were foreigners. A large number of Americans were there; these Americans get into everything over here.

I'll send some pictures that were snapped inside the basilica (if any turn out); of course, it is not allowed to take cameras into St. Peter's but who can tell what a cleric is carrying beneath his robes, which have pockets as large as gunnysacks.

If you wish to read up about Rome, in general, there is a beautifully written book called Ave Roma Immortalis written by Marion Crawford, brother to Mrs. Chanler who wrote Roman Spring. You can begin anywhere and find it amazingly different; he divides Rome into its old sections and describes them.

Love,

Phil

Comments: Letter of March 27, 1937

(1)   These special, charitable concerts usually on Holy Saturday afternoon were extremely delightful. The special guests, clergy and nobility, were always very gracious, appreciative, and very knowledgeable about the music. The performers were the cream of the musical world and very generous with their encores. Italian culture at its best. I like vocal music better than instrumental so it

was my kind of concert.

(2)   The showing of the famous relics is no longer observed. It was an awesome occasion and was very appropriate for the penitential part of Holy Week. We were really connected with the Passion of Christ, although there always was some question about the authenticity of the towel of Veronica. Apparently, a part of the spear of Longinus (which pierced the side of Christ) is kept elsewhere, probably in Germany. It was said that Hitler knew the legend that whoever possessed the spear of Longinus would never be defeated in battle and, therefore, tried desperately to secure it. General George Patton also knew the legend and tried, after World War II, to find it, without success.

(3)   The washing of the altars was a kind of re-dedication of them and was carried out with great solemnity by Cardinal Pacelli who was called "the praying Cardinal" because of his obvious piety.

(4)   Pope Pius XI, despite rumors to the contrary, seemed to be in fairly good health and was cheered uproariously by the congregation, yelling "Viva il Papa" in every possible accent. The thrilling singing of the famous Sistine choir added to the glory of the Mass celebrated in the presence of the Vicar of Christ. We all left with the feeling of the Resurrection fulfilling the ringing words of St. Paul, "When Christ, your life appears, you too will appear in glory."

March 28, 1937
Easter

NORTH AMERICAN COLLEGE
VIA DELL' UMILTA 30

Dear Everybody,
        The reverend students in the North American College are in what is commonly called a "stew". It is rumored about that good old F.D.R. and

the Senate are debating about devaluing the dollar a little more. [1]

This afternoon about twenty of us went to see the Quirinal Palace, the royal palace of Italy. [2] It is rated as one of the most beautiful in Europe. From the outside it looks like a stone barn and is built like a square with a court inside. As soon as one gets inside the very ordinary gate that keeps out the rabble of Rome, the pageantry of royalty starts.

In the first place, all the guards inside are specially chosen for height and build. We didn't see any that were less than six feet six in height; and to accentuate their height, they wear gilded helmets topped with a crest that flows almost halfway down their backs. The uniform is of blue with silver and crimson trimmings, and they all carry swords. It's much better than a musical comedy — especially the way they salute (they exaggerate everything). When one gets inside, some functionary dressed like a headwaiter produces guides out of the thin air and everything begins. It must be remembered that the Popes used to have this place as their residence before the papal states were taken away from them by the forces of the king of Savoy (whose descendant is the present king.) Consequently, it is done in the magnificent style that could only be produced by four centuries of papal rule. There are rows of unbelievably rich rooms: some are covered with silks embroidered by hand, some with brocades and tapestries; some with paintings and marble. The ballroom is unearthly. It is not tremendous, but it has three great chandeliers, draperies, and tapestries that not even Hollywood would imagine, and art objects that would keep a high school kid from dancing. It is a place made exclusively for sweeping trains and dignified dowagers. (I don't know what in the world the Popes used that hall for.) It is not only the magnificence that sweeps one off his feet, — the contrast between the styles of the rooms makes one catch his breath. For instance, one hall will be done in a royal scarlet while the next will be done in a white, satin-like motif that has enough of red in it to harmonize with the previous room. The throne room is not very large or impressive; in fact, one forgets about the throne (a very ordinary piece of work compared to the rest of the work) when looking at the mosaic work in the floor.

The truth of the matter is that though the king stole the place from the popes, he couldn't steal away the spirit of the place — which is certainly not that of Italian royalty. Every room seems to bear some reminder of the former owners of the Quirinal, whether they be sacred paintings or works of sculpture. And I am positive that the king of Italy (I don't refer to his small stature) would look as much out of place in those grand halls as an American iceman; for after all, anyone would know that an iceman was only there by mistake or on a visit, but the king is supposed to be there as lord and owner of all. They bit off more than they can chew, or, to be more exact, they took such a good thing that nobody will ever believe that it is really theirs.

Even though Easter has rolled around, I am going to make a request for a present. Seeing as how Mr. And Mrs. Hannan have (as far as my memory runs) never had good photographs made of themselves, I think it would be a splendid idea if they trusted themselves to the care of a photographer for an afternoon.

Well, I must be on my way.

Love,

Phil

Comments: Letter of March 28, 1937

(1)   The concern about the value of money in a wartime scare is well founded. In 1939 while standing in line at the American Express office in Paris to change my German marks (I had just arrived from Germany) the value of my money dropped in half — and there were only two or three customers ahead of me in the line. The elderly and retired people suffer enormously from war' when I first visited France in 1936, the French franc was four for an American dollar; and in 1944 when our troops entered Paris the rate of exchange was one thousand French francs to a dollar. Gold was so precious in Rome at that time that one of our students took a fifty-dollar gold piece (a present from his family) to a bank to be changed into lira and was shown into the office of the president of the bank who promptly shut the door to prevent the student from leaving while negotiating the exchange.

(2)   The Quirinal Palace, near the College, was the royal palace (now the residence of the president of Italy) and had all the papal insignia (the tiara and keys) above the front entrance and throughout the building. Visitors had the queasy feeling of being in a place under two different sovereigns.

March 30, 1937

NORTH AMERICAN COLLEGE
Via Dell' Umilta 30

Dear Everybody,

A few days ago I went to see a movie at a Silesian Institute with a couple of fellows. First of all, the place was crowded to the point where even the Italians admitted that it was filled; there were no tickets to be had, and no one was even allowed to come near the door. Somehow Ed Latimer got two tickets; and to make a long story short, we five of us crashed with only two tickets. [1] Four of us without tickets went in first and let the fellow with the two tickets bring up the rear; by the time he got to the ticket taker, we were all securely lost in the crowd inside the theater. Needless to say, he took quite a lecture on what a disgrace he was to the clergy, what robbers all Americans are, etc., but he finally got in. It was a Passion Play made by a French film company. All the Italians cried when Our Lord was crucified, and all cheered when He chased the moneychangers out of the Temple. After the show was over there was a big crush, so Ed picked up a little Italian who was getting her new dress and ribboned hair all messed and carried her up the stairs. All the Italians were surprised but got a big kick out of it. The whole afternoon cost us a nickel.

I saw Rome from the top of St. Peter's dome yesterday for the first time. [2] The dome is about four hundred and thirty feet high, and the climbing is a bit precarious. First one climbs to the roof of the front part of the church, the part above the nave and façade (remember St. Matthew's is built just like St. Peter's). And there they have a souvenir store on top of the church. The moneychangers are not in the temple, they are on it. One can mail letters or cards from the office there. Then you can go inside the dome, the base of the dome and take a look at the interior of St. Peter's. It seems so far down that it is more terrifying to look inside than out. Another climb takes you to a higher level inside the dome where one can better appreciate the perfect proportioning of the church. In fact, it is much better to look at St. Peter's from the inside of the dome than from the pavement outside because the front is far from beautiful. The stairs become gradually worse and worse until finally during the last flight you can hardly see where you are going; but from the dark, snaky staircase you suddenly come out on the top of the world. Everywhere stretches the famous Roman "campagna" up to the mountains in the distance and all around is the great Rome. And ancient Rome still exists because some of those buildings look as old as the rocks on which they are built. The Vatican building looks like a house that Old Mother Hubbard built and enlarged on every time there was a new addition in the family. There is nothing splendid about the exterior; it is as homely as an old rock cliff that straggles everywhere until it gets tired and gives up the struggle; but the Vatican gardens and new buildings are magnificent from the dome. You can't appreciate the gardens until you have seen them from the air. The most impressive sight is the old castle by the banks of the Tiber that was used as the defense for St. Peter's during the Middle Ages; it is Castel Angelo built in the fourth century as a burial tomb for the Roman Emperors, but gradually changed into a fort to which the Popes fled every time Rome was attacked. Its gaunt old walls are battered from fifteen centuries of fighting, and it boasts a military record practically unequalled; it was taken by storm only once in those hundreds of years of fighting, and today one can go in and see the old military machines that the old Romans used to conquer the world and make Rome the only city in the world. Then far across the city stands the present royal palace situated on a hill too, but not comparing with the magnificence of the palace of the church. Just as the best way to see New York is to climb the Empire State Building, the only way to get a clear picture of Rome is to climb St. Peter's and find why it was called the city built on seven hills.

While up there, I couldn't help but think how different Washington is from Rome. From the Monument one can scarcely make out the houses and streets because of the trees. It looks as though Washington was young, just growing up in a forest; but Rome seems old, so old that all the traffic and living there had worn off all the vegetation, and there was nothing left but the bricks of the homes and the stones of the pavements. The houses seem built on top of each other, as they certainly were, in an effort to get together for protection.

Love,

Phil

Comments: Letter of March 30, 1937

(1)   Ed Latimer was a seminarian from the Diocese of Erie, a very energetic and impulsive fellow who not only took advantage of opportunities but created them. He was the genius who began the house publication, Roman Echoes, and I was his assistant editor and later editor.

(2)   The ascent to the top of St. Peter's by the dome is made possible by the construction of the "double dome" of St. Peter's, that is the inside dome separate from the outside dome; and, therefore, one can walk up the very narrow steps inside the inner dome to arrive at the outside pinnacle of the dome. It is one of the marvels of design and construction by Michelangelo who designed the dome. The view inside the dome is as spectacular as the view outside at the pinnacle of the dome.

April 2, 1937

NORTH AMERICAN COLLEGE
Via Dell' Umilta 30

Dear Everybody,

I don't know where I left off, or where to begin, so I'll just start backwards and ramble around. On Tuesday after Easter, six of us went down to Ostia (now called Lido) a little seacoast resort about fourteen miles from Rome. We arrived at the station five minutes late for the nine o'clock train so had to wait for the next one. The Protestant cemetery is across the street from the station so we went in. It is a magnificent little spot — it is very stately, very simple in its Greek beauty, very pagan, and since it is mostly English, very respectable. I went over especially to see the tombs of Keats and Shelley who are both buried there; they have very sentimental inscriptions on their tombs, and Shelley's (considering his life) is very confident. There is a pyramid on one side of the cemetery, built by a Roman emperor as his tomb; there is a sort of moat around it and in it was a horde of cats. I counted thirty, but the census was not complete.

Well, we got down to Ostia, saw a children's sanitarium march out for recreation (little shavers not more than five years old drill and are commanded by kids of their own age), and fell in with an Italian priest who was waiting for a young American priest – which priest at that moment was in Palestine. He was a chaplain and insisted on showing us the town; the "town" for him meant the military airport. So without knowing just where we were going, we were railroaded into taking about a three-mile walk to see an Italian airport (the airport from which Balbo sailed when he came to America). [1] After that we had dinner; then somebody got the wild idea of showing off their ability to ride a bicycle. One can hire a bicycle at the rate of about eight cents for two hours. Since there were no cars in the town – it has large avenues, but this is the off season for bathing – and not too many people to laugh at a beginner, I took a deep breath and sailed off. Didn't fall once, or even have to stop; bicycling is the easiest thing I ever tried. [2] And remember, I learned with a cassock and Roman clerical hat on. There is a very wide avenue along the beach at Ostia, so we cruised along that. It was the first time the natives had ever seen such goings on and didn't know what to make of it. The Traffic policeman was a bit puzzled at first, but when he learned that we were Americans he understood everything. The outstanding event of the afternoon was the attempt of a big fellow from Denver, six and a half feet tall and weighing about 270, to learn to ride on a bike too small for him. Coming back we discovered a way of keeping a whole electric car to ourselves; we got on early and opened all the windows in the car – and the fresh air scared every Italian away from the car.

A few days ago they started to put in another water tank or to fix the water system, and we had a real glimpse into the efficiency of Italian plumbers. They started to work in the trunk room, didn't move any of the trunks, didn't cut off the water, just opened the pipe and started to work as though nothing in the world were wrong. Luckily a couple of fellows walked by and saw a few trunks floating around so they dragged them out. Not once did the plumbers even stop to find out what was happening to the trunks. No wonder the government has to control almost everything over here.

Just a few days ago when there was a newspaper report about some scandal concerning Mussolini, I heard some things about his censorship of the press. The Paris edition of the New York Herald Tribune is sold in

Rome, but it is suppressed any time there is something in it against the government, and you can't buy that paper for any price here then. Sometimes they even censor the use of the radio; during the war against Ethiopia last year, it was forbidden to listen to broadcasts from other countries for fear that one might hear something condemning the war. Occasionally I read some statement made by an American blabbermouth about the danger of a dictatorship in the U.S. or that Roosevelt is a dictator – nobody knows how much pure nonsense that is until they have lived in a country under a real dictator. It would be impossible to put any sort of dictatorship in the U.S.; the Italians just can't understand our kind of government, and we just can't understand how anyone would want to live under their kind of government. The government even controls all tobacco and salt sold in Italy, and they charge about twice the price that is placed on it in the U.S. And sugar is so expensive that one never (except in the best hotels) finds sugar containers on the table.

Love,

Phil

Comments: Letter of April 2, 1937

(1)   Balbo was a famous Italian pilot commander of a crew that flew from Italy to the U.S. and elsewhere as a publicity gimmick for Italy.

(2)   I had never learned to ride a bicycle because my oldest brother suffered brain damage from an accident while riding a bicycle.

May 1, 1937

NORTH AMERICAN COLLEGE
Via Dell' Umilta 30

Dear Everybody,
        I just returned from serving High Mass at a convent of perpetual

adoration near the college. The nuns (mothers, to be exact, like the nuns at the Sacred Heart College) are all from either noble families or wealthy people; they must have a dowry before they are admitted. The church is really very beautiful; the whole altar is built to give emphasis to the Blessed Sacrament exposed and everything is shined as though ready for inspection. The curious thing is that on the carpet covering the sanctuary there are all sorts of *fleur de lis* (lilies) worked into the pattern and the royal coat of arms of France; the *fleur de lis* is the emblem of the deposed monarchy in France. Now all that sort of thing gets me irked with the pious girls. Why not give up all this fantastic yearning for the dead monarchy that has been out of commission for over a century and which was such a rotten thing when it was alive; why not try to cooperate with the present order and do something instead of sighing for the past. The type of person who hides his face and retires into a corner when things go wrong doesn't impress me a bit. The whole affair reminded me so much of the Sacred Heart Convent. First of all, they had a nun trying to sing bass that just sounded like a horn with a hole in it but the rest of the choir was excellent. Then the vestments worn by the priests were very beautiful, very costly and very un-liturgical. Instead of having the prescribed cross on the back of the chasuble they had a large picture of the Blessed Mother — all of which is not allowed. Then afterwards came the refreshments, very good Marsala wine and cookies. They have an excellent organization, do marvelous work but they would please me more if they called themselves simply "sister" and did something for the poor or other positive work. [1] They are having a tough time in Spain; formerly, they had about twenty-one convents there, but since the war began they haven't heard from eleven. Everything went off very well for our service there; but unfortunately, they complimented the deacon on his singing and told him he should cultivate his voice — that's just what he has been doing around here at the expense of everybody in the community. I shall never forgive the dear nuns for that compliment and advice.

A few days ago the Rector went down to Naples to meet his sister and brother-in-law who are making a tour of Europe. Just about a day after he left the Vice Rector had a party for some of the American priests at the Gregorian University. When the cat's away, the mice will play. But they were all well-behaved little boys. From my room I can see the room of the Rector — where the party was held — and everybody went home before ten-thirty. Next week the Rector of the house of graduate studies for American students is giving a party for a couple of cardinals, etc., up there. I don't know the occasion for these goings on but I hope they work everybody into a good humor.

I think that even if I were to live in Europe for fifty years, I would never get accustomed to some of their customs in eating. When some of the fellows go out in the morning to serve Mass or do something for a convent or institution and are invited to breakfast, they get a glass of wine with breakfast. And the wine doesn't come in after the meal, it usually comes in first. Imagine sitting down to a breakfast of wine and eggs (only they don't get eggs for breakfast in Rome). Some country. I am waiting to show Dad the kind of muddy water they call coffee over here. [2] Coffee is very expensive here, and they squeeze everything but the color out of the coffee beans; and to make the things produce more, they toast them until they are almost black. A usual cup of coffee at a cafeteria here is just about as inviting (to me) as a hot cup of crankcase oil. As somebody said, it tastes like the inside of the handlebars of a bicycle.

According to the recent reports in the papers, the mark (German money) is going down a bit; and it seems as though the French money is to go down more. All of which means that an American dollar will buy more this year than it has in a long time.

Love,

Phil

Comments: Letter of May 1, 1937

(1)   Despite my criticism of the Sisters, we students very frequently prayed there and asked for the prayers of the Sisters. At exam time the chapel was packed with nervous students of all nationalities.

(2)   Pure coffee was a rare commodity because it was imported. Eventually the Fascist government conducted a campaign against the use of coffee — "it is not a real Italian custom but imported."

May 6, 1937
Ascension Thursday

NORTH AMERICAN COLLEGE
VIA DELL' UMILTA 30

Dear Everybody,

A few days ago an incident occurred that makes living in a foreign country interesting. There is an alleyway that runs next to one of the walls of the college; the people living in the apartment that is on the other side of the alley have a habit of dropping everything they don't want out of the window. There were some dead fish and heads of fish out there a few nights ago when a cop came along. The only person he saw was a fellow in our college reading in his room; the cop asked him if he had thrown the fish out the window. The fellow didn't understand his Italian so to get rid of him he said yes. That got the cop all stirred up, of course, and he began to say a few very pleasant things. A priest who is a graduate student here heard all the carrying on so he leaned out of his window and tried to explain to the cop the situation. He told the cop that this was a college, not a fish store, that students never kept fish in their rooms, that the kitchen of the college was on the other side of the building, etc. Somehow the cop wouldn't take his testimony and stewed all the more, insisting that some students had thrown the fish out. By this time people were leaning out of the window of the apartment enjoying the whole scene and yelling at the cop — all of which didn't help his disposition. [1] The affair ended like all those things do — in a sandstorm of words that finally settles when everybody is tired of talking. But that wasn't the end of it. The next day after High Mass the Rector very dramatically asked the community for its attention and really began to go to work on the "students who had publicly insulted the police force, had posed as the Rector and had been guilty of throwing garbage into the street." The police had come to see the Rector saying that they had been insulted, etc., etc., etc. Of course, they gave him a very jazzed up account of what had happened. The Rector made no investigation to find out the facts, believed all that the police said, insisted that there was no doubt about the facts in the case and worked himself into a fine lather of rage. The funniest part of the affair was that he insisted that any student that did such a thing showed that he was unqualified to remain in the seminary and should go home — the priest implicated has been here ten years. So now the next thing to watch is how the Rector can get himself out of this gracefully; I'll bet that cop gets told enough to keep him quiet for a year. I was worried for a while because we are supposed to have about three free days to go on a trip around the feast of Pentecost and this mess would have ruined that.

The Rector reminded us of the rule in the constitution forbidding students to look out of the window. (2) A seminary is the only place in the world where no one has to make new legislation for any emergency at all; the only thing they have to do is look back into the by-laws and dig up something there. The Sulpician order is the prize lawgiver of all orders. They can dig up legislation to cover any incident; they have a rule that forbids seminarians to fight with bartenders (what boys they must have had in those days) and another to prevent students from looking into or getting into the carriage of the queen.

It won't be long before the family has another college graduate and another professional man.

I have to hit the books for a while.

Love,

Phil

Comments: Letter of May 6, 1937

(1)   What added to the emotion of this fish incident was the fact that to put a dead fish at a door was a great insult and among the Mafia a sign that one was marked for execution.

(2)   The law forbidding sems to look out the windows was another of the incredible anarchisms.

May 10, 1937

NORTH AMERICAN COLLEGE
Via Dell' Umilta 30

Dear Mary and Rob,

   After pestering the city with two air raids in a week, the Fascist government decided to pull a real one on Sunday evening (they must be jittery about the vulnerability of Rome). At dinner, or rather supper, the lights went out leaving us to slobber soup over our cassocks and spear potatoes by random shots in the dark. The lights remained off for an hour and a half while the "enemy" must have done everything but sweep the streets of Rome. Despite the inconvenience it was a relief to have that infernal city quiet for a few moments. I am afraid the Rector was fearful of some outbreak of anarchism in the college, so he had candles lit and placed in strategic points. After all, it would have been an excellent time to give somebody's dignity a nice jolt. The amazing thing about these raids is the discipline of the population; there is no robbing or rowdyism at all, and there is a complete silence. I can imagine what would happen in the U.S. if an air raid was conducted three times a week, the last one lasting for an hour and a half.

   As spring comes, Rome becomes more attractive. Very excellent weather here; and do you remember what fashion parades pass at the Pincio and Borghese Parks every day? On Sunday they have concerts at the Forum and in the Pincio; everyone turns out to walk and listen to the band; then when the Ave Bell sounds the day is over. Sunday afternoons on the main streets remind me a lot of Connecticut Avenue. If only this place had our trees, and our government buildings and monuments, what a place it would be. The more I look around here, the more I become convinced that the Italians are cursed by a mania for bigness, a real megalomania. They are like giants living in a pigmy land and won't accept the circumstances. These people have real taste in music and almost all forms of art except architecture (I mean the modern Italians); the most horrible example of their taste is the Victor Emmanuel Monument which fits in with nothing and expresses almost nothing except their respect for size. [1] Whenever I hear the solons and sages from Squeedump and Crested Butte rave about the beauties of Rome, I think of the vistas from Lee's mansion or the Tomb of the Unknown Soldier, or from Meridian Park, and sigh as they pour out their raving. They rush through D.C., grabbing a look at the Capitol and Monument, on their way to see art and beauty in Europe. I'll have to write me a book some day on Washington.

Love,

Phil

Comments: Letter of May 10, 1937

(1)   The government of the House of Savoy, the dynasty of this present king, has never produced any great artistic building. The Palace of Justice (Palazzo de Giustizia) near Castel San Anglo is a gingerbread building, which was hailed as the gem of architecture of the regime of the House of Savoy.

May 12, 1937

NORTH AMERICAN COLLEGE
Via Dell' Umilta 30

Dear Aunt Maggie, [1]

Your magnificent fruitcake was a very pleasant surprise. Almost everyone on this floor — including the Vice Rector — sends his thanks. Almost any food different from this Italian menu is a great treat, especially a fruitcake since it is impossible to buy anything like it in Italy. Furthermore, the cake arrived in the nick of time. We have a new disciplinarian here, a new Vice Rector, who happens to live just a few doors from me; he began his career by being very strict to the dismay of everyone. But just a few days ago, perhaps by the grace of God, he contracted some sort of a fashionable illness that confined him to his room but did no serious damage to him. He leads a lonely life, anyway, so a couple of us went in to see him. That afternoon your cake came, so I took a piece in to him just before his tea time. He could hardly believe I was actually paying him a courtesy instead of asking for something; even when I was leaving I could see that he was expecting me to ask for some sort of a permission. That piece of fruitcake was a very good investment in good will.

I just received a letter from a fellow in the Seminary in Washington and he tells me that the Sulpicians, the Archbishop and the Baltimore Catholic Review had a three-cornered fight about the editorial (on the Supreme Court) they printed in the Review against Monsignor Ryan of the Catholic University. Besides keeping the Review out of politics, I think they should keep it out of circulation altogether and develop another diocesan paper. When they try to write on popular questions of the day, they have just as much dignity and sense as a funny paper.

This Wednesday they are to celebrate the anniversary of the founding of Rome. These Roman holidays are nothing like our celebrations in the U.S. They always have a big parade — in which the soldiers march very raggedly — that finally ends in front of the Palazzo Venezia, the home of Mussolini. There is all sorts of flag waving, shooting of salutes, cheering and yelling. Finally Mussolini comes out on the balcony to give a speech, which he does magnificently. Before he even says a word, he is cheered madly; he simply stands and throws out his chest, then after a while gives the famous Fascist salute. After that there is even more cheering; finally Mussolini speaks. He speaks with his whole body — legs, hands, head, and shoulders all seem to have some part in the pronunciation of his words. He never speaks long from his balcony, partly because nobody could speak for a long time if they worked as hard as he does in speaking, and partly because there isn't much to say that they haven't heard from him before. After he finishes, bedlam breaks loose again, everybody yells until they get tired and the party is all over. All this business takes place early in the morning. Normally parades are over before ten o'clock and the whole affair is finished before twelve. Nothing happens in the early afternoon; not even Mussolini could get the Italians to come out during siesta time immediately after dinner.

Sincerely,

Phil

Comments: Letter of May 12, 1937

(1)   Aunt Maggie was the sister of my father, a very devout and cheerful

lady whose life gave a good name to sanctity. She was very hospitable to the clergy and it seemed that every priest knew where her home was and visited there.

May 23, 1937
Trinity Sunday

NORTH AMERICAN COLLEGE
VIA DELL' UMILTA 30

Dear Everybody,

I spent most of my birthday in a very unusual way — studying Hebrew for an exam. But, of course, I didn't waste the whole day on that dot and dash language.

Al Smith is scheduled to be in Rome today, and the rumor says that he will come to the American College for a visit. We shall see.

Last night we had the usual weekly movie, but it was unique for me; it was the first time I had ever seen Greta Garbo. It was just a series of poses by the Swede, but there's no question about her ability to do that; and she can act a certain type beautifully. We used to kid Father Gustafson because Greta Garbo's real name is Gustafson. Well he needn't be ashamed of his namesake, what a woman.

I believe that I didn't tell you all about our trip to Tivoli. We met an American fellow, graduate of Fordham, who was teaching at a school in Tivoli and attending some classes at the University of Rome, who showed us all around the town. One of the most interesting things to me was the public laundry where all the women of the town came to sing, and incidentally, to wash clothes. (Some of the enclosed pictures will give you an idea of what some of the fountains in the villa d'Este are; an explanation of the pictures is on the back.)

This American, of Italian descent, had some very interesting things to show us. Around Tivoli are the ammunition dumps and airplane centers for the defense of Rome; they are very cleverly built and disguised, and it seems that Italy has enough airplanes to blow another nation off the map. [1] Another thing he showed us was an artificial waterfalls made by a Pope. The little river that flows through the town used to flood part of it, so the Pope (who had a villa near there) decided to change the course of the river. He tunneled right straight through a mountain and made the water flow in a different direction, and also caused a very nice waterfall. Then along came this nobleman, the man who built the villa d'Este (the Count d'Este) and decided to get the river water for his fountains. And he tunneled for water. The result is that the poor little river was just gobbled up completely. Tivoli is on the side of rather mountainous hills and thus gets a lot of water from the rain coming from the Mediterranean. Consequently, it is a good grape section; we saw stretches of vineyards that must have been about five miles long. You can't see the ground at all; the whole countryside seems to be covered with grape arbors. They are supposed to be the finest eating grapes in the world.

Our American friend was also telling us about the political meetings he has been attending. He has a graduate degree, speaks Italian perfectly, and since he is an American he enjoys rather a nice standing in the community. Consequently, he is on the "in" about things. An education really rates in Italy; until recently about eighty percent of the people could neither read nor write. So now the game of the college graduates (even though they are from the south of Italy — the northern Italians almost despise the southern Italians) is to get a rich widow. This fellow was telling me how many of the young fellows who are instructors with him at the school at which he teaches propose rather regularly to any rather wealthy woman. Furthermore, he insists that Fascism will not last; or rather will last just as long as Mussolini lasts. For instance, they can't understand why Italians should be going to fight in Spain, but as long as the Duce says so then it must be all right. But they are all convinced of one thing — that the Italians are the chosen people, the most intelligent and most cultured in the world. Proof: Duce says so. When you and Dad come to Europe you will notice that almost every nation over here thinks that it is the elect of God. But whenever they speak of the merits of nations they never mention Americans; we just belong to another world entirely. Altogether, the Germans are the smuggest lot of the bunch. A delegation of French people were in Tivoli the day we were there, and there were Germans there too. Despite the fact that Italy has signed a treaty with Germany and is supposed to be decidedly unfriendly to France, the Italians much prefer the French to the Germans. Despite all the howling about that treaty, the truth is that the Italians get along much more easily with the French than with the Germans.

The more I write the more it seems that my letters are just like a fourth rate political sheet — but what else is there to write of?

Today, Trinity Sunday, is the customary day for the third year fellows to treat the rest of the house to free beer. It is all supposed to be done on the quiet, but, of course, the faculty knows all about it since they used to do it themselves. Everybody goes in the afternoon to the back room of a German beer hall; it is almost like a speakeasy — in the rear of a courtyard, and one must knock twice, no more no less. And nobody ever uses that back room but American students.

Love,

Phil

Comments: Letter of May 23, 1937

(1)   My estimate of the military power of Italy, especially in aircraft, was woefully incorrect. The story in Rome was that when Mussolini made a tour of inspection of the Italian air force, the head of the air force had a couple of their best squadrons fly ahead of him to each airfield he inspected, giving him a very inflated and wrong assessment of the strength of their air force. Another famous story concerned the flight by a squadron of French air force planes over northern Italy to influence Italy not to declare war on the Allies as a partner with Germany. Mussolini was enraged and ordered the Italian air force to be alert and shoot down every plane that invaded the air space of Italy. The next day the Italian anti-aircraft batteries in Naples shot down two planes, both Italian. The Italians said, "The Italo-Italian war has broken out."

May 25, 1937

NORTH AMERICAN COLLEGE
Via Dell' Umilta 30

Dear Everybody,

For the past few days the betting has been that the whole community will be shipped back to the U.S. in warships before September, due to the bombings of Italian and German warships. But things have quieted down again after the newspapers ran out of epithets and names against Russia and the Reds. It seems that Germany and Italy are not quite ready to take on Russia, etc.; otherwise they would have acted on this occasion. It seems that Russia is really baiting Germany and Italy; when it was announced in some German newspapers that their ship had been hit by two bombs. Communistic papers contended that four bombs had hit the ship — proud of their marksmanship! The Jesuit authorities on Communism say that the war planned by the Russian government is to begin in France, and is scheduled to begin this year. Well we shall see. If Europe is to be seen anytime, this year seems to be the right occasion; it might get blown off the map before many years have passed.

Somebody over here is going to be really disappointed if no war comes off. [1] In order to pay for the Abyssinian war a special tax was leveled on property owners; the government forced all property owners to give them a "loan" that amounted to five percent of all they were worth. That was to pay for their war and get the country in condition just in case. ... Everybody here pays taxes <u>six</u> times a year; taxes are collected every two months so that it won't seem so much. If a person doesn't pay, they take anything you own, leaving only a bed, a chair and a table. Furthermore, every day the government is given so many "gifts" by large corporations and societies; these "gifts" are given outright with no provision for their use. There is no bribery, though; it is all used for uniforms and guns. At least they don't have any racketeers here.

It just occurred to me that Baccalaureate Sunday has already occurred. Who gave the address? I just read in the papers that Monsignor Healy just died. Almost all of the Old Guard have passed at the University, and there are rumors that the Rector plans to shake up almost everything there. Before he begins his plan of renovation, I hope he recognizes the merits of some of the men that have really helped the University. I am afraid that the present rector is too partial (from reports I hear) to the members of the clergy and is inclined to put Roman collars in every post where it is possible.

Love,
Phil

Comments: Letter of May 25, 1937

(1)   The wild rumors about war were an everyday occurrence in Rome. The newspapers carried articles about some of these rumors, confirming and nurturing expectations of a war. All these rumors were grist for the mill of the Fascists who wanted a war and sought every opportunity to nurture a willingness to go to war. Mussolini erected a large series of maps near the Forum depicting the growth of the Roman Empire with the idea that Italy should regain an empire. Despite all this propaganda, the vast majority of the Italian people thoroughly detested war.

May 27, 1937
Feast of Corpus Christi

NORTH AMERICAN COLLEGE
Via Dell' Umilta 30

Dear Everybody,

Well this morning after a heavy session of religion in our chapel, we went up to the American Church to see Al Smith and his wife attend Mass and to hear Monsignor Fulton Sheen. [1] The place was packed, mostly with English, Irish and American priests and seminarians. Al was planted in the first pew with his wife, painted like a country barn. The pastor, a dreamy old Paulist, is the prize bungler I have ever met. His announcements are marvels of jumbled expressions; one Good Friday he made this announcement, "This afternoon in this church there will be Benediction of the Most Blessed Sacrament, except that there will be no Blessed Sacrament here — no, I don't mean there will be Benediction, I mean that we have a relic of the true cross and that there will be veneration of the relic." Then he usually repeats his announcements "to make everyone remember" and makes the same mistakes all over again. He arose to welcome the "foremost citizen of the United States" and after acting as though he were in a trance, he left the pulpit to Monsignor Sheen.

Monsignor Sheen swung into his usual form and just bowled them over. I was especially pleased to see the effect he had on the English; I have heard some of their foremost speakers, and they just can't be compared to Sheen. Almost everything he said was old (at least to me), but that voice and his gestures were working in their old form. Modern Rome has heard nothing like him. A few weeks ago the foremost orator of Italy harangued a crowd of students in one of the large churches here, but half of the game with them is yelling. I was proud of smoothie Sheen. It was interesting to watch the reactions of some of the yokels here who had never heard him and were inclined to deprecate him.

After the Mass, Al Smith and his wife and Sheen held a rather informal reception in the sacristy; we went in and shook hands with both, or rather I didn't shake hands. Instead of getting in the line and passing out quickly, I stepped aside to see how they would act. Well, I think the whole Irish College was in there to shake Smith's hand, and he appreciated their welcome. But he is slowing up greatly, hasn't any of the old pep and fire that he used to have. He got off only one good crack about the "Bowery". Monsignor Sheen was his right-hand man, introducing people and carrying the whole affair. Both of them are very good friends. Mrs. Smith stood behind them, not shaking hands but smiling at everybody; she seems much younger than Al. Smith seems completely finished as a power in the nation and finished physically. He and Monsignor Sheen were admitted at the papal summer villa, Castelgandolfo. Monsignor Sheen was carrying a couple of his books to present to the Holy Father but didn't get a chance. And that reminds me that before you come you should get a letter from Archbishop Curley asking for a papal audience. If the Pope is well enough, you will certainly get one.

Al Smith is scheduled to come to the college for dinner sometime this week. As usual, the Rector has fubbed up matters again, and there seems to be no chance of having Monsignor Sheen speak to the students. We expect to have Smith give a short little talk after or during dinner; I hope this Italian wine loosens him plenty.

Many of the fellows from the college went to Orvieto today, a little town not far from here where they have a large procession through the town. (2) I decided not to go in order to see Smith and Sheen and am plenty glad that I made this choice. The biggest event of the morning was to see good American money in the collection basket. Smith put in a five or ten dollar bill — which means one hundred or two hundred lira, enough to run the parish for a week.

And speaking of money, there are rumors that the American money is to go up — which will mean more European money to the dollar. I found out that I can get all the reductions for traveling in France that you can, and by paying for tickets with tourist lira I get a further reduction. So I will buy all the tickets and have them all set before you come to Europe; that will take away the necessity of bringing over a lot of money with the further risk of losing it. There are some fellows here who know all the ropes about reductions, etc., so we will get the best possible deal. I won't buy any tickets until about the first or fifteenth of July so that we will profit by all the special rates.

The Italian newspapers gave Smith and his party quite a good write-up. Evidently they had someone write the article who was well-informed because they called him the "happy warrior" (translated of course) and talked about New York just the way it is associated with Al Smith. There are so many relatives of Italians in New York that they speak of it as though they had half a title to it.

Love,
Phil

Comments: Letter of May 27, 1937

(1)   The American Church was Santa Susanna, conducted by the Paulist Fathers. Americans and other English-speaking persons considered it "their church". I had attended some of the classes of Monsignor

Sheen at The Catholic University but did not know him personally. He was at his peak and made a marvelous impression on his audiences in Rome. Al Smith had his own particular charisma and was very well received.

(2)   Orvieto, about fifty miles north of Rome, is famous for its gorgeous cathedral, gothic style but with a mosaic that practically covers the front of the cathedral. The Cathedral contains the relics of the celebrated "miracle of Bolsena," the conversion of the bread and wine at a Mass into the actual Body and Blood of Christ by a German priest who was having doubts about the Real Presence of Christ in the Mass after the words of consecration. The Mass was said in Bolsena, a town not far from Orvieto, and the Bishop ordered the Body and Blood to be brought to the Cathedral in Bolsena. Fortunately, the Pope, Urban IV, who declared the feast of Corpus Christi to be celebrated throughout the world in 1264, had visited Orvieto and had seen first-hand the miracle.

By a providential occurrence, Urban IV had been the archdeacon of the Cathedral in Liege, Belgium, who had, as Jacques Pantaleon pleaded with the Bishop, to start a Mass in honor of the Presence of Christ in the Eucharist at the pleading by a Sister Juliana who had received an apparition of Christ ordering her to propagate devotion to His Presence in the Eucharist.

June 2, 1937

NORTH AMERICAN COLLEGE
Via Dell' Umilta 30

Dear Everybody,

At last Al Smith arrived at the college. What a time! His whole party, except Mrs. Smith (blame the seminary rules), was here for dinner and a short visit after dinner.

To start off with, they were about fifteen minutes late — so everybody had a chance to really get set for a welcome. We gave him a good cheer, him and his New York cronies (who all look like typical big New York political bosses) and Monsignor Sheen. Then we sat down to a special dinner; the "special" for us being simply that in addition to the usual spaghetti we had an entree of two sardines.

There was another eminent guest, Bishop Walsh, the head of the Maryknoll organization, and he took the place of honor away from Al Smith but not the attention. Before dinner began, after everybody was seated, the Rector introduced Al Smith and Al Smith got up for a little speech. He was excellent, in old form. First of all, like a typical New Yorker, he took a crack at the Bostonians. And after he got a big hand for some crack he said, "Well, I guess I made a big mistake for not running for some position around here." Then he proceeded to tell us about his public and private (he did get a private) audience with the Pope. Says he, "At last I got a look at the man that I was accused in 1928 of trying to take to America." According to Al, he was completely flabbergasted by the Pope; he said, "in all my political career I have been elected twenty-one times to public offices and called upon to give important speeches. I have met every European big shot that has come to America and I can talk up to any of them. But when the Pope said to me, and talked to me in English, here is a present for you and gave me a picture of himself, for the first time in my life I just couldn't say anything. And I didn't say anything. And when I went out the door I could just feel the Pope thinking, "I wonder if this could be the guy that gave all them speeches." Even yesterday at Santa Susanna's he was talking about the picture that the Pope gave to him and the pearl rosary (pronounced "poil") the Pope gave to his wife. In fact, he made his wife show everybody the beads yesterday. All through the speech, Al used his New York slang and "ain't". He was in excellent shape the whole time and posed for all sorts of pictures. I'll send some when they are developed. [1]

But that wasn't the end of the doings. After dinner, we waited for the party to come out, and greeted Al with the "Sidewalks of New York". He got a tremendous kick out of it — and you'll only realize how good it sounds to hear such things only after you have come to a foreign country. He stood up and sang along too, with a big cigar in his hand. And Monsignor Sheen, in the background, was singing too. First time I had ever seen Monsignor Sheen in such a mood. They took Al Smith into the sun to take his picture, and that left Monsignor Sheen alone. Then somebody got to work on him, dragged him into the sun for his picture. That let Smith out of the picture and brought Sheen in. Everyone got around him so that he couldn't break away gracefully; and he started to talk. He was in rare shape too. He told us about the trip first; everybody in the party got seasick. They even got seasick while unpacking the flowers that were in the stateroom of Al Smith. One big politician crawled under a bed to grab a box that had slid under there, got seasick and couldn't come out under his own power. Then Sheen got started on his favorite topics; and before everybody knew what was happening, he was backed in a corner and giving the dope about everything he knew. He told us of his latest encounter with the Communists, a very startling story. You probably read in the Baltimore Catholic Review his answers to the questions proposed to him by the Communists. Well, while in New York one time, he managed to meet the head of the Communist paper, and after quite a while of bickering finally had him out to dinner. After talking nicely all through the dinner, Monsignor Sheen finally pulled his joker on him. Sheen knew that this fellow had been a good Catholic, had come from a very good family (and had been disowned by them for giving up his religion), had adopted a girl whom he put in a convent in New Jersey for her education, had given up his faith to marry a divorced woman, and then had gone into Communism. Then, he proceeded to tell the fellow about the Communists' secrets; somehow or another Monsignor Sheen has gotten hold of their secret constitution and by-laws. He says he is going back to meet the rest of the Communist leaders in New York. Whether or not all his stories are true is a question, but he certainly can handle them well and keep an audience interested. He had positively no preparation, was just grabbed after a heavy dinner, but he came through beautifully. That man has real poise.

After seeing these prominent men in action, it certainly is easy to see how they got there. While Monsignor Sheen was still talking to the fellows, Al Smith and his party came down to leave. So Monsignor Sheen asked Al to tell us his famous joke — one he was supposed to have told to the Pope. And Al pulled it; here it is:

A Jew had a dream (I knew that it would be about a Jew) and an angel appeared promising to give him anything he wanted; but whatever he got, his enemy, Levy, would receive two of the same thing. That put him in a mess; if he got a big car, old Levy would get two; if he got a big clothes store on Fifth Avenue, Levy would get two. The angel broke in and reminded him though that he could just forget Levy, and even if Levy did get twice as much as he, he would be well off anyway. But that didn't comfort him any; he hated Levy and wouldn't take a favor if Levy would profit from it. Finally the Jew thought of an answer — he asked the angel for a glass eye.

Almost every American priest of any rank was at the college for dinner; the president of the Gregorian University came trotting in after dinner, the general of the Franciscans, etc. But nobody was looking at the clergy.

According to Al Smith, the Pope is in very good shape. He can walk and is very alert mentally. So be sure to get a letter from Archbishop Curley. Furthermore, there is no need for Dad to bring full dress; the audience you will get will not be private, and in a public audience nobody dresses formally. And even in a private audience, one may dress simply in black. Mom will simply have to drag along a dark blue or black dress with sleeves in it. Ask Mary about it. And be sure to bring a good camera over. Don't buy a small camera; tell Tom to get you a really good one, large enough to get a rather large picture. And, of course, bring the movie camera along. It sounds like a lot of luggage; but since there will be three of us, it will be very easy to manage.

Love,

Phil

Comments: Letter of June 2, 1937

(1)   In those days, especially Al Smith and his famous companions, had great luster and appeal. There was no air service from the U.S., and America seemed so distant. Al's visit was a great emotional lift.

July 11, 1937

NORTH AMERICAN COLLEGE
Via Dell' Umilta 30

Dear Everybody,

At last I have gotten through the general madness and mass hysteria that grips this place once a year, to wit, examination time. (1) Unfortunately, I was up last; and it is no cheering sight to see the fellows coming back with, as they say in America, the posterior portion of their anatomy dragging. For nine solid months, the first year men had been steadily indoctrinated with the dogma that no first year man ever flunks, that the profs are as benevolent and generous as F. D. Roosevelt before election time, that the oral exams were as cheerful and light as a *tête-à-tête* in a Paris salon. All their promises and assurances were as ineffectual as a burp in a windstorm; the casualty lists were heavier this year than ever in the history of the college. I got by very handily, but just to show you how much of an indication these exams are of one's knowledge of the year's matter, I'll recite my tale of woe. In canon law (the exam lasts for ten minutes) I did very well until the prof asked me what Leo XIII thought of the Church in America compared with the Church in Europe — none of which had been treated either in class or in the textbook. Then in the dogma exam I had none of my profs as examiners (my Hebrew prof examined me in Revelation), and one fellow asked me some very detailed stuff that was not even included in the conspectus for the exam.

In dogma you have three examiners, each one examines you for ten minutes in any of forty-five theses. It may either be childishly easy or impossibly tough, depending on the profs and their mood. One fellow was actually examined by three profs on the same thesis, but I got probably the toughest assignment handed out this year in the exams. I found that it is very easy to speak Latin, but sometimes difficult to understand the prof's questions (especially if he is a Spaniard). The real hazard is the possible paralyzing effect of jitters on one's mind; I have seen fellows read one thesis and then give the proofs of an entirely different one – never realizing what they were saying. One fellow was asked to name the adversaries of a certain doctrine, and he said,"Suarez" (the leading intellectual genius of the Jesuits). But the Italians can certainly rattle off the Latin, it flows out as easily as their native tongue. The most curious thing at the University is the attitude about cheating; none of the Latin races considers it wrong. And to cope with the situation they have to hold oral exams. It is useless to try to get them to swear that they will not cheat, they won't be bound to conscience about such a matter. The fact is that their career seems to be largely determined by the marks they get, and if they fub an exam, it may be costly. The personnel that works in the Vatican is recruited from the bright fellows in the Seminary; if a young priest has a bit of backing and shows superior intelligence, he is started in some minor post and gradually works his way up. Some of the cardinals in the key positions have never been parish priests.

I recently pulled a real *coup d'etat* and acquired a two-pound box of chocolates. A visitor from Washington, the wife of the Mr. Donohue who runs some automobile agency in Washington, called at the college to see Father Cowhig, who was then in Naples. I went down to see her and received the candy intended for Cowhig; it was Whitman's, so we had a real lay out that night.

Love,

Phil

Comments: Letter of July 11, 1937

(1)   There was only one exam in the courses at the Gregorian University — at the end of the year, in July. The exams were open to the public, oral and always in Latin. Because of the numbers in each class, there were several professors to administer the exams. Each professor was seated at a small table, and the student sat opposite him. Anyone could listen to the exam and generally there was a ring of listeners near each student. It was a custom for the students of the North American College not to listen to the exams of their fellow students. An appreciated courtesy. The tensions were high and produced unexpected results; one example, a first year student being examined in philosophy was asked by the professor to define philosophy, "*Quid est philosophia?*" (What is philosophy?) The nervous student blurted out the only phrase he could remember in Italian, "*Chi lo sa.*" (Who knows.) The audience roared.

In my four years at the Greg I never had one of my professors administer the exam.

A few yards from the Greg there was a chapel of Perpetual Adoration and during exam time there was a steady stream of nervous students making a visit. A few pious beggars stood close by offering to say a prayer as they extended their hands. They always made a rich harvest.

October 3, 1937
Lourdes, France

Dear Everybody,

When I last wrote I hadn't seen the cathedral at Chartres. [1] To say that it is simply the crowning glory of French architecture is like saying that Michaelangelo painted some nice pictures. The exterior is not so breathtaking as other great cathedrals, but the interior is a knock out. The statuary is marvelous — there is a series of statues enclosing the sanctuary that required 200 years to complete, and if they had spent 2000 years I don't see how they could have improved them. But actually I didn't notice the statuary until I had been in the church for two hours; the windows just hold you spellbound. In gloomy weather they glow like a mountainside of heather in late afternoon, and in the sunlight they simply burn. They are the only things I have seen that really conquered the sun. Most stained glass seems to show up its defects under a strong glare, but even the most merciless light only adds to their beauty.

The Blessed Mother was the inspiration of the whole work; she is featured in many a window, and the windows behind her shrine are so intense it seems that the artist went half mad with the glory of his thoughts. After seeing a bit of France one gets the impression that almost all of French inspiration comes from an ideal womanhood: the early painters and architects learned their trade on the Blessed Mother, St. Genieve built Paris, Joan of Arc saved France from the English, St. Therese and St. Bernadette and St. Margaret Mary saved it from irreligion. Without this ideal inspiration, they have achieved almost nothing. What can the Communists ever hope to achieve by making the French woman simply an equal, a "comrade," of the French man instead of leaving her on her pedestal.

Now where was I? After seeing Chartres I went to Rheims. Tremendous place, still incompletely restored after its destruction during the war. The beauty of the building remains, but the glory of its windows is almost gone. Only a few were saved. And not all of Rockefellers' millions can restore one window; they simply can't make them.

Now I am in Lourdes; came here with a fellow from the college. (Paris was full of American students, but I preferred to see the cathedrals alone. I was afraid that, like the guides, they would insist on getting simply the facts instead of the feeling of the place.)

The most pathetic sight I have seen is the entrance to the Shrine here filled with sick and crippled. Everything is done from charity — nurses and doctors give their services freely, the hospital costs the sick nothing, and men practically fight to carry the sick or wheel them. Here is the return of primitive Christianity; every tawdry bit of human selfishness is left behind. I was proud of my Irish ancestry after watching the Irish pilgrimage attend and sing their Solemn High Mass. Everything was orderly, everything respectful.

I don't know how I shall ever get accustomed to the Italian way of attending Mass after seeing all this.

Needless to say, I am remembering all of the family and the relatives, at the Grotto. Rome is the center of Christianity for doctrine, but this is the center of Christianity for fervor and devotion.

Love,

Phil

Comments: Letter of October 3, 1937

(1)   I visited the great Cathedral of Chartres before going to Lourdes. It was a huge delight, and I became so enthralled with it that I consider it to be my favorite cathedral in the world — of course, excepting the Basilica of St. Peter in Rome.

It was a sunny day and I was so enraptured with the stained glass windows that I stayed in the Cathedral long enough to see all of the windows through a bright sun. It's a marvel that cannot be repeated, in my opinion. However, a very sad operation was being prepared during my visit — they were making plans to take out the windows in case of a war and placing them in a safe refuge. I was told that they probably would be placed in one of the deep caves in the Champagne area.

I later learned after the war that an American officer had prevented the shelling of Chartres by the Allied forces. Thank God for him!

October 6, 1937
Carcassonne, Southern France

Dear Folks,

Lourdes was one of the greatest experiences possible in my life. I didn't tell you about the ceremony of the blessing of the sick at about 5 o'clock in the afternoon, and the procession with torches at night. Both are very impressive. The sick are brought out in front of the church and lined up in a great square; then the Blessed Sacrament is brought out in procession while everybody sings and prays. After the procession, the sick are blessed with the Blessed Sacrament (meanwhile special prayers are recited by the whole mob). The climax is reached when the priest leads everybody in the prayers, "*Faites que j'entend; faites que je vois; faites que je marche.*" (Lord make me hear; make me see; make me walk.) This final appeal for a miracle is heart-rending and beautiful. Everything — prayers, songs, appeals, intense devotion — conspire to make one of the greatest religious moments imaginable.

The greatest attraction at Lourdes is the spirit of charity towards the infirm. I was at Lourdes for 4 days, and in those 4 days there was not more than 4 hours of dry weather — it rained during every public exercise. But even in the rain, despite every obstacle, the sick were taken care of perfectly. And all this is voluntary and free work. To be allowed to wheel the sick or carry them on stretchers, you must make an application in advance. As the attendants pull the sick to their places, they pray aloud (recite the rosary) with them. The only reason why the Lord wouldn't hear a prayer here is that the favor would not be advantageous to the one asking.

The procession with torches (candles) at night is very picturesque. Sometimes the processions are so large that only pilgrims in a certain tour are allowed in them. My last night at Lourdes was the occasion of a tremendous display; there was a special French pilgrimage on hand. The procession (with persons about six or eight or ten abreast) was considerably over a mile in length. The route of the procession is always fixed — from the grotto (where the Blessed Mother appeared to St. Bernadette) across the front of the basilica, down a long parkway and then back to the basilica. To see thousands of people in line carrying candles, and all singing the special song composed for the occasion is a sight one can't easily forget.

No matter how much one spends to get there, Lourdes is worth it. The situation of the town is dream like — set in a valley of the Pyrenees Mountains, whose snowy peaks form a magnificent background. And that business of snowy peaks is no figure of rhetoric; the peaks are covered with as much snow and ice as I saw in the Italian mountains when I went skiing. The Blessed Mother picked a real spot in which to appear.

I got a bottle of the Lourdes water (from the stream which the Blessed Mother caused to flow miraculously) and had some medals blessed there. [2] I'll send them when I get the chance.

I am traveling with an excellent fellow. We have had extraordinarily good fortune — our hotel bill at Lourdes (for room and 3 meals) was not quite $1 a day, thanks to the fall of the French franc, and everything at Lourdes is free. Coming from Paris on the train we had a good time; the waiter tried to charge us for a full meal (we refused to eat meat on an Ember Day — Lourdes is the only place in France where they keep the law of abstinence from meat). We refused to pay and deduced 6 francs each from the bill (Mom and Dad can imagine how much kicking and squawking that caused). When they found that all their squealing was doing no good except to make us refuse all the more, they told us that they were going to throw us off the train. "All right," says we in our best French, "we are ready any time you want to start that." Of course, we didn't pay the bill and didn't get thrown off.

I have learned to press clothes by wetting them and putting them under the mattress during the night. Instead of paying for baths, we get up early and take them before the unsuspecting proprietor is around.

Carcassonne is a completely walled-in, old city. Very interesting as a perfect example of ancient fortification. They still have a city within the fortifications.

I am going by the southern route back to Florence — Marseilles, Nice, Genoa.

Love,

Phil

Comments: Letter of October 6, 1937

(1)   I was so impressed with the fervor of all the pilgrims at Lourdes as well as their care of the sick that I went to the office of the Shrine to volunteer to be a "brancardier" (stretcher bearer for the sick). I may as well have asked to be ordained to the priesthood on the spot. The official Irish pilgrimage was present and all the openings for volunteers were filled with many waiting to serve.

I stayed at a French pension and remarked rather triumphantly and breathlessly, at dinner, "I heard that there was a miraculous curing of a small boy." The owner replied, "Why are you surprised? It happens all the time here."

(2)   In shopping for medals, I entered a shop dedicated to the Little Flower whose proprietress was a Madame Nieudan (actually she had inherited it from her mother). She was very interesting and informed me that her husband was a doctor, the secretary of the commission, which registered the "miraculous cures." Later, I met him and we had a long talk about the number of cures and the process for judging them. He recounted that in securing the details of the cure they insisted on having a description of the disease and this process revealed that there were a number of "unregistered diseases" which baffled the medical profession in France. That friendship with the Nieudan family developed subsequently to the point that the Nieudans later visited me in Washington, D.C.

During the war they became followers of Marshal Petain and named their son after him, Philip Petain. Their assessment of the program of Marshall Petain was the exact opposite of the general condemnatory attitude of most of the French people.

I still welcome the Christmas card I receive each year from Dr. Nieudan and the Little Flower store conducted by Philip Petain Nieudan.

November 1, 1937

NORTH AMERICAN COLLEGE
Via Dell' Umilta 30

Dear Everybody,

At last I have gotten my studio in shape for the year. The room that fell to my lot was in such shape that not even I could stomach it for a year. So I plastered the holes in the walls, enough to keep the room from looking like a piece of Swiss cheese, and proceeded to paint it all. One receives a very liberal education over here. I have learned to plaster and put paper on walls with absolutely no practice or instruction; I must admit that my technique in plastering would not be approved by the best authorities. The only instrument I could find to slap the stuff on the walls was a paper knife; so with a paper knife and my thumbs, I smeared the plaster on. The crisis came when I had to put a little paper border on but I handled it rather well. The final task was the making of curtains. Curtains seem like a sheer luxury, but they are a real necessity in my room. The street is about ten feet wide and there is an Italian apartment house (at least one family to each room) across the street. If I had longer arms I could reach across and slap their brats. So in order to prevent myself from feeling as though I were as exposed as a goldfish in a bowl, I had to put up curtains on the windows. The material I bought for the curtains is rich stuff – cost ninety cents for five yards of it. I cut it and stitched the ends of it myself – until I got tired of the job and decided to invent a new style with ragged edges.

Today was the day for visiting the Campo Santo, the large cemetery in Rome. The cemetery is very beautifully kept; and easily kept because there is almost no space unoccupied. In many of the places the bodies are placed five or six deep. In some sections they file the bodies like cards in a filing system. Once a year all the relatives turn out to decorate the graves with flowers and wash the tombstones. They make a whole day affair of it, standing around until it gets dark. As each family or person carries in his flowers for the dead at least one flower is thrown in front of a large statue of Christ just inside the central gate. At dusk the statue is deep in flowers; very pretty practice, except that it reminds one too much of the Italian love of kissing statues.

Mary, or any teacher of history, or Latin would be interested in a large exhibit now open in Rome showing the advance of the Roman Empire. There is an exact reproduction of a Roman house (like the houses in Pempey) complete to the last detail, even to the dirty poetry written on the walls. They have a whole room dedicated to reproductions of the war engines used by Julius Caesar and his method of capturing cities. The whole thing is very thoroughly done but I don't like the dirty implication that the present government is a continuation of the Roman Empire and can maintain its expansion by war.

There was a big time in Rome on the occasion of the sixteenth anniversary of the Fascist march on Rome (when Mussolini came into power). All sorts of bands and uniforms were in evidence. The important phrase of Mussolini's speech was his pledge to back Germany in her demand for colonies. There were large numbers of Nazis in Rome for the occasion. There was a troop of Nazi girls in town and, of course, many of them went to St. Peter's. The Italian soldiers gave them a real reception and gathered in crowds around them demanding autographs. Most of the girls were very plain looking — just the normal German type with braided hair and cheeks scrubbed red. I don't know what would have happened to the morale of the Italian army if they sent some pretty girls down. A delicate problem is going to arise in the future when Hitler comes to Rome (as he has promised to do). Everyone who is anybody is almost bound to visit the Pope, or at least St. Peter's. But will the Pope receive Hitler? If he does, I should like to be hiding behind a curtain and listen to what he says. Even when General Goering, the German minister of war, was in Rome he visited St. Peter's even though he believes in nothing but German might.

I feel a thousand percent better this year. Maybe it was the trip, maybe it was just getting accustomed to a new way of living; anyway, I am feeling like a man instead of a dried fish. Maybe it was Lourdes, or maybe it was just a couple of good beefsteaks.

Love,

Phil

November 24, 1937

NORTH AMERICAN COLLEGE
VIA DELL' UMILTA 30

Dear Mom and Dad,

Today there was another large parade — as a commemoration of the imposing of sanctions against Italy last year during the Ethiopian War. Just a polite way for Italy to thumb her nose at the nations that imposed sanctions, especially Great Britain. That sanctions business worked in the exactly opposite way; instead of weakening and humiliating Italy it strengthened her. There is much ugly talk about war, but that seems impossible since these people are taxed to the limit now.

If everything goes well the religious articles I bought should be at St. Matthew's Rectory (I addressed them to Father Stricker) in about three weeks. Excluding the postage, the whole business cost about six dollars — about 120 lira. Although there is an amazing array of stuff in Rome (and students from the American College get a 20% discount), I didn't want to ship anything that you may not like. So this is more or less of a sample package; take the best piece or pieces as Christmas presents from me – or use them as Christmas presents to the relatives. Anything I sent can be duplicated or if there is a special type of anything in that line wanted, I can get it. They have some magnificent "Della Robbias" (porcelain work with a garland of fruit and flowers for a border, like the piece in Mary's dining room in Hartford) here for six dollars. The largest piece I bought, and I think it is magnificent, cost only three dollars and a quarter.

There is a famous institution in Rome here called the rag market. There is a special section of the city set off once a week for venders; everything is sold (from eels to swords), everything is supposed to be very cheap, everything is very noisy and very dirty. A fine place to shop if you have a strong nose and thin pocketbook. Last year one of our fellows bought a sword, Lord knows why, and every time the fellow goes near there the salesman jumps out and shows him the mate that is supposed to match it. I had a very gratifying experience there yesterday. One greaser kept pestering me and pulling my arm (trying to sell me satin and silk!!!); I got tired of having him around, asked him if he spoke English; when he assured me that he couldn't understand a word of it, I told him to go straight to h - - - and stop bothering me, in English of course. He got the idea, not the words. A visit to the rag market makes one understand canon law regulations about abstaining from buying and selling stuff on Sundays; buying and selling of goods that is marked at a definite price is allowed, for a certain amount of time, because there is no haggling and carrying on. But selling and buying of goods that has no special price is altogether wrong; nothing in the rag market has a price stamped on it and an Italian would faint if you paid him all he asked. And, of course, they positively can't sell a thing without all kinds of squawking.

There is a rumor around that Roosevelt is going to devalue the dollar more. Well if he does intend to do that, you should invest in some lira if you expect to travel next summer. By juggling the currency one fellow here went from Rome to Cherbourg to New York for only twenty-five dollars this year.

Since Christmas will be rolling around soon, I want to warn you not to send cash over for a gift. In fact, we are warned to tell everyone concerned never to send money over except by a personal check. Anyway, please don't send me anything (except a fruit cake, if it can be done, and it makes no difference if it is broken up) since the postage and import duty would be so much.

Love,

Phil

Comments: Letter of November 24, 1937

(1)   Mussolini delighted in reviling the League of Nations which had condemned strongly his invasion of Ethiopia. At one time he said that the League, which was dead, ought to be cleaned up and taken away as a matter of good hygiene. The League was destined to fail because it had no system of effective sanctions. I visited the headquarters of the League of Nations in Geneva and was much disappointed in it. Its symbol was a magnificent painting on the ceiling of the general assembly room showing hands and arms extended in a handclasp.

The whole peace effort after World War I was influenced largely by President Woodrow Wilson who proposed and lobbied the "fourteen points" to secure peace. Premier Clemeceau of France, a cynic, said, "God gave us Ten Commandments and we have broken all of them. Wilson has given us fourteen points ... we shall see."

November 25, 1937

NORTH AMERICAN COLLEGE
Via Dell' Umilta 30

Dear Mom and Dad,

On Sunday, the twenty-second of November, I assisted at a Mass at St. Cecilia's which was sung by a recently appointed cardinal. It was a riot of fun. It was the first time that the cardinal had pontificated in his church, it was the feast day of the parish, and everybody was there — it could also be added that hardly anyone there knew the score. In the first place, they always have about four times as many jobs as are necessary; the Italians just don't seem to feel right about things unless there are monsignors piled up four deep and priests just falling all over themselves. Then to make sure that there will be enough around for decoration they appoint honorary deacons, honorary assistants, honorary everythings. (Of course, all the honoraries are decrepit monsignors that must be shifted around like so much stage furniture.)

When we got to the Church the whole nave was filled with people, so much so that it was impossible to form a procession to go down and meet the cardinal at the door of the Church. But the pastor had expected that – he had six policemen come into the church and make a path down to the front door of the church. The cardinal pulled up in a fine car and the population jumped at him to kiss his ring; the nuns were the greatest offenders in this. I saw one little Jennie sneak under the arm of a policeman and grab the cardinals hand; the policeman just grabbed her by her robes, dumped her back into the crowd then kissed the ring of the cardinal himself. The cardinal was not so good at blessing the people; you could see it was his first public appearance. The mazy motion of his hand resembled the waving of the old fellow near home who gets tipsy, and then has to balance himself with his hands and arms. After innumerable delays, we got things all set, got the cardinal all the way down to the gate to the sanctuary only to find that some brilliant sacristan had locked the gate, had the key on his person and couldn't be found.

The Mass went on as all masses seem to in Italy — nobody pays the slightest bit of attention, don't even kneel at the elevation. Things ran into a snag when it was found that the first assistant, a little old monsignor who was not five feet tall, could hardly walk when they covered him with a cape. The poor old boy had a frightful time trying to change the book; he couldn't get his hands out from under the cape nor could he get up and down the altar steps because his robes dragged about a foot. The problem was solved by assisting the assistant to the point of hoisting him up and down the steps. The second assistant was quite a character also. He didn't have any eyebrows. A man looks terribly plain without any eyebrows, especially when his muscles in that section of his face are very active. I could see hardly anything but those twitching hairless eyebrows. Our job was simply to vest the cardinal, despite the assistance of a couple of papal masters of ceremonies who were present, and to keep from being shoved out of the sanctuary – or at least to keep in the church.

I don't see how anybody gets any devotion out of one of these feast day masses with a cardinal pontificating. There was not a moment during the whole Mass when the people were entirely quiet and these people would rather kiss a cardinal's ring than receive Holy Communion. They genuflect more to a cardinal than they do to the tabernacle. Great people. I'd hate to be a priest in Rome.

Rome continues to be an interesting place, but it certainly is not as beautiful as Washington is. If a person can't enjoy the flavor of ancient things, he had better skip Rome. Outside of St. Peter's and a few other buildings, there are no beautiful sights (at least from the exterior) to be seen. Everybody wanted to live within the walls even when there was no reason for it, and actually the government had to knock down part of the walls of some cities to make the people spread out a bit. There are no safeguards against fire either, except the construction of the buildings themselves. In all Rome, there are only two fire stations. And they are simply for ornament since, there are very few water hydrants.

When Cardinal Pacelli arrived in Italy after his trip to the U.S., a monsignor from the college went down with cardinals, etc., to receive him.

He passed up the Italian cardinals and spoke all the time with the American monsignor. Mrs. Nicholas Brady and the U.S. impressed him very much. It shouldn't be long now before there is a Vatican representative to the U.S. in Washington. [1] I suppose there is talk about that now among the red robes in America.

Love,

Phil

Comments: Letter of November 25, 1937

(1)   The hostess for Cardinal Pacelli in New York was Mrs. Nicholas Brady also known as Countess Brady, the title given to her by the Holy See because of her charitable gifts. The Cardinal was enthusiastic about the U.S. but his visit did not, as I surmised, lead to the establishment of a Papal Nuncio (ambassador) to the United States.

December 2, 1937

NORTH AMERICAN COLLEGE
VIA DELL' UMILTA 30

Dear Everybody,

As I write now the last lingering aroma of the fruitcake disappears amid the odors of Italy. Brief is the life of a fruitcake in a student's room. The magnificent package reached here about the first of December. Whoever was the unfortunate person that had to bake the cake and then pack it, I sympathize with deeply and thank heartily. The size of the package and its contents was a real surprise. What was even a greater surprise was the fact that the Italian customs charged me only thirteen cents for the package. They apparently were rushed and didn't bother to open it. Last year when they troubled themselves to open the package you sent, they charged over sixty cents. Consistency is not one of their virtues. Everything arrived in excellent shape, and for two days this room had a very delicious odor; smelled like Christmas time. The cake came at a very favorable time. About ten fellows were going on retreat that night for ordination; the cake helped to put them in excellent physical shape at any rate.

For the first time in the history of the college, the whole building has been warm in the winter. The rumor is that a new furnace man has been appointed and only knows how to turn on the heat, doesn't know how to turn it off. Unless it blows up, everything will be excellent. Our only fear is that he will learn how to turn the heat off.

A college magazine has been launched (or is being launched) and it looks as though I shall have something to do with it. Ed Latimer, who gets four ideas a day (and bothers everybody else with them), is at the bottom of this business. He talked the Rector into giving his permission and support. So the only thing left to do is to write it and get it paid for. Letters were sent out to some of the alumni asking for advice, donations, etc. Some of the replies were classic. All of them took the opportunity to wave the flag for the good, old Del Nord (that's what they call this place), and some of them gave advice — most of which can be safely disregarded. What we wanted was the money. One letter was particularly glowing; it seems that the writer was in favor of anything that was ever done by the college — he was willing to pledge his support to anything and proved it by stating that he hadn't missed a reunion of the alumni in fifteen years. (I still don't know just what that had to do with this magazine.) One was the most complete crank and pessimist I ever heard. He wasn't in favor of anything, saying that people nowadays don't read anything but headlines and pictures and that they wouldn't look at anything that was not put out by Hearst. He then said that he couldn't see where anything we had to write could possibly interest anyone and closed with the cheering suggestion to try our hand at discussing philosophical problems. (And the old walrus didn't include a cent of donation.) My suggestion was to make an article of extracts from the letters received. I guarantee that the next time we asked the reverend gentlemen for advice and donations they would be very cautious. I have none of the work and am in a fine position to have the fun. The rector was in favor of the idea, if it would cost him no money and no trouble. Our total assets at the time are simply good will and a certain amount of unknown and untried talent. No matter what happens I shall at least learn how not to proceed in organizing such a venture. I really think that we can put out a very creditable magazine.

Within the past few days we have done some furious sightseeing.

On the feast of St. Francis Xavier (a holiday because we attend a Jesuit university) the community went over to the Church of the Gesu where St. Francis' body is preserved. It's a strange looking sight to see a whole community walk out in the dead of night (it's so early in the morning that it seems like night) and prowl through Rome. And it's always the same system — everybody climbing over each other to hear Mass, and all the holy clerics stealing your seat when you go up to Communion. The law of charity works everywhere except in Church. Then after Mass half the community stops by a place called "Poison Annie's" to buy a couple of buns. [1] I think the place is rightly named. The proprietor at "Poison Annie's" knows the schedule of the community as well as we do; every morning that we go out to hear Mass she has an extra supply of stuff on hand. It would cause nothing less than a depression, if the Rector decided not to let the fellows go out to Mass.

An air of mystery is brooding over the house. The Vice Rector has become a real night prowler. He is the law enforcement committee around here and this year he seems to have gotten very conscientious – prowls around the corridors every night finding who is out of order. It would be an easier job finding who is not out of order, because he always seems to catch half the community in the wrong. Someone turned the lights out on him last night as he was walking around, but it didn't stop him at all – he pulled out a flashlight and kept going. But he's always a gentleman; whenever he finds fellows having a "scald", he never demands that they clear the food away (he knows that they would sneak back anyway); but he always asks them the next morning where they got it. He ought to know himself; he did enough buying of it in his time around here. The rector has a different system; twice a year he comes out of retirement, reads the rule, insists that it be enforced, promptly returns to his den and is not seen until the next year. He is out in the open just about as much as a groundhog.

Love,

Phil

Comments: Letter of December 2, 1937

(1)   Poison Annie's was a coffee and sandwich bar across the street from the College. It did not deserve the name we gave it, but I never

heard an Italian name for the establishment.

The family owning and conducting the bar — husband and wife and teenage daughter — were always very congenial, except on one occasion. A new seminarian from Brooklyn (whose name I shall not submit) was just beginning his study of Italian and went into Poison Annie's to get a "maritozzo" (a sweet bread) but got confused and asked for "meritrice" (a prostitute). As soon as he asked the clerk, the daughter, for it, she screamed and charged into the kitchen to get her father, who came out with a knife. Fortunately, an older seminarian happened by and explained the mistake with multitudinous apologies.

December 8, 1937

NORTH AMERICAN COLLEGE
Via Dell' Umilta 30

Dear Mom and Dad,

Eighteen fellows were ordained in the College chapel this morning by a cardinal. Ordinations over here are a magnificently thrilling event. In the first place, there is none of that mass production hurry and bustle, as at the Shrine, which amounts to an all day picnic. Everything is very solemn and has the charm of a family affair. Many of the parents of those ordained were present owing to the ridiculously low rate granted to the group that came over. Roundtrip from New York to Rome and return over the northern route (with railroad fare paid down to Rome included) was about two hundred dollars!! And the return ticket can be used any time. After ordination and breakfast, the newly ordained priests go up to their rooms and receive the fellows. The room has been fixed up before by the fellow diocesans, flowers, etc., and the presents from the fellows and telegrams from home are all arranged for him. He supplies candy and ordination cards and American cigarettes to all those who visit him. Of course, his parents are also in the room and are introduced to all the fellows who come in. It was the first time that ordinations had ever thrilled me. I enjoyed as much as anything else, the pleasure of the fellows' folks who had come over.

To make it doubly enjoyable for them, a priest who graduated from here last year and who is now studying for his doctorate went up to meet the incoming boat at Cherbourg and helped pilot them down. He is an amazingly interesting and cultured person so they had a perfect trip. [1]

To make it a genuine American College affair and to give the visitors the true atmosphere of the place, no heat was turned on, even today. It was a good thing that they had other things to divert their attention from the coolness.

But there is always a fly in the ointment. In fact, there was a whole cloud of flies in the ointment today. Only eighteen of fifty fellows were ordained, the others being detained until next spring because their marks were not as high as the others (they didn't flunk in anything — the rector is just trying to develop a spirit of competition). At one time in the morning, I was afraid that some of the disappointed deacons were going to stab him in the back. The air just crackled and sizzled with bad feeling. Another boner he pulled was to refuse permission to the recently ordained priests to go on trips with their parents — which has always been granted, since even the Jesuits (who run the Greg University) grant their men a holiday of four weeks from class after ordination. Outside of these two things the Rector is o.k. I hope he is appointed to Buffalo.

The American ambassador, a very smooth looking man, was a guest at dinner with Cardinal Fumasoni Biondi (who used to be Apostolic Delegate to the U.S.).

Our camerata celebrated in its own unique way. In the afternoon we went around on our floor — we have no superior for the present — and dragged out all the house officers who were asleep during siesta. If any showed resistance, they and their mattresses were dumped into the corridor. We have a 260-pound fellow in our group so we are invincible.

Well, I must hit the books for a time. *Merry Christmas.*

Love,

Phil

Comments: Letter of December 8, 1937

(1)   The "graduate from last year" was Father John Wright of Boston, later the Auxiliary Bishop of Boston, the Bishop of Pittsburg and

finally a Cardinal in the Curia in Rome. He was an excellent linguist and brilliant theologian whose only problem was that he could not master the German language. Years later, he and I were members of a three-man committee, which wrote the annual statement for the U.S. Bishops at their annual meeting of the N.C.W.C. (National Catholic Welfare Conference later named the N.C.C.B., National Conference of Catholic Bishops), and I also served with him on the Committee for the Press at the II Vatican Council.

December 11, 1937

NORTH AMERICAN COLLEGE
Via Dell' Umilta 30

Dear Everybody,

Last night I heard the King (former King), Eddie the Eighth, make his famous address to the people. A fellow down the hall has a crystal set (which seems perfectly allowable over here, if you don't make too much noise about it), and we listened in. The King really told them that he was a home-loving man, didn't he? There is another fellow on our corridor who has a new short wave radio with which he can get everything — from Japanese news reports to headaches from staying up too late. We are now in touch with things in America more than when we were in the Sem in the U.S. The Italian stations, for the most part, use women radio announcers. It works very well; their voices are much clearer than the men's. I may develop a British accent over here from listening to the English broadcasts in Rome. There is no advertising over the radio. Everyone who buys a radio must pay a tax that is used to maintain the stations (which are government controlled.) If you have any imagination at all, you know where I'll be on Christmas morning when Midnight Masses, etc., are being broadcasted in the U.S.

I am told that Ireland has given the door to its Governor General. Won't our Irish patriot relative cut loose! By the way, in the papers over here the former king's love affair was always referred to as "the constitutional crisis". [1] Just like the English to coin such a long, respectable phrase for such an ordinary thing. They were scared to death that an American woman would some day wear the robes of the queen. After all, I think that the world has learned a lot in causing revolutions for getting rid of kings. Whenever a nation should want to get rid of their king, they only have to get a clever girl from Hollywood to lead the man off the throne; and a shipload of pretty American girls ought to be enough to ruin all the monarchies of Europe. The old time clumsy and grisly way of starting a bloody revolt to kick out the king ought to go out of style.

On December 8, the Feast of the Immaculate Conception, a number of us went to assist at a solemn benediction at the Franciscan Church (Cardinal Marchetti, who is often mentioned as a candidate for the papacy gave the benediction.) The governor general of the Franciscans, an American, was there and gave us a hearty welcome. He was very glad, says he, to have somebody around who combs their hair. The Franciscans over here – as most of the clerics – shave off everything but a fringe of hair. They all look a little mangy. The American governor general is trying to get them to change the custom and is doing his best to show the way by keeping his hair long. But the poor fellow is having a tough time — his hair is all falling out. This practice of making your head look like a billiard ball for the sake of sanctity is rather queer, I think, since the Russians and Easterners grow long bushes to show their sanctity. Who's right? I think the pay-off is the solution, or compromise, offered by some monks who cut off the hair on their head but grow long beards. That's diplomacy.

The Rector was inspecting rooms again this morning (what a job for a bishop!), so I must get it cleaned up. Anyway, we are the only institution that has a bishop for a janitor.

Love,

Phil

Comments: Letter of December 11, 1937

(1)   There was surprising interest in Italy about the abdication of the English King, Edward VIII and the Italians ascribed his downfall to the wealthy leaders who were afraid that his views about helping the poor ran counter to their own plans.

They also gave considerable credit to the Premier for engineering this event without any serious political crisis. It all proves that England is still a dominant power in the minds of all the common people and that whatever England does will have an influence on them.

Christmas Day, 1937

NORTH AMERICAN COLLEGE
Via Dell' Umilta 30

Dear Everybody,

The great day of the year has come and is slipping away quickly and silently like a spent wave. (I am not typing this because it is afternoon and everyone is in bed.) But to begin at the beginning:

The diocese decided to use my room for the "scald" after Midnight Mass. A royal spread with all the trimmings was decreed and the room was scheduled to be decorated. By some clever slight-of-hand work, we secured plenty of decorations; in fact, I am now deposited in the shambles of a "decorating" orgy that swept through like a cyclone. Four fellows started hanging things as though they meant to wrap up the four walls and strewed enough streamers around to make the interior look like a quaint spider web. In fact, the decorating developed such a fast and furious pace that we finally had to haul my bed and desk out of the room, and if the room didn't have my name on the door, I would never have known it was mine. It looked more like a Chinese emporium than a student's room. Besides the usual crêpe paper, Santa Clauses, etc., we had a small Christmas tree with electric bulbs, a crib, a radio, and a phonograph. And around all this were arranged enough tables for nine fellows. Then came the job of re-heating the food we had bought — sweet potatoes, gravy, turkey with dressing, mince pie and coffee. We also had fruit cup, cranberries, and fruitcake. Too much stuff. The evening passed quickly and pleasantly — we ended about six-thirty in the morning, crawled into bed until nine o'clock then went to Mass again. [1]

The Midnight Mass was a really grand affair. The chapel was decorated very tastefully, and we indulged in some mild theatricals — during the procession into the chapel, the only light was that from an illumined star above the high altar. The singing was not brilliant but was good enough not to detract from the service.

However, as with most events, the enjoyment came in the anticipation. For me, my cup of joy was filled the day before Christmas Eve — all my Christmas mail arrived at the same time. I had not received but one letter in five weeks up to that time, then it all poured in together. In the same mail, I received three or four letters from Mom, and letters from Mary, Frank, Bill, Jerry, Denis. Even Dick Ginder and Father Gus came through. So I was in such a glow that it didn't make any difference to me what happened. Everyone was so magnificently generous that I was more than slightly dazed. I could have eaten bread and water on Christmas and enjoyed myself perfectly. Altogether it was one of the most pleasant Christmases I have ever spent. Such is the difference that remembrances make.

Before I forget, I didn't receive that anniversary copy of the <u>Post</u> yet. Too bad, maybe the Rector grabbed it. Thanks anyway.

Our one-day retreat for Christmas this year was the most colossal flop, failure, and fake I have ever seen. The retreat master, a Benedictine, was mortally afraid of making a positive statement. He would begin a sentence, then start to qualify and apologize until you didn't know what he was saying. Everything was as disconnected and separated as the articles in an encyclopedia. His whole act seemed to consist in trying to get his hands and arms free of those long flowing sleeves. If he accepted any money for the two conferences he gave, he should make it a matter for confession. If every speaker were like him, it would be almost a blessing to be deaf.

On Christmas night there was a movie with an introductory act by the students. Santa Claus came to give a few presents; but before he gave them, he asked a few questions. He began on the faculty and did a real job on them. I was amazed at the way they took the faculty apart — even though it was in good fun. The Rector was in a tough position, but he came through very well. I think that this is the only institution in the world where the faculty takes a public beating every time an entertainment is put on; and the faculty enjoys it as much as anyone. (After all, they are forced to take it well.)

On Monday I am going on a "bum run" to Assisi. St. Francis owned that whole territory, and now they have some wonderful pieces of art and mosaic work there. Besides, it's always good to get a change.

There goes the bell for High Mass.

Love,

Phil

Comments: *Letter of December 25, 1937, Christmas Day*

(1)   Christmas is always a "family" or home feast inspired by the example of the Holy Family. Christmas was not celebrated in Rome with all the ornaments we use in the United States, and so we tried to recreate a bit of an American Catholic celebration for ourselves; and the bond among us made it a very warm and spiritual event.

December 30, 1937

NORTH AMERICAN COLLEGE
VIA DELL' UMILTA 30

Dear Everybody,

Just arrived back from Assisi, where I had never intended to go this year and had decided not to do the things I did; but despite all that we had a really marvelous time. I always used to think that visiting a monastery in the middle of winter was about the last word in stupidity.

Assisi is about one hundred and twenty-five miles from Rome, set on a spur of the Umbrian Mountains with a grand stretch of valley in front and an imposing background of snow-topped mountains. It is a typical hill town, with hardly a level yard of paving in the whole town, with streets slithering in all directions and often ending in street-stairs; after about three days of walking there in the snow and ice, you develop a gait like a sailor or duck. However, snow is unusual in Assisi; when we arrived it hadn't snowed in four years, but we had been there only two hours when it began to snow and it continued at intervals for our whole stay. We stayed at the American Convent there and proceeded to eat the establishment out of house and home. When I tell you that I was usually the first one finished, you can realize what a noble job of eating was done there. The nuns even gave us sandwiches and hot chocolate at night, about ten o'clock.

Assisi was the birthplace of St. Francis, and almost the whole town belongs to him. He started his monastic career in the very small church of "Portiuncula" (the church is about twenty feet long and about sixteen feet wide), and it was here that he was given, in a vision, the gift of declaring an indulgence to all those who came and prayed at this little church. Later the privilege was extended to all Franciscan churches but restricted to the first and second of August. But therein lies a story. St. Francis was meditating in the little chapel when he was beset by a strong temptation, and to rid himself of it, he ran outside and jumped headlong into a clump of briars and rose bushes. When he was tangled in the middle of the bushes and briars, two angels appeared to him and led him back into the "Portiuncula", and there Our Lord and the Blessed Mother appeared to him, and gave him the privilege of declaring that all who should receive Communion and pray at the little chapel, should receive a plenary indulgence for themselves or for the souls in Purgatory. And as a sign of this gift, the rose bushes into which he jumped, were to lose their thorns. He went outside, found that the rose bushes had lost their thorns, picked some of the thornless roses and went to show it to the Pope, who was then visiting nearby Perugia. He proved his point and was given permission to declare the indulgence. We saw the spot where he jumped into the rose bushes and saw the thornless rose bushes — they still grow today on that spot without thorns. And a man told us that his sister had gone to America and taken a bush from that spot, and transplanted it, but it grew thorns immediately.

Another interesting spot, in the Church of San Damiano where an old crucifix spoke to Saint Francis; they still have the crucifix. And there is another crucifix there with an even more amazing history. An old monk made a crucifix very hurriedly but didn't complete it, left the head undone. The next morning when he came back to his work, there was a marvelous head finished with a face that has three different expressions – the right side shows Christ in pain, the front view shows him in death, the left view shows him at peace after death. The wood, out of which the head is made, is different from that from which was made the body and arms; and the difference in sculpture between the body and arms and the head is tremendous.

Another story connected with the same church concerns the origin of hot cross buns. St. Clare founded a convent at St. Damiano's and attained a tremendous reputation for sanctity. One day the Pope came to visit there and to eat in the refectory, but at mealtime he refused to bless the food in the presence of St. Clare, insisting that she do it and gave her his papal ring to put on her finger as she blessed the food. She obeyed and after she blessed the bread each piece had a cross on it — and that miracle is commemorated by our practice of having hot cross buns on Good Friday. This is also the place where Saint Clare stopped the Saracens, when they came to pillage, by raising the Blessed Sacrament in benediction; those in the front ranks were struck blind and those on horse were knocked off.

But despite the efforts of Saint Francis, everything did not go peacefully in his order after his death. (I forgot to mention that St. Francis was a very short, thin man – only about five feet tall.) The great number of pilgrims who came to Assisi used to leave money at his shrine so one faction wanted to build a great basilica to him; the others insisted that it would be an insult to the spirit of his poverty. But those who were in favor of building got the upper hand by the simple trick of driving the others away. The monks apparently had not learned the virtue of peace or tolerance; those who favored strict poverty used to smash the vases holding the offerings of the pilgrims, and those who favored the building project would beat the opposition. But the climax came when the brother in charge of the building stole the body of St. Francis and hid it; he buried it at night and wouldn't tell anyone where he had put it. And the place remained unknown for 800 years; it was only in the last century that they found it after extensive digging.

St. Francis had a mania for meditation and solitude, so he selected a lonely spot on the mountainside as a retreat. It is called the "carcere" — prison. And the name is eminently fitting. We climbed the hill in a biting wind and snowstorm, but it was worth it. He had a little rock cell, used as a chapel, built on the side of a deep gorge in the mountainside. And it was there that he battled with the devil, for today the old monk who stays there will point out the deep hole where St. Francis said the devil used to live and would come out to torment him. A wilder, bleaker, more desolate spot would be harder to find; and even the little man who was not afraid to battle the devil stayed there for only a short while. And I don't blame him at all.

Assisi is famous also for the great paintings found there. Giotto, the first great Italian master, covered the basilica of St. Francis with pictures. [1] The quaintest of the series I think is the one depicting the vision of Pope Honorius III who saw St. Francis holding up the Church. The Pope is asleep in full ecclesiastical regalia with mitre and robes on, and the little mite of a man that St. Francis was is holding up with his shoulder the huge church of St. John Lateran, the mother church of the world.

Altogether we had a magnificent time, thanks also to the congenial company. It was good to see a whole countryside of snow; it was also good to see the place where was begun the practice of having Christmas cribs (I forgot to mention that). Another place that should be seen by visitors if they are to learn the spirit of Italy and Catholicism. Curiously enough, we found many English at Assisi; they have a great devotion to Saint Francis, and I couldn't imagine any saint more unlike an Englishman that St. Francis. One reason why they like him so much is that they contend he was a heretic (which would scandalize that little saintly man to the last degree), and no one can deny that he did have some difficulty in having his radical ideas accepted.

The more "bum runs" I take the more I enjoy Italy and the college (rather a left-handed compliment to say that I like the college because I can leave it frequently).

Love,

Phil

Comments: Letter of December 30, 1937

(1)   The Basilica of St. Francis in Assisi is one of the most ecumenical churches in the world. St. Francis is venerated by Catholics, Protestants, Buddhists, the Dalai Lama of Tibet and practically every religious denomination in the world. For this reason, Pope John Paul II convoked special prayer meetings at Assisi to pray for world peace. The meetings were very successful in attracting leading members of almost all the religious groups in the world but the Pope received rather sharp criticism from a number of

Cardinals and other prominent Catholics saying that his invitation to pray with all those groups, even for an excellent purpose, nurtured a feeling of syncretism and relativism, namely that all religions are equally right in their doctrines. The Pope quietly and without comment ceased the calling of the "Assisi Meeting."

Camerata walk, George Spehar and Jim Clark, 'Beedle' leading Camerata.

Camel Corps of Italian Army on parade in Rome.

Car wreck near Assisi, 1937

Students awaiting visit of Cardinal Pacelli, Secretary of State.

"Bum Run" group to Villa d'Este near Tivoli

1938

January 6, 1938
Epiphany

NORTH AMERICAN COLLEGE
Via Dell' Umilta 30

Dear Everybody,

As we expected, the Archbishop pursued us across the ocean with his new prohibition drive on the clergy and clerical students. The long arm of the law finally nabbed us. The Rector called us all in one morning (all the members of the Baltimore diocese), and as soon as we had shuffled into the royal presence, we knew by his expression that news of the first importance had arrived. The Rector introduced the question rather smoothly saying that at the bishops' meeting in Washington a resolution had been passed urging action against drinking, especially against women drinking. And so, we are asked to give up everything with even a smell of alcohol in it so that the fair and tender sex may be saved from the demon drink — I feel inexpressibly noble and chivalrous. We all signed our names to a pledge that removes us from all danger of drink until we have been ordained ten years; which means that particular problem is solved for me for the next twelve and a half years. We are pledged to give up all intoxicating liquor, everything that has alcohol in it — including beer and light wines. (1) But as long as we are studying in Europe, we are allowed the use of beer and light wine; as soon as we step on the boat that hauls us back to the U.S., we say goodbye to even beer and light wine. I guarantee that the pledge didn't worry me any, but six years ago I never dreamed that I would have to give up even 3.2 beer as something evil. Everybody knows that the Archbishop had good reasons for forcing everyone to take the pledge: a violent disease requires a violent remedy.

Usually talking about the weather is an ordinary thing, but it no longer is ordinary here. We are having the coldest weather that Rome has experienced in over six years. (2) The water pipes are freezing and bursting.

Of course, that wouldn't excite anybody in the student body except for the fact that we have to shave in cold water; and if you think that shaving in water that's just at the freezing point is fun you ought to try it. After a nice brisk shave at five-thirty in the morning, one feels more like a piece of meat in cold storage than a human. O pioneers. Some of the capitalistically inclined are thinking of flooding the corridors and starting skating rinks. Even at that our college is supposed to be one of the warmest in Rome; most of the other colleges have no heating systems. In fact, they had to discontinue the heating system in the Gregorian University one year because the colleges protested that their men were catching cold by sitting in heated classrooms and then going home to unheated colleges. The people I admire in weather like this are the monks who walk around barefooted; they give me a shiver that bends my backbone out of joint. For the first time in many a moon there are icicles on the fountains around Rome.

Tonight we are having a typical entertainment; a "slop show" interspersed with music has been arranged. As ever, the faculty is to be taken for a ride, and I am to act the part of Archbishop Curley (who also gets taken on a one-way ride). The orders of the Archbishop about the pledge will form the background for the affair. Of course, the faculty will not be present — not that they can't but that they understand that they are not wanted. There never will be another place like this in which the faculty stands for so much good-natured beating; they not only give permission but actually allow the fellows time off from exercises to fix up this sort of thing. If they ever had an entertainment in which the Rector and Vice-Rector did not get a drubbing they would probably faint. (And as far as prospects go at the present reading they'll never faint.)

Epiphany is celebrated by the Italians as much as Christmas. [3] In some sections of the city they have "fairs". Last night some young fellows were going through the streets singing Christmas carols — but I don't think it was due to the Epiphany, simply to strong wine.

Many thanks for the package. By the way, the rosaries I enclosed in Dad's ties were blessed and bought at Lourdes. And I think there were a few medals from Lisieux, home of St. Theresa (they can be identified, if they were enclosed, by the name on them); the medals from Lisieux were not blessed.

Love,

Phil

Comments: Letter of January 6, 1938

(1)   The decision of Archbishop Curley to request the seminarians of the Baltimore Archdiocese to pledge in writing that they would abstain from drinking any alcoholic beverage was hotly contested concerning its effect. Everybody agreed that the decision was legitimate, but the argument developed about its binding force. Was one bound under pain of sin to abstain from an alcoholic drink and could the Archbishop make the pledge a condition for ordination. Years later, in the School of Canon Law in The Catholic University in Washington, the argument was still alive. One professor, who was known to have an occasional drink (he was in his fifties and not subject to the pledge), contended very strongly that the Archbishop did have a right to make the pledge a condition for ordination. Actually, the pledge was operative for me only for the brief two years from my arrival in the United States in 1940 until my entering the Army in 1942. It was agreed that it did not apply to one in the armed forces. The successor to Archbishop Curley dropped the obligation to take the pledge; he died in 1947.

(2)   During this snowfall we had a good snowball fight in the Piazza of St. Peter's. The Americans vs. everybody else.

(3)   The feast of the Epiphany was very well kept because the people had a good understanding that they were gentiles, and therefore, the Magi represented them. Recitation of poems by children and other presentations were held in many churches.

February 4, 1938

NORTH AMERICAN COLLEGE
Via Dell' Umilta 30

Dear Everybody,
        Saturday will be the anniversary of the Pope's election to the papacy and a big time is expected. Practically, for us, it means a holiday. They are

still repairing St. Peter's, as they were when you were in Rome, but today I noticed that they no longer allow the pieces of marble to fall on the floor or to be scooped up by visitors.

Our class gets tonsure on Saturday, but due to the Rector's mistake in mislaying some of the dimissorial letters from the Bishops, there are a few of us who will not get it. It was rather embarrassing for me for a while when my diocesan was notified that he would get tonsure and still no notice came for me. So I went up to see the faculty to find the difficulty, and they said that the dimissorial letters (letters from the Bishop enabling his students to receive orders) had not come from the chancery in Baltimore. The Vice Rector then sent a rather testy letter to the Chancellor demanding the letters or a reason for not sending them. Then in a few days the Rector found that he had them all the time on his desk, but had misplaced them. So the Rector put both the Vice Rector and myself in a tough spot. However, I am rather glad that this little mix-up occurred, since it does give me a handle by which to demand his good will in case I have to ask for any permissions; after this little blunder he is a bit obliged to me. So I am one up on the faculty right now. I am not the only man in our class not getting tonsure; two fellows from New Jersey, Marty Killeen and another fellow, are not receiving tonsure because for the time being they are men without a country. The dioceses in New Jersey were shifted and they don't know who their bishop is; they have received no word from anyone.

Archbishop Mooney is coming to Italy on the Rex. The big question is what will be said about Father Coughlin at the Vatican. [1] Archbishop Mooney is a big man over here, and according to common opinion is picked as one of the coming big shots in the church in America. He was spiritual director at the college for a while before the Vatican took him into their "foreign service" and sent him somewhere as papal legate. The stories about his inability to learn to sing the Mass give me some encouragement. He was almost tone deaf, but gradually worked himself out of it.

I recently located the pictures taken of us at Castelgandolfo just after the audience with the Pope. [2] In a few days, I'll send a copy of them home. They turned out very well, except that Mom looks a bit caved in.

The Rector has just come out with a new decision that may seriously clip the wings of the students on "bum runs" during the year. He cut down our vacations at Christmas, and he is practically eliminating them at Carnival time; it's an old custom to have a few free days just before Lent. Formerly the fellows could go out for three days. According to the latest news, we can only go out for the day — leave after breakfast, must be back before supper. All that a "bum run" means now is that one can have a meal outside the college, which is something. And at Easter time, we only get one day. If I keep reciting my woes, I'll swing into a crying jag soon.

This college magazine has produced some real stuff in the line of poetry. One fellow turned in some stuff that even with the combined efforts of eight of us, could not be figured out; finally we elected a committee to ask him what he meant (not that we were going to publish the tripe but just out of curiosity). I still contend that he isn't even a Christian. Maybe it would be a good thing to publish such stuff and ask the readers to send in their impressions — nothing like starting a good fight to stimulate interest.

Love,

Phil

Comments: Letter of February 4, 1938

(1)   One of the first problems confronting Archbishop Mooney after his appointment as the Archbishop of Detroit was the enormous following of Father Coughlin, famous pastor of Royal Oaks, Michigan. His popularity developed from his radio talks about economics (he condemned roundly the rich, the policies of President Roosevelt, etc.) The Archbishop was very adroit and charitable, solving the problem with no serious trouble. The public was divided in its opinion of his talks — my parents disapproved, but my Protestant relatives thought he was wonderful.

(2)   The health of the Pope was declining; and after his death it was learned that he did not take the medicine prescribed for him by the doctors. Furthermore, he worked constantly despite the warning of the doctors.

February 25, 1938

NORTH AMERICAN COLLEGE
Via Dell' Umilta 30

Dear Everybody,

The famous lamps on St. Peter's are being prepared for a canonization; the basilica is not lighted with electricity but by oil. [1] Maybe Mom and Dad remember seeing the holders for the oil lamps on that famous day that we climbed to the top of the dome. Anyway, I have been thinking seriously of buying fifty feet of movie film and taking pictures of St. Peter's when it is all illumined for a canonization. I can then send you the films and let you see them. The film would cost me about two and a half dollars; I think it would be a good investment (that is if I can borrow or rent a movie camera from some store in Rome — which usually can be done). But a further difficulty is that perhaps they are only going to light up the dome of St. Peter's and not the whole church and colonnade; if the illumination is only partial it may not be worth the trouble. The only reason for grabbing this opportunity is that one never knows when another canonization will take place. (The official announcement for this one has not been made yet, but all the preparations are being made.) I hear that it costs ten thousand dollars to light up the whole works; the Vatican does not pay the bill — the order to which the saint belonged pays the bill, or the nation to which he belonged. And if they don't come through with the price, then they just don't do anything.

Another historic event is taking place in Rome. The very, very renowned beer hall near St. Peter's, Gambrinus', is being torn down. We had beer there one day, but perhaps Mom and Dad don't remember it. It was a very noble institution and did noble service to many generations of thirsty American seminarians. In fact, most of the fellows paid more visits to Gambrinus' (they had German beer) than they did to St. Peter's. The Italian government is making a very nice approach to St. Peter's; all the old houses in front of it are being demolished so that a good view of it can be had. The famous old Borgo section is being knocked down. If they do nothing at all but just leave a park in front of St. Peter's, everything will be splendid. But that's asking a little bit too much of the Italian temperament;

they will start immediately to pile up a heap of decorations that will be worse than the Borgo. Already they are beginning work on an arch — just after tearing down the other stuff to allow a view of the church.

We walked through Vatican City today and were amazed to find that they have <u>five</u> little parish churches for the people living in Vatican City — and all of them are not more than ten minutes walk from St. Peter's. We even had a cup of coffee in the bar for the Vatican City. [2] Maybe it will shock you to know that they actually have a bar set up in the sacristy of St. Peter's when they have great ceremonies there. The reason is obvious; most of the old cardinals are just about done under by one of those ceremonies that last half a day. The only thing a bar means to me now is a place to get a cup of coffee. We almost popped over on finding that they have a very nice plumbing supply and hardware store in Vatican City. Actually it costs just about half as much to live in Vatican City as it does to live in Rome — because there are no taxes. The men who have jobs in Vatican City guard their jobs jealously and pass them down to their sons. Their living quarters are very neat. But to work and live in there, one must become a full-fledged citizen of the Vatican State; he must give up his Italian citizenship (which doesn't cause any tears to most of them). They also issue passports in the Vatican State.

Best wishes to Dad on his birthday.

Love,

Phil

Comments: Letter of February 25, 1938

(1)   The illumination of St. Peter's was the climax of a canonization and caused intense excitement. Vantage points to see the illumination were carefully chosen beforehand — the Pincio in the Borghese gardens was our choice. We went there just before dusk to get the full effects. The "sanpietrini" (the workers in St. Peter's) carried out the lighting of the oil lamps that were placed all over the exterior of the Basilica including the crucifix at the summit of the dome. The real stars of the event were the two workers who lighted the lamps on the cross; poised at the very top of the cross, one descended the

cross lighting the lamps on his way and the other gave a leap (he was in a harness) that propelled him to the lamp on the extreme end of the cross bar of the cross and then after lighting it, he kicked himself out to swing over to the other tip of the cross to light the lamps.

The whole operation required only a few minutes, and it was timed to compare it with other illuminations. The effect was breathtaking. The Basilica stood out like a heavenly light against the darkness of the sky. The lamps lasted for about forty minutes, and the real professionals raced around town to get pictures from various angles of the illumination. Unfortunately, the illuminations were stopped because they were considered a waste of money.

(2)   The Vatican City was a very interesting place to visit. Everything was very orderly, new and inviting. The coffee bars had food and drinks at an amazingly cheap price because there was no duty imposed in the City. I enjoyed very much my "official visits" to the printing shop in the Vatican for the publishing of the Magazine, **Roman Echoes**, the magazine of the College.

March 2, 1938

NORTH AMERICAN COLLEGE
Via Dell' Umilta 30

Dear Everybody,

Before I begin getting wrapped up in an account of a one-day "bum run" I took, I want to tell you about the fellow who is coming through Washington and will, I hope, bring you a package from me. His name is LaTourette — French name, but his mother is Irish. [1] I don't see how it is possible for him to deliver all the packages that he has in his trunk, but he assured me that he would look after mine.

And now about our "bum run", which happened two days before Ash Wednesday. It cost me nothing — the diocesan priests, who have been ordained recently, always send over enough money for one of these affairs;

the whole diocese goes out together. We hired two cars (there are nine fellows from the Baltimore diocese over here) and went to Gennazanno, Subiaco, and Tivoli.

The first stop we made was at a little town, Gennazanno, that is completely untouched by the industrial age. We stopped to see a famous shrine to Our Lady of Good Counsel. The story connected with the shrine is interesting: There is a picture of the Blessed Mother and Child that is supposed to have miraculously detached itself from a wall in Albania (across the Adriatic Sea from Italy) and come across the sea. It happened during the time of invasion by the Turks; two Christians went into this little chapel to pray for help, and while they were praying the picture (which was not painted on canvas but on the surface of the wall) detached itself from the wall and rose in the air. The pilgrims, in an ecstasy, followed the picture, which simply flew across the water, the pilgrims also crossing the water miraculously. The image came to Rome and then disappeared. The two pilgrims didn't know what to do, but meantime it was noised abroad that an image of the Blessed Mother had miraculously appeared at Gennazanno, so they went there to investigate. And sure enough, it was the same picture that they had followed. Even to this day, the picture remains unattached to any wall, canvas, or material of any kind, but is contained in a very elaborate and beautiful shrine.

And another story is connected with the same church. A drunken soldier, enraged by losing his pay at gambling, came into the church and began to slash with his sword a picture of the crucifixion. Wherever he slashed the painted figure of Christ blood began to flow, and the sword of the soldier became bent. A few days later, in the presence of the Archbishop of that section, a blacksmith heated and straightened the sword, but immediately after he had straightened it, it went back to its old bent shape. The bent sword and picture are in the church.

Then we continued on to Subiaco, through very rough, rugged country. At one place we stopped to take a picture of the crowd in the snow (it had not snowed recently but little drifts were to be found occasionally). One of the drivers (all Italians in Rome act like kids when they get near snow) playfully threw a snowball at Marty Killeen — I forgot to mention that he was along because he took the place of a fellow who had gotten sick. So Marty started heaving back, and that poor Italian took the worst snowball drubbing he ever suffered in his life. The Italians are no good at throwing anything; they are clever with their feet and legs, but are very awkward with their arms — as this driver soon found out.

Subiaco is a little town perched on the side of a rocky mountain; famous only because St. Benedict went into a cave there and lived the life of a hermit for a long time. A monastery and shrine is built over the cave in which he retired when only fourteen years old; food was brought to him by an old monk, and he didn't stir from his cave for over three years. This was in the fifth century. At that time they had no rules for monks — each man led his own life, and some lived in communities. After a while the monks of that section asked St. Benedict to be their superior; he refused, but at last gave in to their request. But things were not to their liking. He was too strict, so they tried to poison him twice and both times he was delivered miraculously. After that, they gave up the poisoning as a bad job. It was St. Benedict who made the first set of rules for a religious order, and they served as a pattern for other religious orders for centuries. The trust they have in him is marvelous; for instance, the stone cliffs overhanging the monastery began to crumble. Instead of removing the crumbling rock, the monks simply erected a statue of St. Benedict facing the cliff and inscribed under the statue the words, "Stop, cliff, and do not harm any of my sons." But the Italian government was more or less a doubting Thomas and went to work and removed some of the rock. But the fact is that although many pieces of rock have fallen from the cliff, they have not harmed any of the monks. Which may be sheer luck, and may not. But great things have happened there — the story is told of a monk who walked out on an adjoining lake and rescued a drowning man.

We ate at Subiaco and then continued to Tivoli. Visited the famous Villa d'Este with its hundreds of fountains. The first time I went there I was charmed with it, and the more I go the more the place grows on me. It was built in the sixteenth century, and its shaded ilex walks, and fountain-lined paths are rich with the memories of the great figures of history. The composer Liszt used to haunt the villa garden and give concerts there; and when he became a priest, it was his favorite spot.

Then, in the purple twilight with the setting sun like a great Japanese lantern, we returned to Rome. A perfect day.

The order of examinations in July has been posted, and I am glad to see that I shall be up early this year, probably within the first ten days of July. The Saturnia arrives in Naples on the twenty-first of July; that would be convenient for me, if Bill or anyone comes over. But that's looking very far ahead.

Love,

Phil

Comments: Letter of March 2, 1938

(1)   Frank LaTourette, who had a very engaging personality, later got into television and had some very popular success.

March 8, 1938

NORTH AMERICAN COLLEGE
VIA DELL' UMILTA 30

Dear Everybody,

I am in quite a tough spot at present; our magazine is coming out shortly and all the work of correcting, etc., fell on me — the supposed editor and his assistant had to go on retreat in preparation to receiving minor orders. And editing magazines is something not exactly familiar to me. I don't approve of all the articles in it, but I am not supposed to use my judgment on throwing them, only on correcting them. [1] There is always one convenient way of getting out of any difficulty, and that is simply to say that the Rector doesn't approve of it. That poor Rector is going to carry the burden for everything.

A peculiar incident occurred during a soccer game last week; our team was playing an Italian College, and all during the game there was one Italian who was roughing it up. Occasionally the Americans would protest to the referee, but the referee would only shrug his shoulders and do nothing about it. Finally the fellow who was playing opposite the Italian, a hot-headed Irishman, told him (he can't speak Italian but he showed him by unmistakable gestures) that he'd knock his block off the next time he starts any dirty playing. After the game was over the Americans found out that the rough player was none other than the Vice Rector of the Italian College; that was the reason why the referee always refused to reprimand him or penalize him. Well he doesn't know how close he came to getting a drubbing from that Irish fellow.

Now that Lent has started there is a Station church every day at which one can gain a plenary indulgence. We make them all. I used to see old General Lenihan last year at them, but apparently he is not in Rome any more, or doesn't get to the churches when we get there.

Love,

Phil

Comments: Letter of March 8, 1938

(1)   My complaints about the editing of the magazine, **Roman Echoes**, were relieved by my visits to the printing press in the Vatican with subsequent stops at the bar. I also discovered that the best means of getting an outstanding job from the printers was to give them a bottle of good wine — which I did.

March 13, 1938

NORTH AMERICAN COLLEGE
Via Dell' Umilta 30

Dear Everybody,

At last I can forget about the first issue of our forthcoming college publication. But I shall need a bodyguard when the rag finally is put into circulation, because just a few days before printing I was given half a dozen articles to be fixed up before being printed. Well, I fixed them; about the only thing I didn't change was the name of the fellow who wrote them. When he sees his stuff in print he won't recognize it. I was surprised to find the number of fellows who do not have an adequate command of English. Reminds me of a few years ago when one morning after Mass I asked Father O'Hara why he didn't write a letter of protest about something that had gotten into his craw, and he very honestly said that he didn't think he could write a dignified letter of protest. Any of the alumni who expect a finished job of this first issue are in for a surprise; I don't even like the name of the magazine, **The Roman Echoes** — sounds to me like some bi-weekly, two-bit midwestern sheet. I should be the last person in the world to pan it because I think the first article in it will be mine. Just to show you how many difficulties always present themselves in editing such a thing, I'll tell you what happened just as Ed Latimer was taking the stuff over to the printer. Just five minutes before he arrived, the chief printer and boss passed out in a dead faint and couldn't be revived for quite awhile. That was a fitting climax to the whole history of the publication.

If it weren't such a tragedy, this latest affair in Austria would afford a good plot for a comedy; all the news in Italy about it is strictly censored, and according to the version that the ordinary Italian gets one would think that Germany was saving Austria. For instance, this is the sort of applesauce that is printed in the papers, "The German army in Austria is at the disposal of the Austrian government to preserve the freedom of the country." And according to the Italian press, the whole Austrian population greeted the Nazis with cheering, flags, etc. Everything is such an outrageous lie that it almost amounts to humor. The Austrian servants in the college consider it as almost the death of Austrian freedom; they are going around as though they had lost everyone in their family. I think this would never have happened if Mussolini had not allowed it. When Germany tried the same thing some time ago, Mussolini rushed troops up to the border. But this time no troops were sent up, and some two weeks ago it is said that Mussolini called Schuschnigg on the phone and told him that the game was up. Things like this make one thank God that he lives in America. It is now a crime to try to get out of Austria. Of course, this will just about strangle the Church in Austria. [1]

Recently a new law about clerics has been published in Rome. It is forbidden for any cleric to watch parades, or public spectacles, or even to read movie ads. This law is effective from March to November. Everyone knows what it's for. It is to prevent any priests or seminarians from watching and cheering the giant parade that is to be staged in honor of Hitler when he comes to Rome in the beginning of May. [2] Already they are beginning to erect great standards, etc., along the route of the march. They are even fixing up a place for landing at Ostia (Hitler is coming by water — I suppose they are afraid to let him come by land) and building a new road to Rome just for the occasion. The sad part is that some of the clergy in Italy are all for Mussolini and this treaty with Germany. During the Ethiopian War they say that some bishops gave their pectoral crosses to the government to help. The whole business just sickens me. Everybody at the college is in favor of going in a body to the parade (if possible) and giving Hitler a great big Bronx cheer as he passes. But that would get us right out of the country — as everyone knows. Anyway, the Pope is doing all that he can possibly do to oppose Hitler's reception. They say that the Pope is going to move out to Castelgandolfo as a protest.

Anyway, all this business makes it interesting to live here. And it also is good to show just how well off the Church in America is where we have no one trying to dictate to us. Europe is a good place to see and enjoy, but a heluva place in which to live.

Ordinations are at the end of this week. Three fellows from Baltimore are being ordained. This will be an expensive affair for me. According to the rules of courtesy at the college, I will have to buy five ordination presents — books. Without a doubt, this place takes more money than any place I have ever heard of. I must buy a present for the three diocesans, for my prefect of last year, and for another fellow who has asked me to his first Mass and breakfast.

We are getting some very interesting inside dope on the war in China from a missionary who has just come from there. He was in Peking before, during, and after the Japanese occupation. The missionaries are being very discreet and diplomatic in their attitude towards the war because I think they are just about convinced that Japan will take over China, and so they don't want to offend the future government. They say that it is very easy to get along with both the Japanese and Chinese.

The visitors are beginning to pour into Rome. Spring is here.

Love,

Phil

Comments: Letter of March 13, 1938

(1)   The "Anschluss", or union with Austria by the Nazis, outraged most

of the Italians. Mussolini was allowed to take some parts of the Austrian Tyrol as the pay-off for not objecting to this rape of Austria. Italy needed hydroelectric power from Tyrol and this was the reward for Mussolini's inaction. The Nazis were brutal in their take-over, having shot Premier Dollfuss. This event is further complicated by the inaction, or quiet approval of Cardinal Innitzer of Vienna, who did not protest it. The rumor here is that the Holy Father will certainly summon him to come to Rome and explain his silence.

The feeling was then that war was not far away.

(2)   The preparations for the visit of Hitler were enormous. The government was painting many of the buildings in Rome and arranging cultural events, as concerts and parades, in honor of Hitler. Of course, this also means that the Germans will send enough security men into Italy to protect Hitler and also to learn how to control Rome.

The Pope is doing everything possible to discourage crowds from watching the triumphal entrance of Hitler. There is reported unwillingness of some of the best operatic stars to sing at the operas being prepared to honor Hitler.

The Italian temperament and their culture are completely opposed to the Nazis and although Mussolini will force them to have an impressive welcome, there will be no "heart" in it.

March 15, 1938

NORTH AMERICAN COLLEGE
Via Dell' Umilta 30

Dear Everybody,

There was an incident that happened here which I think is the funniest I have ever heard. There is a graduate house of studies for American priests in the Vatican City, and consequently any packages sent to them come in duty free. Sometimes they would receive a package for a fellow at the college so that he would get it cheaply. But there was a sudden rift in diplomatic relations between the college and the other house which ended in their sending down to the Vice Rector some packages received by them and intended for fellows in the house here (the practice was officially condemned before but winked at). So, of course, the Vice Rector confiscated the packages and put them in his office. But the fellows here were determined not to let the matter drop, feeling as though they had been double-crossed. So night-by-night someone has gone down and grabbed a package, emptied it of its contents, re-loaded it with books and put it back in place. To date just half of the packages have been emptied without the Vice Rector knowing it, although he has them practically under his feet all day long. I suppose he is wondering why the fellows owning the packages never come in to demand them. If he only realized it, he would never start a practice that must necessarily end in his defeat — the fellows have every action of his timed perfectly, even knowing exactly what minute he goes to bed at night.

For a long time one of our neighbors living in the third floor of the apartment house opposite us has kept us awake by coming in at about ten-thirty or eleven at night and yelling up for the key. After a number of yells someone leans out the window and throws down the key; then after more yelling they find the key and get in. It was decided that something had to be done about it. So one fellow went around making a collection of old keys; he had a bunch big enough to open every lock in Rome. Then they waited for the opportunity. Two nights later the person came at the usual time, started yelling for the key. The fellow leaned out of the window and threw down about two dozen keys just at the time that the real key was being thrown down. Of course, the keys got hopelessly mixed up. Then was there some squawking!!! What a life. [1]

Love,
Phil

Comments: Letter of March 15, 1938

[1]   The episode with the keys was more important than it appears. The street noise and the practice of neighbors across the narrow street playing radio music with the radio placed on the window will and singing at the top of their voices was the cause of a nervous breakdown in one of our seminarians from Baltimore. He lasted

only a year. Although we were not so sensitive as the seminarian, we wanted to give the neighbors a lesson about noises after eleven o'clock at night. The seminarian who masterminded this key operation was Johnny Linn, my classmate from Baltimore.

April 5, 1938

NORTH AMERICAN COLLEGE
Via Dell' Umilta 30

Dear Everybody,

In my last letter I forgot to put in an Easter greeting — not that I forgot about Easter coming, but only that I have not yet learned to live two weeks ahead of myself. Already they are getting St. Peter's ready for the canonization. Inside they are hanging chandeliers all down the nave, and the nave is also decorated with red draping edged in a golden border. It's the most colorful scene I think I have ever seen (if they would only sell the movie rights for taking pictures inside St. Peter's, they would make enough to run the Church for a year). And, of course, the outside is being fixed up as usual, oil lamps all over the façade.

The preparations for Hitler are also going ahead. That will be a real Roman holiday. The people are a bit bitter about all this money being spent on Hitler (50,000,000 lire for his welcome), but they will all enjoy it and yell their heads off when the time comes. All along a couple of the principal avenues they are putting in special gas mains to illuminate a series of huge lamps. It makes me sick at my stomach to see all this nonsense going on despite the poverty in Italy. Your remark that the American newspapers think that Mussolini was fooled by Hitler was interesting. Mussolini made a speech after it was all over and professed to know all about it even before it had come off, but there is a rumor going around that he was so taken by surprise that he rushed troops up to the Brenner Pass, not knowing what was coming off. But if Hitler pulled one over on Mussolini, you can bet your boots that the Duce will make up for it sometime in the future. I heard the speech that Mussolini made after Austria had been taken, and it did not get much cheering at all; it will take a long time for the people to get used to that deal.

By the way, today we met some Austrians who had just come from Innsbruck, and they gave us the dope on Hitler's little party in Austria. They say that everyone will vote for him — they predict that the vote will be 100% for him — but that they are all very sorry to do it. It is very difficult to get out of the country, and only a very small amount of money can be taken out (so little that it is almost impossible to travel). Furthermore, all Austrians are supposed to be back in Austria very shortly to take part in the vote. The way these people spoke, it was very dangerous to even keep away from the polls; they were going back just to vote.

Our proposed school magazine will be out shortly. Must go to work on the final proofreading now.

Happy Easter.

Love,
Phil

April 10, 1938
Palm Sunday

NORTH AMERICAN COLLEGE
Via Dell' Umilta 30

Dear Everybody,

At last the much awaited, over worked "Roman Echoes" is ready to delight the expectant world. I shall send a copy home in short time — I mean that I shall start it on its way in a short time; the exact date of its arrival will depend so much on the will of the Italian postal service and the special providence of the Lord that I can predict nothing except that it will probably reach America before I do in 1940. You will notice that it carries my name as associate editor, and as author of two articles; but actually I re-wrote four of the articles and had all the correcting of most of the others. I am not at all proud of the literary standard of the magazine, but I didn't have a free hand in the ordering of the material (officially I am just one of the six associate editors). But as an initial effort, I think it is creditable. However, since the alumni of the college are very loyal and make it a point of honor to cheer madly for everything that issues from this place, it will be well received — I hope. They have put enough snap shots of groups of fellows to make it sell very well in the house here. The dear little magazine will cost each member of the alumni one dollar; if that isn't too big a strain on their loyalty, it will establish it on a firm financial basis. [1]

The colorful Palm Sunday atmosphere of Washington is notably lacking in Rome. It is a miserable day, and if Easter Sunday is as chilly and wet as this one, the canonization ceremony will be hindered.

I understand that Father Speer Strahan (who taught Tommy and me English — the prof that Tommy couldn't stand) is going back to Yale to get his Ph.D. [2] That's the end of a long story. He used to come to class and take the Ph.D.'s for a big ride. Then when he started to give sermons on the radio, he took more than one opportunity to belt them in the rear. And now he ends it all by going to work for one himself. That's just like him. He has a lot of talent and brains, but little common sense.

Tommy's letter was a honey. I'll answer it sometime soon. (Contrary to what most people think, there is a lot of work in the Seminary — if one does it.)

Now the rumors are starting to fly about where the new college is to be built. [3] Nobody knows when the old one is going and if the Rector does, he is not letting anyone else in on it — maybe for fear that the students will start the process of tearing the college down before the wrecking company gets to work. One story is that we might move into the old Propaganda College, which is right next to the Piazza di Spagna (not far from the Hotel de Russie where we stayed in Rome). The Piazza di Spagna is one of the busiest places in Rome — precious little studying would be done there.

The clippings about Dr. Walsh of Georgetown were very interesting; maybe we will see him in Rome — if we get into St. Peter's for the ceremony.

I have been watching the news about Spain rather closely. It would be nice to see a bit of Spain before leaving Europe, but they must do much cleaning up before it will be ready for visitors. There is nobody at the college who has ever seen Spain, despite the great cathedrals they have there. [4]

We don't know if we will get permission for "bum runs" at Easter;
I am afraid that we will spend a very quiet Easter time.

Love,

Phil

Comments: Letter of April 10, 1938

(1)   Roman Echoes was a success, and it continued through the years,
        always redolent of Rome; and therefore, always popular with the
        alumni.

(2)   Father Speer Strahan was a very talented poet and writer who taught
        English to our class. He taught us even the rudiments of writing a
        novel and made us, on successive weeks, write the first chapter, the
        climatic chapter and the last chapter of our novel! The greatest surprise
        was that he became a chaplain for the U.S. Army. Near the end of the
        Roer campaign for our 82nd Airborne Division, I received a summons
        from our Colonel to see the Corps Chaplain (a Corps had then about
        four divisions and so the chief chaplain of the Corps was as very
        important person.) I got rid of my dirty combat uniform, dressed up
        in regular duty uniform and went with some unease to see the Corps
        Chaplain. I found him in a very comfortable and safe office many
        miles behind the line of combat and dressed in a combat uniform.
        The chaplain was Chaplain Lt. Colonel Speer Strahan. After the usual
        polite pleasantries he said, "I learned that your division went through
        München Gladbach, and I heard that they had some fabric shops
        there of high quality. I am making a new set of vestments and I want
        to know if you saw any of their fabric shops?" When I returned to
        my post, the Colonel, worried about this very important order to me,
        said, "What did he want?" I couldn't tell him the truth.

(3)   The rumors about building a new college were preposterous. No
        building materials were available, no money was even in prospect
        and nobody was interested. The new building, the present North
        American College in the Vatican City, was built after the war, largely
        through the efforts of Cardinal Francis Spellman of New York.

(4)   Spain was in terrible shape as a result of the war.

April 24, 1938

NORTH AMERICAN COLLEGE
Via Dell' Umilta 30

Dear Everybody,

Things have been rather interesting here lately. As I told you, we put out an issue of the "Del Nord Digest", and it caused more of a stir than if the Rector had been shot. It was a revolutionary pamphlet — revolt against the attitude of some students, not against authority. There is some distinction between new men and old men around here, despite the fact that the old men say there isn't. The third year men are especially conscious of their dignity and seem to spend some time in contemplating their excellence. As a matter of fact, the third year is in charge of handling most of the "business" around here — hiring movies, etc. We thought the best way of killing their false dignity was to suffocate it by laughter; so we ridiculed them for about twenty pages, and did it so effectively and cleverly that they have no comeback. The whole business went over magnificently, partly because other issues of the same publication have been hopelessly dull, partly because almost the whole house wanted to see the third year laughed at. The funniest thing was that all the fellows we hammered had given us permission to mention them in the publication; when they gave permission, they acted as if nothing we could ever write would affect them. They think differently now. I was very glad to have the opportunity to write an article about some of their shows around here; I ended my criticism with the sentence, "Unfortunately the lines were distinctly spoken." [1]

Yesterday, we went up to the field owned by the college to play baseball, and fell in with a very stupid cab driver (who thought he was clever). We told him where we wanted to go; he started to take us by the longest way, we told him he was going the wrong way. He protested vigorously that it was the best way. Finally, he went by such a fluky way that he got himself lost, but took us on a very beautiful drive. After I had enjoyed the scenery enough, we got him straightened out and arrived at the field. Then the battle began. He insisted on giving him just what it would have cost if he had come directly. He said, "All or nothing." "Fine," we said, "you get nothing. Thanks for the ride," and walked off. That sent his temperature up to a thousand degrees; so we gave him a little less than what we had intended to give him in the first place and let him stew. It will be a long time before he tries to cheat any other American seminarians.

One of the Baltimore fellows who was just ordained, and went to the Holy Land, brought back the Baltimore diocesans' rosaries from the Holy Land that had touched the Holy Sepulchre and were, therefore, highly indulgenced. I shall send mine home to you some time shortly. The rosaries are very plain, wooden beads. But the wood is from olive trees, the same variety of olive tree that is grown in the Garden of Olives.

There is a fellow at the college who knows almost everything about the Roman forum, and a few of us are going through it with him. [2] By the time you come I ought to be able to make something out of that yard of broken marble; the most interesting thing we met was the floor of an old temple that had green metal scattered on it. The green metal was copper (turned green from age and weather) from money that had been in it when it was burned. But now there is almost nothing left and what is left in the forum is about as orderly as a junk pile.

Occasionally I hear about the great art museum that Andrew Mellon is donating to Washington. [3] The site is supposed to be next to the Smithsonian Institute, I believe. Have they done anything about it besides talk? And whatever happened to that suggestion of the Holy Name Society to build a great statue of Christ somewhere in Washington?

The next time I write I shall have some information about rates, etc., for traveling in Europe.

Love,
Phil

Comments: Letter of April 24, 1938

(1)   The "Del Nord Digest" never had a second edition. The subjects of our criticism were very understanding and good-natured and in our opinion were very indulgent towards our rebel camerata.

Actually, the customs that we criticized were subsequently discontinued when the new college building was completed.

(2)   The expert on the Roman Forum was Henry Beck, a very intellectual student from New Jersey who was later a history prof.

(3)   The museum I referred to became eventually the National Art Gallery in Washington, an excellent and world-renowned gallery.

April 28, 1938

NORTH AMERICAN COLLEGE
VIA DELL' UMILTA 30

Dear Rob and Mary,

(News flash: summer trips will not be cut out, simply shortened a bit.) A number of us went to Orvieto, shortened from "*Urbs Vetus*," for the feast of Corpus Christi. [1] The façade of the cathedral is reputedly the most brilliant in the world; Italian Gothic style, a rainbow in stone. The procession is the main feature, and amounts to a display of the native genius in pageantry. The organizations and costumes are as varied as Madolin's May Ball; it looks as though everyone just empties the old trunk or attic and enjoys the excuse for traipsing around the town. Real medieval costumes are used and are very picturesque, but I think our modern dress is far more becoming and kind to the human figure — a man must be an Apollo to wear more or less tight fitting hose, breeches, etc. And as I noticed amply, there are few Apollos in Orvieto.

Very shortly I am to be named editor of our recently established college publication. If my ideas do not coincide with the Rector's, I shall very gracefully resign. I should like to make the thing representative of Roman and European culture in regard to the Church — articles on recent discoveries in the catacombs which conclusively prove the doctrine of the primitive church, etc. I want a substantial, intellectual but readable (I abhor "scholarly" writing — a poor excuse for being dull) publication. I would welcome the opportunity of working for something respectable (and I am quite sure the Rector would wish it that way), but if they want merely a college gossip sheet, they can dispense with me as editor.. [2]

The Rector just arrived from a trip to America where he attended the annual alumni meeting. According to him our last publication was hailed as the greatest thing published since the Bible. Well, we shall see — I foresee a few very busy sessions with His Excellency, the Rector.

Don't forget to send me the address; I should like to write for accommodations before we started on our trip. Much obliged.

Sincerely,

Phil

Comments: Letter of April 28, 1938

(1)   The trips to Orvieto were always very inspiring and rewarding. The genius of Italy is at its highest when it combines their love for the past with the Catholic faith. I think that the celebration of these feasts, especially those concerning the Blessed Sacrament, have preserved the faith to a large degree. It seems to me that it is impossible to attend one of their celebrations, with their very visible and human emotions demonstrating their basic and deep faith, without being inspired.

(2)   Frankly, I was very much surprised by the success of Roman Echoes and the fact that the Rector and Vice Rector were so supportive. They agreed also with my idea about the development of the annual magazine and allowed me whatever was needed to insure its success.

April 30, 1938

NORTH AMERICAN COLLEGE
Via Dell' Umilta 30

Dear Everybody,

We finally succeeded in getting our magazine printed, but it has not yet been folded and assembled. The most amazingly unexpected things bob up; for instance, we suddenly discovered from the director of the Vatican

Press that nothing could get out of Vatican City without the official permission of the Vatican officials. It took us quit a bit of smooth talking to show them that this was only a private publication and that the Church would not be blamed for anything in it. I also found out on the same afternoon that no package at all can be carried out of Vatican City without an official stamp: this is to prevent smuggling. Vatican City is the cleanest, most modern little affair I have ever seen. Those who say that the Church is backward in the affairs of the world ought to take a look over here. The streets are immaculate, living conditions perfect, and last but not least, I think they have the cheapest and best little bar and coffee shop in the world. An excellent place to live. (Coffee costs 2¢ a cup, and no alcoholic drink, even of the best stuff in the world costs more than 8¢. The secret is that nothing is taxed.)

The crisis for our printing job came on Saturday night. They had told us that it would be done then, but we came early on Saturday afternoon to see if it would — it wasn't ready, just as I had feared. So, we did a little cheer leading. The secret is to make them think that they are as good as Americans in efficiency and then keep prodding them along. We sold them that sort of stuff for about four hours and finally got the printing all done — I was more tired than the printers. Luckily, the assistant editor is a perfect man for such occasions; he has a marvelous sense of humor and never is discouraged. We took time out and went over to get a couple of coffees and buns and then came back to the press. Believe it or not, we made them establish a speed record in printing; they said that our job would take fifteen days, and they finished it in four!!!! I see a new future in printing for Italy. They kept telling us that it was impossible, but we kept giving them the old line of how good they were; now they are as proud as kids of themselves. We intend to have some sort of memorial made and erected in the printing room. Anyway, we succeeded in having five copies made for Saturday night (after those two cups of coffee, we really swept them off their feet) and got the Vice Rector to take them to America with him for the annual Alumni Association Meeting to be held in Brooklyn on May 9. [1] Sometime during the coming week I shall send you a copy of our publication; when the bill comes back for the printing, I'll have to wear smoked glasses before looking at it. It will cost (for 1550 copies) between 15,000 and 20,000 lire. All I must do now is pay for it, but that will be very simple.

Now about the international situation. Hitler's speech did not make much of an impression over here. The people are tired of all this war scare stuff and things have been whooped up so much that the whole show has started to bore everybody. All they need and want now is a good long sleep. [2]

I have realized for a long time that Mother's Day is coming, but it seems that I shall have to take it out in wishing and praying. I have been trying to send a little picture home but that is hard to arrange since it must be proved that it was paid for in lire that was bought at 19 to a dollar. We'll see. If nothing arrives by the 14[th,] or shortly thereafter, you'll know that I was doing my best. Best of everything to Mom.

Love,

Phil

Comments: Letter of April 30, 1938

(1)   After securing the first copies the <u>Roman Echoes</u> I did a bit of celebrating at one of the bars in the Vatican City where the coffee, dolci (sweet buns) and liqueurs were unbelievably cheap. The most expensive drink cost 6¢ in our money. The most important part of the job was to get the first copies to the Vice Rector, Monsignor Allen Babcock, in time for him to take them to the annual convention or meeting of the North American College Alumni. His taking them there was a guarantee of their acceptance and eventual success.

(2)   Hitler's speeches eventually lacked interest in Italy because of the difference in national backgrounds — Germany had lost the war and was mercilessly penalized by the reparations imposed on it, whereas, Italy had been a member of the victorious Allies. At best, Italy was only interested in sharing the spoils of a German victory, not in sharing their complaints against the Allies. In addition, the Italians were sufficiently cultured to abominate a real war.

May 2, 1938

NORTH AMERICAN COLLEGE
Via Dell' Umilta 30

Dear Everybody,

The Vice Rector, a neighbor of mine, was taken ill with something or other and confined to his room. I took him a piece of cake; he was stopped completely. There he was propped up in a big chair nursing a big toe that had been infected and trying to read. He didn't know whether I had come in to get a permission or simply from charity. We got along very well; he told me about shows he had seen in New York before sailing, then about his sore foot. When I got tired listening about his sore foot, I went back to rescue the remainder of the cake from the fellows in my room. (Don't tell the Collins this, but as a matter of fact they carted the Vice Rector off to the hospital the day after I gave him the cake — I don't know whether there is any connection.) That wasn't the only peculiar dealings I had with the faculty recently. The Rector paid me a sudden visit, unannounced, the other morning when I was hardly in condition to receive him nicely. We had a hard baseball game on Sunday; the pitcher was so terrible that the outfielders (I play left field) had a track meet. The next morning both my prefect and his fellow officer (who are supposed to wake up the fellows in their camerata) overslept; I had loaned my alarm clock to a fellow next door who had to serve Mass at five twenty-five. Consequently I didn't hear the measly, asthmatic bell that rings at rising time — first time I hadn't heard the bell in six years in the Sem. Ordinarily the Vice Rector stops in at the rooms on our corridor as he goes down to the chapel to see that everybody is up, but this morning he was in the hospital. So the Rector himself took up the task, a possibility that no one thought of. Well to make a long story short, he acted as my valet that morning, and he doesn't make a very pleasant one either. The first thing I knew to reassure me that I was still living under Seminary routine, was the face of the Rector near my bed. I was so soundly asleep that I hadn't even heard him knock. When I saw him I said the most natural thing in the world, "Good morning." That surprised him more than his appearance had surprised me. The next thing he did was to ask me if anything was wrong with me; I was still so completely sleepy and befuddled that I never even thought of the possibility of my somehow being out of order, so I gave him another answer that stopped him, "I don't know. Is there?" He didn't know what in the world to say or think, but after grunting a while he said, "What are you doing in bed?" Then my mind turned over enough to realize that I wasn't supposed to be in bed at that time. "I suppose I didn't hear the bell," was my very obvious reply. He left with only a warning to keep my alarm clock in my room. He was secretly much pleased with himself for having proved that he is wide-awake and checking up on the fellows.

Last night there was a special meeting held just across the street from the back of the college in the piazza. There was much yelling for Mussolini and speech making. The doorkeeper said that the meeting was to get volunteers for Spain. According to some treaty almost all of the European powers are supposed to keep a "hands-off" policy in Spain and to control the Spanish coast to keep ships from sending troops there. But on the day on which that control was supposed to go into effect, it was rumored that Italy sent 45,000 Italians to Spain. The only thing that happened last evening was the distribution of volunteer slips (so they say) for duty in Spain. Newspaper correspondents say that Mussolini admits what everybody knows, — that there can be no settlement of things in Europe until the business in Spain is settled. (1)

Love,

Phil

Comments: Letter of May 2, 1938

(1)   The war in Spain was of the greatest interest in Italy. Eventually, the forces of General Franco won, and a great public celebration was made in front of the Spanish Embassy near the Spanish steps. The Italians recognized the war as a struggle against Communism as represented by the "Republican" regime in Spain; the regime had seized all the gold from the Spanish treasury and sent it to Moscow. Their atrocities against the priests and religious in Spain were colossal. One of the current stories concerned the heroic defense of the fortress in Tolido. The Catholic commanding officer

was ordered by the Republican regime to surrender, and if he refused his only son was to be executed. The Republicans then ordered the son to speak to his father and the young son said to his father, "Long live Jesus Christ." His father replied, "Long live Jesus Christ" and heard his son shot to death.

May 7, 1938

NORTH AMERICAN COLLEGE
Via Dell' Umilta 30

Dear Everybody,

This is the fifth consecutive day that I have stayed indoors to avoid being one of the rabble welcoming Hitler. A fellow can hardly walk out on the street without running into a parade, a demonstration, or a function staged by the government. And I don't care to appear even in a crowd that is cheering for that dressed-up Charlie Chaplin (did you know that all the films made by Charlie Chaplin are banned in Germany because that silly mustache Chaplin wears looks so much like Hitler's). A number of the fellows have seen him accidentally as his party was going to attend some function. They say he looks much more intelligent than his pictures would lead one to believe. He received a tremendous welcome, but if one has seen a really excited Italian crowd he would know that the people did not give him a fervent welcome. There was cheering, but none of the delirium that usually attends the demonstration of an Italian crowd. No matter how much they try to cloak it, the people don't forget that they were fighting against Germany in the World War and that they took a couple of very bad defeats at the hands of the Austrians and Germans. Furthermore, the people are definitely "griped" at the huge outlay of money for his welcome. So whenever Hitler and Mussolini appear, they get a hand, but everybody knows that it is for Mussolini; the first time that Hitler rode into Rome he was accompanied by the King — Mussolini was not with him — and all the people yelled the old, familiar, "Duce, Duce." There was no individual yelling for Hitler. [1]

I have to admire the superb theatrical style of these Italians; they really know how to lay it on thick. When Hitler came they let him know that he was entering "the sacred soil of ancient Rome" and not just another big city. He came in by the gate at St. Paul's (we were there last summer) and the governor of Rome, old Piero Colonna, the head of the Colonna family that bossed things in Rome from the eleventh century was there to meet him. Colonna is the governor of Rome and was dressed in his medieval outfit; beside him were representatives from all the old sections of the city (Rome was formerly divided into sections) dressed in the ancient uniforms and wearing the colors of their section. Their uniforms were designed by Michelangelo. They must have just knocked the German's eye out because they say he was almost bowled over by the sight. Then he was accompanied by the King's bodyguard of cavalry who are even more richly uniformed than the King's guard in London. [2]

As I am writing this now an air review is going on just over my head. We are very near the center of the city, and it seems to me that every airplane in Italy is going over the college. Actually they are flying so low that they are rattling the windows. Italy has not the largest air force in the world; but they do hold most of the speed records, and they love to show off in colorful formations.

Just what old political-adviser Phil predicted in the last letter (about Muss using this German alliance to panic England and the rest of Europe into his lap) is really coming true in a hurry. Already they are saying that Hitler is trying to make the alliance closer, seeing that Mussolini right now holds the balance of power in Europe and that if he swings over to France and England thenhe has Germany at his mercy. He certainly has jockeyed them into the right position. I hope he rubs this system of German militarism off the face of the map; just a look at some of their big shots gives me a distinct itch to unlimber a good right to the jaw. They are the haughtiest, proudest-looking set I have ever had the pleasure of despising. There is just as much difference between the Italian and German temperaments as there is between an Irishman and a Chinaman.

The cadet corps looks in good shape — but not as good as the corps in 1932, or whenever I was there. Our companies were larger and looked more impressive than these chipped off squads. But they are o.k.

Another rumor is going the rounds that perhaps next year we will be in a hotel in Rome. They say that attempts are being made to hire a whole hotel, a small one. That will certainly be some stuff, a seminary in a hotel!

They never did have a rigorous system of discipline here, but I don't know what things would be like if we moved to a hotel. Or maybe we will all land out in the park — which seems to be happening to the German College unless somebody comes to their aid. The German College really got caught between the devil and the deep sea. Hitler's government sent word that they must wear swastikas on their arms and that they must be on the welcoming committee to meet Hitler. Then the Vatican sent word to them that they were forbidden to attend any ceremony at which Hitler would be present. Of course, they obeyed the Vatican; but the German government told them that if they didn't appear at the welcome that they couldn't have their passports stamped — which means that they can get absolutely no money out of Germany. So the poor devils are left holding the bag. The Pope will probably have to dig up some shekels for them somehow. By the way, did you hear that the Pope, at an audience at Castelgandolfo, took an open crack at the Nazis and criticized the people for "neglecting the Church"? The other day one of our fellows met the American Consul General and he said that the diplomatic service was certainly admiring the clever battle that the Pope is fighting. As a further protest against Hitler, he shut up the Vatican Museum and the Vatican Palace. [3] That's a tough break for the German visitors because the Vatican Museum is one of the real sights in Rome.

Love,

Phil

Comments: Letter of May 7, 1938

(1) On the whole, Hitler's visit to Rome was not a success, that is, it did not impress the Italian people. The difference in the temperaments of the Germans and Italians was evident in the behavior of the Germans at the cultural events, as the concerts. The Fascists had arranged to have the best singers in Italy sing at a special opera performance and the tepid applause of the German guests infuriated the Italian stars, so accustomed to a delirious reception by the audience. In fact, it was said that at the first intermission in the opera, the Italian cast was so furious that they threatened not to go on stage for the next act. Of course, the Fascists took care that they did.

(2)   The Italian love of history and their pride in the past was a new experience for the Germans. The Germans came to impress the Italians by their force of arms, and the Italians responded in a very impressive show of culture, which caught the Germans completely off guard.

(3)   The visit raised the esteem and pride of the Italians in the Church and the Pope. Pius XI carried out a very dignified but effective campaign against the Nazis. Of course, eventually he was forced to allow the German seminarians to attend the parade for Hitler, but he made his point of disapproval for Nazism very public and impressive. The Pope was especially conscious of the fact that the Church was obliged to demonstrate strongly their total opposition to Nazism, particularly because Cardinal Innitzer of Austria had mistakenly not condemned them when Austria was taken over.

There was eventually also the report that Pius XI had prepared, just before he died, another excoriating condemnation of Nazism, and that he died when at the point of signing it.

May 29, 1938

NORTH AMERICAN COLLEGE
Via Dell' Umilta 30

Dear Everybody,

The enclosed editorial you sent (about the Fascist press and its opposition to the Pope's attitude toward Germany) reminded me of an audience that the Pope gave to a delegation of Germans from Bavaria. He spoke for about twenty-five minutes in German to them and they way that they were so affected that they almost flooded the papal villa with their tears. Everybody in the audience chamber was boo-hooing except the Pope; he asked for their prayers, told them that he prays for Germany every morning and evening, etc. I still can't entirely understand the Italian resentment of the Pope's stand against Hitler. They certainly couldn't have expected the Pope to welcome him and no one denies that the Italians do not like the Germans as a people. [1]

The appointments for the new priests in the archdiocese raised quite a stir around here. Two of the three newly ordained men from our diocese have been sent to Washington, one to St. Patrick's and one to Immaculate Conception. Father Cartwright sent a note of welcome cablegram) to his new assistant who is a good fellow but has not too much push, I think. But he is a good worker and will get along well.

Love,

Phil

Comments: Letter of May 29, 1938

(1)   The editorial in the Fascist press certainly did not represent the popular opinion of the Italians in regard to the Pope's opposition to Hitler. Of course, it was expected that the Fascist press would be loyal to the Fascist political program.

June 27, 1938

NORTH AMERICAN COLLEGE
Via Dell' Umilta 30

Dear Everybody,

At last the fruitcake arrived. As usual it was very cordially received; by this time I think Mom is the most popular person on the corridor. In fact if I were to give the list of fellows commending and thanking you it would take up the rest of the page. Without a doubt, the fruitcakes I have been sent are the best I have tasted — including all the other types of pastry that have arrived for fellows from the U.S. The virtue of fruitcake is that it improves on the way over. A few more sessions at eating fruitcake in my room and we shall be able to cut up the rug in slices and eat it; everybody seems to drop at least five raisins on the rug and then trample them in. A thousand thanks for the box. In the future you need not bother to send chocolate nor any hair shampoo; I have plenty to last me for quite a time. Strangely enough the least expensive object for the customs duty is the most important, the cake. I forgot to tell you that we now have a small store in the college, run by the students, that sells chocolate, shaving cream, etc. The chocolate candy is made by Trappists who have a monastery just outside the city, not far from our villa. It's good chocolate. We also have Coca Cola in the store! A storekeeper in the little village at Castelgandolfo told our storekeeper that during the summer he sold something like twelve thousand bottles of Coca Cola (mostly to American tourists); he made over a lira on a bottle. A few more years at that and he will be able to buy the papal villa.

The student store is quite an institution. It is situated in a room called the poop-deck. The poop-deck is a strange place; to enter the room one must go up about five steps and almost bend himself double to get through the door. But once a fellow gets in, he can never hope to get out within a half an hour — all of which is good for the cash register. The present storekeeper is very enterprising. His latest specialty is hot dog sandwiches; during the summer he advertised ice cream made from the milk of the papal cows. I believe there was an indulgence granted to everyone eating a box of it. The only drawback is that the store is not needed this year. The food has improved tremendously ever since they allowed the recent addition to the faculty to look after the kitchen. Sometimes the fellow gets up at five in the morning and hustles over to market to see that we get the best type of meat and vegetables. The meals now are actually enjoyable.

The rumor here declares that the Rector of the graduate school or house of studies is to be made a Bishop very shortly. His name is Hurley, from Cleveland. He was secretary to Archbishop Mooney when he was apostolic delegate to Japan and has been connected with the Vatican for about fifteen years. So he is due for a bishopric. According to the rumor he is to be made Bishop of Youngstown. Another very faint rumor says that our Rector will be sent back soon as Bishop of something or other. And Archbishop Mooney is slated for New York. [1]

The Rector of the English College is to be made an Archbishop and sent back to England as apostolic delegate. Our Rector is to be one of his consecrators. Just before and after the consecration there will be about a thousand fellows asking permissions — the Rector is always in a good mood when he is given a chance to parade his dignity.

Love,

Phil

P.S. I am sending home a small copy of the Sistine Madonna; I hope it will arrive before Christmas. The other affair will come much later.

Comments: Letter of June 27, 1938

(1)   The rumors about appointments to dioceses in the United States were all wrong. Hurley was made the Bishop of St. Augustine, Florida, Archbishop Mooney was made the Archbishop of Detroit and Bishop Hayes, the Rector, was eventually made the Bishop of Davenport.

July 20, 1938

NORTH AMERICAN COLLEGE
Via Dell' Umilta 30

Dear Everybody,

We are right now in the midst of a whale of a mess. Examinations are now on, and this place is a real mad house. The weather is very hot, the fleas almost infinite in number, the new men get sick from study and worry (almost everyone gets at least a bit of dysentery before the exams), the natives are noisier than ever — and to crown it all, we are to have another apostolic visitor to come around and give us another third degree. From all this you can rather guess that life is a bit disturbed. I had my exam in moral theology and did well. I didn't go around to find my marks, but I know that I did well.

The news about the new apostolic visitor caused a sensation. This is the first time in the history of the college that we have had two such visits in less than a year. The story goes the rounds that the first visitors gave us a very good report, were very well pleased with the college; but the secretary of the Congregation in charge of this work had his own ideas about what sort of an organization was functioning at our place, and he put a bug in the Pope's ear who ordered another grand jury investigation. [1] So far, the good holy priest has not arrived to start his work. But two Dominicans arrived a few days ago to visit a student in the house, and the doorkeeper thought that they were the apostolic visitors and rang for the Rector. When the Rector came down and discovered the error, he almost blew the head off the doorkeeper.

We just had an electrician do a piece of work that I consider a real masterpiece. In the college, there are two distinct electrical systems — one for the night lights in the corridors that are lighted all night, and one for the lights in the rooms that are on during the day. Something happened to the night lights, so they called for the electrician, a queer-looking duck who goes around in golf togs. He came, couldn't find the trouble but got a brilliant idea. He hooked the night lights onto the day light system, so the night lights are on all day and are off at night. It's the stupidest sight I have ever seen — corridor lights burning all day and off all night. But I still think that the Italian plumber who fixed the water pipe without turning off the water was even better than the electrician. This is a country of extraordinary genius.

As you know, we have a summer villa, and it is customary for the newly ordained priests to go out there sometime in May and study for the rest of the term amid good surroundings. They have started the practice of giving the keeper of the villa and his wife and helpers (who are very good cooks and maids) a little treat. They usually send them to the opera, so they did it again this year, sending them to the first opera of the summer season that was opened in Rome amid very impressive circumstances. Mussolini and a number of bigwigs were present. Well, the first thing that the "help" did was to fix a cold supper for the fellows, put it away somewhere and forgot to tell them about it. But that wasn't the worst. They got into the opera, and had very good seats — were within about twenty feet of Mussolini. But these country people weren't accustomed to all these uniforms and outfits and in the intermission the fellow from the villa ordered a general to buy him some ice cream, thinking that he was an usher!

Well, I must get back on the books again. I have but one more exam and will probably be up for it in about three days. It will probably be the toughest exam I shall have to take in my whole course — all about the Trinity, etc. But I know the stuff and have no fear at all. I have never yet been in a position in which I couldn't give some answer — even though we do have to speak in Latin.

Love,

Phil

Comments: Letter of July 20, 1938

(1)   An "apostolic visitor" was appointed by the Holy See to investigate the seminaries, principally in regard to their internal discipline. The visitation comprised everybody, from the Rector to the students in the lowest grades, and included every aspect of the spiritual life of the seminary — times and locations for morning prayer, meditation and Mass; the system of spiritual direction; the rules in regard to recreation and especially conduct outside the seminary; the method of instilling reverence for the Holy Father and the Curia, etc. Of course, the seminarians were interviewed at random by the visitor, and this was a source of anxiety for the students and also for the Rector and Vice Rector.

I think that the main concern was to see that the pagan ideologies of Nazism and Fascism were not affecting the students. In addition, the Americans were considered to be a little bit too casual about discipline in the college.

July 23, 1938

NORTH AMERICAN COLLEGE
Via Dell' Umilta 30

Dear Everybody,

At last I am a free man for another year. Finished my exams in very good style. [1] If I did nothing else, I at least achieved a real ambition by correcting the Latin of one of my profs in the exam; a foolish thing to do perhaps, but it was worth it. He was a young fellow and inclined to ask very difficult questions if he thought you were doing well. I decided to set him back on his heels a bit, so when he flashed the next question I anticipated it a bit and ripped back the answer before he got the question out of his mouth. (This was just about at the end of the exam when I knew that I had certainly passed.) That unsettled him a bit, and in beginning his next question he messed up a word, so when I answered I gave him the correct form of the word he had bungled. He got the idea and smiled.

Our second apostolic visitor has arrived and started to go to work on the community. He gave the faculty an examination that must have even concerned their teeth; the story goes that he gave the Vice Rector a three-hour fourth degree. He even lives in the college at night, and this is the first time in many a moon that everything is as silent as a tomb in this place at night. I wish he were condemned to sleep in my room at night and listen to the low murmur of the neighbors' conversation that almost deafens one. Although he insists that this second visit is not a distinct one from the first, we all know that the explanation is a mere politeness and that he is really gunning for us. I don't know what he is here for; but if he came to check up on any serious abuses, he is just wasting his time. But then again his order (he is a Carmelite) may be having an unemployment problem and he just wants to give the boys a thing or two to do. Some of the questions he had been asking are really blue-ribboners; he asked one fellow if we ate fish on Fridays. The fellow said no, they bring it on the table but nobody will eat it. But the poor old fellow is getting all tuckered out; instead of sleeping in the college at night, he sneaks home. I suppose he can't stand the noisy neighborhood.

I have new neighbors. A new family has moved into the apartment house opposite me and has settled into their normal mode of living. The last family managed to make a good deal of noise by their own devices, but these people go them one better. Not satisfied with playing the radio all day and trying to keep a conversation going at the same time, these people brought along a whole flock of canaries to help them along in this sound production business. I wonder if they would think it an accident if they awoke some morning and found that their birdcage had dropped from the windowsill to the street seven stories below.

A fellow getting ordained this July (whom Dad and Mom met last year at the dock in Naples — but whom I am sure they do not remember) had a real encounter with the native mental capacity. He ordered thirteen hundred ordination cards — twelve hundred to be done in English and one hundred in German (he has relatives in Germany). Of course, the Italian printer did just what may have been expected — twelve hundred in German and one hundred in English, even though he knew the fellow was from the North American College. This fellow is a bit hotheaded, so he went over to the printer and told him that he wouldn't throw him out of his shop but that he would insist on punching him in the nose. These people have a real genius for getting things muddled. And that reminds me of the letter I tried to mail by air some two weeks ago to get home before Mom and Bill left. I took it to the fellow who weighs the mail and sells stamps here, and he couldn't tell me how much postage it would need, but said that he would take it over to the post office himself, mail it by air mail and then collect from me. Then he gave the letter to another fellow, the doorkeeper, and the doorkeeper took it over with some other mail and then mailed everything without putting any stamps at all on it. So, just when that letter will get through is more than I can say. I suppose that I shall be back in America before it arrives.

I am sending very shortly a movie film of the illumination of St. Peter's on Easter night. This copy I am sending is not mine and is to be forwarded as soon as is convenient to Mr. Hiester in Denver (the address will be enclosed in the package), Dad will remember Mrs. Hiester, the lady with whom we rode out to the papal audience and who had her son, recently ordained, with her. But if you want to make a copy of the film do it before you send the movie to Denver. I was to have a copy of the film made here in Italy but it is too expensive and slow. Unfortunately, the best technique was not used in taking the picture and some of the angle shots of the dome need an explanation but one can at least get an idea of the illumination. But please forward the film rather promptly.

I just received Mom's letter telling of the new plans of the government. Well, I hope it turns out all right for our interests — I can see what Dad will be doing this summer.

Love,

Phil

Comments: Letter of July 23, 1938

(1)   My account of the exams omitted a very important part of our preparation — I made a visit to the convent or chapel of Perpetual Adoration next to the Gregorian University and prayed fervently.

The chapel had many other students performing the same preparation. After the exam, I made a donation to one of the genteel beggars outside the University in thanksgiving.

(2)   As we had surmised, the second apostolic visitor made a more thorough examination of the Rector and Vice Rector than the students. The scuttlebutt reported that the visitor, after being welcomed by the Rector or Vice Rector said, "With whom do you wish to start your visitation?" The answer was, "With you. Please sit down."

(3)   My account of the loss of one of my letters to my brother Bill may also account for the lack of any letter to my folks about Easter. Holy Week and Easter were the spiritual centers of the whole year. I personally enjoyed tremendously the celebrations in St. Peter's of the Holy Week liturgies, especially the Easter Mass celebrated by the Pope with the blessing "Urbi et Orbi" (to the City and to the World) which attracted literally hundreds of thousands of people. The crowd extended from the Piazza of St. Peter to the Tiber River, a sea of devout people.

The attendance at the Holy Week events and Easter were very impressive also because of the fear of war. The people were serious and devout and the congregations were filled with uniformed men. The words of the Pope had a special significance about living the faith and the need for a spiritual renaissance in Europe and the world.

The Way of the Cross, performed in the Colosseum where so many Christians had been martyred was particularly significant in view of the Nazi persecution of Catholics in Germany and Austria. A moving figure at these religious ceremonies, especially in St. Peter's, was the figure of Cardinal Eugene Pacelli. He was always at prayer or recollected and deserved the name, "The Praying Cardinal." He was well prepared to take over the awesome duties of the Vicar of Christ after the death of Pius XI, which occurred early in 1939.

September 13, 1938

NORTH AMERICAN COLLEGE
VIA DELL' UMILTA 30

Dear Everybody,

The last time I committed myself to any lengthy statement was just after I made the visit to the chateau; so now to pick up the thread, or shred, of thought. But before I do that, I really wish to express a million sentiments of gratitude for this past summer's experience; I realize fully that it is the generosity of Dad and Mom that made it possible and that otherwise I would be subjected to a summer of Italian heat and cooking (by far the greater evil of the two). The only method I have of showing my appreciation, besides the statement of thanks, is by getting the most out of the opportunities afforded — and you can be sure that I do that. I was sorry that I couldn't make it to Lourdes (we had to give that up owing to lack of time) because it really is the most inspiring and beneficial place, both for one's self and for the family, because the Blessed Mother is certainly not stopped by the distance of an ocean in her disposition of favors. Personally, I hardly ever expect to spend a more delightful vacation (though I was not up to snuff on some occasions) and will always look back on this year's little whirl with a great deal of profit.

Before I start a travelogue again I simply wish to insert the attitude of the fellows at the English College, whom we visited today (each year we pay them a whole day's visit), — they are all positive that a war is coming shortly, that it will be destructive of almost all European culture, and that nothing can be done but to stop it. [1] I have never heard such deep and resigned pessimism in my life. And a German fellow from our college who has just arrived from a stay in Germany says that everybody there expects a war before Christmas. A whole continent living without any hope — except for the faint glimmer that America will furnish enough cannon and airplanes to ward off complete destruction. Whenever a number of seminarians get together over here the conversation always turns to politics and in the course of an afternoon the wildest concoction of stories and tales are unfolded. But before I finish with the English and things English, I must tell you about their language; a window is a "sight", a swimming pool is always a "tank", a cigarette is a "gasper", one does not borrow a cigarette but "drives" a cigarette, etc. But the Englishman who simply stopped us cold was the one who asked Henry Cosgrove if he had ever done a bit of "bricking". We looked startled, gawked a bit, then asked for a showdown; we found that "bricking" means digging around and excavating old ruins. "Why dash it all," seems to be the favorite expression of disgust.

In general, they are real gentlemen, poor conversationalists, as stiff as funeral directors. We arrived there at about ten in the morning (their villa is across the lake from Castelgandolfo), were given wine and little cakes, taken for a walk through their small garden up to see the "tank" where a few of them were waiting to give a very putrid exhibition of swimming and diving — whereupon some of our fellows stripped off and showed them how it should be done. (They all think that every American by virtue of his nationality is a perfect athlete.) Then we ate; in fact, we gutted ourselves. Then after dinner, we had black coffee and liqueur, which left me out in the cold because of my pledge. They had a few musical numbers, their rector singing two songs; he had a good voice but now he puffs like a seal coming to the surface. After that, we wandered up to the homemade golf course they have, sat around and made dirty cracks at the few courageous souls who tried to play the course. Then we returned for the inevitable tea, talked for an hour, then walked home. I was surprised to find them so interested in American sports, and so full of political talk, and when pumped about the Duke of Windsor and his duchess they really became fluent. So much for the visit.

And now for the rest of the trip. Our last stop in France was Nice. Cosgrove left the day before I did because he was supposed to report back a day ahead of me. We couldn't go to Rome in one day because of the abominable train service. Eye hath not seen nor ear heard how impossibly slow the train can go along the Riviera coast. They stop at every station on the map and a few more; Henry insists that the engineer of the train makes up the schedule as he goes along. To go from Nice to Pisa (we stayed in Pisa overnight before going to Rome) requires eleven hours although it is only the distance between Washington and New York. The ride proved rather interesting because I happened to be in a compartment with Italian officers and newspaper men coming from Spain, and I got some interesting information (the Italian troops are not being used now for the heavy fighting, according to them).

Pisa is a ghost town. It has a group of splendid buildings, a cathedral, baptistery, and bell-tower, that were done in the eleventh century, but the rest of the town has vanished. It is still a good-sized city but nothing of the importance it had a thousand years ago remains today. I saw the cathedral and the famous leaning tower for the first time by the light of the moon (helped by artificial lighting too). Everything is softened and purified by the moonlight; the grime, the cracks, the sags are not evident at night, and somehow it takes on a very spiritual appearance. Besides, the whole group stands in the middle of a large lawn without a tree or shrub to distract the eye from the central attraction. There is something splendidly solitary and strong about the great cathedral alone in its setting, the sole remnant of a once great city and a monument to its former glory. It is more than another large cathedral because it was built at a time when the rest of Europe was wandering about in animal skins and done so perfectly that later and more sophisticated ages have used it as a model. The façade is made of rows of columns; but instead of being monotonous, it is very pleasing owing to the ingenuity of the architect. The arches between the columns and the length of the columns are not exactly the same — just enough to prevent the eye from getting tired, although they appear to be the same length and distance. The famous leaning tower of Pisa was intended as the campanile, or bell tower. It leans so much that one instinctively says, "If I didn't see it I wouldn't believe it." As it was being built the foundation slipped; they made one effort to straighten the building then continued to build the tower at an angle. Although a good view is promised any who climbs the tower, I thought that I had seen enough scenery for one summer. There is a very famous cemetery attached to the cathedral, most of its beauty lies in the delicious sentimentality associated with some of the great men buried there. I stayed in Pisa for the night and left the next morning at nine-thirty for Rome. I was much surprised by some of the men in Pisa, tall and broad. As in some other Italian cities where there has not been much influx of population, there seems to be a distinctive type.

I can assure you my arrival in Rome again was anything but thrilling. It became hot, sticky, smelly, noisy, crowded. The tracks were being repaired so the abominable train service became even more abominable. And to create the climax, there was as usual a supposedly popular demonstration going on for some foreign embassy. I think some stooge from Manchukuo was in town and the Duce was engaged in the old game of pulling the wool over his eyes and assuring him that Italy was always his good friend. (That reminds me that the fellows around here are saying that so much wool is being pulled over the Rector's eyes that they are going to have a public shearing this fall — which is true except that I think the Rector knows that the wool is supposed to be pulled over his eyes and tolerates it as long as it doesn't cause any difficulty.) But, getting back to this parade business — it happens to be just that — it ceases to impress me after I have seen the same decorations used four times for four different persons and all with the assurance that it is a great spontaneous public demonstration. After the third time, one begins to get suspicious that this is just a big, paid show. [2] Just what intimate bond of friendship binds Manchukuo to Italy, when ninety percent of the population doesn't even know what or where Manchukuo is, is more than I know. And that reminds me that the people are still sore at Hitler around here because he didn't give them a big hand even after they cheered for him; Mussolini always appears on balconies as long as there are enough to give him a sizable audience, but Hitler just gave them one appearance and continued his poker game.

When I can borrow more paper I shall give you a more detailed account of some of the things we saw after leaving you.

Love,

Phil

Comments: Letter of September 13, 1938

(1) The resigned attitude of the English seminarians was a perfect example of their philosophy of "muddling through" a situation. Even when there seems to be no hope, they continue to live and survive, a trait which helped to enable them to survive the *blitzkrieg* during the war.

(2) The monotony of the performance put on by Mussolini and the Fascists finally became boring. It also became frightening to the Italians who saw the terrible consequences of Mussolini's desire to

profit from the coming war and the alliance with Germany. One Italian monsignor put it very succinctly after asking me what I thought of Mussolini. He said, with a characteristic gesture, "Superbia semper ascendit." (Pride always grows or increases.) He was totally disgusted.

September 15, 1938

NORTH AMERICAN COLLEGE
Via Dell' Umilta 30

Dear Everybody,

Again, we can settle down for the rest of our stay in Rome. This past war scare was a real one. All the fellows in the college were told to get their passports ready (I had mine renewed in July), and we were at least getting prepared mentally for sleeping in hammocks aboard a battleship; the Vice Rector had stated definitely that we would go if Italy were involved. But Mussolini went to see Hitler instead of going to war, so here we are. But the French College had already gone home — whether to enlist or to find a cozy hiding place, I don't know. Some of the fellows have just arrived back from trips through France, and they reported that the people were no little excited; suicide was a very popular diversion, especially among recently engaged couples, and one whole family decided that it was better to fall (though uninvited and under poor circumstances) into the hands of the Lord than into the hands of the Germans.

When Mussolini returned to Rome, after he had helped to squelch Hitler's war plans, he was given a tremendous reception by the people. He was almost mobbed all along the route from the station to the Piazza Venetia, and they say that the British flag was actually flown from the Duce's palace while the crowd cheered Chamberlain. [1] Next to the Day of Judgment, that was the most unlooked for event in Italy. People are still wondering what sweet words Mussolini said to Hitler when he met him at the German border and rode with him to the conference at Munich; [2] the general rumor is that Muss stuck out his big jaw and popped a few ideas about the necessity of peace into Hitler's head. There seems to be no doubt in the world now about who is the stronger man in this Rome–Berlin axis. Hitler learned his theory from Mussolini, and it looks as though he still has a few lessons left to learn in the book. The message that Roosevelt went to both Hitler and Mussolini during the scare received very favorable comment in all the countries of Europe; it was read over the radio from almost all the broadcasting companies in Europe.

Our three diocesans arrived in Naples aboard the Saturnia, were made to land and then given railroad tickets (first class) to Trieste. They came to Rome, called the villa by phone, and we told them to use the tickets (it will be the last time that they will have first class tickets in Europe). After the feast will come the execution.

Yesterday the English College came on its formal, annual visit to the villa. Despite rainy weather, we had a very nice time; in fact, we do such a good job of entertaining that I hardly recognize the place. After dinner we had coffee and a bit of good apricot "liqueur"; that always produces the correct frame of mind for a good impromptu entertainment. In fact, one fellow played a guitar solo without a guitar, which seems to me a feat that somewhat resembles the act of creation; he does it with his nose (I don't mean he makes the guitar with his nose, but imitates it with his nose). Then we had a movie that was far funnier than the producer ever dreamed it would be; it was Deanna Durbin in, "Mad About Music", and there was many a luscious crack about the English in it. Every time one of those happened it brought the house down, so after about two or three hours of that we began to forget about the Revolutionary War, Mrs. Simpson, and the war debt. The English were especially pleased to come over because they thereby evaded seventy English pilgrims to Rome who were due at the English villa. But unless my eyes deceived me, many an Englishman went home with an aching back; they all tried the swimming pool with its diving board, which has quite a spring in it. And it generally landed them right on their backs in the water.

The country air out here must be very healthy; despite the Italian food I am putting on a bit of weight (which I shall promptly lose as soon as we go to the city).

Love,

Phil

Comments: Letter of September 15, 1938

(1)   This account refers to the relief and feelings after the sell-out by Chamberlain, Prime Minister of England, to Hitler. Chamberlain accepted the conquests of Hitler with his famous "assurance" that there would be no more war. Mussolini was seen as a participant in that agreement, and the Italians were delighted that they were not being called to war.

(2)   The dreadful significance of the famous Munich Conference with its consequent encouragement to Hitler's drive to take over Europe was not recognized in Italy by the people. Although they welcomed the fruits of the alliance with Germany, they abhorred the idea of a war, especially with the French. Deep down in their being was the idea that the French were cousins, and they had no desire to fight them. As a matter of history, the King of Italy was the head of the house of Savoy which years ago included a part of France, and the language of Savoy had French and Italian elements.

There was also a rumor that at least one Italian general resigned his commission when Italy entered the war because he refused to engage in a war against the "French cousins."

September 21, 1938

NORTH AMERICAN COLLEGE
VIA DELL' UMILTA 30

Dear Everybody,

Despite the fact that we live amid the most placid surroundings, the college is on edge. The Rector is as nervous as a hen in a thunderstorm about the Czechoslovakian crisis. The weirdest sight in years occurred a few nights ago when Hitler gave his last speech at the Nuremberg Congress. The Rector and his visitor, a monsignor, wanted to hear the speech. The Rector did not bring his radio to the villa, but there is a community radio in a little building not far removed from the main building at the villa. It was raining tremendously, but the Rector was intent on hearing Hitler even though he doesn't understand a word of German. He asked a student who speaks German perfectly to go down and listen to the speech with them. So out into the rain struggled the valiant three. Meantime, parked cozily in their rooms, lying on their beds and smoking pipes while they lounged and listened to their private radios were the students who had very ingeniously smuggled out their radios. To cap the climax the Rector heard only a very small part of the speech — which did him absolutely no good — while the wiser students heard it all. The Rector is having a time for himself— the Fascists decide that his college must be torn down, have notified him that we can stay there only a year more; he can't decide where to build a new college nor does he know where he can get the money; [1] apparently, the alumni association are beginning to badger him with suggestions; now the Sacred Congregation added their little bit by plaguing him with two formal visitations within six months, then sends him a list of regulations for summer trips which he can't enforce; next comes the war threat. Who can blame the man for forgetting yesterday that it was the anniversary of his ordination, then refusing to believe the students when he was told that it was?

By the way, you needn't fear about me if war breaks out. If Italy is involved I guarantee that I shall act very decisively. I have seen quite a bit of Europe in two years, have no desire to experience any air raids, would love to sit down to good American breakfasts again. The first American battleship that has an extra bunk will be graced by my presence, and there shall be "no moaning of the bar when I put out to sea." The shopkeepers of Italy will just have to worry along without my support.

A few seminarians from Innsbruck were visiting Rome a few days ago, and they seem to think that war is assured. The Czechs, they say, hate everything German and are as bull-headed as the Germans. One of their students, a Czech, was slapped in the cooler for six months by the Nazis because of a letter he wrote home — needless to say the government there considers everybody's correspondence just a big family affair in which everything is common property.

Another amusing incident turned up in regard to Mussolini's new campaign against the Jews. They discovered that eleven Jews in the army were generals!! Now they are starting to whip up the people against the Czechs. [2] Until a few weeks ago the ordinary Italian had probably never heard of Czechoslovakia; but when Mussolini gave his speech in Trieste a few days ago, Czechoslovakia was booed tremendously (mainly by stooges). If all this business were not so tragic, it would make the world's funniest comedy. The situation will be this: Some poor little Italian in Sicily who wants to do nothing but eat spaghetti and drink wine will be drafted to fight with Germany (which he despises and which he was always taught to dislike until a few months ago) against a country of which he has never heard.

Love,

Phil

Comments: Letter of September 21, 1938

(1)   The problems of the Rector were caused mainly by the demands of the Italian government for the Americans to build a new seminary. We thought that this was a means to get American dollars. During the war, the Italians actually used the building to house war orphans and refugees.

(2)   The callous manner in which Hitler caused the "sudeten crisis" (accusing the Czechs of persecuting their citizens of German blood living near the Czech border) further convinced us that Hitler would create a war. Mussolini acted like a supine puppet — the ordinary Italians had great respect for the Czechs. The mentality of the Nazis was shown in a conversation I had with a German youth of about twenty years; he said, "I cannot understand the Polish people. They are definitely inferior to us and they would profit by being under our domination." How can you deal with that?

September 27, 1938

NORTH AMERICAN COLLEGE
Via Dell' Umilta 30

Dear Everybody,

The Rector has gone again! [1] And again he sneaked out without being seen, even though we knew on what day he was leaving and we were standing outside the front door waiting and watching. But when he was Bishop of Helena, Montana, he was made an honorary chief of the Blackfoot Indians, and they must have taught him a few things. This time he made his escape by leaving through a side door, cutting across his private garden and meeting the college car at the gate to the villa. In his three years of service here, he has been back to the U.S. four times, I think; he has not stayed in the college more than six months at a stretch, and every time he comes back his little impromptu speech tries to convince the increasingly doubtful student body that Rome is a wonderful place. But the spiritual director's speech on his return from America was a masterpiece in that line; he had stayed in America, and especially New York (his home town), as long and longer than possible. In fact, they were contemplating putting the G-men on his trail to locate him when he finally decided to up-anchor and come back to Italy. Then the night he returned to the college, after he had been given a big hand, he rose and launched into a panegyric of Rome saying that it was a greater place than New York, etc. To prove just how much he meant it he went back to the States this summer and is still there.

This morning one of the local police came in to find out if any Czechs were in the college! The fellow whom we met in Paris, Catich (he was carrying an artist's sketching book in the American Express), is supposed to be in Czechoslovakia and the border is closed — he will probably get back to the college about 1940. [2] That reminds me of another fellow who suddenly found himself confronted with the necessity of changing from his cassock to civilian clothes (he was passing from Italy to some other country) while traveling in one of those motorcars (like we took into Siena). They are as private as a glass-enclosed telephone booth. After he had made the change he noticed that everyone, the conductor in particular, was staring at him, so he decided to check up. He made a hasty investigation of his clothing (he had changed into gray pants and a black mohair sweater) and found nothing out of place; even his fly was securely buttoned. But still the staring continued, so he decided to look into a mirror — and found that he had not taken his Roman collar off! Needless to say, he has become famous already. Then there is the story of two other fellows who went on a mountain climbing jaunt in the northern part of Italy and in crossing a mountain unknowingly crossed the border. They walked right into the arms of the border officials of the other country; and since they weren't carrying their passports, they were walked right into the hoosegow — no further questions asked and no explanations accepted. When they finally forced an explanation on them and phoned for the passports, they were still in a mess because they had no visa for entering the country. And the three fellows coming from our diocese will have a few stories to tell because the Vice Rector refused to allow any of us to go down and meet them at Naples. [3] His reason, of all things, was that they wouldn't need anyone to help them through to Rome! You who have landed in Naples not knowing a word of Italian will know how true that is. I shall send them a letter with complete instructions. I am sorry because I wanted to go down and see that silversmith.

Today the Scotch came to visit us, and we really had a very nice day. Actually they are all Irish, just two or three are genuine Scotchmen, but they all speak with a burr that I find difficult to understand.

The international situation doesn't seem to be so tense now. There is a strange but true story going the rounds about Italy's move to conciliate the Austrians living in the northern part of Italy. They are afraid that Germany will grab a piece up there, so recently the Italian government awarded pensions to all the Austrian soldiers (now living in Italy) who had fought in the World War against Italy. That's certainly bending over backwards to please everybody.

Love,

Phil

Comments: Letter of September 27, 1938

(1)   Undoubtedly, the Rector had gone to the U.S. to consult with the Board of the College to determine the future course of action. The Rector and all the prominent Catholic clergy were total peace advocates. The Rector was quoted as saying that he was convinced that there would not be a war, and Monsignor Sheen, on returning to the U.S., also said, "There will not be any war because the people will not stand for it."

(2)   The farce that the Czechs were now enemies of Italy was proven by their search for our student-artist, Maxie Catich (a Czech-American) who was totally disinterested in everything except art.

229

(3)   The decision to prevent us from guiding the newly arrived seminarians from Baltimore was founded on the fear of the government seizing an American simply to create a political problem. This later occurred when a couple of students were arrested at the border in north Italy. Of course, as soon as the authorities secured some bad press publicity against us, they released the students.

October 8, 1938

NORTH AMERICAN COLLEGE
Via Dell' Umilta 30

Dear Everybody,

Now that almost everybody has returned and things have settled down the stories about trips are starting to float around. Here is a typical one: four fellows traveling in Germany were suspected by the authorities of carrying guns and revolutionary literature, and were searched very thoroughly. (They were suspected, I think, because two of them speak German perfectly.) At the end of the investigation they pointed out the obvious fact that they had been unjustly detained and robbed of an opportunity of seeing the city, and demanded that something be done about it. The authorities put them in a police car, toured them around, got free entrance for them in any place they wanted to visit, took their bags to the station for them, and delivered them to the train. Not bad. A funnier story is one of two fellows trying to steal a ride in a gondola in Venice. They had been thoroughly cheated by a gondolier during the day (you can appreciate that) and decided to have a free ride at night. There were two gondolas tied up outside the hotel, so they got in one and proceeded to push along. Just after they started, the gondolier (who had been sleeping under the little roof) awoke and proceeded to act just as any Italian would in such a situation. They tried to explain that they weren't trying to steal his gondola, just trying to take a ride. The explanation didn't satisfy him at all, so finally they each gave him an American cigarette, and the whole affair was settled. Two other fellows were arrested for speeding in Florence (they had hired a car); as the cop was giving them a ticket, another fellow from the college sneaked up and took a picture of all three. When the cop found out that his picture had been taken he tore up the ticket on the promise that he would be given a copy of the snapshot.

Did I tell you that I returned to Rome the same day that Mussolini returned from Germany? As a matter of fact, we both returned by way of Florence, and I took the train ahead of his out of Florence. What a mess that was. You remember that jam we got into at Milan (the day that about forty thousand were on each car and Dad and I got separated from Mom); well that was nothing compared to the mess caused by the approach of Mussolini back from his triumphal entrance into Germany. What caused the tie-up was the elaborate protection system. They had troops stationed at close intervals from Florence to a point twenty miles outside the city, and inside the station there were uniforms over everything. As we approached Rome things got steadily more involved. There were troops stationed at every little town or railroad stop all the way to Rome. The only way anyone could get a crack at the Duce would be to ride overhead in an airplane. Rome, of course, was on a spree of jitters; you would have thought that Mussolini was coming back with Germany in his pocket. [1]

The four fellows who have just arrived from our archdiocese received a warm welcome in Naples. They were trying to sneak in American cigarettes and got caught. One fellow had forty-six packs on his person; they were supposed to be fined heavily but fortunately an official intervened and let them off with light fines because he knew that they were students and did not intend to sell the cigarettes. Otherwise, they may have landed in the clinker instead of the North American College. [2] Everything went haywire (as Dad and Mom can understand); it required three and a half hours for them to get through the customs. There are now nine fellows from the archdiocese at the college; and strangely, I am the only one from Washington. One fellow, who went to Basselin and lives in Baltimore, is very homesick for Washington. There's no use telling him, but I can guarantee that it will be a long time before he sees anything in Europe to rival it.

It's too bad that we didn't have more time in Florence (when we were all there). Some of those galleries are almost unbelievable; the Pitti Palace, built as a rival of the Uffizi (which Mom visited) is the most beautiful I have seen. Actually, the marble tables are so beautiful that they take one's attention away from the pictures. I shall always remember Florence as the place where I took my first extended bicycle ride. We both wanted to see (I was with a friend) a park shortly outside the city where Dante took his last look of Florence as he went into voluntary exile. The other fellow persuaded me to ride a bike; it was night and there was no traffic. In the first place we had an awful time hiring bicycles. The first shop we went to told us very blandly that they didn't have any bikes at the time but that if we came around next springtime they could probably rent us two. At last we got hold of two and started out. I did very well, I think; I didn't run over anything or anyone, didn't fall once, and got to the park without breaking any blood vessels. We passed one cop who told us to ride in single file, not abreast. I felt like telling him that if he knew what a time I was having just keeping astride the bike, he wouldn't demand anything of me.

I didn't return alone through Europe. In Paris I met plenty of fellows (there were at least sixteen from the college in the city). I traveled from Paris to Rome with a classmate; in Florence I met twenty students from the college in that large piazza (where they have the music and the tables in the street). (3) I arrived in Paris in time to say goodbye to two fellows who were leaving for the States because of ill health. As a matter of fact, they spent their time in Paris in bed because of the rainy weather. It is a distinct advantage to travel with just one or two fellows (or alone). Otherwise you get in each other's way.

Many thanks for the check. Even after paying for the pictures I sent you, I returned to Rome with over thirty dollars in my pocket. Good financing even if I do say it myself. I found that I had traveled (after leaving you) about three thousand miles, counting side trips, and had lived very comfortably for five weeks — even gaining weight — for about $150. And it was the first time I had traveled in those places. And things would have been much cheaper if I hadn't crossed two channels.

Love,

Phil

Comments: Letter of October 8, 1938

(1)   The extreme measures taken by the Fascists to protect Mussolini after his trip to Germany showed their fear of an assassination. Many Italians who had supported his domestic policies were totally against

his alliance with the Nazis.

(2)   The predicament of our seminarians in Naples justified our fears that they would encounter problems. Actually, we did not strongly blame the Rector for not allowing us to go to Naples because of the quixotic nature of the government, which occasionally seemed intent on causing bad publicity for Americans by grabbing a student on a false charge. The Rector was so worried about the safety of the students that he adtually mailed some funds by way of the American Express office to a group of students in Paris, saying, "That group was on a starvation trip. I don't know how they expected to live on the few dollars they had."

(3)   Despite all the political problems the touring students always achieved their primary goal of visiting the churches and important shrines and institutions in Europe. The policy of the College was always to allow the students the opportunity to profit from the culture of Europe.

October 11, 1938

NORTH AMERICAN COLLEGE
VIA DELL' UMILTA 30

Dear Everybody,
       The three new fellows from Baltimore arrived a few days ago. One looks as though he had swum across the Atlantic; already some are betting that his health will break before Christmas. All are excellent fellows but need a bit of standing on their own feet — which they will get. They seem to be resourceful; before coming back to the college they made a little trip to Florence and Venice, even though they didn't know any Italian.
       I am getting sicker of the international situation every day. I have been trying to send just a little plaque to the French family who were so kind to me this summer, and it is almost impossible to get it through the border. Just why it can't be sent is more than I can find out, and of course

the Italian officials are particularly brilliant at such a time. I must get some sort of a permit at a bank in Rome to allow me to send it, but the bank officials don't know how to make it out. I shall probably end by hanging the thing on my wall.

Tomorrow our class is to go to Frascati for a class "bum run". You should remember Frascati, the lovely little village that has the lovelier wine. These class "bum runs" end up with half the fellows sick from over-eating and all of them hoarse from over-singing. But everything in the college is very peaceful.

The rest of the vacation will be spent in meeting the new men. I feel rather sorry for one young, but tremendous Polish fellow from around Scranton. He is built like a wrestler but is very gentle, with a very soft voice. And now he has gotten a good, strong case of homesickness; they say every time he starts to write a letter home he breaks down. All that will clear up when he must go to the Greg University and get completely bewildered by the Latin lectures.

But the fellows at the German College think that this last incident is by no means the end. We shall see. During the recent scare all the people in the street thought that fighting had already begun but that the government was keeping it quiet. Even the doorkeeper at the college was called to service in the army. [1] Everything seems more settled now, but the wailings and groaning of Italian merchants are really tremendous.

We have about 800 members of the college alumni association to contact for subscriptions to our magazine. I hope the grace and mercy of the Lord moves them to respond promptly and in the affirmative. Otherwise we shall be left holding the proverbial bag.

Love,

Phil

Comments: Letter of October 11, 1938

(1)   The war jitters continued and had their repercussions among the workers at the College. As the workers were called into the Army, they were given a gift and then they would appear at a dinner dressed in their uniform and thank the College. Generally, they would speak only a few words, but one gave a short speech saying that

God supported the Italian cause. He didn't give any proofs. The students always empathized with them and gave them a hearty burst of applause. It was always an emotional scene and brought the impending war close to us.

October 13, 1938

NORTH AMERICAN COLLEGE
VIA DELL' UMILTA 30

Dear Everybody,

Someone in the student body, or the faculty, decided recently to do something about a few poor people who hang around the college asking for alms. (Curious thing is that the students of other colleges are never troubled by beggars, but as soon as the North American College uniform comes into sight there is great cause for rejoicing.) Anyway, a St. Vincent de Paul Society was formed to take care of them. The proposition was to use all the spare food from the tables, and to have contributions of small amounts from the fellows. Everything was prepared; a room was fixed up on the first floor to receive the poor and dish out the food, and we certainly had plenty of poor people lined up. But a little unforeseen difficulty occurred that should have been anticipated — there wasn't any food left over from the table. The bank of the organization went bankrupt after the first meal. The only thing that issued forth from the kitchen of the college was a shred of meat not thicker than a stamp and hardly any longer in length. Instead of appeasing the hunger of the poor that little bit would have caused a riot over its disposition. Just how the committee met the crisis is more than I can say, but to all appearances it looks as though the St. Vincent de Paul Society is getting a rabbit punch on the pate before it even gets going.

An event of cosmic importance happened today at the Greg. One of our profs in moral theology, a typical German who even coughs at a regular, appointed time, didn't show up for class. After ten minutes they decided to investigate; he wasn't in his room, he wasn't in the library, he wasn't in the corridors. Finally somebody remembered that he always came down in the elevator. Sure enough, the elevator had gotten caught between floors, and there was our prof marooned safely in the elevator. For all I know he may be there yet; he hadn't been liberated by the time class was out — and from what I've noticed of Italian efficiency and workmanship, especially in matters of electricity, I wouldn't be surprised if he starves to death in the elevator. The class was rather interesting in its reaction; the English started the fireworks off with imitations of a barnyard. They had one fellow that could crow better than any rooster I have ever heard. But we have a farmer boy from way back in the sticks who must have learned to imitate animals before he could talk. He could do everything a cow could do but give milk. The contest ended when the Dean of Studies came in to find out what professor was teaching class in such a way.

Recently, I have been hanging pictures on the walls, not as decorations primarily, but to cover up the holes. I bought a print at the Rag Market that cost the huge sum of a cent and a half and decided to glue it on the wall. I borrowed some glue that was guaranteed to hold bricks together; it may have been good for that because it certainly did not do me any good. The picture stuck for two days; on the third day it fell — the glue had somehow pulled off two coats of paint, and there was the picture on the floor clinging to two coats of paint but with no wall to hold on to. I am afraid to use the stuff again for fear it will eat a hole into the wall.

The most interesting diversion this year is watching the reactions of the new men as they visit the big churches in Rome. A long time ago, I read a saying of Emerson that I have found to be tremendously true, "A man can travel the whole world and not find beauty if he does not carry it with him." I have noticed that a beautiful church or picture does more to reveal the mind of a fellow than an examination in studies. If he has not an inborn appreciation for beauty and refinement, he may as well have stayed home in Kankakee or Oshkosh; Europe will never do him any good. The acid test is to take a fellow down in the catacombs. If the only thing he gets out of it is a chill and an ache in the back, he may as well stay in his room for the rest of his course in Rome.

There is supposed to be a new decree out by the Sacred Congregation of Cardinals to the effect that no early ordinations (at least none before Christmas) will be tolerated any more. That used to be the reward for coming to Rome — early ordinations; lately, at our college, it has been made the reward for getting high marks. I don't know what they'll do about it; a number of fellows from our college are supposed to be ordained on December the eighth.

A new book has been going the rounds in Rome written by a clever Englishman who has been connected with the Vatican, or at least had access to all the great personages there. He has an interesting little story explaining why Archbishop Curley will never be cardinal. According to him, the Holy See does not want any more cardinals in the U.S. than it has at present for fear of their strength. Of course, it is a fact that Pope Leo XIII wrote an encyclical against what he called "Americanism" directed towards the American clergy criticizing them for the American way of doing things. [1] But it was Cardinal Gibbons who straightened him out on that point. And it was Archbishop Curley who resisted The Apostolic Delegate, Archbishop Fumasoni Biondi, when he wanted to make seminarians and priests wear the cassock as they wear it in Rome and Europe. And the present Pope actually forbade the assembly of all the bishops and cardinals at the annual N.C.W.C. Conference in Washington if one man was to be made the chairman of it. [2] Now they have a cardinal presiding over it for a few days at a time; then another man takes his turn, etc. The policy of the Holy See is to center all power in itself, even in administration, and prevent any one country from building up a self-governing policy. Lot of diplomacy in this business. These people are cardinals over here not simply because of their holiness.

There goes the bell for Cam walk.

Love,

Phil

Comments: Letter of October 13, 1938

(1)   "Americanism" referred to a feeling that the Church in the U.S. had its own special form and privileges. "Modernism" was a much more serious danger; it meant that Catholic doctrine could be understood by the elite in a different way in which the non-elite understood it. This error was firmly resisted in the U.S. despite the fears of some quarters in Rome that it had taken hold in the Church in the U.S.

(2)   Our scuttlebutt explanation of the opposition of Rome to the
        National Catholic Welfare Council was wrong. Rome did not like,
        for good historical reasons, the word "council" because of its
        connotation of an ecclesiastical body with official authority given
        by Rome. The difficulty was eliminated simply by changing the
        name to the National Catholic Conference of Bishops — the word
        "Conference" had none of the connotations involved in the word
        "Council".

October 15, 1938

NORTH AMERICAN COLLEGE
Via Dell' Umilta 30

Dear Everybody,

Today we had our annual class "bum run" to Frascati. It couldn't be
other than a great success. We had our meal in the same hotel at which we
got the wine and ice cream the day we visited it with the Cosgroves. Our
trip brought back vivid memories; and I am proud to say that I redeemed
the family honor by drinking a respectable portion of the stuff that has
made Frascati famous (do you remember how I bought ice cream that day
because I had had enough wine?). The meal lasted from twelve thirty until
about four — now, we didn't eat all the time. There was scheduled and
unscheduled entertainment. I gave them a couple of jokes; since dinner
was finished I let them have Monsignor Buckey's story about the pea soup.
I did not make a visit to the famous crypt in Frascati this time; the crypt is
a wine cellar that seems to be as endless as Purgatory to which all the
faithful go to pay their respects to Frascati wine.

But no one has ever been to Frascati the right way until he has
gone by the tram. The tram tools and grunts around the curves and hills as
though it had an acute case of appendicitis. The difficulties start as soon as
you try to pay for the ticket; the conductor has no change. He never has
any change, so no one expects it; he begins by canvassing the car to see if
anyone has change. Of course, no one has change; it doesn't phase the
conductor any because he didn't expect anyone to have change. Now he

begins his act in earnest. He juggles and arranges finances so that everybody in the tram has some part in paying for everybody else's fare. This would go on indefinitely if someone didn't offer the conductor a cigarette as an incentive to finish with this messing.

I weighed myself in Frascati (before the meal) and found that I now weigh about 165. The air is very healthy.

We begin our retreat tomorrow night; for six days we will observe complete silence. For the first three days it is difficult; on the fourth day one gets resigned to it all; on the fifth he forgets that he ever talked in his life; on the sixth he feels as though he doesn't give a d - - - n if he never talks for the rest of his life. We are to have the Rector, or abbot, or general, or whatever they call him of the Franciscan order to manage this excursion to the higher realms of spirituality. Personally, I don't mind retreat at all, rather enjoy it. [1]

At the end of the retreat we have a traditional play that is a sort of a send-off to the deacons. The little skit I am in involves the old days of the college — Pace, Hanna, O'Connell are in it. I am Pace. The person who will enjoy it most will be Archbishop Hanna who is at the villa again.

Love,

Phil

Comments: Letter of October 15, 1938

(1)   I thought that the retreats in Rome were excellent, and they occurred at the right time, just before beginning classes and immediately after the summer vacation with its trips through Europe. There was an added solemnity and fervor because of the war fever. I did not write about that to my folks for fear of disturbing them.

The war fever or jitters assailed one every time there was a radio newscast or as soon as one walked out of the College. On the streets there was always a display of many types of military uniforms and the Fascists had plastered signs everywhere urging the people to support the Italian cause, the Berlin-Rome Axis. The lack of enthusiasm for the Axis led to almost frantic efforts by the government to whip up support for it.

October 16, 1938

NORTH AMERICAN COLLEGE
Via Dell' Umilta 30

Dear Everybody,

Here it is the middle of October with the weather gorgeous and the weather crisp, and no opportunity to use them. School begins the third of November, so until then, we can live deliciously on the memory of the summer trips and the dreams of future trips.

We had a class "bum run" a few days ago to a little hill town about twelve miles from the villa. Except for the congenial company, everything was haywire. We started at eleven in the morning and went first to Frascati (a gorgeous little town where the rich Italians have villas), changed trams and then went to Montecompatri, a place that seems marooned up in the hills. It looks as though the whole little town had been caught up in a flood and left on top of a high hill. By the time we got there, it was two o'clock, and we were ready to eat the countryside. But the wary Italian innkeeper had waited until he saw the whites of the eyes of the customers before he would begin to prepare anything. At two thirty, the first course rolled in — a kind of spaghetti that was as tough and as edible as blowout patches. But we were ready even for blowout patches. At last the dinner came to an end, or rather our endurance became exhausted, and then the real business began. Four Scotch fellows (from the Scotch College) happened along — their villa is near there — and sang us some real Highland tunes. One came from way back in the heather, and none of us could understand a word he said; but there was one of the fellows who interpreted for us. That sounds a bit exaggerated, but it's the truth; when they get that real, thick burr in their throats the only way to get their meaning is to have them write down what they want to say. We toasted the Queen of England for them (since she is Scotch), and they replied with a toast to Wally Simpson. The Scotch are very sociable fellows, much different from the English; they don't seem to agree with the Italian temperament. A story is told about some Scotch fellows who got into a brawl some years ago (before Mussolini got into power) in a little town out this way. There was a lot of Communism in the town, and consequently much anti-clerical feeling.

So when the Scotch walked through there one day, they were received with the usual abusive language and stones. One brawny Scotchman decided to do something about it and got tangled with a young Italian. The fight ended, so the story goes, with the Scotchman killing the Italian. Maybe it's just another Roman story. Anyway, I was surprised to meet some American ladies this summer who had traveled in Italy, especially Rome, before the rule of Mussolini, and there wasn't one who hadn't been hit with a stone. Anyone who wore good clothes was considered an enemy of the "people", and there was violent anti-clericalism even in the "Borgo", the old section of the city in front of St. Peter's.

Anyway, I started to tell you about our "bum run". The pay-off came when we discovered that we had talked too long and had missed the only tram that went to Frascati. Consequently, we hoofed it for about four miles back to Frascati and there got a car back to the villa. But I was glad of the walk; these Italian sunsets are glorious. We were high in the hills and could see across the whole Roman campagna in the misty twilight, with Rome in the distance and the sea on the horizon. The sun seemed to set fire to the whole sky before it extinguished itself in the sea; and before it had gone down, the moon had risen making the olive orchards a soft olive silver. To add to the effect the tinkling wine carts came winding down the road on their all-night journey to Rome. I often wonder whether the Italians like their countryside as much as I do.

The student body this year is interesting. There is almost an Irish colony in our midst. Five Irishmen, studying for dioceses in the States have arrived. They are all excellent fellows, are not interested in arguing politics, make good conversationalists, and are interested in sports. But already they live in dread of the Italian summers. One fellow comes from Ballybunnion, another from Newmarket — about fifteen miles from Limerick. One thing that gets them down is the lack of tea after meals; as you know we have only wine with the meals. [1] Most of them are slated for dioceses in the far West, Washington and Oregon. It's too bad that we don't have their Seminary system here; they get up at six or six thirty in summer and seven o'clock in the winter. We get up at five-thirty the year round.

Our retreat starts tomorrow; a whole week of silence, punctuated occasionally by the talks of a man who reads his sermons and insists on giving Italian quotations in a miserably flat voice. But I suppose that half the merit comes from suffering the retreat master in silence. [2] I feel as though I made my retreat this year already — at Lourdes. I didn't tell you the full particulars of that at the time because I thought you would get worried. It rained the whole time I was there, four straight days of deluge. My fellow traveler and myself were soaked three times a day, at least, but suffered no ill effects at all — due to the grace of God and the help of hot water and rum taken before going to bed at night. Even in all that rain we couldn't get positions as stretcher-bearers; but I did carry a fainting old lady, dying from cancer, all the way up the steps of the basilica. All the while her son, a man of thirty-five, stood wringing his hands and jabbering; I felt sorry for him but couldn't help thinking what a dolt he was. The most amusing thing at Lourdes was the pilgrimage of French peasants who were up before dawn (for no reason at all) and just marching around to pass the time away before going to Mass.

We had the movie "Maytime" last night at the villa. Very beautiful; don't miss it. (I have seen more movies here than I did during my vacation.)

Love,

Phil

Comments: Letter of October 16, 1938

(1)   The Irish had a real difficulty at first with the food — there were no potatoes, only pasta.

(2)   There was a mix-up about the time of the retreat. It actually began on October 17, not October 16. Despite my gloomy prediction, the retreat was very inspiring and helpful.

October 26, 1938

NORTH AMERICAN COLLEGE
VIA DELL' UMILTA 30

Dear Everybody,

Retreat is just over. The scheduled retreat master had to send a substitute who turned out to be an extraordinary man — he had no teeth at all in his upper jaw, his lower jaw jutted out like a rain spout, and his nose bore evidence of some very hard usage inflicted during the formative years. If you can imagine Popeye the Sailor dressed in a black Franciscan's robe and minus his pipe, you have a rather good idea of our friend the retreat master. Add to that the fact that he had spent so much time in Italy that some of his English was faulty, and you have a complete picture of him. His material was very good, and his stories were a distinct relief from the usual ecclesiastical brand; for instance, this crack about jealousy in the clergy when one is made bishop, "One gets the red and ten get the blues."

As usual, Archbishop Hanna came out and sat in the Amen corner during the whole retreat, amusing and edifying all about him. The old man is very kind and thoughtful; I did the reading at one of the meals (we have reading during the meals) and was standing waiting for the community to leave, afterwards when he came up, shook hands, thanked me for the good reading, etc. Very kind of him, I thought; I could blow three or four pistons but the faculty would never notice the effort. I also pushed through an idea that I had been nursing a long time. Every year one of the sacristans is detailed to look after the Archbishop, to show him to his room, give him his place in the chapel, etc. This year I asked the fellow detailed for that service to corner the Archbishop in his room and drag in one of my associate editors to get an interview with him about his famous debate with Monsignor Pace in the presence of the Pope (then Leo XIII). [1] I sent an associate editor who knows shorthand. The old man was in just the right mood and gave them everything and more. (I forgot to mention that the Rector had refused me permission to see the Archbishop last year because "his memory is gone and he couldn't do you any good anyway." But the Rector is now safely tucked away in America.) Incidentally, the debate was of far more importance than I had ever thought; it marked a turning point in Catholic philosophy. [2] The Pope, Leo XIII, was very much interested in having the philosophy of St. Thomas accepted by the Church as its official philosophy. So he sent up to northern Italy for his former philosophy professor and put him in charge of philosophy in the Roman seminaries. This, of course, stirred up the Jesuits and other orders who wanted the liberty of teaching their various systems. So a debate was arranged; two students from Propaganda College (Hanna and Pace were selected) were to defend something like 212 theses against the big shots in

Rome. The Pope was to preside. Actually, it was a defense of the philosophy of St. Thomas against all the opposition. First of all the other nationalities were very sore because two Americans were picked, but as Archbishop Hanna says, "We could speak Latin better than we could English." Furthermore, the Archbishop was so good at classical Latin that he could be-fluster the opposition by his answers; as he said, "Those Jesuits tried to trip me up, but I shot back Latin that they couldn't understand."

Some of the stuff he said in the interview could never be printed. When asked what part, if any, Cardinal O'Connell (who was also a student then) had in the proceedings he said, "O'Connell — why he was only a boy in short pants." Can you imagine what a howl that would raise if it were printed?

News has just come that we are to receive a new disciplinarian at the college. The Vice Rector is to be changed to the house of graduate studies but will come to the college every day to give permissions, etc. The new disciplinarian is a fellow who graduated from here two or three years ago and enjoyed the reputation of being the biggest talker that ever came here. [3] I know him well; he is the one who invited me to the chateau in France this summer. He will serve in his capacity only until Christmas (lucky for him). What a position for such a fellow.

Love,

Phil

Comments: Letter of October 26, 1938

(1)   Pace later became the professor of philosophy at the Catholic University and finally the beloved and respected Vice President of the University.

(2)   The sequel to that interview with Archbishop was that Pope Leo XII was very much impressed and finally the philosophy of Thomas Aquinas was adopted as the system to be taught in the seminaries and Catholic colleges. Of course, other systems of philosophy were taught in Catholic schools but Thomistic philosophy was the official system of philosophy.

(3)   The disciplinarian was Father John Wright, later Bishop of Pittsburgh
        and then a Cardinal in the Curia in Rome.

October 27, 1938

NORTH AMERICAN COLLEGE
Via Dell' Umilta 30

Dear Everybody,

I received your letter immediately after retreat; it came at an opportune time. The retreat was lightened by such things as floods, storms, and the cracks of Archbishop Hanna who came out to make the retreat with us. Just in the middle of retreat a rather sever storm swept this region; the rainspouts became clogged and the water flowed off in one spot. But directly beneath this spot someone left his window open and the wind swept in the river that was flowing from the roof. The water was ankle deep in the corridors on one floor. The electrical storms always happened in the middle of a sermon, invariably putting the lighting system out of commission. All would have been well if the retreat master did not have the habit of reading his sermons; so when darkness came the end of the sermon came.

But, of course, Archbishop Hanna was the whole show again. His memory is even worse than it was last year. At the Archbishop's suggestion the Vice Rector tried to improve his memory; the plan was this — every time the Archbishop repeated a question the Vice Rector was supposed to say, "I refuse to answer" and make the old man try to think of the answer he had received before. Just after they had agreed on this they went down to dinner, and in the middle of the meal the Archbishop asked, "How many students do we have here now?" "About a hundred and fifty," says the Vice Rector. About half a minute later the Archbishop asked as again, "How many students do we have here now?" The Vice Rector came back with a snappy, "I refuse to answer." "What, what's this?" said the old man, "You mean to tell me that you refuse to tell me how many students you have," and promptly got into a huff. He had already forgotten about the little plan to cure his forgetfulness and was insulted because the Vice Rector gave him such a short answer. As usual, the old man kept up a running commentary on the sermons. And, of course, he needed someone to show him to his room all the time; but he got stopped short one day when he asked a new man where his room was, and the new man said, "I don't know; I'm new around here too." (Archbishop Hanna was at the American College for eight years as a student and then taught for a number of years at the Propaganda College in Rome).

The show at the end of retreat, given in the benefit of the whole house by the graduating class, was a big success. Of course, the whole theme is a satire and ride of the faculty; it's traditional that the faculty gets its ears trimmed on these occasions. But the faculty wasn't alone in their drubbing; everyone from Mussolini to Hitler was kicked in the rear end. The theme of the show was a trip to Rome by Hitler to visit the Duce during which visit, among other things, Hitler was engaged to marry the ex-Queen of Ethiopia. The climax, as far as we were concerned, came when Mussolini was trying to buy the Hofbrau (the biggest beer hall in the world, in Munich) from Hitler. Mussolini offered Hitler the Rector and Vice Rector of the college and everybody was asked to vote on it. There was a rising unanimous vote by the students to make the trade. And the Vice Rector was the first one to stand up; maybe he is as tired of the job as the fellows are of him. Anyway, he is an excellent sport. The last two days at the villa are a panic; the seven day retreat of complete silence causes a bedlam at the end of it and the next business on hand is to take your room apart — literally. When you move from the villa to the city you move everything, even mattresses and pillows. All the stuff, mattresses, chairs, trunks, bags, blankets, dishes, are hauled into the city in five-ton trucks and the whole load just poured out in one big soup in the middle of the college. The trick is to grab as good a mattress and pillow as possible and lug it up to your room — the only difficulty being that you don't know which room to haul it to because the rooms are changed. Consequently one spends about half a day dragging a mattress and pillow around the corridors finding his room. The next thing is to haul down his furniture from his room of last year. To be in the middle of 150 fellows trying to haul tables, desks, beds, books, wash stands, chairs, etc. all at the same time is as bad as standing in a crowd waiting to see the Pope. For a day, everything is just a great big mess, as shapeless and formless as an American Legion Convention. (By the way,

I noticed that quite a few of them are still tramping around Rome, still wearing their uniforms.)

Tomorrow, the 28ᵗʰ of October, is the Fascist New Year, the day on which they took Rome. It looks like another one of these Roman holidays. The Duce gave a speech this afternoon to a horde of Italians and Germans. A large delegation of Germans are here, all wearing the black swastika.

This year I have a very warm room, very fine. But it is on the busiest street around here, and the people are just as noisy as the gondoliers in Venice. (Remember that fellow in Venice who came along about three in the morning singing at the top of his lungs.) The street is very narrow, with very heavy traffic and everybody opposite me has a radio. I know the kids in the opposite apartment house — Giovanino, Graziella and Anna Maria. When things get too noisy, I have a way of shutting everything up; I open the window and sing at the top of my lungs. That holds them. A good dose of my singing will keep them quiet for an hour.

It's interesting to watch the new men come in. One of them is a Roman who was born in Brooklyn. His family moved back to Rome when he was nine years old and instead of wanting to be a priest in Italy he wants to be an American Priest (for which I don't blame him at all). He is crazy to get back to the States. There is one fellow who will take a real beating when he comes — a Californian who came all the way to New York and missed his boat. His reputation is made before he sets a foot in the college. I know him; he went to Basselin. I thought at first that he had gotten cold feet at the last minute, but he hadn't. There is a fellow here now who almost missed his boat; he went down early to the dock, took a look at the boat, got depressed at the sight of it, went back to Broadway to see a good show, got back to the boat when the last gang plank was being hauled away. I think he would have been glad if the boat had been gone.

Love,

Phil

Comments: Letter of October 27, 1938

(1)   The system of moving from the Villa to the College in Rome was traditional — there was a scramble to get a good mattress after the truck arrived from the Villa.

(2)   The celebration of the anniversary of the taking of Rome was an overkill. Mussolini and his followers had no great difficulty or fight to take over Rome. The people were disgusted with the current regime and welcomed Mussolini. Of course, he is owed the credit for recognizing that the previous regime was incapable of ruling.

November 1, 1938

NORTH AMERICAN COLLEGE
VIA DELL' UMILTA 30

Dear Everybody,

At last we are established in the city again. The war cry was that this is the last year in the old building, but almost as soon as we arrived, we found that the Fascist government had decided to give up the idea of building a road through the College owing to lack of money. So it will take an earthquake or some other act of Providence to remove us from the "venerable" building. My room is on the third floor, opposite the Jesuit Biblical Institute; I painted it a French gray but I don't know whether it looks more like a bathroom or a Dutch kitchen.

Every year, just before we come in from the villa the list of cameratas is read off; each camerata has a prefect and an assistant (who is called a beedle, which is a contraction for "bidello" — a janitor). [1] I am in almost the same camerata in which I was when I came, and I am neither prefect nor beedle — which pleases me to no end. Last year the prefects and beedles were appointed according to marks received in the exams, and according to that system I would have been a prefect or beedle this year, but the system was changed. I have too much to do besides being burdened with a job like that. The appointments caused no end of griping; for instance, the Vice Rector is from the diocese of Detroit and there are three students from that diocese here; all of them were made either prefects or beedles and none of them is at all outstanding. The most logical man in the house for the position of beedle is a young Italian from Rome (studying for the diocese of Brooklyn because he was born in Brooklyn) who is a very intelligent fellow and knows Rome perfectly; but he was lost in the shuffle. So goes life at the college. Our college is the largest it has ever been, I think; we have about 170 at the college here and quite a few at the school of graduate studies.

The work is going around that the Sacred Congregation for Seminaries is preparing a new list of rules and regulations; a nice little surprise package will come through the mails some day and make us all happy. The last regulations succeeded in converting the normal disorder into a real chaos. It was ruled that the Vice Rector has to stay at the graduate house of studies, but he was left as the sole disciplinarian of the college, even though he doesn't live here any more. To make things even more intelligible he insisted just before we came in from the villa that the strictest discipline was to be enforced this year by himself — even though he doesn't live at the college. This is the sort of set-up that the Marx brothers would fix if they were given a seminary to run. Meanwhile, the latest addition to the faculty, Father Wright (who was a student just three years ago), is proving to be a real godsend. He is an excellent fellow and has already started to give us better food. I was talking to him for quite a while a few nights ago and he told me about the family in France with whom I stayed for a few days. They have a greater history than I thought, but it's a long story, so I shall save it for another letter. Anyway, I have been invited back there anytime I am in the neighborhood. I shall go back sometime, but I hope to have my French in better shape.

I wrote again to the company in Naples; they are shipping the package.

Love,

Phil

Comments: Letter of November 1, 1938

(1)   It was a distinct honor to be chosen as the prefect of a camerata or as the beedle (derived from 'bidello' an assistant, even a janitor, a term and job used in very old colleges), the assistant to the prefect.

November 13, 1938

NORTH AMERICAN COLLEGE
Via Dell' Umilta 30

Dear Everybody,

The accredited representative of the Holy Ghost from Chicago is still blessing Rome with his presence. Incidentally he bestowed the unutterable privilege of dining with us in the refectory — but Cardinal Pacelli stole the show. And it was such a good show that it really deserves some treatment.

Cardinal Pacelli and Cardinal Mundelein were finally cornered and brought over for a very formal dinner. The best caterer in Rome handled the event and almost did a perfect job on it — no one could ever do a perfect job on serving a dinner in that refectory.

The main reason for the dinner was not to rub His Eminence for a new college (though that was not neglected in the least); Cardinal Pacelli and Ambassador Phillips, American Ambassador to Italy, have been trying for a long time to have a real get-together out of range of newspapermen. [1]

Cardinal Pacelli has been especially anxious since the recent war crisis. A direct visit from the Ambassador to the Vatican would cause a lot of comment, and they wanted to work things out privately. This provided a good excuse.

The ambassador escorted the cardinal to his place in the refectory while Monsignor Babcock took the moneybag from Chicago in tow. I was in an excellent position to notice them and did plenty of unabashed gawking.

As soon as the meal started, the Cardinal started in on the ambassador. It was no merely formal conversation; Cardinal Pacelli did not make even a pretence of eating for the first fifteen minutes (we timed him). He did not even look at the food, but his jaws were certainly going at top speed; he was so intent on the conversation that he pulled his chair out and sat sideways.

And the ambassador did very little eating either. Both really had something to say, and they said it. Cardinal Pacelli makes a very charming, dignified appearance; and the ambassador is no slouch. Apparently things went well, because I overheard the ambassador speaking to one of his attaches after the meal, and he said that everything was splendid. Just what they said or did I don't know, but if anything happens shortly it is due partly to the little talk they had.

It is no secret that both have been trying to get together on neutral ground for some time. Obviously, Cardinal Pacelli was not even faintly interested in speaking to Cardinal Mundelein. It was a very important get-together and the college was honored by their presence. All together there were forty guests, and it's no small affair that rates the attendance of the Cardinal Secretary of State.

Today we attended the beatification ceremony of Mother Cabrini. [2] About five of us were just about twenty feet from the Pope. We had wonderful seats. The story goes that Cardinal Pacelli secured the tickets for us, and when asked to get us seats in the apse (where the papal throne is) he said, "Certainly, if it will keep the Americans from getting into the diplomatic section."

I didn't know that we had such a national reputation for gatecrashing. Anyway, I and forty other fellows from the college were ushers and general utility men; we ushered nobody except ourselves, and we did a magnificent job of that. I planted myself as closely as possible to the throne and stayed there.

Cardinal Mundelein celebrated the solemn Mass this morning — the first American cardinal ever to attain the privilege of saying the Mass on such an occasion. As you see, the Americans took over the situation.

This afternoon there was solemn benediction attended by the Pope. I had a magnificent view; we were almost on the altar steps. Behind us sat the sister, sister-in-law, niece, and grandnieces of the Pope. The niece of the Pope (a middle-aged woman) is very pretty; she is a blond with very good features. All the grandnieces are small, not over ten or twelve years old.

Apparently they were given orders not to applaud or cheer as their granduncle was being brought in; the older women maintained a very reserved composure, but the kids let go rather often. They were not present at the function in the morning, so we had used their box — without knowing whose seats we were using.

Then about an hour after the afternoon ceremony our choir broadcasted to the U.S.; Cardinal Mundelein gave a brief talk, and the choir filled in before and after the speech.

I have just given you the main events sketchily. The next time I write, I'll pack in the details. The news about the fruitcake package is very welcome; much obliged. They have not turned on the heat in the building as yet, so a bit of extra food will be much appreciated — not that I need it; I am now stronger and heavier than I have been since my first year in Basselin. That stomach ailment seems to be definitely on the mend. I am not now so hungry as I used to be, and when I eat, I actually feel as though I had gotten something to stick in my stomach. Occasionally, I have a bad day, but I soon snap out of it. You can be sure that I have said many a prayer of thanksgiving.

Love,

Phil

Comments: Letter of November 13, 1938

(1)   The meeting of Cardinal Pacelli with the American Ambassador to Italy was a very serious effort on the part of the U.S. to enlist the help of the Vatican in a final peace effort. Although no press notice was ever made, everyone understood the meaning of the visit.

(2)   The beatification of Mother Cabrini was a very popular and joyous event. Mother Cabrini, an Italian, spent years in the U.S., especially in Chicago, assisting the Italian immigrants by developing schools and institutions to take care of their needs. Cardinal Mundelein was given the honor of celebrating the Mass because of his position as Archbishop of Chicago.

November 22, 1938

NORTH AMERICAN COLLEGE
Via Dell' Umilta 30

Dear Everybody,

I forgot to mention the fire in St. Peter's last Sunday and was reminded of it by a shameless exaggeration of it in the Paris edition of the

Herald-Tribune. Now the moral of the fire is that either a miracle happened or that someone is a great liar. Just at the end of the ceremony a little smoke then a flame issued from the giant bronze casing, which holds the chair that St. Peter used. The fire was not near the chair — it was about thirty feet from it. When it started no one believed it; it took about five minutes for one of our fellows to convince a Swiss Guard that something was actually on fire. By the time flames were a foot high they conceded that something was somewhat wrong. The first attempt at something constructive (or rather, destructive) was typically Italian. A fellow came out with a short rug to beat it out, but soon found that he couldn't reach the blaze to smother it so he did a very nice job of fanning it. Of course, instead of getting water or a fire extinguisher, he still had faith in his idea so he went after a larger rug; by the time he got back with that, the fire was doing quite nicely; in fact, so nicely that he would have burned the rug if he tried to smother it. It was then formally decided by the assembled force, in formal conclave, to drag out a hose which was easily accomplished, since it was almost directly behind the high altar where all this took place. But the usual difficulty presented itself; the hose was too short. After a bit of maneuvering they finally hit the blaze with the water and that was the end of the entertainment.

All during this little affair the Americans were getting increasingly disgusted; just when we were ready to throw the Italians into the fire and do something about it ourselves, one of them said very comfortingly, "No danger at all; it's all bronze." You figure it out.

I had a very good chance of observing the Pope at close range — all during solemn benediction. He can walk unassisted, though shakily, and he was able to incense the Blessed Sacrament very easily. But he is thin and worn out, and the affairs of the past week even have been tough. (The Italian government openly broke the Concordat with the Vatican; they had agreed, of course, not to meddle with the Church's law on marriage, but recently they published a law annulling all marriages between Jews and Italians. Before it was drafted, the Vatican wrote a letter to both the King and Mussolini indicating what an open breach of the Concordat it would be, but they went ahead. [1]) He is the only man I know who at eighty years and in such a tremendously important post still remains so keen; there is nothing wrong with his mind at all.

Tonight our Rector makes his triumphal return to his little den. The unsuspecting and innocent new men asked if we were all to go to the station as we did for Cardinal Mundelein and cheer as he came in. If that ever happened, the Rector would climb out of the back of the train and sneak down the tracks. In his absence he has become rather popular — simply because the Vice Rector has become tough and everyone knows that it is easier to handle the Rector than the Vice Rector. And now the rumor reports that the Vice Rector is making arrangements to go to America for Christmas. You can see that no one on the faculty is afraid of the ocean or boats. It takes less of an excuse for them to travel 6000 miles than for any person I know to travel a hundred miles. [2]

I have been in the market for a Christmas present for the family, but I am afraid I must send home a make-shift remembrance until it is possible for me to get hold of what I intended to send for Christmas — again Italian service has come through magnificently.

Love,

Phil

Comments: Letter of November 22, 1938

(1)   The breaking of the Vatican Concordat Lateran treaty of 1928 was flagrant and ridiculous. The Jews were popular in Italy, and the absurd attempt of the Fascists to copy the persecution of the Jews in Germany was absurd. It further discredited the regime of Mussolini in the eyes of very many Italians. In fact, many Jews came to Italy from Germany seeking refuge knowing that the Church would try to protect them.

(2)   The reason for the high interest of the students in the trips of the faculty to the United States derived from the rule that students coming to the North American College would never be allowed to visit the U.S. until after the completion of their courses and ordination in Rome. Actually, some dioceses decided to call back to the U.S. their students at the College because of the war scare.

November 27, 1938

NORTH AMERICAN COLLEGE
Via Dell' Umilta 30

Dear Everybody,

So far the fruitcake has not arrived, but I continue to enjoy it in anticipation — which will be nothing compared to the actual enjoyment of demolition. I feel in a begging mood these days; I just wrote a letter to the Del Nord alumni of the diocese, through Father Stricker, setting forth the plight of the Baltimore men here now. It is an ancient custom for the diocesan alumni to send over enough money to give us a "bum run" sometime during the year. And since I am now the dean of the diocese here, it was my duty to write a report to Father Stricker (who requested it). Needless to state, I sent the best tearjerker I could manage, hoping that it will be a good money-jerker.

A few nights ago we had the annual "New Men's Mix" which is supposed to serve as a sort of introduction of the new men to the College. As with all the shows here, the audience furnishes most of the entertainment; as a matter of fact the new men serve merely as a target or opportunity for cracks from the audience. The entertainment was held in the library and to make the new men feel comfortable as well as to set the tone for the evening, the librarian announced just before the show started that everyone was requested not to throw the large books in the library for fear of damaging an old statue of Pope Leo XIII in the back of the room. The show lived up to all traditions; the silliest act was that of the Five Dionne Quintuplets, each of whom was over six feet tall and weighs more than 200.

Today our class received our final minor orders, exorcist and acolyte. [1] It seems that after about seven years in the seminary. I am only now a full-fledged altar boy. Rome moves slowly. The ceremony was climaxed by a funny incident. Almost at the end of the Mass, the ordaining bishop gives the kiss of peace to one of the fellows ordained who passes it on to the rest. The master of ceremonies came over to get one of us; he picked out one of our six foot six giants and trotted him up. When the bishop, a man of about five feet four inches, turned around and met this mountain, he almost called for a ladder. After the ceremony we all went over to a good restaurant and did considerable damage to an American breakfast.

There is much talk in the newspapers about the condition of the Pope and a civil war in France. Lovely continent on which we are living. The only way to get the true dope is to listen on the radio to the foreign news accounts.

Love,

Phil

Comments: Letter of November 27, 1938

(1)   The II Vatican Council re-arranged the orders leading up to priestly ordination — tonsure has been dropped as well as subdiaconate and the former "minor" orders have been dropped. We have the institution of readers and acolytes, an admission of candidacy to the sacred order, diaconate and priesthood.

December 10, 1938

NORTH AMERICAN COLLEGE
VIA DELL' UMILTA 30

Dear Everybody,

We had ordinations here on December 8th. Ten fellows were ordained; two of them were in the class ahead of me at Basselin. The ceremony went along in its usual smooth manner except for the fact that the Rector, who did the ordaining, is fast and half the community swears that he doesn't give the Holy Ghost time enough to get in. The abbess (whom you must remember because I know I have described her before) was here in all her glory. She was dressed in one of her more outlandish and impossible outfits. She struggled around with a coat that could have been used as a tent for her and the general effect of the whole affair would lead one to believe that she was starting out for the opera. The abbess still can't understand why women can't be ordained. There was a young couple at the ordination who has almost become a part of the college. The husband is a professor in Boston (teaches English somewhere) and is spending a year in Europe brushing up on his culture; he got himself married just before coming over to a very cute girl. But the strain of getting all this culture is beginning to tell on the girl. Europe or no Europe, she is beginning to get homesick; and she is so tired of hearing foreign languages and seeing foreign faces that she comes to almost every exercise she can at the college. I'll bet she never expected to spend part of her honeymoon haunting a seminary. Father Wright has been very thoughtful and done quite a bit for them, managing at the same time to have a good time laughing at them; for instance, they came for the ordination ceremony and breakfast and the girl remarked on how nice the pie was. So Father Wright goes down to the kitchen and gets them a whole pie, large enough for twelve, and gave it to her. She very innocently said, "Thank you, Father," and proceeded to go around getting blessings from the newly ordained priests lugging this pie with her. She went out the door still clutching the pie. I'd love to have heard the comments at the hotel as she can trotting in the front door with a big pie.

We are now having the privilege of learning how a "popular demonstration" is created by a government in Europe. As you have probably read in the newspapers, the Italians are supposed to be clamoring for Corsica and a part of the French Riviera. Of course, they have no idea of ever getting Corsica or the Riviera; they want to be given a few concessions in Africa as a reward for not pressing their demands. They give instructions to the students in the university to go out and produce some demonstrations. First, they went to the Parliament when the French ambassador was in attendance and started screaming for Corsica and Tunis. The French government protested; Italy replied that it was a "popular demonstration". Then they branched out. They went around the city in groups yelling their fool heads off. They staged a demonstration in front of the office for a French steamship company; the police came along and gave the manager of the office a bawling out for causing the disturbance and demanded that he close his shop. The manager appealed to the French ambassador who told him to defy them. Then a few days ago, a group of the students got out in front of the Greg University and shouted — probably for the benefit of the French students. It's going to be a sad day when they get an idea to carry out any anti-American demonstration.

Well, I must get to work. A few Christmas cards are beginning to come in and so far I have a clean conscience; I have sent cards to all from whom I have received them.

Love,

Phil

Merry Christmas and a Happy New Year

Comments: Letter of December 10, 1938

(1)   I explained at length the process of creating demonstrations in Rome to allay the fears of our family if they should read of riots or demonstrations against the Americans. The demonstrations are arranged, and therefore, there is never a fear of real violence. I witnessed a couple of "anti-American" demonstrations, standing just across the street from the demonstrators and waving to them at the end. After the demonstrations they promptly returned to their classes at the University of Rome. One Italian gentleman remarked, "Students get credits for making demonstrations."

December 12, 1938

NORTH AMERICAN COLLEGE
Via Dell' Umilta 30

Dear Everybody,

All prospects at the present moment, about nine o'clock in the evening, indicate that this will be a tough night for the college. Mussolini is scheduled to make an important speech at ten (which means that he will start sometime after eleven) from his quarters in the Palazzo Venezia. The troops were given orders to gather at nine, and the place for the falling-in is just around the corner of the school. All of this is supposed to be a voluntary and spontaneous gathering, but it usually is just about as voluntary as a headache. The troops get their notice to be at a certain place at a definite time; the only thing or the only person who attends these meetings of his own free will seems to be the man who runs them — Mussolini. Maybe that's putting it a bit too strong because there usually are a number of visitors in town who go to see him. I also found out how they run these vast "spontaneous" gatherings in Germany where about 200,000 people suddenly find themselves moved by a common impulse to gather in one place and shout themselves hoarse for their leader; the minister of propaganda or whoever it is who acts as national cheer leader in Germany sends the people notice that "they are to gather spontaneously" at a certain place. Half of the people in these crowds don't see any more than the back of the person in front of them. I was straining and stepping on everybody's toes at one of the gatherings to see Mussolini but couldn't see anything but the perspiration dripping off the faces of exulting Italians; then a little Italian woman asked me to take my hat off, so that she could see better. The only difference was that she could see more of the back of my head. Everybody seems to have a good time making a big audience for the Duce. According to common rumor (which is as uncertain as the weather in Washington) Mussolini should say something about Germany's right to colonies. [1]

The latest news from the States about changes in dioceses has caused a crisis here. The dioceses in New Jersey have been changed so much that I suppose not even the bishops know where they belong. That brings unexpected difficulties over here for the fellows from those dioceses; the college supplies no furniture, it's all hereditary in the diocese. So now the question comes up, who owns what? Four fellows belonged to the Trenton diocese; two of them still do, but one now belongs to another diocese, and the last one belongs to another one too. The matter might be settled nicely if furniture could be divided evenly, but after all a chair or a desk is no good to anyone if it is sawed in half. Another Solomon is needed; I'd venture to predict that the matter will be settled in the European way — grab what you can hold and defend.

A fellow whose folks are over to see him ordained said his first High Mass in the chapel this morning. For all those who hail my attempts at singing as the gawkiest, shakiest effort ever produced, should have been here. On demand, I at least can make a loud noise that may sound like a freight station agent or a barrack-room performer, but anyway it is sound. Now this fellow couldn't even do that (at least this morning). His voice quavered and got clogged in his throat, and he bumped, bounced and jarred all over the notes. He always managed to come out on the right note at the end; reminded me of Father Hemelt (the big German who used to be at the Sem) who would suddenly swing off into a little composition of his own, ramble up and down the scale awhile but just at the end would come back to normal again. It always keeps the organist on his toes (and ear too) trying to figure out where he will end.

It seems that the newly ordained priests are having a few difficulties saying their first Masses at the tomb of St. Peter's. There is a little Italian altar boy over there who insists on keeping an eye on everything, and of course manages to get in the way all the time. A newly ordained priest must have a priest to assist him at his first three Masses, so the first duty of the assisting priest is to can, strangle, or tie the Italian altar boys. I saw one in action over there who was serving three Masses at the same time and making more noise than all three priests. But the worst I've heard, was an old lady who came to hear Mass, couldn't find a kneeling bench so she parked herself on the top step of the alter. If the priest hesitated before anything, she would pull his alb and tell him what came next. She had to be removed too.

I am told that all the demonstrating and doing last evening was to give proper emphasis to Mussolini's statement that Italy is withdrawing from the League of Nations — which hardly could be called a surprise to anyone. [2] (An argument is now going on between the fellow up above me, an Italian, with a family across the street who always take Sunday morning as the occasion to wash laundry. He tells them they are wrong for working on Sunday; they tell him he is doing wrong too by studying — I wish they could convince the Greg of that.)

Love,

Phil

Comments: *Letter of December 12, 1938*

(1)   Hitler and Mussolini agreed in demanding colonies for their countries but Mussolini had the more dramatic strategy, recalling the greatest days of the Roman Empire and erecting series of maps near the famous Forum showing the growth of the Empire. Neither Mussolini nor Hitler had any compunction about seizing lands and peoples without any regard for their rights.

(2)   Mussolini had defied the League of Nations when he conquered

Ethiopia, a war against a nation with practically no weapons. He declared in his speech that the League was dead, and that for hygienic reasons they should get rid of the corpse. It was a brutal speech, delivered with a great deal of strutting and bravura.

December 19, 1938

NORTH AMERICAN COLLEGE
VIA DELL' UMILTA 30

Dear Everybody,

Christmas is coming and a real crisis is facing the college — we still do not know whether we shall have the usual "bum run" or not. All indications seem to point that we won't, which is very bad news. The only recreation during the holidays, if the worst comes to the worst, will be a long camerata walk — and we have camerata walks every day (and everybody grows increasingly sick of them). If we are allowed to have "bum runs" I think I shall get me up to Perugia, a little town in the Umbrian hills past Assisi. I have never been there, and a change of scenery is always appreciated; as you know I suffer with the travel bug rather acutely. However, I must say that the loss of a "bum run" will not affect me too much; I have too much else to think about, but I can just hear the stomping and griping when the Rector refuses permission for the "bum runs".

It's rather interesting to watch the reaction of the new men to their first Christmas season in Rome. Everyone in America very naturally thinks that it is celebrated with much ceremony and fanfare; the fact is that it is the most neglected, matter-of-fact, ordinary, down-at-the-heel celebration of any of the large feasts. There is almost no build-up for it in the stores — reason: no good Jewish merchants and no extra money. [1] What is more surprising is that there are almost no Christmas hymns on the radio. The Italians preserve their normal spaghetti-level of life during Christmas time. Consequently, the new men are constantly waiting for the Christmas "spirit" to develop; and they will just wait, and wait, and wait, and wait. In fact, after two years of this type of Christmas, I find myself sinking into the same rut. As usual our diocese will have a "scald" after Midnight Mass in the college chapel. But we all agreed to go easy on it this year. A very heavy meal at two in the morning makes one's stomach feel like a corrugated washboard the next day. So our simple little repast will include cereal, ham and eggs, fruit, mincemeat pie. Last year we had a real buster, and I think the diocese was burping for a whole week after. A "scald" is a substitute for the American way of celebrating Christmas, but a d .... poor one.

I am much encouraged by the recent performances of the newly ordained priests in singing a Solemn High Mass. Almost all the fellows who were in the choir do rather poorly; and all the fellows who were not in the choir are at least passable. Of course, I still believe in originality and will probably invent three or four new scales before I get to the last Gospel.

Right now our diocese is engaged in a very serious investigation. We had accumulated some very fine implements for preparing "scalds" and had carefully stored it all in a villa box (a large wooden box that is used to haul one's belongings to the villa in the summer). The villa box with all its contents has disappeared. The difficulty is that at least nominally all that stuff is contraband; consequently, we can't appeal to any authority around here to recover it for us — like going to court to recover bootleg whiskey. We could forget about it if we didn't have such a fancy collection; there was enough stuff there to carry out a banquet — little stoves, pans, dishes, frying pan, stove to heat a room, knives, etc. We started a thorough search and came across something unexpected; we found someone else's villa box that had a fine set of stuff for furnishing a room (the fellow had left some three years ago). My part of the swag was a curtain for my window and a lamp — but we can't cook a "scald" with stuff like that.

Love,

Phil

Happy New Year to everyone.

Comments: Letter of December 19, 1938

(1)   We all regretted, especially at Christmas time, the lack of good Jewish merchants because we were confident that they would have made a difference in the merchandise in Rome. As I noted before, there were Christmas "shepherds" who strolled some of the busy streets playing bagpipes; the shepherds of Italy played bagpipes, but they lacked the power of the British bagpipers.

December 28, 1938

NORTH AMERICAN COLLEGE
Via Dell' Umilta 30

Dear Everybody,

Midnight Mass was very impressive. The sacristans are a stage crew and they do an excellent job of strewing the whole chapel with festoons of laurel, bay leaves, holly, pines, etc. To add the final Hollywood touch only the lights on the main altar are lit while the college files in. The candlelight on the rich marble draped in Christmas greens is very effective. The whole Mass was excellent.

After the Mass the work came. As someone said, it's like falling off the high altar on one's belly. We had a sensible "scald", but some of the barbecues arranged almost defied description. I am told (I didn't see it, and I wouldn't believe it entirely unless I had seen it.) that one group, eleven fellows, put away three turkeys in the course of the evening. One of the eleven was Joe Spitzig who was at the University either last year or the year before last.

The day was climaxed by the combination shoe and movie; the movie was "Snow White and the Seven Dwarfs." But the short entertainment before the movie was concocted by the fellows. The object was to give the faculty presents; of course, much went on before the presents were handed out. Then the Rector was given a toy train that went down the track and came straight back (in honor of the short "bum runs" this year); that almost tore the house down. The Vice Rector was given a little soldier's suit because he always plays the part of the policeman in the house. All this was carried out with appropriate cracks. When the Rector was given his present, the Vice Rector laughed all over — but not for long, because his came right at him.

The library, where all this is held, was decorated very elegantly by our class. All in all it was an extremely successful Christmas. I think that movie of Snow White is one of the cleverest things I have ever seen. The Italians are crazy about it.

Happy New Year to all and many thanks for the perfect Christmas.

Love,

Phil

Comments: Letter of December 28, 1938

(1)   The chapel was perfect for the celebration of Christmas — the beautiful marble walls blended with the Christmas decorations and the gem-like picture of the Blessed Mother, our Lady of Humility, focused attention on the Birthday of the Divine Infant. The war rumors nurtured a spirit of unity and home-like feeling among the students. The Masses at midnight and in the morning with the Solemn Benediction in the evening gave us a full and inspiring Christmas.

Cardinal Pacelli entering the College.

Visit of Cardinal Pacelli, Secretary of State, in center. Cardinal Mundelein, Chicago, on his left. Ambassador of U.S. to Italy and assistant on his left, 1938.

Cartoon of North American College Student - also called "Del Norder" a contraction of the Italian name of the College, Collegio Americano del Nord. Cartoon by student artist Maxie Catich.

Archbishop Michael J. Curley of Baltimore with his seminarians, North American College, 1938.

On a "bum run" to Florence; Phil Hannan in the back seat, right.

1939

January 16, 1939

NORTH AMERICAN COLLEGE
Via Dell' Umilta 30

Dear Everybody,

Your foreign correspondent has put in a very busy week. To begin with the least important: I saw Chamberlain when he came to Rome — if seeing an open car streak by with two people in it at such a distance that they could have been two of the original apostles for all I know can be called really seeing anyone. The English flag was very prominent all over Rome, and just a year ago they were ready to fight England! Chamberlain had an audience with the Pope, lasted half an hour so they say, and left him very much impressed. I was much surprised to find that the Italians flocked out to watch Chamberlain at the few functions he attended. [1]

During the past week we had an exceptionally excellent talk on Communism by a French Jesuit — they say he is French but he speaks so many languages that even he has probably forgotten which is his native tongue. The Rector introduced him and was in his normal good form; he thanked the priest for the excellent talk that he gave last year — the only difficulty being that he did not give us a talk last year. But no use fighting about trifles. The high points in the fellow's speech were that Communism in Europe was definitely on the decline and that they are now concentrating on the U.S., especially in New York and California. The tremendous information of this priest was amazing; he knew all about the Dies committee investigation in the U.S., the tactics of Communism in Costa Rica, the proceedings of the last meeting in Russia, etc. Without mentioning his name he gave Father Coughlin a terrific drubbing about the facts he quoted trying to prove that the Jews were responsible for Communism; he contends that the facts he quoted are just Nazi propaganda. He ended by making a big plea for prayers for Russia. This year is the 950th anniversary of the conversion of Russia, and he wants to get some priests back into the country. [2] Risky business.

Again the rumor is revived that this building will be torn down this year. [3] That was soft-pedaled for a while, but now the Rector has said that the place will go (not publicly). When the accumulated furniture of the ages starts to pour out of this den, it will look like Old Mother Hubbard on the move.

I received a very unusual letter today. The assistant director of the N.C.W.C. wrote and asked if I could write two articles about the celebration of Easter and Christmas in Rome at the North American College. Of course, that will depend on the permission of the Rector. I could write them an inside article that would singe their beards, but it wouldn't be what they want. If I told them about some of the all-night feeds that some of the dioceses have after Midnight Mass, it would give them a husky jolt. They don't know what they're asking for but I suppose I'll give them the type of thing they want, though it's the most unappetizing subject I have hit in a long time. The Rector will probably keel over when I show him the letter.

Love,

Phil

Comments: Letter of January 16, 1939

(1)   Chamberlain was popular because he capitulated to Hitler and the Italians thought that this would prevent a war. They still did not understand that Hitler was determined to have a war, regardless of the surrenders they made to him in his demands for more territory.

(2)   The fact was that the Church was sending priests secretly into Russia. There was a Collegium Russicum (Russian College) that trained priests to get into Russia secretly. Of course, they never gave any press releases about their activities.

(3)   Despite the rumors, the old building was not wrecked and is actually still in existence, completely refurbished and is the residence for some American priests doing graduate studies in Rome and is also the office for Americans to receive tickets for Papal Audiences. Its name is Casa Santa Maria.

January 23, 1939

NORTH AMERICAN COLLEGE
Via Dell' Umilta 30

Dear Everybody,

How do you like this little incident? One of the cooks ate some of the fish that was served at the faculty table on Friday and got very sick. The faculty remains as healthy as ever. If the poor cook had eaten some of the fish for the students, I guess we should have had a funeral Mass by now. None of the students got sick.

Speaking of food reminds me of a letter I received from one of the alumni. We sent out letters asking for subscriptions to our magazine and one priest from Chicago sent me a food chart that he had drawn up himself and a number of letters of recommendation. He explained it by saying that he had spent six years in Rome and that it had ruined him for life (although he has been a pastor for some time). He quoted the Bible to prove that he was right about his theory on food. I took the letter down to the Spiritual Director, and he enjoyed it; however, it seems that he isn't the only priest crazy on the subject of food in the U.S. I can easily understand it, because I don't doubt at all that the students here a number of years ago just spent an endurance contest. But that reminds me of the oldest living alumnus who is a monsignor in Baltimore; he spent one year in Rome at the del Nord, 1879, and left for France to die. He had consumption, but he is still alive! I was told that the former counselor at the embassy in Rome was a whack on dieting and his theory was that one was supposed to eat food of only one kind at a meal. One day he came to dinner at the college, for some feast or other, and he ate nothing but duck. He ate a whole duck, and not a thing else — not even celery or bread. A nice guest to have.

Last night they held a big reception at the royal palace for one of the princesses who is engaged to be married to an Italian-French count. [1] Whenever they have such a reception they park the cars just in back of the college, almost directly under my room. It always turns out to be a near riot. They have about twenty policemen directing the parking, and, of course, each cop has his own plan and ideas. The chief director of them all is a fellow who does everything but swallow his false teeth when he gives an order; for some hitherto unknown reason he always wears a sword. I can't imagine what he would do with it other than puncture tires if he got sore at the chauffeurs. The princess is very pretty, and she is engaged to a real dope, so they say. Royalty will never amount to anything until they get new ideas about this marriage business.

The carving that I had made for the family at Christmas time has been sent. This time I had to make out four applications to get it through the customs.

A few days ago we met an interesting English priest in the forum; he had been educated in Spain and is now teaching in Paris. He had just gotten out of Spain when the war broke out, and he had some pretty awful stories. His Bishop was hacked to pieces by women armed with axes, and the seminary at which he taught was taken over by the Feds. The stories he had about France were just about in the same style. The clergy and nuns in France are ready for anything; the nuns have civilian clothes all ready in case of a Communist uprising, and the priests have taken the same precaution. [2] But recently Communism has decreased greatly in France owing to the war threat; whenever a war threatens, the French believe in loyalty to the nation first.

We are enjoying a little rest now. The Vice Rector has gone away on a little trip and the Rector is in bed with a cold. "It's an ill wind that doesn't blow somebody some good."

Love,

Phil

Comments: Letter of January 23, 1939

(1)　　The Italian princess was Princess Margherita; and the Prince had a long name ending in Borbon y Borbon; and by the strangest coincidence, I met him at the end of the war in a woods in Germany where I was celebrating Mass for our soldiers, as well as for a group of refugees. Among the refugees was the Prince, and I asked him about his wife. He said that the Germans had put him and his wife in a small house in the woods as a kind of house arrest and that she was not well; and therefore, could not come to the Mass. I told him that I remembered their wedding, which really surprised him.

(2)   The stories about the Civil War in Spain were wrenching and very widespread. The reason for the worry of the French about them was that the remainder of the Republican Army (the army of the Communist regime in Spain) was maneuvering to take refuge in France. Actually, many of them were interned at the border of France, but a large number of their Communist sympathizers were in Toulouse. It should also be remembered that the government of France was Socialist and, therefore, well inclined to the Reds.

January 30, 1939

NORTH AMERICAN COLLEGE
VIA DELL' UMILTA 30

Dear Everybody,

This morning (Sunday) we went for high Mass to the American church, Saint Susanna's, and heard the best exhibition of fubbing that Rome has seen in a long time. The pastor of the church is a Paulist named Father O'Neill, known to members of the clergy as "Repetition" O'Neill, and known to the college as Mother O'Neill. Whenever he gets up to make the announcements he repeats them all about three or four times, and each time he has a different account of them; today he was in rare form. He was trying to get over the point that Benediction was to be some time in the afternoon. First he announced that it would be at 5:45; the next time he read the announcements he said, 5:30; the third time he read them ("to make sure that everyone will know the time of the services") he said quarter to six. But he is a genius compared to the assistant he used to have. The assistant was a thin fellow who always had at least twelve jokes to tell — all of them old. He would always laugh before telling the joke, during it, and afterwards. The sight of him was enough to break up a whole gathering.

We hear quite a few ructions about the agitations to abolish the arms embargo to Spain. Well it won't make much difference in a couple of weeks. The taking of Barcelona was hailed by a public holiday in Rome, I suppose in all Italy. They even put stands up in the PiazzaVenezia, the large square in front of the palace in which Mussolini has his office. They had a demonstration and speech there the night that Barcelona surrendered. But instead of taking the stands down after the demonstration was over, they started to put up more. I think they are getting ready for the final victory of the war. And will have a real "buster" here in Rome when everything is finished. As a special feature, they had the orphans of some of the Italian troops killed in Spain.

For the past few weeks, they have had a big exhibition of the resources of Italy in Rome. Supposed to show that Italy is independent and can stand on her own resources during a war. According to the exhibition, they are all set for anything. A few days ago at the Greg University, one of the German fellows said he had received a letter from a friend of his in the army saying that no one says anything about it, but that they all expect Germany to show her might in 1940 — I hope I beat them to it and get out of Europe before things start. Meanwhile, Italy continues to keep working up the propaganda against France. It all leads but to one conclusion, unless things change radically, and there is no doubt what side the U.S. will favor in the next war.

Love,

Phil

Comments: Letter of January 30, 1939

(1) The placing of the stands for the victory celebration for the surrender of Barcelona in Spain in the PiazzaVenezia shows how open was the admission of Italy for assisting the forces of General Franco in Spain. It also showed how widespread was the support of Franco throughout Italy among the ordinary people. Nevertheless, I was somewhat surprised by the openness of the Italian government in showing their favor toward Franco because there was a large group of Communists in Italy, but their voice had been muted or disregarded.

(2) The struggle of Italy to become independent was doomed to failure. Both Germany and Italy were hampered by the lack of high–octane gasoline for their warplanes. There is no substitute for high–octane gas, and gradually during the war it became evident that Allied

pilots had an advantage, because their gas was more powerful than that of the Axis powers. The capture by Germany of the Ploesti oilfields in Romania did not compensate for their lack of high-octane gas.

February 7, 1939

NORTH AMERICAN COLLEGE
VIA DELL' UMILTA 30

Dear Everybody,

Before I begin to give you a small description of what ructions Roosevelt's reported statement that "France is our boundary" created, I must warn you that a couple of bottles of hair tonic will arrive at 1501.

The report on Roosevelt's speech set off a tremendous explosion of word slinging. There is no doubt that he scared Italy purple. I am convinced that we could preserve world peace simply by re-arming and threatening to use our strength; we should never be called to use it, because it wouldn't be necessary. The editorials and articles in the Italian newspapers were the last word in bluster and hypocritical indignation at the "hostile move" of Roosevelt. But in such a contest of ballyhoo, there is always one newspaper that reaches the apex, and in this case it was the radical "Il Tevere" that wrote a huge editorial on the front page that went something like this: we can't understand the politics of Roosevelt until we understand the man. Now the most important thing about the president, and one that is often forgotten, is that he is a paralytic; this infirmity has ruined his whole character. Suffering from this ailment, he has developed an alarmist attitude, a tendency to fear aggression, because he can't defend himself and naturally this personal fear has reflected itself in his foreign policy. It was the most fantastic piece of political observation that has dirtied a newspaper in recent years. Of course, there were other editorials that, even in sheer hysterical effort, surpassed this. What I can't understand at all is why Italy and Germany should jump on Roosevelt as a warmonger. It's positively sickening to read all this rant over here about Germany and Italy being the big powers for peace when everyone knows that Germany is trying to get her hands on

Ukrainia now, and hasn't a shadow, or a pretense of a right to it. I am sorry that Roosevelt denied his statement, because he certainly called the bluff of Germany and Italy, and we are the only nation capable of scaring them.

This incident caused a bit of feeling at the Greg University. Some of the more stupid Italian seminarians wouldn't speak to some of the Americans after Roosevelt's speech was reported. Of course, that was true in only two or three cases, but it shows how a national feeling can be stirred up to wipe out every trace of clear thinking. Propaganda can make black out of white. Although our form of government has many faults, I think it is far better than any dictatorship in Europe.

Last night we had "Annie Oakley" for the movie show, and it was the funniest thing I have seen in a long time. The Rector was made an honorary chief of one of the Indian tribes and at the end of the show, as he walked out, the whole college began to give Indian war whoops and shouts. He enjoyed the joke (lucky for the community.) When a man signs up to be on the faculty here, he automatically agrees to take a ride from a community that never gets tired and never gives up.

Love,

Phil

Comments: Letter of February 7, 1939

(1)   It was a surprise to me that the speech of Roosevelt, despite the fact that the U.S. had practically no army, could cause such a sensation in Italy. It firmly convinced me that the U.S. had a very potent force for stopping war by simply threatening. Italy especially was cognizant of the strength of the U.S. resources because of the large number of Italians in our population and their dispersal or presence throughout the U.S. Politically, it was not possible for Roosevelt to back up a real threat against Italy and Germany but it would have been effective. The German generals, to a large extent, opposed the plans of Hitler, because they thought they were too grandiose to succeed. They would have been emboldened by a real threat by the U.S. to oppose Germany and Italy. After the war, we found that the German generals had hoped that France and England would have reacted against the seizure of the Ruhr by Germany, in defiance

of the Versailles Treaty after World War I. They thought that any strong military threat could have stopped Hitler.

(2)   The reaction of some of the Italian seminarians showed how sensitive they were to any reflection on Italy. Even though they were against the war and the militarism of Mussolini, they were still very proud of their native country and resented anything that seemed to be offensive to Italy's prestige.

February 13, 1939

NORTH AMERICAN COLLEGE
Via Dell' Umilta 30

Dear Everybody,

As the world knows, the Pope is dead. What the world does not know is the dramatic suddenness of his death; actually, the morning that he died they were putting up the big notices around town that there would be a big celebration commemorating the anniversary of his coronation and the signing of the Lateran Pact. Just the day before he died, they had draped St. Peter's in ceremonial red and erected the throne; the throne was still there even on Saturday morning. There was an aching loneliness and vacancy about that throne. We received the news at the college before almost any college in Rome. Just before morning prayers began at six, the Spiritual Director said very simply, "I have the sad duty to inform you that the Pope died at 5:30 this morning." A Requiem Mass was said for him then.

The body was to be laid out in the Sistine Chapel before being taken to St. Peter's, so we went over to see if we could get in. Some got in on Friday afternoon; I got into the Sistine on Saturday morning. He was laid on a bier about six feet high dressed in red vestments with a golden miter on his head. The layout was simple, the only note of color being the uniforms of the Guards. The Swiss Guards in dress uniform and full armor kept the visitors moving while the Noble Guards (dressed in shining hip boots, white breeches, gold-trimmed coat and golden helmet with a long horse hair mane falling from the crest) were the guard of honor around the coffin. We walked in with Bishops and Cardinals, the only distinction being that they sprinkled the corpse with holy water, then knelt in a specially reserved part of the Sistine Chapel. We were lucky enough to meet a very nice usher (the ushers are dressed in 16th century Spanish outfits) who told us we could stay as long as we wished. I stayed for about fifteen minutes, but I know of some fellows who stayed for an hour and a half! — an imposition on kindness I thought. The Sistine Chapel was lighted beautifully. All the pictures and walls were beautifully illumined, the great works of Michaelangelo, Raphael and others, making a very effective setting; the most impressive characteristic of such an affair is the blending of the centuries, for the unbroken continuity of the Church is evidenced in the liturgy, the uniforms, even the building.

It may interest you to know that the old custom of pillaging the papal apartment immediately after the Pope's death has also been carried out quite efficiently (and I use the word "quite" in its original meaning of completely). Unfortunately, there were hundreds of Italian bishops and cardinals in Rome, having gathered for the intended celebration of the Pope's coronation and the 10th anniversary of the signing of the Lateran Pact. Hence, the vultures were more than ordinarily numerous. The Pope's apartment was cleaned out completely — rugs, chairs, lamps, toilet articles, personal effects, everything but the wallpaper. Souvenir hunting is not an American invention, as so many people think; in fact, we have much to learn from the methodical pillaging carried on in Rome. They say that his aged sister either did not get, or was not interested in getting, anything. But I hardly believe that, for the Pope had also nieces and grandnieces, and I am sure that they were interested in getting some mementoes of the famous member of their family. It was also discovered (maybe this has already been published in the newspapers) that the Pope never took the medicine prescribed for him by his doctors; they found the untouched bottles neatly stored away. He had too great a confidence in his physical strength, and had a curious distrust of doctors. There is no doubt that he had a real mountaineer's strength and that his tremendous will kept him going longer than it was thought possible, but he actually killed himself working. He was given strict orders not to do a thing on Wednesday and Thursday, but he dragged himself out of bed and worked over documents all day long. [1] That was the end of the road. Thursday night he became worse and died Friday morning.

Whatever may be said in praise of the Pope, and hardly any praise is too great, it can be truly said that hardly any Pope was called upon to rule in such a troubled time and that he was equal to every crisis. His authority was challenged and assailed by more dictators and governments than probably any Pope in modern times, but he met every challenge and left the Church more unified and militant than when he ascended the throne. (2) He certainly lived up to the motto of the <u>Osservatore Romano</u>, "They shall not prevail."

Already there is talk of a possible candidate for his successor. Cardinal Della Costa of Florence seems to be in the running, and also Cardinal Schuster of Milan. Cardinal Della Costa is a very holy man, and a strong anti-Fascist; it would be very interesting to see how Italy and Germany would receive him. Cardinal Schuster has Fascist sympathies, but recently condemned very strongly the race theory of Fascism. The Italians say that the newspapers will try to play up Cardinal Della Costa's name before the conclave because any such popularity, or newspaper talk, will kill (as it has done) any possibility of his election. We shall see. Nobody today can doubt that the papal election is run strictly according to the rules of secrecy and with no political engineering — could you imagine any of our American Cardinals being dictated to be a government in Europe? I, myself, would like to see either Cardinal Pacelli or Cardinal Gerlier of Lyon, France, get it (Gerlier is a real man — war veteran, lawyer, priest, made cardinal because he was so effective in organizing Catholic labor unions in France to combat the Communist unions). But the Italians would go crazy if a Frenchman were to get it; I think it's high time to get away from this tradition of Italian Popes.

This morning, Sunday morning, the Pope's body was moved from the Sistine to St. Peter's. I'll go over to see it this afternoon.

The college awaits with great interest the advent of the three American cardinals, none of whom agrees with each other although all are Roman students. What a cargo of freight to ship across too! A story goes the rounds that some years ago both Cardinal O'Connell and Cardinal Dougherty had dinner at the College. During the course of the dinner, Cardinal Dougherty leaned over to the Rector of the College and said, "What are the rules about smoking?" The Rector said, "The boys are not allowed to smoke anywhere except in their rooms." "Make them cut it out entirely," said Card. Dougherty. Then Cardinal O'Connell leaned over to the Rector and said in a clear voice, "Allow the boys to smoke, Rector, there's nothing wrong with it." So you see how they agree.

During the week, the day before the Pope died, I had a very interesting talk with Monsignor Wilpert, the foremost Christian archeologist in the world. [3] The Monsignor is now 83 years old, very alert, still working steadily. I spoke to him in his room in the Anima College (a German outfit, Wilpert is a German). We had a long talk about many of the big shots in his field — he wasn't backward in giving his honest opinion — and finally became very friendly. Finally, I suggested that he have his most recent work (which shows all the evidence in the catacombs and old basilicas for the teaching and practices of the early Church) translated into English. After a while, he asked me to see if I could look after it. So now I must write to a priest in Oregon who wanted to do it and have it printed in America; but Wilpert doesn't want to send all his illustration (his book has 155 illustrations) to a press in America. So now, I have to see what can be done about it all. Very interesting work for this summer. Anyway, I shall learn a lot in a number of ways.

Love,

Phil

P.S. I shall send you accounts of all the events in Rome during the next few days. Maybe it will be worthwhile to save these next few letters.

Comments: Letter of February 13, 1939

(1)   There is no doubt that Pope Pius XI spent his last hours trying to complete a statement, possibly a formal condemnation of Nazism and other forms of dictatorship, as well as a rallying cry for the Catholic world to oppose the coming war. There is a solid tradition that unless a Pope has written and signed a statement to be published, the writing should not be published, hence the lack of any attempt to find and disseminate what he was writing when he died.

(2)   The mourning in Italy was very genuine. The Italians had a very high respect for Pope Pius XI's integrity, courage and opposition to

all forms of dictatorships. They had relied on his direction and strength to curb the effects of Fascism and Nazism.

I thought that the funeral arrangements were perfect; they portrayed his august position as the formerVicar of Christ and they did not indulge in any undue embellishment. The gesture that was most definitive to me was the breaking of his ring immediately after his death. Of course, this is to prevent any possible counterfeiting of statements by him and an affirmation that his tenure of office is terminated.

(3)   In regard to Father Joseph Wilpert, he spent his priestly life in the work of exploring the catacombs as a work of evangelism. His book, "*La Chiesa Nascente*" (The Church A-borning; orThe Infant Church) deals with the evidence in the catacombs of the activities and beliefs of the very early Church. He was prescient about the work of excavating the catacombs. He made a great discovery of the fresco in the Greek Chapel, which is the earliest picture of the celebration of Mass, and he felt that many more similar discoveries could be made. I owe him a great deal of my interest in the catacombs.

February 20, 1939

NORTH AMERICAN COLLEGE
VIA DELL' UMILTA 30

Dear Everybody,

Before I begin on the ceremonies at St. Peter's for the burial of the Pope, I'll tell you the story about Saint Gregory's Church. Saint Gregory was a very wealthy and pious man who turned over his home to the poor and helped feed them himself; later he was made Pope, and among other things sent the monks who converted England; he was noted for his devotion to aiding the souls in Purgatory and on various occasions he saw souls liberated from Purgatory after he had said Mass for them. They preserved the altar on which he celebrated Mass and preserved the custom of saying Mass there for the souls in Purgatory; later, by miracles and other signs, it was shown that St. Gregory was still interceding for souls for whom Mass was said on his altar, so the practice was finally approved by the Church.

The Pope was buried with great solemnity, in fact endless solemnity. Masses are still being said every day for the repose of his soul; usually a cardinal says the Mass, which is always celebrated at the high altar in St. Peter's. Today, Sunday morning, there were forty-two cardinals present at the Mass. A number of the cardinals have been very friendly when meeting the fellows from the college on the streets. A number of the fellows met Cardinal Innitzer — who is, by the way, a very powerful man; he is built like a typical large German. Cardinal Verdier, from Paris, is also a very gracious man to meet. But the fellow who is causing all the talk is Cardinal Della Costa of Florence (whom I told you about in my last letter); he is a very saintly man and doesn't care whom his remarks hit. A story is told of him that he walked into a Fascist meeting and promptly told them all that they should be thinking more of their souls. However, most people think that he will not get it. The rumor goes around that a party is forming behind Cardinal Maglioni. Strangely enough, not very much talk is heard about Cardinal Pacelli, a man whom the whole world knows to be a saintly man and a finished diplomat. There are a few remarks about the cardinal of Portugal, a young energetic man of only 52. I should like to see Cardinal Pacelli get it; he has a strong leaning towards the democratic countries and is a very shrewd man (one of the reasons why the Nazis in Germany hate him so much).

Now about the American Cardinals. The Rector certainly got himself in a mess, but blind luck got him out of it again. When he heard that Cardinal O'Connell was not coming (the first rumor here was that he would not come), he promptly cabled an invitation to Cardinal Dougherty to stay at the college. Just after he had done that he heard that Cardinal O'Connell was coming. . . . . and Lord knows this building is not large enough to hold both of them. But Cardinal Dougherty arrived last night and went to a hotel next to where Mom and Bill stayed last summer. The real event is yet to come — the arrival of Cardinal Mundelein; if he expects to get a hero's welcome as he did last November, he is sadly mistaken. The college didn't budge an inch to welcome Cardinal Dougherty, and it remains to be seen what will be done for the Eminence of Boston. We can be sure of one thing — if the college does nothing for Cardinal O'Connell and pretends not to take public notice of his presence, the Cardinal will certainly do as he pleases with the college. He just takes over the joint when he comes over. He was Rector here at one time; and whenever he comes back, he simply starts where he left off. He gives the students hell if he catches them doing what he thinks is not proper and does the same for the faculty; the fellows are very anxious to see him around, just to see how the faculty behaves under fire. The last time he was here he stayed in the college <u>25 days</u> — the faculty almost had a nervous breakdown before they got rid of him. Then, as though that is not enough for one year, the faculty will have the pleasure of meeting Archbishop Curley of Baltimore (for whom they have a tremendous respect). It looks like a tough year for the faculty. For twelve years we have been waiting for the Archbishop to come over; I only wish that there were some public occasion at which he could tell the world where to get off. Everyone will be disappointed if he doesn't blow off at least once over here.

To add to the general excitement, the story is heard that Lloyds of London is giving 2 to 1 odds that there will be a war within the next two months!! And here am I loaded up with subscriptions for a publication that will certainly be nipped in the bud if war comes. A very quiet, easy, uneventful life.

Love,
Phil

Comments: Letter of February 20, 1939

(1)   Although there was talk about the possible election of Cardinal Della Costa, the prevailing opinion was that Cardinal Pacelli would certainly be elected. There was great need to continue the opposition of the Church to all the dictatorships, and Cardinal Pacelli was completely linked with the Policy of Pius XI against the dictatorships. In fact, there was a debate about what sign could be given that he had been elected, so that the workers in the conclave could signal easily to their confreres in the press to let them know who had been elected.

(2)   The presence of the American cardinals drew attention not only at

the College but wherever they stayed. Cardinal Dougherty stayed at the Hotel Majestic on the Via Veneto, and the hotel always flew the Cardinal's flag from the entrance of the hotel. This courtesy was also a good ad for the hotel. The cardinals did not form any kind of a bloc for the election of the Pope, and so there was no great amount of patronizing of them by the press.

February 28, 1939

NORTH AMERICAN COLLEGE
Via Dell' Umilta 30

Dear Everybody,

At last they have finished with their air raids and taken to playing cards to take up their time. During every raid the Rector and Spiritual Director came up to the apartment of the Vice Rector on the top floor; I don't know whether they were afraid to be alone in the dark or feared an uprising from the student body, but as soon as the lights went off they rushed up there. The last raid was the best; it lasted longer and caused far more inconvenience to the city. When the lights went out the last time we were at dinner, and our table finished cleaning the plates with the help of two acolyte's candles. [1]

A month ago I was surprised to find how the students went up and racked the rooms of the departing Vice Rector. This morning I found that it is an old Roman custom. Whenever the election of the new Pope was announced, the rabble in the streets would rush to the home of the cardinal who had been elected Pope and pillage his home because he would have no more use for it. If the newly elected Pope had not been a wealthy man, there was all sorts of disappointment and grumbling. The nobles and wealthy people used to bet on the Cardinals as future Popes, and the banks in Rome acted as bookies and betting centers when the election was on. Further, when a Pope died and his death was announced by the tolling of a bell on the Capitol hill, a real carnival and riot started. The police and those in charge of the jails liberated all those imprisoned (because the crowd would if the police didn't) and ran to their homes to take shelter. There was no law in the time between the death of a Pope and the election of his successor; any man who had a private grudge, or spite against anyone, availed himself of the opportunity, and it was a case of Lord help the chief of police if he had been guilty of any severity. After every man had his little fling at his enemies, the city settled down to having a carnival and betting on the new Pope. There was a case of one old Pope, a strong man, who contracted some fatal disease but didn't die quickly enough to please the people. Further, he had started the hated Inquisition in Rome, and as some would say, "nobody liked him nohow." So the crowd burned down the jail, burned down the palace of Inquisition, and wanted to burn the college of the Dominicans (who had been in charge of some of the proceedings of the court of Inquisition) and kill the Dominicans. Then they gathered and rioted in front of the papal residence until the old man finally died. It must have been great stuff in those days to have watched a papal election. But if the old Rome was like the present Rome in some spots, I don't blame the people for rioting. The conditions in which some of these people live are terrific; walking to some of the old churches is sometimes anything but edifying.

They have revived an ancient practice at the college; as I told you the whole college is organized into "cameratas," and one usually goes anywhere and everywhere with his camerata, and without his camerata he goes nowhere. Now they even go down to chapel in camerata formation; no one starts down to chapel until the whole group is formed and then goes down with it. I am curious to learn the reason for the origin of this lock-step business. I have no objections to it because I like the fellows in my camerata, but what a bore it would be if the fellows weren't congenial. The whole seminary system in Rome seems to begin with the supposition that a seminarian, if left to his own inclinations would promptly and certainly do everything to disgrace the clergy and send himself to hell. We believe in free will as a doctrine of faith, but they seem to ignore it in practice here. The only objection to it is that if a fellow must go to the same church or same place as the camerata wishes, even though they go to dismally out-of-the-way spots. (Such is not my case, but I take my hat off to the fellows in the other seminaries in Rome who are not used to the discipline and must put up with it for four years.)

We had an unexpected break on the night before the birthday of George Washington; the chaplain to the American Catholic medical students in Rome (of whom there are quite a number) gave them a show "The Texas Rangers", but had to hold it at the college because he was forced to use the college projector and screen; so that night we saw the show again. Cowboys, Indians, shooting, riding — hot dog!! Reminded me of a few years ago at the Immaculate Conception when they used to have shows for a nickel and Brother Louis ran the machine; the only difference is that we make more noise here. We went to school, of course, on George Washington's Birthday, but we celebrated by giving the English a good ride; the Scotch were all behind us. Fortunately, the Rector has almost a boyish enthusiasm for movies, especially those with lots of fighting and shooting; it's a very good way to work off extra energy or a grouch.

Love,

Phil

Comments: Letter of February 28, 1939

(1)   The repetition of the air raids always reminded us that the government knew that a war was impending. It also seemed to me to mean that the war would begin in the fall because the air raids were held also in the winter when the sun had set before seven o'clock. Obviously, they were getting the people ready to have air raids in the evening and at night.

March 2, 1939

NORTH AMERICAN COLLEGE
VIA DELL' UMILTA 30

Dear Everybody,

    We saw the new Pope elected — as much as could be seen. I'll give you an account of the whole day.

    The conclave was to open with Mass in the morning at 9:30 followed by the first ballot, which was to be finished about eleven. If there was no election on the first ballot, then a second was to follow immediately. After the second, even if it was negative, there was to be a signal from the famous smokestack erected on the Vatican Palace (by the way, the smokestack is ridiculously small). Therefore, if a signal came after the first ballot at eleven o'clock, we were certain that a new Pope had been elected. As the hour approached, the whole crowd became tense, but eleven came and went and nothing happened. Evidently the first ballot had not accomplished anything. The next ballot was to be finished at 12:30. By this time the huge piazza was filling because the rumor was that Cardinal Pacelli would be elected on the first day; a few of the Italian cardinals were outspoken in their belief that the conclave would last only a day. Finally, at about 12:25 smoke started to roll out of the smokestack. The first few puffs were white, and the crowd, a little too amazed at the sudden election, was slow to get excited; the excitement was short-lived because soon great puffs of black smoke came billowing out. No Pope yet. The suspense and excitement is intense. Always, the first smoke is white, and the tension between the first few puffs and the final billowing out is tremendous. White smoke means the Pope is elected, black means that he is not. So everyone asks everyone else, Is it white? Is it black? Half are yelling that the Pope has been elected, half are settling down to wait for the results of the next ballot. We were lucky enough to be standing near an old Italian who seemed ancient enough to be able to remember St. Peter, and he told us that it was black, no Pope. Thus the morning passed, and the crowd going home to dinner began to say that the chances for Cardinal Pacelli were dwindling. [1]

Meantime, while waiting, we had picked up a pleasant conversation with some newspapermen. I met a fellow named Barry (he introduced himself as General Barry, but although he did have a couple of war wounds — shot off fingers, etc. — he didn't seem old enough to have been a general) who was the representative of the British newspapers for the conclave. He tried to speak Italian to me; I thought he was German, from his accent, and replied in German. But the little German I know stopped him completely. Then it dawned on me that he was English. He tried to get the dope from me, and I pumped him for some of his stories. Announcements were being made by the Vatican on a broadcasting outfit for the occasion, and I translated them for him. Among other things he told me that three English reporters had tried to crash the conclave, had been escorted to the limits of Vatican City and then escorted to the border by the Italian Government. The French reporters couldn't get into the country. The only reporter who ever scooped the news of the election was a reporter for the New York Herald some years ago on the occasion of the election of Pius X, who had been cardinal of Venice. This reporter had it fixed up with a servant, who was in contact with another layman who had access to the cardinals, to give him the name of the newly elected Pope by a code of signals. Now the signal for the cardinal of Venice was a motion of the fingers like scissors — the cardinal's name was Sarto, which means "tailor." So the servant slipped the reporter the signal, and the Herald got the news long before anyone else.

But, back to the election. The balloting in the afternoon was to start at 4 o'clock; and therefore, would be finished at about 5:30. We arrived early. Hardly a soul was expecting the election on this ballot. Finally, the smoke started to come, very slowly and very sparingly. The crowd hushed completely, waiting to see if the black smoke would come after a minute's pause. It was late in the afternoon, and in the waning sunlight the smoke was very indistinct. A little more white smoke came, then it all stopped. Some began to scream that a Pope had been elected; most waited because visibility was poor. Meantime, the cameramen had been grinding away steadily; and in front of us was the Fox Movietone man who had a radio in his car, and he received the news on the radio that the Pope had been elected. He made the announcement in very American language, "Well, folks, they shot the works." Meantime some of the personal servants had run out on the roof of the Vatican Palace and began waving and shouting wildly. Then one of the liveried servants or men-in-waiting, jumped up on the railing of the roof waving a red cloak — it was the discarded mantle of Cardinal Pacelli. But the distance was so great that no one heard what name he was shouting. By this time, the tremendous crowd, ever growing by people swooping in from every angle, was seething. Then somebody started a very familiar, popular Italian hymn, and that swept through the crowd like a tidal wave. Immediately after this hymn a group started the "*Te Deum*" ("We Praise Thee God") and everyone took it up. The sound welled up, recoiled from the great façade like a huge sounding board and rolled down the huge piazza between the colonnades of Bernini. By this time we had been standing for over an hour, yet none felt tired in the least. Just as the last note of the "*Te Deum*" rolled off into the clouds, the balcony was draped and out came Cardinal Caccia-Dominiani to announce the election. I have seldom heard such a moment; the tension was so thick that one could cut it. He strode to the end of the balcony, took up the microphone and in a ringing voice called out, "I announce to you a great joy. We have a Pope, the most Reverend and Eminent Lord, Lord Cardinal Eugene ... (he never finished the last syllable of Eugene because the crowd screamed so loud that New York must have heard it; but after a short time he continued) Pacelli, who has taken the name Pius XII." [2] When the crowd heard that he had taken the name Pius, then all the old enthusiasm for the dead Pope sprung up and expressed itself in a tremendous shout. If there had ever been a doubt that the old Pope did not own the hearts of the Italians, it was certainly dispelled by that ovation. [3]

Before I tell you about the first papal benediction by the new Pope, I must tell you that it was announced that March 2 was the birthday of Pope Pius XII. That increased the enthusiasm past the breaking point.

When the Pope came out to give his blessing, everyone shouted everything they could think of; everyone was waving hats, scarves, handkerchiefs. But when he started to give his benediction, a great hush immediately settled on the whole piazza, and all those who could possibly manage it, kneeled. Then the shouting started all over again. I was directly in front of the balcony and had an excellent view of all the proceedings. But the Pope started to give his blessing again, and again everything settled. By this time it was deep dusk, and the moon had just come up flooding the young night with a soft glow. So ended the Pope's first public appearance. But our day was not yet ended.

The newspaper extras had already made their appearance by the time we had started home. And just at the side of the colonnade was a fellow with a few papers left; he was crouching on the papers trying to keep the crowd from snatching them before paying. The crowd was very dense, but I determined to get two of them, one for myself and one for the fellow with whom I was walking. I knifed my way through the outer fringe rather easily by a free use of my elbows. Then just separating me from the man crouching on his papers were three Dominicans. They suspected nothing, and were completely interested in getting the papers. The situation was perfect. I picked the first fellow up bodily and eased him over my shoulder, letting him fall gently into the crowd pressing behind me; he still has no idea what happened. I did the same with the second, and he also disappeared in a small cloud of flying white robes. I don't recall what I did to the third, but I have a hazy recollection that I tripped him up backwards — I say hazy recollection because by this time my interest was focused entirely on the papers. I got the papers and turned to fight my way out. How I ever made it with all my paraphernalia intact is more than I can understand. I do remember that my companion had to help drag me out. A wonderful experience; a great sense of exhilaration after such an accomplishment. [4]

I neglected to tell you what a grandstand play Cardinal O'Connell made in his dramatic entrance to the conclave. He made himself as late as possible in coming over, one of the reporters on the boat said that there was absolutely no reason why he could not have taken the Aquitania and come down to Rome through Europe in plenty of time for the conclave. When he arrived in Naples he simply brushed aside the ecclesiastics sent to greet him, though he did give a big blow to the member of the faculty from our college sent down to meet him. The Italian government had a special train waiting for him and the two South American Cardinals who came with him. But his Eminence stepped into a private car and drove to Rome.

He arrived in Rome about noon. The conclave was supposed to start about four-thirty. He refused to leave his hotel until about twenty minutes after four. Then he breezed majestically like a clipper ship into the room; in fact, he breezed in so fast that he sneaked by the Swiss Guards who were supposed to escort him from the door to the large waiting room where all the cardinals were gathered. But his Eminence didn't fool the Guards long. They stopped him, brought him back to the door and escorted him in according to the usual custom. His Eminence was one of the three cardinals who asked Cardinal Pacelli if he accepted the papacy. And now, for some unknown reason, the Cardinal is not coming to the college for dinner; he will visit it, but not for dinner.

Of course, the usual rumors are floating around about the voting. This seems to be the most reliable story: Cardinal Pacelli and Cardinal Della Costa of Florence were the two candidates, with the votes about evenly divided. After the first ballot, during the ten-minute recess, Cardinal Della Costa frowned at the cardinals who voted for him. No discussion of the voting is allowed in the intermissions or at any time in the conclave; no "lobby" is permitted under pain of excommunication. But Della Costa simply showed his disapproval. But they voted for him again on the next ballot, and again he showed a sign of disapproval. Then, in the third ballot it was almost unanimous for Pacelli. The story sounds credible. More later.

Love,

Phil

P.S. Bishop McCarthy of Portland, Maine, just asked to see me along with the two men from his diocese here. Very gracious, asked us to dinner too. He spoke for quite awhile about Rob, Mom, Mary. Please save this letter; I could use it for a diary.

Comments: Letter of March 2, 1939

(1)   The background of the immense interest in the election was the question: Will the cardinals elect someone with the same attitude of Pius XI towards the dictatorships, especially Nazism?

The Nazi government of Germany was openly and viciously against the election of Cardinal Pacelli who was seen as almost a clone of Pius XI in his attitude towards Nazism and the other dictatorships; that's the reason why at the end of the first day of voting it was felt that maybe Cardinal Pacelli would not be elected.

(2)   There was a very unusual reaction to the announcement of the identity of the new Pope. We were not aware of the fact that there were two Cardinals with the same first name — Cardinal Eugene Pacelli and Cardinal Eugene Tisserant. When Cardinal Caccia-Dominiani began the announcement of the identity of the new Pope and began to recite his name beginning with his first name, Eugene, there was a delirious whoop of joy by a group of French people thinking that Cardinal Eugene Tisserant had been elected. When Cardinal Caccia-Dominiani finally completed the name of the new Pope, Cardinal Eugene Pacelli, the French were very crestfallen. Of course, a few moments later they joined in the general celebration.

The announcement itself was in grand style. Cardinal Caccia-Dominiani had a wonderful baritone voice and the Latin language, with its sonorous vowels, enabled him to fashion a glorious announcement which so impressed me that today I still remember it in Latin — "*Annuntio vobis gaudium magnum. Habemus papam. Eminentissimum ac Reverendissimum Dominum Cardinalem Eugenium Pacelli qui sibi nomen imposuit Pium Duodecimum.*"

(3)   The joyous shout by the crowd at the time of the election was also a tribute to the former Pope and a resounding approbation of his reign as well as an agreement with the choice of name by the new Pope.

(4)   The action I took in securing the newspapers would have been impossible under any other circumstances. The pressure of the crowd, their complete lack of order and their intense pre-occupation of getting a newspaper made them completely oblivious of what was going on around them.

March 12, 1939
The Coronation

NORTH AMERICAN COLLEGE
Via Dell' Umilta 30

Dear Everybody,

As usual, there was a tremendous push to get tickets for the ceremony. Although the coronation ceremony occurred only about ten days after the election, they had an unprecedented demand for tickets — about 500,000 applications were made before they stopped counting. The basilica holds around 70,000. To add to the suspense and excitement, tickets were not issued (for fear of counterfeits) until about two days before the ceremony. All sorts of rumors got around — the college had no tickets, wouldn't get any, not even the royal family had gotten all that they had asked for, etc. Finally the tickets for the college came, and we all had tickets; I succeeded in getting myself opposite the main altar where I could see the Pope celebrate Mass.

The crowds started to pour into the basilica in the early hours of the morning. We arose at five, had Mass and a hurried, but plentiful, breakfast. One of the servants in the college, in coming to work, had gone by St. Peter's at four in the morning and told us that we should hurry; the basilica was being filled even then. And later an American priest told us that at five in the morning the number of taxis in the piazza had caused a jam!! Some from the college got over there by six thirty; I arrived before seven. So great a crowd was anticipated, that one could not even cross the Tiber unless he had a ticket. All the approaches to the basilica were blocked and wartime barricades were erected with whole companies of soldiers stationed all along the route. The immense colonnade around the piazza of St. Peter's was ringed with soldiers in between the columns. And the crowds did not disappoint them. It is estimated that about a million people were there at the coronation ceremony (which was held on the balcony of St. Peter's). You can imagine the sight, I can't describe it, except to quote what I heard a French lady exclaim, "Look, the whole world!"

The ceremony was supposed to begin at about 8:30; but, of course, the calculation must be made according to Italian mentality. The crowd was really interesting, and made the time pass very quickly. Almost all around us men were dressed in top hats and tails with the women in long black gowns. And most of them had come prepared to preserve their dignity — I saw more sandwiches and food dug out of the ample folds of ladies' gowns and men's formal dress than from delicatessen shops. The prize went to an old Frenchman, with an 1850 style dignity set off by a flowing mustache, who produced ham sandwiches from his high silk hat better than a magician. He couldn't have surprised us more if he had made a rabbit jump out. I might also mention the nun near us who saved one of our fellows from being chased out; this fellow had been standing in the corridor and the order was given to either find a seat (there were none at that time) or to go back. The nun saw the predicament of the fellow, fumbled around in the folds of her habit, drew out a folded campstool! Anything and everything happens in a crowd at St. Peter's. I have never been there yet when it didn't fall to my lot to carry somebody out. Yesterday was no exception. About half way through the ceremony, I saw a young couple trying to get out; both were well exhausted. By the time the lady got near me she was walking as though a column had hit her, and the guards were simply looking at both of them. I carried the lady out, but for all I know the fellow may have been trampled to death.

At about ten fifteen the Pope entered the basilica, went to the Blessed Sacrament altar, then to the altar of St. Gregory where he vested for Mass, the Cardinals paid him homage, part of the Office was recited. Then, he started his procession down the main aisle — and then, it sounded as though the roof was falling down. The procession is stopped three times while the master of ceremonies lights some flax, allows it to burn to a crisp, then says to the Pope, "Thus passes the glory of the world" (Sic transit gloria mundi.) If the Pope needed a reminder that both he and the glory of the world are mortal, he certainly received it when he passed near the main altar under which lies the body of Pius XI.

Finally, the Mass at the High Altar began, amid a setting that would remind one of the gathering of the tribes for the Last Judgment. There were eastern Bishops apparently dressed in silken rainbows, patriarchs who wore vestments rivaling the magnificence of the papal outfit, cardinals and canons, the Crown Prince of Italy, the Duke of Norfolk, mobs of uniformed diplomats, the Prince Assistant at the Throne (Prince Colonna), besides the normal magnificence afforded by the Swiss Guards and Noble Guards.

The Mass, unlike the Mass at some great events, was very edifying. The history of the ages is packed into the ceremony of a Mass celebrated by the Pope on the main altar in St. Peter's. It is a tremendous thrill to hear the Pope refer to himself in the prayers at the Mass — especially in the prayer, "O Lord, who gave to <u>me</u> the power ....." Then the ceremony of having a Greek assist and sing the Epistle and Gospel in his own language is very impressive (the Gospel and Epistle are also sung in Latin). And the Greek was vested in the vestments proper to his rite. Just before the singing of the Epistle, a Cardinal goes down to the grotto just about the tomb of St. Peter and sings a Litany composed for the occasion, and he sings it just above the tomb of St. Peter. By this time, there is certainly no doubt that all the Catholics really believe that the Pope is the successor of St. Peter. Then the Pope receives the homage of the Cardinals. The ancient elaborate ceremony of testing the bread and wine used at the Mass to make sure that they are not poisoned is also observed. And the Pope takes the consecrated wine through a little golden tube (just like a straw). The Elevation is also very impressive: the Pope elevates the Host and turns in three directions — he celebrates the Mass facing the people, then turns to his right and left.

And for once that huge basilica was very quiet and reverent. The blessing near the end of the Mass is another very solemn moment.

At the end of the Mass, the cardinal arch-priest (who has charge of the basilica) goes up and presents the Pope with a little purse — an offering for the Mass "well sung" (I like that clever little phrase, "well sung", I wonder what would happen if they were really truthful?) The Pope, by the way, has a very good singing voice; he must have been in a choir in his student days. But the Pope never keeps the offering; he always gives it to the cardinal assistant — in this case to Cardinal Gerlier of Lyons, France. The story was that the offering this year was a number of little jewels.

The Mass was not the only part of the ceremony. The coronation was to take place on the balcony of St. Peter's. After cheering for the Pope as he passed out of the basilica, the crowd rushed for the piazza; why there weren't scores crushed against the door supports is a mystery to me. Half a dozen fellows from the college prevented a near tragedy by some hefty work; the crowd knocked a number of women and children sprawling with the consequent danger of having them trampled but our fellows managed to pick them up out of danger. When fifty or seventy thousand try to push out three small doors ...... you should be in the middle of it to appreciate the pressure. I had an excellent position in the piazza, just in front of the balcony, and consequently I saw everything.

The Pope is seated on the balcony. After a prayer, a deacon comes and removes the miter the Pope has been wearing and places on him the tiara. It is a very simple, very solemn affair. A tremendous cheer goes up from the assembled crowd — in this case, from a crowd that extended from the doors of St. Peter's almost to the Tiber river. Then the assisting cardinal reads the granting of the indulgence to all those present, then the big moment arrives — the blessing of the Pope "to the city and to the world". Instead of remaining seated, the Pope arose and walked to the edge of the balcony. Bedlam broke loose. Even the princes, cardinals, ambassadors, etc. gathered on the roof of the Vatican palace let out a big howl. Every language under the sun was a part of that cheer. It was probably one of the largest crowds ever assembled. The Pope gave a few more blessings, then turned and departed. It was then about two o'clock in the afternoon. We had been at St. Peter's for over seven hours! And it was no sedentary occupation attending the ceremony. The strain of excitement, to say nothing of the physical strain of carrying on a minor war trying to get in a good position — and all on an empty stomach — is enough to wear down a giant.

There were a couple of notable incidents in the procession coming out. The Crown Prince and Princess, who make a very handsome couple, walked directly behind the Pope's chair, and when the people tried to cheer him he very gracefully stopped the demonstration, thus preventing anything that would take away from the homage given to the Pope. But Count Giano, Foreign Secretary for Italy was not so polite; he gave everyone the Fascist salute, one of the most ill-placed and ill-timed gestures I have ever seen.

So it all ended, certainly one of the greatest manifestations of devotion to the papacy that the world has ever seen. If a battle is coming, and almost no one doubts it, there will be plenty of force on the side of religion.

Love,

Phil

Comments: Letter of March 12, 1939

(1)   To understand the electrifying feeling of the gathering crowd for the first official Mass and coronation of the newly elected Pope, it should be remembered that it occurred in March which meant that the crowd actually started assembling long before daylight. It was an eerie feeling to hurry along with an excited crowd in the dark.

(2)   The ancient form of the procession for the newly elected Pope was impressive (no longer used) especially when the three candles were lit at various intervals with the reminder to the Pope, "Thus passes the glory of the world." This action is actually a recall of part of the ceremony used at the coronation of the Roman emperor in ancient times. Such customs, including the genuflection before the Blessed Sacrament, which replicates the gesture made before addressing the Emperor, show the antiquity of the Church.

(3)   Remember that the Mass was celebrated according to the Tridentine Mass, the Mass was in Latin as was determined by the Council of Trent which ended in 1565, and is much longer than the present Mass with Eucharistic Prayers I, II, III and IV.

(4) The coronation of the Pope is almost infinitely more solemn and meaningful than the coronation of a king or emperor. The supernatural character of the papal office and the power inherent in it, as well as the perpetuity of the office, confer a feeling of awe that is unique. These facts, as well as the moral dangers facing the world through the existence of three great anti-religious movements — Nazism, Communism and, to a lesser degree, Fascism created a feeling of enormous moral significance.

(5) Crown Prince Umberto was an avowed Catholic far different from his father. Many years later when he was the head of the House of Savoy, and therefore the owner of the Holy Shroud of Turin, he graciously gave his permission to have the Shroud as a part of the Vatican Pavilion in the 1984 World's Fair held in New Orleans. The Cardinal of Turin refused permission to move the Shroud to the Vatican Pavilion.

Count Ciano was always considered to be a puppet of Mussolini, and held a position in the Fascist government comparable to that of the Secretary of State in our government.

March 18, 1939

NORTH AMERICAN COLLEGE
Via Dell' Umilta 30

Dear Everybody,

St. Patrick's Day reminded me of Dad and Patrick Jeremiah; the method of celebrating the feast here is nothing less than weird. They always give us green spaghetti! But the celebration does not end with the meal at dinner. There is an "Irish club" that holds a traditional "scald" in a very remote corner of the building, and the feast is celebrated until the small hours of the morning. I didn't go in for that stuff this year because I had to take some material for our magazine over to the printers the next morning.

Today (Laetare Sunday) ordinations were held at the college. The last half of the deacon class was ordained. Ed Latimer was among them; he invited me to serve his second Mass and go out to breakfast with him. I haven't found out yet where he is saying his second Mass. Now that Ed is ordained, myself and Marty Killeen are the oldest seminarians in the college (have been in the major seminary longer than anyone else). Getting old and bald.

Do you remember Father or Monsignor Bernardini who used to be Tur's great friend? [1] He has been apostolic delegate to Switzerland for some time, and recently I decided to contact him. He comes to Rome very seldom, but he has friends here, of course, who might be able to do things — for instance, get some good tickets for functions at St. Peter's. Maybe I shall have an opportunity to see him sometime. He is an alumnus of the same college that the Pope attended, the Capranica College, the oldest in Rome. That college now controls everything in Rome.

The great event of the past week was the reception of Ambassador Kennedy at the college. [2] The college gave him a formal reception (some say that the Vatican gave orders for it) that was attended by six cardinals and many big shots. It was some affair. Our hideous refectory, done up so that one would not recognize it, was the reception room. The students, of course, did not attend, but Kennedy gave us a little impromptu talk. He has a very winning personality but is not a great speaker. The cardinal Secretary of State, Cardinal Maglione was here, and he seems a very nobel, intelligent person. The English cardinal, a very democratic old man also attended. John McCormick was also on hand, but stayed for only about five minutes. The sandwiches must have been bad. It was really rare to hear the remarks of some of the guests about how wonderful the college must be, after they had attended the reception and eaten the refreshments. The mother of one of the newly ordained priests attended the affair and then gave her son a bawling out for having told her that the building was cold, the service in the refectory poor, etc. Another woman told us how lucky we were for living in such a comfortable college! There was only one person who saw the real part of the college, the son of Kennedy who came out of the reception and said he was sick of that stuff. [3] One of the fellows showed him the other side of the college life, and he was certainly glad to get out of the building. The caterer did a really splendid job on the reception; but if anyone thinks that that is the sort of service we get every day, he should come around some day when the college is normal.

The recent war scare has made things jittery again. It's my opinion that Germany may yet drive Italy into the arms of France and England because, so far, they have gotten nothing out of this Rome-Berlin axis while Hitler has been grabbing handfuls. This business of grabbing can't go on forever.

Love,

Phil

Comments: Letter of March 18, 1939

(1)   Tur refers to Bishop William Tuner of Buffalo, a cousin of my mother, who had been professor of philosophy at the Catholic University and was given the name Tur by us children in the Hannan family.

(2)   At that time, Ambassador and Mrs. Kennedy were considered two of the leading Catholics of the United States and none of us knew that the Ambassador was severely opposed to the U.S. having a role in the coming war with Germany.

(3)   The son of the Ambassador was Joseph, later killed while flying in a bombing mission to destroy the launching pad of the V bombs at Peenemunde in Germany.

March 23, 1939

NORTH AMERICAN COLLEGE
Via Dell' Umilta 30

Dear Everybody,

We were given a "bum run" just before Ash Wednesday. I felt like taking a few days off, so it came as a very welcome relief. Six of us went to Pestum — a place about fifty miles south of Naples — where there still stand the ruins of old Greek temples. Pestum was a Greek settlement, begun about the seventh century before Christ; almost all

Southern Italy was a Greek colony, and many traces of their settlements are still left. Pestum has the best-preserved Greek temples in the world though, of course, none of the three still standing is in perfect shape. We arrived there late in the afternoon with the sun almost setting. Of course, the gates were closed, but we hadn't come one hundred and seventy miles just to look at the temples through the gate so we went right over them. Three of the fellows in the party have excellent cameras, and they ran like mad to get good views of the temples. As soon as everything was all set for a picture of the temple, the old gatekeeper came hot footing it along, demanding the entrance fee. So, they paid him the fee, asked him in no uncertain language to get out of the way so that a picture could be taken and got all set again. He disappeared, and they got a few pictures. Then they drew off to a distance to get a good perspective picture, and just as all things were set the old boy comes legging it back again — he had forgotten to give us those d - - - silly tickets that they give you for everything in Italy. Here we were inside the temple, had paid the entrance fee, had seen everything, had even taken a few pictures, were out in the middle of open country (Pestum is right in the middle of nowhere, not even a tree is within miles of the old deserted settlement) and he insists on the stupid formality of giving us a ticket! If he could have understood the remarks one fellow gave him as he walked up in front of his camera to give him his ticket, the old boy would have passed out.

There is something almost ghostly in going through those old temples, set in the solitude of the sky and fields. In the late afternoon sun, they turn a rich brown and seem to rise up twice their height, framed against the nearby mountain range. Then they seem to merge slowly into the parent mountain from which they were dug.

In going to Pestum, we passed through Salerno (not far from Pompeii) and enjoyed a real thrill. The body of St. Matthew is buried in the old cathedral and is done in a very ornate and expensive style. Salerno was a very important place in the eighth century, and fought a bitter but losing battle against the power of the Mohammedans, who finally took the city and established their power by building a fortress above the city — the old ruins are still there. The body of the great Pope Gregory VII is also buried in the old cathedral.

Gregory VII was one of the greatest Popes of the church, having served in various capacities under two or three Popes before being elected Pope himself; he was hemmed in by the foes of the church in the north and by the Mohammedans in the south. He died in exile at Salerno, chased out of Rome. I hope to get the full story about the cathedral — when it was founded, how they got the body of St. Matthew, etc. — and then send it to Monsignor Buckey. I shall try to get pictures of the cathedral and the tomb from the rector of the cathedral. I think the old monsignor would get a big belt out of it. [1] But that can't be done in a week.

Cardinal Dougherty is now amazing the college and Rome. He has a number of students here. They were all duly summoned to appear before his eminence, for which occasion there was all sorts of furbishing. They went in good order to the hotel at which he was staying, ushered into his presence, each one was asked his name then promptly dismissed!!!!!! Not one word of friendly conversation was exchanged. The cardinal had made a rule that his men could not travel in Europe during the summer, so they were watching for an opportunity to ask him to reconsider. As they neared the door, one of them turned and began, as politely and smoothly as he could, whether he was of the same opinion. The cardinal told them in just so many words that he was, and then asked for the name of the fellow who had dared to ask the question. So far the cardinal has not deigned to bless the college with his benign presence. When he comes, and if he comes, he will certainly get a cool reception from the fellows. Neither of the American cardinals now in Rome (Cardinal O'Connell has not arrived yet) has even come near the college; we are certainly basking in the warmth of their affections. I am enclosing a couple of the pictures taken during the time when the Pope's body lay in state. I know that the papers will carry the usual stuff.

Love,

Phil

Comments: Letter of March 23, 1939

(1)   The "old monsignor" was our pastor, the pastor of St. Matthew's church (later the Cathedral), Monsignor Edward Buckey.

March 26, 1939

NORTH AMERICAN COLLEGE
Via Dell' Umilta 30

Dear Everybody,

I don't know if I told you about the kindness of Bishop McCarthy of Portland, Maine, who asked me (together with the two fellows he has studying here) out to dinner with him. He was staying at an old hotel, the Hotel Minerva, that used to be the hangout for the bishops and important people who came to Rome. It is the only hotel in Rome that has its own private chapel, given to it by Pope Pius IX. Anyway, the meal was very good — the chief event of the day, as far as I was concerned. Bishop McCarthy was very gracious; I shall never forget what he said to the Rector when he was at the college. Bishop McCarthy came at about three, or three thirty, in the afternoon; he was shown into the visitor's room instead of into the Rector's apartments (where bishops are usually entertained). Then he apologized for intruding into the Rector's busy day — the Rector was then taking a nap — and when the Rector finally pulled himself out of bed Bishop McCarthy spoke to him for only a couple of minutes because he "knew that he was taking up his time." Well, if he only knew how busy the Rector's day is, he would have stayed until midnight.

Today, Sunday, March 26, they are having a big celebration in Rome, and some real fireworks may result from it. Mussolini is expected to demand Tunis from France. But despite all this war talk, the ordinary man in the street is completely unwilling to fight and doesn't believe that a war is coming. The Italians seem to have the idea that the French are afraid to fight. [1] If a war were to come now it would find me in a very embarrassing situation. Our college magazine is now being printed but won't be finished for a couple of weeks; if anything happens and we have to go, it would be impossible to carry the copies with me, and they wouldn't receive them in the mails. I am praying like the dickens for peace right now.

Some of the best rumors I have every heard are now flying around. One report has it that 43 trainloads of German troops went through Italy on the way to Sicily to help the Italians take Tunis from the French. Another is that there are three American destroyers waiting down at Naples to take the Americans out of Italy in case of war. Then a few days ago the word got around that Rumania had been taken by Hitler (but, of course, everybody knew that it wasn't — not yet). (2)

I am getting sick of these war jitters. A fellow doesn't know whether to pack up or to study. In case of a European war we are to be sent home, and I know that during the crisis in September the American ambassador had gotten in touch with the college to make preparations to send us home. But I don't want to go home on a battleship. The chances that I shall be ordained in Europe look rather slim right now. I don't think that Germany and Italy can hold up their armaments race like this very much longer. Did you know that the windows were taken out of the cathedral at Chartres last September? (3)

One of the newly ordained priests in the college is well over six feet — about six feet six. His brother, a priest, came over for the ordination. Two days ago this fellow sang his first Solemn High Mass in the chapel, and there wasn't a man in the sanctuary less than six feet three. The deacon was six feet six; the master of ceremonies was six feet five, etc. No wonder the Italians think us a race of giants.

Love,

Phil

Comments: Letter of March 26, 1939

(1)   The failure of the French to protest vigorously and to demand the return of the territory taken over by Hitler (the Ruhr) begot the idea that France would never fight, or could not fight, among the Italians. The fact also that France had a wavering government, Socialist, nurtured that feeling about France.

(2)   These rumors were characteristic of the giddy feeling then in Italy.

(3)   I referred in an earlier letter that the French were preparing to take the famous stained glass windows out of the Cathedral of Chartres to hide for their protection, as they did with many of their national treasures.

March 30, 1939

NORTH AMERICAN COLLEGE
Via Dell' Umilta 30

Dear Everybody,

This is an Easter Card. I didn't see any around Rome, so I finally decided to send a note. Despite all predictions to the contrary, it seems that we shall celebrate Easter in Rome. For the past two months, all the talk was about being home before Easter, but here we are yet. All of which goes to prove that everyone is either too poor or too sensible to fight. But before I forget it, I must tell you about the night of Mussolini's speech; they had assembled all the young men in the army to hear it, and they really put up a demonstration. The trouble was that they didn't stop the demonstration with the speech; they were walking and shouting through the streets even at one and two o'clock in the morning. When the speech was still going on some were yelling, "On to Paris!" [1] But the funniest thing about the speech was that Mussolini promised them hardships, more sacrifices, more taxes, and they cheered like the devil for it. Try to figure that one out. This business of stirring up war fever and excitement is simpler than I had ever thought.

But, back to Easter. The Pope is scheduled to celebrate Mass in St. Peter's on Easter, so that means another big day (and a headache in the afternoon). There is a rumor going around that the Pope may possibly crown the King; the Italian King has never been crowned, because there was always that rift between the royal family and the papacy. But no one knows when the coronation will be.

Happy Easter to everybody. I suppose Tom and Bill will be in the choir as usual. When Palm Sunday starts to roll around, I always think of the procession at St. Matthew's; that has always been the symbol of the opening of Holy Week for me.

Love,

Phil

Comments: Letter of March 30, 1939

(1)   The insane yelling of the Italian youth, "On to Paris", shows how volatile is the Italian temperament. Nevertheless, the older Italians have absolutely no wish to fight anyone, especially the French.

April 3, 1939
Palm Sunday

NORTH AMERICAN COLLEGE
Via Dell' Umilta 30

Dear Everybody,

The real business of Easter starts today at St. Peter's. Palms, by the way, are not used today in Italy; they use olive branches, more plentiful and cheaper. In the afternoon, the Cardinal in charge of the Sacred Penitentiary sits in a confessional with his long rod and taps the heads of those who kneel in front of him — 300 days indulgence. Then tomorrow, we have the famous seven church walk, [1] in the course of which one walks about ten or twelve miles, produces a whole pad of callouses on both feet, ends up by eating a huge dinner at some restaurant, and gets a plenary indulgence. It might also be added that one is usually no good for about two days after. After such a start for Holy Week, it is easy to see how everything else during the week is considered very easy.

During the past week, there was a big celebration in Rome for Franco's victory in Spain. The Spanish embassy was all decked out in flags and drapes (all of the drapes had the crown of the King of Spain on them) and a whole crowd of students were sent up to give a big cheer for Spain. These "popular demonstrations" by the students are very queer things; the fellows at the university are told to go out in a crowd and do all this stuff. They don't even bother to drop their books before they start out; they have three leaders (students) and about four large flags. Their Italian lungs supply whatever else is needed. The whole program consists of marching through the streets yelling for Franco, singing Italian songs, jamming up traffic, having a heluva big time out of the whole affair. The poor cops simply have to stand aside and put up with whatever the students do (there's positively no rowdyism or rough-neck stuff — the Italians never fight, they waste all their energy in shouting). Then, after they are all tired, they march home, and the newspapers give out the flaming news that a great popular demonstration took place. I was at the dentist the morning this demonstration happened, and the dentist (who speaks English and who was educated in New York) told me that attending the University of Rome is great stuff; you have to be willing to march and shout; that's all.

The war scare is not so bad as one would think from reading the newspapers. Despite all the talk, the Italians are not willing to fight the French — they can't bring themselves to think of them as a traditional national enemy. Besides, Tunis is hardly worth a war. But Germany may drag Italy into a war. It is said that Germany has quite a few spies in the Italian government to keep Hitler informed of the drift of things down here — and that story is not at all incredible. For the time being, Italy will not fight France for Tunis; the Italians did not expect the French president, Daladier, to make such a strong statement. The French really set the Italians back on their heels when they said that they did not intend to give up a bit of French territory. They say that the Pope is praying night and day for peace.

The report you have that the lamps in Rome are green is wrong; they are now a blue, which makes it impossible for enemy airmen to see them from the sky. Despite the very serious war scares and the fact that the Italians are calling their reserves to the colors, I do not think that Italy will fight France. Such a war will prove unpopular among the older and wiser Italians. Besides, Mussolini would be in a difficult position if the war proved very difficult and long. [2] If there is no war by the time I can travel in the summer, I am going to try to see as much as possible; because peace will not last much longer.

Love,

Phil

Comments: Letter of April 3, 1939

(1)   The "seven church walk" is maintained in many places in the United States except that in some places the walk includes fewer churches.

(2)   The remark that Italy would not tolerate a long or costly war was validated by the reaction in Italy after a few years of war. They did not have the resources to fight even a short war against a determined foe, as in their war against Greece in which they needed the help of the Germans.

April 11, 1939
Easter Sunday

NORTH AMERICAN COLLEGE
VIA DELL' UMILTA 30

Dear Everybody,

Before starting on the ceremonies for Easter, I must tell you about the "burial of Christ" I saw in the Greek church in Rome on Good Friday morning. They have a whole crucifixion group in the sanctuary — Our Lord, the Blessed Mother and Saint John. One priest gets up in the pulpit and chants the passion in a very curious, oriental chant (everything is sung in Greek). This is accompanied by a whole group of clerics in the sanctuary who join in at various times, or keep up an accompaniment, to the singing of the priest in the pulpit. At the end of the passion, they take the statue of Christ, put it on top of a richly decorated coffin that is there in the sanctuary, and four priests carry it around the church. A procession is formed that chants a number of dirges as they march in procession. The coffin is put down in the sanctuary and the book of the passion put on one side of the coffin. Then everyone comes up to venerate the buried Christ; three genuflections are made and then the statue and the picture of Christ on the book of the passion are kissed; then each one receives a couple of flowers from a priest stationed at the coffin (the flowers are all over the top of the coffin). All this takes place in the morning; something also happens in the afternoon to complete the ceremony, but I did not have an opportunity to see that. The chanting is particularly impressive; it has a real swing and a very characteristic eastern throb. I saw the chant books and the method of marking the notes is not anything like our method. The vestments worn by the Greeks are much more flowing than ours.

Good Friday was the occasion for the publishing of the news of the taking of Albania by Italy — it was rumored around that Italy took it four days before, but kept it quiet. It certainly was a jarring note in the celebration of Good Friday. [1]

The avoidance of using bells of any kind is rigorously avoided in Rome on Good Friday. Even a huckster, or peddler, was using a wooden clapper instead of the usual bell (that insistence on an external ceremony is typically Italian).

Holy Thursday was celebrated with more devotion in Rome than in any of the three years I have been here. The Italians are past masters at arranging carpets of flowers for the repository and to see all the churches is almost a full course in the art of decorating. St. Peter's was crowded with Germans and Americans; there are so many Germans in Italy now that if a plebiscite were held, Rome would probably be declared a German city. In the afternoon I stopped in at the Vatican Press where our college magazine is printed and found that the call to arms in Italy had taken away their best printers! I am a thorough pacifist now.

The Tenebrae services in the great basilicas are almost like operatic performances. [2] The services of Holy Week are held at the various major basilicas — St. Peter's, St. John Lateran, St. Mary Major, St. Paul's. Consequently the choir at these places, when it comes their turn to have the services, puts on a real exhibition. It was announced that in St. Peter's on Thursday (I believe) a couple of opera stars would be in the choir. I don't know if they were there, but it was a splendid performance. After Tenebrae at St. Peter's on Holy Thursday, they wash the altars with a mixture of wine and spices (I recall very vividly how stately Cardinal Pacelli did it last year) and then they show the great relics preserved in St. Peter's — the relic of the Cross, the spear of Longinus that pierced the side of our Lord, the veil of Veronica.

Good Friday was very impressive. I told you what I did in the morning. In the afternoon I went up the Holy Stairs on my knees; [3] the physical part of the job is easy — putting up with the pushing, coarse natives is the real burden. I admire their faith, but I certainly do not like the way they exhibit it. You never saw such kissing of a statue as most of them engaged in at the top of the Holy Stairs (an exposed crucifix is placed there). All this emotional display doesn't impress me at all. I should be far more convinced of their piety, if they went to Mass on Sundays regularly and stopped their statue kissing.

After I went up the Holy Stairs, I visited the Church of the Holy Cross where they have the part of the Cross on which the inscription was carved, a couple of thorns from the Crown of Thorns, and a nail from the Cross. We ended the day by hearing the end of a Three-Hour Sermon preached in the Church of Santa Susanna (the American church).

The only discordant note in the solemnity of the day was the singing of the celebrant at the ceremony in our chapel; when unveiling the Cross and singing the antiphon, "Ecce lignum cruces" he misunderstood the master of ceremonies who was telling him to lift the cross higher; he thought that the master of ceremonies wanted him to sing higher — and did he make an attempt! Positively, it was the worst performance I have ever heard; he got the idea that he could hit the note if he put everything he had into it. Well, he almost blew a piston in the attempt, but he didn't come anywhere near any of the notes. Despite the gravity of the occasion, everyone smiled, snickered or giggled. The choir was so disrupted that they couldn't make the response.

Holy Saturday went off in the usual way; there were times when I thought that they wouldn't be finished in time to allow us to go over to the papal Mass at St. Peter's on Easter morning, but the ceremony finally ended.

Easter morning, we all went over to St. Peter's to see the Pope celebrate Mass. A great innovation was attempted; instead of the usual shouting and screaming, they tried to substitute the singing of an Easter hymn. [4] The singing went all right until the Pope came into the basilica — then the old style came into action. The Pope tried to stop some of the noisy demonstration, but there are some things to which his powers do not extend. They say that Pius X once stood up on the <u>sedia gestatoria</u> and shook his fist at a section that was being particularly noisy; but Pius XI approved of the custom of yelling (Leo XIII thought it was great stuff too). But the present Holy Father is more of an aristocrat than Pius XI; I don't mean that as a reflection on Pius XI at all, because I much prefer the old system of shouting allegiance to the Pope. Pius XII has not the easy grace of Pius XI, who was always like a kindly old grandfather. Pius XII is a bit more rigid, more stiff in his dignity; they are different types, though certainly each is, or was, an undoubtedly great man. Did I ever tell you that Cardinal O'Connell almost predicted that Pius XII would prove to be the greatest pope we have had in centuries — and that is certainly saying a lot considering what a tremendous figure Pius XI was in the affairs of the world.

But, back to the Mass. Our Vice Rector and Spiritual Director helped to carry the canopy over the Holy Father, a real honor. A huge delegation of Germans came down for the Mass, and there were a number of American sailors from the S.S. Sacramento (a very excellent group of fellows; I was speaking with most of them). I think I described a papal Mass before — singing the epistle and gospel in Latin and Greek, tasting the wine and bread before presenting them for the use of the Holy Father, receiving the Precious Blood through a golden tube, receiving Holy Communion on the throne, assisted by a Prince (in this case, Prince Colonna) etc. I had a very good seat, thanks to the simple little trick of jumping barricades when the Holy Father came in and all the guards were looking at him. Furthermore, the fellow next to me had an excellent pair of field glasses. I could even make out clearly the ring on the Pope's finger.

After the Mass the relics were exhibited while the Pope interrupted his procession out to kneel while the ceremony was in progress. [5] I saw the veil of Veronica very clearly through the field glasses, and since we are not obliged to believe the authenticity of the relics, I remain unconvinced. The image of the head is clear (a little too clear for credence, I think) and shows Our Lord as a partly bald man with the face of a Greek. It looks like a Byzantine painting to me — although I am told that perhaps the image we see is a copy on the outside of the container of the real image on the veil. I don't know for certain, but I don't think that the image I saw is the genuine article. Of course, I wasn't there when it all happened, so I am completely ignorant; but the picture of Christ on the veil of Veronica does not correspond with the image on the Holy Shroud at Turin, in my opinion.

The Pope received a tremendous ovation when he appeared on the balcony to give his benediction to the world. He left his seat and came to the edge of the rail so that all could see him better — and the crowds gave him a tremendous hand.

I forgot to say that the Pope read a rather lengthy speech at the throne, and the typical Italian service neglected to have the amplifying system in order to broadcast his speech to the crowd in the basilica (there is a loud-speaking system in St. Peter's now).

Love,

Phil

Comments: Letter of April 11, 1939

(1)   The Fascist government could not have chosen a better time or announcement to demean it in the eyes of the Catholic Italians.

(2)   Tenebrae services are the singing of the liturgical hours of Matins and Lauds sung in the evenings (vigils) before the feasts of Holy Thursday, Good Friday and Holy Saturday. The candles are extinguished as the ceremony continues so that the ceremony builds up to a climax with the death of Our Lord. The Italian choirs in the great basilicas are splendid, and the ceremonies are an excellent preparation for Easter.

(3)   The Holy Stairs are the stairs in front of the palace of Pontius Pilate, which were ascended by Our Lord before His passion and death. The faithful ascend these stairs on their knees and recite prayers of penance and contrition. They kiss an exposed crucifix at the little chapel erected at the top of the stairs. The Holy Stairs are near the front of the basilica of St. John Lateran.

(4)   Pius XII and later John XXIII tried to suppress the shouting of the congregation in St. Peter's as the Pope was carried in. Pius XII ordered hymns to be sung and John XXIII ordered the Nicene Creed to be sung, but both attempts failed completely. The people sang the prescribed hymns and Creed until the Pope arrived, when they all shouted "Viva il Papa" (Long live the Pope). I confess that I joined with the people in shouting, "Viva il Papa".

(5)   The relics are the veil of Veronica with which she wiped the face of Christ during His carrying of the cross, the spear of Longinus used by the Roman soldier to open the side of the crucified Christ, a piece of the cross on which St. Andrew (the brother of St. Peter) was crucified and a relic of the true Cross. These relics are kept in the walls of the great four supports of the dome in St. Peter's. These relics are also shown during Holy Week.

April 17, 1939

NORTH AMERICAN COLLEGE
Via Dell' Umilta 30

Dear Everybody,

During the past week we had a very realistic air raid. The first air raid took place in the day, near noontime. Everyone had to leave the street and stay indoors while airplanes "attacked" Rome and dropped fake bombs that went off like giant firecrackers; all the while the anti-aircraft batteries were going at top speed. The fellows who took the worst beating were the carriage drivers who had to un-harness their horses and tie them with their heads facing the backs of the carriages; as soon as the first raid was over and they had re-harnessed their horses, the whistle for the second raid blew, and they had to do it all over again — you should have heard their comments!!!! The night air raid was even better. The street lights were extinguished except for the small blue bulbs that have been put in next to the large white bulbs; the blue lights are left on for about fifteen or twenty minutes to allow everyone to leave the street (all traffic is cleared off the streets) and get into some shelter. Then the whole city is darkened, and Lord help you if you don't extinguish all the lights in your room. The darkening of the city was perfect, and it lasted from about eight o'clock to about ten. Then the real fireworks began. Planes droned above dropping "bombs" (flares to show where they had scored hits) and the anti-aircraft whaled away at them. It had all the excitement and noise of a real air raid and none of the damage.

The college is in a particularly central position; we are near the royal palace and the palace where Mussolini has his offices, the "Palazzo Venezia". There are anti-aircraft guns stationed very close to the royal palace, so that the noise near the college was like that at a Democratic national convention.

The tension is easing a bit over here. America seems to be more concerned and worried than Europe at present. [1]

Love,

Phil

Comments: Letter of April 17, 1939

(1)   The curious result of these realistic air raids was that it begot a sense of security. This was true also in England. The people felt that they had prepared for a war and, therefore, were not in great danger or at least were prepared for the worst. Actually, this feeling was very misleading. The reality of war was far greater than the preparation for it by faked air raids.

May 10, 1939

NORTH AMERICAN COLLEGE
VIA DELL' UMILTA 30

Dear Everybody,

All the talk in Italy now is about the future dismemberment of Jugoslavia. (1) No one doubts that the taking of Albania was just a step to secure a foothold next to Jugoslavia. Jugoslavia has a considerable minority in the north, Croatians, who dislike the rule of the Serbs, the ruling nationality in Jugoslavia. The Croatians are very large people and are very good Catholics. They don't want to be taken by Germany, and the story goes that when Italy took Albania, they immediately started to fly the Italian flag — at least showing that they would rather be gobbled up by a Catholic than a non-Catholic country. Sooner, or later, they will be "liberated" from the rule of the Serbians.

A World's Fair for Rome in 1942 has been announced. (2) Mussolini started the advertising campaign just a few days ago. Rome's world fair will be practical; the buildings will be converted into apartments, or offices, after the fair is over. I don't know whether they are serious about this fair or not. Just where the money is coming from is more than I can make out. Of course, the exhibits of the fair will be no trouble, because Italy has so much art stuff that they can simply haul the stuff down from Florence and Venice. They intend to build a new railroad station in Rome that will be huge. If they ever do all the stuff they have planned with the little resources they have, it will almost amount to an act of creation.

This is the beginning of the tourist season for Rome (the ideal tourist season), but business seems to have fallen off considerably. The English speaking parties are very few, and to the dismay of the Italian guides and taxi drivers, there are a great number of Germans. The Germans are notoriously poor tippers and gruff towards servants, all of which is repulsive to the millions of Italians who live off the pocketbooks of tourists to Italy. Even though Roosevelt is considered the archenemy of Germany and Italy, Americans still remain popular — and will remain as long as they have big pocketbooks.

Work on our publication should be finished in about a week — barring all wars. We have been having a real time trying to hurry the natives; a few days ago I went over and, among other things, told them that I couldn't understand why they were so slow. "Slow!" the fellow said, "We have broken three records already in pushing your work through." I let him know that I expected him to break about five more before he was finished. The difficulty is that they start to run out and hide on me whenever I go over now. Everyone except the office boy suddenly leaves on important business.

The college is ready to celebrate the departure of the Vice Rector for America. For the past week he has been unusually strict, so the celebration will be worthy of the best traditions here.

Love,

Phil

Comments: Letter of May 10, 1939

(1)   The disappointment about the dismemberment of Jugoslavia was typical of the war — the whole country was taken over by the Communists under Tito (a Croation) and remained a Communist country until the demise of Communism.

(2)   The incongruity of announcing a World Fair for Rome in 1942 showed the fatal delusion of the Fascists and all the Italians that a war would not be long. The Italians also thought that they would have the Olympics in Rome.

May 27, 1939

NORTH AMERICAN COLLEGE
VIA DELL' UMILTA 30

Dear Everybody,

Rome is a great place, and the American College is the greatest place in Rome — I am not maudlin or sentimental. These are the facts: last night we had a free concert in the street, and today an old, doting alumnus gave us a tremendous banquet, just to show his devotion to the place. The free concert happened about ten-thirty at night, obviously just after the star of the performance had finished off quite a party. He rolled off a long song from an opera; everyone leaned out of his window and gave him a cheer. Then, he got serious (as serious as he could get in the condition in which he was) about the business of singing. Of course, his efforts soon brought the police; he saw them coming and ducked into an alley, leaving a few spectators in the street to meet the police. The police didn't know which one to grab, so they appealed to the fellows in the college who were hanging out the windows, and the fellows got the police so fubbed up that they gave the job up and went home. The singer promised to come around again. He really had an exceptional voice.

The fellow alumnus who provided the feast is quite a character. He is an elderly priest who got leave of absence to take a trip around the world and his only difficulty seems to be that the world is not large enough. A returning alumnus is allowed to "set up the house" to a meal, and they always try to make up for the poor meals that they suffered in their time as students.

By the way, I am getting myself more excited about the advisability of getting a good camera. I have made some inquiries in Rome and find the situation all set for a very cheap deal. There is a Kodak shop at which one can buy stuff at less than half price! (The cameras are not second-hand — all completely new.) Things are so cheap in Italy now that it seems a shame not to invest. I shall tell you more about prices, etc. in a few days. It would be excellent to get some color film and take pictures of some of the very colorful processions that are held in Rome; just last Thursday (Ascension

Thursday) I was only two feet away from the Pope as he went into the basilica of St. John Lateran to take possession of it.

And that brings up the ceremony on Ascension Day. [1] The Pope was scheduled to take formal possession of St. John Lateran in accordance with an old tradition; after they were elected, the Popes used to ride in state to the Lateran, throwing coins to the populace (they long since gave up that little trick). The Pope left the Vatican at 8:30 in the morning in an open car and drove through Rome to the Lateran. The route was all planned and indicated so crowds could gather to see him — and the demonstration was very impressive. He went up the famous Vis del Impero on which all the great parades are held (the parade for Hitler passed along this street) and the contrast between him and the dictators is tremendous. Absolutely no precautions were taken to protect the Pope; there were no soldiers, no closed car, no machines filled with secret service men. Two motorcycle cops rode ahead to clear the way — that's all. Coming back from the Lateran the Pope's car was mobbed; crowds poured out in front of the Coliseum and blocked the street, but the immense and commanding dignity of the Pope always prevents anything that might amount to a disgraceful mob scene. He just blesses them all; they kneel, then shout like the dickens for him. It is difficult to imagine a time when the power of the Pope was stronger; no celebration or demonstration for any visitor to Rome (as Hitler, Horthy of Hungaria, Prince Paul of Jugoslavia, etc.) even compares with the spontaneity and enthusiasm of the very edifying devotion paid to the Holy Father.

I had gotten myself wedged into a place just in front of the main door of St. John Lateran; the Pope was carried in procession from the Lateran Palace (just next to the basilica) to the church. Dick Hiester, whom you must remember, got some good movies of the procession (I'll try to get a copy of the films). As the Pope came just in front of me, he was let down and walked into the basilica. The poor cardinals who walk directly behind the Pope got a real jolting; the crowds pushed in on them, and the pious old boys had a rough time until a cordon of papal guards swung into position.

Love,

Phil

Comments: Letter of May 27, 1939

(1)   The ceremony on Ascension Thursday, was the Pope's taking possession of his cathedral, St. John Lateran. The Popes used St. John Lateran as their cathedral and palace until after the time of their residence in Avignon.

A very funny thing happened to us at the ceremony. We were near the Holy Father as he descended from his car, and we agreed among ourselves that we would hoist one of our group to a high position so that he could take good pictures of the Pope, which we did with a great amount of work. Afterwards we found out that our photographer had forgotten to put the film in his camera!

End of May, 1939

NORTH AMERICAN COLLEGE
Via Dell' Umilta 30

Dear Everybody,

It is only now that I am beginning to appreciate the life of the ordinary person in Rome. The crowded apartment house across the street is really coming to life. Every night for a week, they had either a fight or a party in one of the apartments opposite me. Then, the first night that everything was silent, the fellow rooming overhead had a "scald" in his room, and they did everything but rip up the floor. After a year of this, I could sleep soundly in a sawmill. The climax came about a week ago when the family opposite me had a real, old-fashioned fight. It started off merely as a discussion about money, but things didn't remain long in that uninteresting stage. Somehow, or another, the young child got into it, couldn't stand the pace, became hysterical. The woman tried to beat the hysterics out of the child, succeeded in calming the child to the point where the kid tried to jump out of the window. The woman decided that she wouldn't be outdone by anybody in the family and promptly got herself a case of hysterics, in the middle of which, she showed her affection for her husband by picking up a potted plant with

319

which to caress his face. This excitement called for attention on the part of the neighbors, who proved themselves equal to the occasion. Windows were opened, heads bobbed out, addressed the fighters in soothing tones that could have been heard at the rock of Gibraltar. Finally, some man took it upon himself to go in and act as peacemaker, or if he failed in that mission, to be umpire to see that the fight was conducted along fair rules. As a peacemaker, he was just as successful as the League of Nations. It was at this time that the bell rang for night prayers. When I came back, everybody was quiet — from exhaustion. Such are our friendly neighbors.

Then there is the young fellow who runs large parties that start at three in the afternoon on Sundays, and gradually increase in tempo and noise until twelve at night. The music is so loud that a person could dance to it a mile away. Another fellow is trying to learn American jazz on his saxophone. He has the most varied, intricate extensive assortment of sour notes that I have ever heard; but he was silenced by five fellows who banded together with all sorts of instruments, and in the middle of one of his concerts let out a blast that was still re-echoing a week after.

I heard of a fellow a few days ago whom I didn't envy. He was studying for his degree in Scripture and was up for oral exams. The Pope decided to use his right to preside at the exam and ordered it to be held in his presence at his villa. They didn't tell the fellow about it until the morning of the exam for fear it would upset him. It so happens that the Pope is a very good scholar in that line and takes a keen interest in such studies. The exam started well enough, but soon the professors started to show off before the Pope and proceeded to take the student apart. I understand that they did everything but take his appendix away from him. Fortunately, he was an able fellow. Then the Pope rounded off the affair with a fifty-minute speech in which he rambled around the world twice. I think the student's bishop will be forced to give him a year's rest.

Love,

Phil

June 6, 1939

NORTH AMERICAN COLLEGE
VIA DELL' UMILTA 30

Dear Everybody,

This is just an experiment to discover just how quickly a letter can be sent. After a few more years of improved transportation, a fellow will be able to send a letter from Rome at five in the afternoon and have it arrive before noon in New York (noon of the same day). At last we are getting to the point where we can beat our own shadow.

I just received Mom's account of the wedding; must have been a very elegant affair. But what ever happened to the cabled blessing I paid for? I was assured that the blessing would reach Washington about the eighteenth of May, but apparently it didn't. Live and learn.

Archbishop Curley arrived in Rome on Saturday, the third of June. He came to Rome from Naples by auto, and is staying in an old but fashionable hotel called the Minerva; he made a mistake in choosing his hotel, I think. The Minerva is next to the Pantheon and is in a low section of the city. If he had gone to the Majestic ,or a hotel in that section, it would be much more cool. The priest that accompanied him, Father Manns, came around to the college shortly after he arrived in Rome. I am very sorry that the Archbishop didn't stay in the college, as he thought he might do (according to Father Manns); that would have afforded a real picnic for the student body, because it is no secret that the Archbishop is a much-feared man. With the Archbishop in the college the Rector would have been as comfortable as a beefsteak in a lion's den.

The Archbishop himself came to visit the college at about eight-thirty Saturday night. Whether he knows it or not, he arrived in time to interrupt the Rector's seeing a movie we were having. The Rector was so interested in the movie that he refused to budge, at first, when he was told that he had a visitor awaiting him downstairs; and if the visitor had been anyone other than the Archbishop or a cardinal, the visitor would have either waited until the end of the movie or have gone home. As it turned out, the Archbishop merely wished to borrow an ecclesiastical coat (the

Roman kind). So far, the Archbishop has not sent for us. I hope that he will be able to take us in for an audience with the Pope — the Archbishop has a private one with the Pope; but besides that, a bishop can get a semi-private audience if he cares to.

Love,

Phil

June 13, 1939

NORTH AMERICAN COLLEGE
VIA DELL' UMILTA 30

Dear Everybody,

The past few days have been almost epoch-making. Thursday the Archbishop worked us into a private audience with the Pope, and Sunday afternoon the Archbishop gave us an audience that lasted for two hours — and he was in rare shape.

But before I begin on all that, let me describe the particularly comical madness that is going on in the college now. Every year when the weather turns suddenly hot, there is a slight epidemic of stomach disorders in the college. This year was no exception. What was exceptional was the behavior of the Rector who became genuinely worried and went on a crusade to locate "the bug that is causing all this sickness." He brooded and planned his campaign, then swung into action. The first thing we knew of this health crusade was when we walked into the chapel and found that Lysol had been put into the holy water to disinfect it! ! ! ! ! ! Then he visited the sick and put each one through a questionnaire to determine what had caused their illness — and this showed that he was on another track. The upshot of that was the padlocking of the student store that sells Coca Cola; he even went so far as to have a doctor come and examine the store with him. The Rector blamed the sickness on the cold Coca Cola (it was all right to drink warm Coca Cola but harmful to drink it when cooled) and the cookies they sold to go with it. The doctor settled that point by eating a few of the cookies and saying that they were the best he had tasted in a long time. But all this was just a build up to the Rector's final scheme: he plans to drain the two small fountains and pools we have, clean them with carbolic acid, fill the pools and stock them with a special kind of gold fish that eats marine growth. All that is supposed to stop the stomach trouble. Just when he was marshalling all his forces for this last attack on the bug, his whole plan had to be dropped — everyone got well. The sick fellows had slight cases of dysentery caused by sleeping without sufficient cover at night; anyone could have told the Rector that but he was having too much fun tracking down the bug.

Now about the audience. We owe a great debt of thanks to the Rector and to the Archbishop. When the Archbishop was making arrangements for his audience with the Pope, he asked if he could take in his Seminarians with him, just to receive the Pope's blessing. He was refused — they do not wish the bishops to bring along their Seminarians. The Rector advised him to try it anyway. So we all went over to the Vatican, got by the guards by saying that we were going to the Anticamera Pontificale (where one arranges for audiences) went up and waited at the entrance for bishops and special guests on their way to private audiences. When the Archbishop came along, he told the Swiss Guards that although he had no tickets for us, he was going to get permission from the Pope himself for us to come in and get the papal benediction. So all of us trooped down to the antechambers just outside the Pope's private audience room, all the time receiving the military honors accorded persons on the way to private audiences (I think only bishops are entitled to military honors at the Vatican). Finally we were left in an outside room while the Archbishop went into the Pope's room. His audience was scheduled to start at 11:15 a.m. They didn't ring the calling for us to come in until about 12:10 — an exceptionally long audience. A bell was rung by the Pope and his attendant Monsignor popped in to answer it; it was for us to come in. Father Manns, the Archbishop's secretary, and the nine of us trooped in. Myself and Father Manns were nearest the Pope. When we entered the Archbishop was still talking to the Pope, who was seated behind his desk; they seemed to be having quite a confab. We genuflected (not a sign of adoration but of respect) and half of us started to kneel for his blessing, half stood waiting to go up and kiss his ring (the Monsignor had told us we could kiss his ring). Father Manns kissed the Pope's ring, and I was just about to take the Pope's hand and kiss his ring when the Archbishop hustled off his seat, grabbed me, told us all to kneel. Then the Archbishop asked for the Pope's blessing. The Archbishop was really nervous — the first time in my life I have seen him really nettled by a situation. The Pope was ready to have us all come up and kiss his ring, but it was the Archbishop who cut things short by telling us to kneel. The Pope gave us his blessing and fumbled for a few words in English; finally he said, "I will give you my blessing," and after he had given it he said, "God bless you all." The Pope was extremely gracious and kindly, gave us another blessing, seemed ready to do a little talking to us if the Archbishop hadn't started to bustle us out. The Archbishop was frankly (as he afterwards said) amazed at the way the Pope received us. Since the Vatican had turned down the Archbishop's appeal to have us in at the audience, he expected at the most that the Pope would only give us his blessing; consequently, the Archbishop wanted us to take up as little as possible of the Pope's time. But that wasn't the way the Pope felt about it at all. In the first place, when we entered the room the Pope stood up to greet us, just as though he were receiving visitors of his own rank (I couldn't help but make some comparisons between the Pope's simple, kindly reception and the lord-of-all-I-survey attitude of some ecclesiastics I have met). As a matter of fact, it is still evident that the Pope is still delightfully "green" in discharging the duties of his office; for instance, he used to walk to the door with his guests and see them out instead of remaining in his place as befitted his dignity. It is almost incredible to think that the highest and holiest official in the world is so accessible and so simply and quietly dignified; he is certainly a Pope "to the manner born." His ring, by the way, is really gorgeous, reminded me of the crown jewels of England; his cassock does not fit him around the collar. Our exit from the Pope's presence was really extraordinary. We were supposed to genuflect and leave. The Archbishop called the signals. We genuflected, started reluctantly for the door, which is very close to the Pope's desk. I myself thought that we should back out, paying the courtesy that people do to a king by not turning their backs on him, so I began to walk backwards to the door (which was only five feet from me). Things got jammed up, and the first thing I knew, the Archbishop was plowing his way through us towards the door like a fullback in a football game. He certainly wasted no time on courtesy and curtsies in ripping his way out. As it was, I was the last one out, and used the time in sizing up the room. The room is not the ordinary one for papal audiences, because the Pope's apartments are being repaired; the room was as large as our dining room, reception room and parlor put together, and had a desk at one end. In a private audience such as we had, everything is very personal — there is no entrance by the Pope surrounded by Swiss Guards and Noble guards; he is simply seated at his desk and one walks in to see him. A really memorable experience. Perhaps, what rendered the Pope even more affable than usual was the fact that the Archbishop carried in the check for the Peter's pence and presented it during the audience. Incidentally, we were the first Seminarians to receive such an audience — it was just like being a bishop.

Now about the hardly less remarkable audience given us by the Archbishop when he came to visit us Sunday afternoon, the eleventh of June. He came at four-thirty in the afternoon and talked for two hours to us. First of all, he asked us about the food, and I answered him, since I am the senior man of the diocese. Then he passed on quickly to telling us stories about the diocese and everybody in the diocese. Among other things, he imitated Monsignor Buckey and told us about the Monsignor's visit to ask him to come to the Calvert School — "mind you, not St. Matthew's School but the Calvert School" was the way the Archbishop told it. Of course, he ended with a tremendous compliment to Monsignor Buckey and remarked on his tremendous vitality and lack of white hair. After a while he asked us about our parishes — he knew I was from St. Matthew's and recognized me immediately. Later, just when he was about to leave, he told me he had seen Dad rather recently at some affair, inquired about the whole family, asked me how many brothers were married, was amazed that only one was hitched, asked about Mary and how she liked Hartford, wanted to know how the doctor in the family was doing (that man has a marvelous memory!) and finally ended by asking why St. Matthew's never had any vocations. He told us a number of stories about the Propaganda College, [1] even went so far as to tell us about the time he sneaked a swim in Lake Albano. He was at his best when he described how and why he called the former Spanish ambassador to the U.S. a "common, ordinary liar." [2] He insisted that he didn't say that when he was in a huff — said he had been waiting for months to get an opportunity to call the ambassador for his tricks. Just before he left, we had our pictures taken with him; if they come out I'll certainly send you a copy. He wanted us to sure to tell our folks that he had come around to see us. The most important point in the whole talk was that he told us we could stay over for graduate study in anything we wished, if we care to do it. So I told him I may be interested in studying history — but that's a long way off. Anyway, he was certainly generous in his offer.

Love,

Phil

Comments: Letter of June 13, 1939

(1)   Archbishop Curley had attended the Propaganda Seminary in Rome and, therefore, was very fluent in Italian, which enabled him to speak easily to the Swiss Guards and officials in the Vatican. Among the stories he told us about life at the Propaganda was his temporary revolt against their system of watching the students even in their rooms. For that purpose there was a small looking-hole in the door, which the prefect would use as, he made his rounds of inspection. Mr. Curley secured a syringe, filled it with water, and the next time the prefect looked through the hole he squirted him with water. He didn't say what penalty, if any, they imposed on him.

(2)   The former Spanish Ambassador was noted for his untrue statements about events in Spain during the "Republican regime". Archbishop Curley, after one of the Ambassador's flagrant distortions of the truth, called him a "common ordinary liar" because, as he explained it, the ordinary people would understand those words better.

July 2, 1939

NORTH AMERICAN COLLEGE
Via Dell' Umilta 30

Dear Everybody,

I think I forgot to tell you about the show we were given a week ago; it is customary for the class below us to present a play, if anything as low-down as that thing can be called a play, the night that we receive subdiaconate. The show ran true to form, just about as complimentary to

us as a prison indictment. It was a great success, the most enjoyable part
being the cracks at the faculty. The Rector had censored the play and had
given it his o.k. — then the fellows took it and put in all the cracks about
him. He seemed to be no little surprised at the unexpected turn of events.
The play that really caught him napping was the parody on the way he
sneakily cleans his teeth after dinner; he holds up a napkin and tries to clean
his teeth behind it without being noticed. When they rolled on that part of
the act, it almost stopped the show — then I thought the Rector was going
to stop the show. The whole point of the show is to step on the coming
Deacon class, and the form of the play can be mangled in any way to achieve
that end; this particular frowzy affair had three acts with about sixteen scenes!

Old Archbishop Hanna is paddling around the villa. He came out to
see the swimming meet, and the day of the scheduled meet, for the first time
in about six weeks, it rained. Everything was postponed. The Archbishop
looks healthier than ever and is piloted around by the Rector. This swimming
meet is the real sporting event of the summer, because a number of visitors
from other colleges come to see the doings. The most interested spectator of
the crowd is always the Rector, who likes to mess around in the water himself
(but not in front of a crowd). Needless to say, I am not entered in the events;
I am not properly streamlined for speed in the water.

The war scare in Europe seems to have definitely died down. As I
told you some time ago, some of our servants were mobilized; one was sent
to northern Italy, and the other was sent to Albania. Both are now back at
the college again — a good sign that no immediate trouble is contemplated.
The same spirit of ease and calm seems to prevail all over Italy, so the summer
looks safe.

I was talking to some Seminarians from France some time ago, and I
asked them about the military service there. It seems that every man, including
Seminarians, is called into the army for military training — for a period of
almost three years! Patriotism is so high in France that the men go very
willingly, even though it means interrupting their career, or business, for quite
a length of time. In Italy, Seminarians are exempted from military service.
But the Church authorities in France very wisely favor the system of taking
the Seminarians, because it makes the Seminarians tougher and gives them a
real opportunity to see if they wish to continue in the Seminary or not; only
five percent of the Seminarians who enter the military service do not return

to the Seminary — a very small percentage. The Americans with whom I was speaking favored the system of sending the Sems into the military service, said it changed the fellows in the right way. Maybe they should try the same thing in Italy. (What a howl the bishops would set up.)

Some time this week I shall start on my trip. I'll keep you informed all along the route. I hope to arrive in Budapest in time for the great national feast of King Saint Stephen, the national patron. Budapest is supposed to be really decorated for the occasion. I hope I can get some good pictures of the events — I won't stay for the whole celebration, which seems to keep up until the point of exhaustion is reached, and I don't know how long it takes to exhaust the Hungarians.

Love,

Phil

July 9, 1939

NORTH AMERICAN COLLEGE
VIA DELL' UMILTA 30

Dear Everybody,

At last, I can sit down to write without counting the seconds. My exams are over. By a strange coincidence I was up for exams on the Fourth of July. The profs did the celebrating (if there was any celebrating). Then three days later, I was up in another exam. These exams are like earthquakes — it isn't the length of the event but the uncertainty and danger that make them so feared. Every set of exams brings its list of incidents: one fellow passed out in a dead faint just as he reached the door of the University, after a number of fellows got sick from some bad meat at dinner one day the Rector (who had just given a strong talk urging everyone to study to "maintain the honor of the college") went around telling them not to make themselves sick by studying, but "at least learn how to bluff the profs," etc.

My examiners were not particularly difficult people to please, but were complete strangers to me and to the Gregorian University. The system of examinations over here is a riot; as you know, the examinations are all oral and the examiners, for the most part, are complete strangers who have not the slightest idea how the matter of the exam was treated in class. In three years, I have never been examined in the matter for the whole year in the space of forty-five minutes; there is one thirty-minute exam and another fifteen-minute exam. In the thirty-minute exam, one is examined by three different profs who work on you for ten minutes each. Now, the amazing thing to notice is that one of those three men can make you repeat the exam in the matter for the whole year (even if the other two examiners find you very good in the stuff in which they examined you). Some of the examiners are very easy; others are extremely tough. I have never had any Santa Claus, but I am quite sure I did well this year. It is beginning to look more and more as though this summer will be our last in Europe. One of the young priests visited folks in Germany on his way home, and he says that they are just waiting for the harvest before they get serious on this business of Danzig. Therefore, I shall try to make my trip early and also try to track around quite a bit because a war wrecks so many things. Why the devil don't they get interested in sports, love, drinking (even religion if they think they can stand a bit of it) instead of the business of blowing heads off? War will come now, I think, without much resistance on the part of the people who have been accustomed with the idea for months now. [1]

I am getting a little pad of fat on my stomach — despite the fact that I beat on the books at all hours of the night in preparation for my exams. I seem to be made of contradictions. That reminds me of the supper we had a few nights ago. A number of the fellows had been sick at their stomachs so the Rector decided to make up the menu for the supper; and this was the supper — an egg, lettuce, custard, and, of course, the usual wine with the meal. Five died of hunger that night. It takes about three years to get completely accustomed to living in Rome; after that one begins to enjoy it.

There goes the bell. I know you understand why the film is to be sent to Father Dick Hiester in Vatican City rather than directly to me. Sorry I haven't had the chance to write much lately.

Love,

Phil

Comments: Letter of July 9, 1939

(1)   The length of the war jitters in Europe had finally caused a kind of fatalism about the war, and the reports from Germany were taken very seriously by us. I planned my summer vacation trip so that it would be finished about the beginning of September. The war began on September 1, 1939, with the invasion of Poland by the Nazis.

August 23, 1939
Paris

Dear Everybody,

Despite the worst train service in the world (owing to the war scare with its consequent troop movements), I arrived in Paris again on the twenty-second of August. [1]

I was passing thru Germany on the train when the papers announced that Germany had made a non-aggression pact with Russia — it knocked the Germans on their ears. [2] By the way, never be alarmed about me in case of war — I am registered at the embassy and can always claim a place on a battleship, if I can't get passage on a steamship. Furthermore, I am going to Switzerland in a few days, and that little spot of mountain land is as safe as being in our kitchen.

I met Henry Cosgrove and some other fellows from the college in Paris — we have almost enough to charter a boat.

Budapest is a very lovely city. It is typically Hungarian — has a touch of the East in it. Their material feast day was very colorful, and I was fortunate enough to get a good seat for the procession. The dizziest thing I saw was a squad of street cleaners following the cavalry up the street. The ruler of Hungary, Regent Horthy, walked in regal style in the procession. He is very popular, very anti-German, and determined that Hitler will not get Hungary. More power to him. [3]

I couldn't tell you by the mails in Italy that I really juggled the currency on this trip — no smuggling of marks into Germany or anything like that — but I just used all the possibilities of securing reductions. The results were these: it cost me about $13 to travel from Budapest, thru southern Germany to Paris, then from Paris to Geneva. I'll explain it all to you some day; it involved about four transactions — buying tourist money with other tourist money until the price is almost worn away completely.

Living is much higher in Germany this year. The Austrians are complaining to those whom they trust. We met an Austrian woman in Hungary, and she gave us some very interesting information. We also met a group of *Hitlerjugend* (Hitler Youth) who were going to Bulgaria to help work that country into the proper frame of mind for a treaty. They were very decent, upright fellows but too simple — stupid. They believe everything they hear, and they always hear the wrong thing.

Many Italians believe that Hitler is trying to bluff the world — I hope they are right, but I noticed that the Italian frontier forts in the Brenner Pass are in excellent shape.

Don't worry about me. I'll tell you where I am and what I shall do in case of war — if the cables are not too busy. I shall be safe. I have the checkbook with me.

Love,

Phil

Comments: Letter of August 23, 1939

(1)   I traveled directly from Budapest to Paris in accordance with the advice I received from a good lady passenger on the train ride to Budapest. She had a number of bundles to carry, and I helped her off the train in Budapest and gave her some money to take a taxi. Whereupon, she said, "Are you really an American?" I assured her that I was and showed her my passport. Then she said, "You did a great favor for me, and so I will tell you that you should leave Budapest immediately after the celebration of the feast of King St. Stephen, and don't stop until you get past Germany. I am fleeing Germany. I saw the troop trains being readied for an invasion of Poland. Get out of Germany before it happens." I took her advice.

(2)   On the train trip from Budapest, the train stopped in Munich. The Germans at the station were enormously excited and worried. One of them, seeing that I was a tourist, came up to me, showed me the

headlines of the newspaper, <u>Der Voelkischer Beobachter</u> (The People's Reporter), which had the headline, "Germany Makes a Pact with Russia". The same newspaper in its previous edition on the previous day had carried a long article condemning furiously the Communist government in Russia. The German said to me, "What does that mean?" He could not believe his eyes. Of course, I could not give him any sensible reply. It was the famous double-cross of Communist Russia by Hitler making a non-aggression pact so that they would not interfere with his taking of Poland.

Our train stayed four hours in Munich to allow the troop trains to pass on their way to invade Poland.

(3)   Budapest is a lovely city, and the celebration of the feast of the famous King Saint Stephen was very elaborate and colorful. The King brought Christianity into Hungary, and the procession in honor of the crown of the King was a review of the history of Hungary. They had detachments of soldiers wearing the national military uniforms through the centuries beginning with a group wearing mail uniforms. The Cardinal and the Regent (not a Catholic) were the main figures in the procession, having the place of honor next to the crown of King Stephen.

The celebration lasted all day. After the Mass, they had folk dances and other entertainments all done in their native costumes. Hungary, a partner with Austria in the Austro-Hungarian Empire before World War I, was strongly opposed to the Nazis.

August 25, 1939
Paris

Dear Everybody,

This is to prevent any worrying.

I am leaving tonight or tomorrow morning for Switzerland, the safest spot in the world. [1] Then I shall proceed to Rome, because I am registered at the Embassy in Rome, and therefore, they are bound to get me a safe journey home (possibly on a battleship).

In any event, there is no danger because the frontiers are open (I can always get into Switzerland to stay) and the officials make every concession to allow Americans through. Furthermore, there is no anti-American sentiment at all — which will prevent any possible difficulties.

I am trying to pick up a few articles for you, but it seems as though our baggage will be limited — if a war does break out.

In a heluva hurry.

Love,

Phil

Comments: Letter of August 25, 1939

(1)   In Paris I decided to go back to Italy by way of Switzerland in case the war became general. A couple of seminarians joined me, Henry Cosgrove and Joe Goodwine, and we decided to stop at Zermatt, at the base of the famous Matterhorn, a very scenic place and also very cheap. When we arrived in Zermatt, the weather was unusually clear, and so we decided to walk up the Matterhorn, without any climbing gear or tough shoes. It was a spectacular walk, and so we ascended to within the ice cap and then decided not to risk a storm, so we promptly walked down. Of course, we stopped at a little refreshment place and had a very enjoyable cheap lunch.

We saw the Swiss troops getting into their mountain position facing Italy. They were carrying machine guns, and I was very surprised to see that this was their only defense against Italy.

September 4, 1939

NORTH AMERICAN COLLEGE
VIA DELL' UMILTA 30

Dear Everybody,

My vacation this year was ended abruptly, and if it hadn't been for the letters awaiting me at the College, I should have regretted very keenly my return to Rome.

Now, to begin at the end, because it is fresher in my memory. From Paris we went to Switzerland, then to Italy. We pulled out of Paris at about nine at night — things were getting decidedly hot in Paris and the French government had asked all foreigners and all those whose presence in Paris was not necessary to leave — and traveled all night to Geneva, Switzerland. Paris was very calm; the French were determined that Hitler was not going to get away with another little surprise. But we certainly learned what war means to a nation. We went to Chartres to take pictures and found them working like mad to take the windows down; it was interesting to watch, if one could forget the reason why they were being taken out. Chartres was more impressive this time than ever (this was my third visit); it has always been one of the chief shrines of the Blessed Mother, and the French were beginning to pour in to ask the help of the Blessed Mother in the coming war. The next day, I went to the Cluny Museum in Paris and found that they were already shipping the stuff to some of the distant chateaux in France to be kept at a distance from Paris. But the greatest surprise was at the American Express Office — where not a dollar bill could be had for anything. As soon as the crisis came everyone rushed for American money, not even steamship companies would accept French money (things have been organized by now, I suppose), and of course, there was no American money to be had. We in America always think naively that money is worth what it is supposed to be; but when one is pushed up against the wall in a crisis, it is very easy to find out just what money is. The price of German money was falling by the hour. I had a little left over from my travel in Germany, and I unloaded it as soon as I could (the morning after I arrived in Paris); but in that short time it had taken a considerable drop. And I shall never forget the foolish American fellow who had exchanged all his American money to French francs and was left holding 9000 francs that couldn't be exchanged; the only thing he could do was to live in France until the money was exhausted, but he wanted to get out of France immediately. I advised him to buy jewelry and carry it out that way.

By this time we had passed out of the lovely valley scenery, above all vegetation, and were at snow level. Strangely enough we were getting a terrific sunburn, despite the cool air from the snowfields. The air is very clear at over ten thousand feet and the sun is strong. I was perspiring very much despite all the snow around us. We finally arrived at a point where we could see glaciers and snowfields stretching away to the horizon. Up there at about 13,000 feet there is nothing but the solitary splendor of snow and rock, no shrubs, nothing green at all, not even moss; the only thing with movement up there are the clouds. From under the glaciers trickle out small streams of water that finally unite and grow until they rumble and boil down the mountainside to the valley far below. We didn't reach the top of the Matterhorn, nor did we intend to, but we did almost reach the little cabin perched way up on the backbone of the mountain in which people stay overnight and then make the final ascent in the morning. The mountain peak is always clearest in early morning and gradually clouds up in the afternoon. I hope I got some good pictures of it. The view from up there was the greatest I have ever seen; in fact, I saw so much scenery that I have no desire to see any more. The crushing force of glaciers must be tremendous because we passed over long stretches of boulders and gravel fields left there by the action of the ice.

Strange to say I didn't feel any dizziness from the thin air, but we did notice that at the very high altitude, we tired very easily and had to rest often — not enough oxygen in the air for vigorous exertion. Another strange thing was the tameness of the sheep and goats we met (domesticated, not wild); they didn't move at all as we passed among them. All in all, our little jaunt up the Matterhorn was very interesting, and I hope to send you some good films as soon as things clear up.

We rested a bit the next day (Joe Goodwine couldn't bend his knees, but I didn't feel any ill effects and Henry Cosgrove seemed to be as fresh as ever) and then started out for Italy. We were afraid of the frontier being closed and war was now almost certain. It was a very sinking and hopeless feeling that swept over us as we came back into hot, crowded Italy. We pulled into Milan at night and the whole city was in complete darkness — practice air raid. There is something sinister and foreboding about seeing a city with over a million people positively black at night. The taxis had their lights painted a deep blue but all the darkness didn't keep them from careening around in their usual mad way.

I forgot to mention that as we came down the Matterhorn, we met detachments of soldiers struggling up the mountainside under full packs. The Matterhorn is almost at the Italian frontier and Switzerland has all sorts of anti-aircraft guns and machine gun nests planted way up there in the mountains. From all recent developments, it seems as though Switzerland has nothing to fear from Italy.

Back to Milan. All Italy was paralyzed with fright; they dislike the Germans despite all this Rome-Berlin axis business and hate to see Poland beaten. We walked through the Brera Gallery in Milan and met only one person in the thirty-four rooms of the museum. It was the same story all through Italy. We stopped at Florence and found the city like a cemetery. You know how busy the Ponte Vecchio is with all its shops during peacetime; we walked across the bridge and found only one customer in all the shops on both sides of the bridge — some shopkeepers didn't even bother to open their shops. We stopped in at the shop where we bought that ceramic ware last year and had a lengthy bull session with the owner who told us that Florence was ruined for the present. I bought some stuff from him in the hope that I shall be able to get something through eventually. In that large square where they have orchestras every night and all sorts of coffee and beer shops, the tables and chairs have been removed. Not a soul was there. The same thing was true in Venice. Some of the Italian cities live on the tourist trade, and war means ruin to them. When the announcement was made that Italy would not fight with Germany, there was tremendous relief all through Italy; none were willing to fight for Germany but many were willing to fight against her. The common opinion throughout Italy is that nothing will force her into the war, at least for a long time. The King of Italy is supposed to be very definitely urging a policy of peace for Italy. At the moment, Mussolini seems to be the shrewdest man in Europe — he played along with this Rome-Berlin axis until he got what he wanted (Albania, the evacuation of the Italian Tyrol by the Germans, a big demonstration for Tunis) and then Hitler gave him a perfect opening to get out of his obligations by signing this German-Russian pact which has disgusted the Italians. Only the most ardent Nazis could swallow that double-faced dealing with Russia; many over here seem to think that Hitler's fatal mistake was that pact. Fellows coming back from Germany say that the Catholics are more alarmed than ever.

I must stop this letter because I wish it to go by the Rex, which is sailing Saturday. Our position at the College is completely safe. If there is any danger of Italy's entrance into war, we shall leave immediately and be escorted out under the care of the Embassy — that means under some sort of military convoy. There is no shortage of food or any inconveniences. The only decree is that no meat is to be sold or eaten on Thursdays or Fridays (the first time the Italians ever kept that prohibition of meat on Friday), and very soon that decree will be abolished.

I'll write soon again and tell you about the first part of my trip — to Vienna and Budapest. Don't worry at all about me.

Love,

Phil

September 6, 1939

NORTH AMERICAN COLLEGE
Via Dell' Umilta 30

Dear Everybody,

My last letter finished off my trip — or rather, recounted the end of my trip. Now I'll begin with the beginning.

As I told you, we started out for Budapest. We found that the easiest and cheapest way was to go north through Italy, pass into Austria by the Brenner Pass and cross Austria to Hungary. We stopped to see Ravenna (I think I told you about that), a very old city built on what was marshlands. When the Roman emperors in the fifth century began to feel uneasy about invasions, they moved up to Ravenna to have an easy escape to the East. Some of the churches they built are gorgeous, decorated with marble and huge mosaics. The most interesting thing up there is the old tomb or mausoleum of Theodosius. He wanted to have a tomb with a dome, but the stone masons had lost the art of making a dome; so they went to a quarry and cut out a huge stone which they cut in the form of an arch, or dome, and capped the building with that. I took a good picture of it. Ravenna has more bicycles than any town in the world. The streets are narrow, the roads leading to the town are also narrow, and so almost everyone uses a bicycle.

We stopped at Verona and attended an opera in the old amphitheater; fittingly, the opera was <u>Romeo and Juliet</u>. We also visited the supposed tomb of Juliet, and the chapel where she and Romeo were married. The guide who showed us the tomb insisted that everyone put his hand on the tomb and make an oath "to Love." (This was just about ten days after we had received subdiaconate.) I and the fellow with whom I was traveling laughed like hyenas to the complete bewilderment of the guide; I think he is still sore at us. Next day we went into the Tyrol. I was anxious to see what the Brenner Pass is like since I had heard so much about it during these years of war talk. It provides a really excellent place for a fort — just exactly what the Italians have done there. There is just a narrow pass in the Austrian mountains, and the Italians have planted their fort directly in the middle of the pass. If Mussolini can block that pass, he is safe from attack on almost half of his northern frontier. The scenery is very lovely up there. There are no rugged, rocky peaks but lovely wooded mountains. A real tragedy was being enacted as we passed through that section. There are, or were, large numbers of Austrians living in that section of Italy (the territory was taken by Italy after the World War). Ever since Hitler has gone on this crusade of conquering all territory occupied by Germans, the Italians were always fearful that he would try to grab that section of Italy. Consequently, after the signing of the Rome-Berlin pact, the two governments agreed that the Germans, or Austrians, should be moved out of that territory. These people, about 386,000 of them, had been living in that section for a thousand years. Suddenly they were told that they must move either to Sicily or into Germany. No details were ever given what arrangements were made, except that they could go to Sicily (where they would certainly die from the tremendous change in climate) or into Germany. Furthermore, it was never published in the German papers what was happening. No one blamed Mussolini from trying to get rid of an excuse for Germany to take over some of his territory, but Hitler certainly proved to be a double-crosser to his beloved German people. I met a German in Switzerland who was furious at the German government for agreeing to such treatment of the Tyrolese. It was impossible for anyone to stop in the Tyrol while that evacuation was being effected, so I suppose no one has the exact information on the subject.

It was raining when we pulled into Salzburg, but we could see enough to appreciate the lovely situation of the little town. The town is in a valley surrounded by mountains, and in the middle of the valley on the crest of a steep hill is the fort that protected the town. The music festival was on, and the town was crowded to capacity. We were forced to stop at a rather expensive hotel, and when we asked the man at the desk if the room he had given us included a bath he puffed up with his German pride and said, "What do you expect for three dollars? What would you expect to get at the Mayflower in Washington for three dollars?" (The fellow spoke good English and had traveled very much.)

"I'd expect to get courteous treatment," I told him. "A small, cheap room like that doesn't have a bath in it," he snapped at me.

"Does it have a bed?" I asked. He shut his mouth on that one. He was very polite to us the next morning. I wished that Bill were along with me during that little incident; we could have given that German the merriest little whirl he ever experienced.

The next day, we went to Vienna. At Linz, we got off the train and took a boat on the Danube to Vienna. Once and for all time let me tell you that the Danube is not blue; it is the dirtiest, muddiest old stream of coffee that I have ever seen. From Linz to Vienna it passes through some very pretty territory — old castles on wooded slopes overlooking the river and curious little villages on the shore — but the Danube is never pretty and never blue. Strauss was either drunk or color-blind when he wrote the Beautiful Blue Danube — or maybe he was in love.

But the ride on the river steamer was very interesting and enjoyable, because of the group of young German fellows we met who were going on a trip of propaganda through Bulgaria. There were about a hundred of these *Hitlerjugend* (Hitler Youths). Many spoke English, especially one whose mother was an Irishwoman. They were all fine, robust, healthy, decent young fellows (about 16 to 18 years old), but all were equally stupid with the unutterable stupidity of simple minds. They believed without question everything the government told them, had very receptive minds for an enormous amount of mis-information, just wallowed in Prussian military pride, were altogether the biggest goober-heads I have ever met in my life (although very likeable kids.) These were the chief ideas on which they dwelt:

The German soldier is the best in the world. We can beat France, England, and the rest of the world any time we wish.

America doesn't like us because it is controlled by the Jews.

Roosevelt is a Jew; his real name is Roosenvelt. He hates Germany because he is a Jew. The trouble with the U.S. is that it loves the Jews (I'd love to have old man Fitzpatrick in New York hear that one.)

Hitler is right in anything he does.

The German people are the best in the world, in strength, in intellect, in cleverness. Etc., etc., etc., etc., etc., etc., etc., etc.

The minds of these kids (as with all the youth in Germany) have been completely spoiled by Nazism. Therefore, my sympathies and prayers are all with Poland, France and England (although England has grabbed too many colonies.). When these fellows started to talk about the coming Olympic games and how many events the Germans would take, I reminded them that Jesse Owens, an American Negro, had beaten their best German supermen in the last Olympics. Their answer always is that a Negro is not an American — they can never get it out of their thick skulls that a man with black skin can never be equal to a man with white skin. I also reminded them that Joe Louis had beaten Max Schmeling. Then somebody mentioned tennis, and I conceded that if they hadn't put their best player, Von Cramm, into jail because he criticized the Nazi government, they would have a good chance in international competition. Whenever they get a question thrown at them, or are told a fact that is new to them, they are completely stumped. Their Nazi-formed minds travel only in the narrow orbit of Nazi propaganda, and if they are jarred slightly off the track, they are completely lost. If that stuff is German education, they can have the whole wretched assortment. I asked one of the fellows how much time he spent at home in the course of the year, and he told me that he spent none, except when he was going to school — all their holidays, whether in the school year or during the summer, are taken up with camp life or drilling. No wonder Pius XI fought the German Nazi government so continually. But the pretty little story we heard from an Austrian woman was the tops: A Hitler Youth about fourteen, or fifteen, years old came home about three o'clock in the morning; his father went into his room to give him a shellacking, but the boy forbade his father to touch him "because he was wearing the uniform of Hitler." So the old man played cagey and waited until the kid had taken off the uniform and then paddled him. The next day the boy reported his father to the local tribunal, and the father was told that if he ever dared to touch his son again that his son would be taken completely out of his custody. Nice pleasant home-loving people, these Nazis.

Vienna is a very beautiful city, the capital of a very easy-going, music-loving people. Unfortunately, Vienna is now dead. It has ceased to be a capital and is only a museum. All the lovely parks and magnificent buildings erected by the great Austro-Hungarian Empire are still there, but they are only monuments of a past that seems to have no hope of return. The Parliament building, a lovely white marble structure, was being repaired when we were there — certainly not being repaired for use, because there is no free speech and certainly no public demonstration of opinion on any decree of the government. The famous Rathaus, or city hall, is magnificent, much more elegant than the Rathaus in Munich and set in a beautiful park. We went to the Ratskeller for supper one night and had a wonderful time; there is music and wonderful food. At the end of the hall, is a very large barrel, or keg, for beer — capacity is about 5,000 gallons!! The Austrians are very likeable people; the orchestra played some American songs for us (we were the only Americans there) — "Dixie," "The Stars and Stripes Forever," and "Sweethearts." The Austrians gave "Dixie" and "The Stars and Stripes Forever" a big hand. They have special wine containers that are quite a trick; they are glass, square containers with a long stem that ends with a faucet — no pouring needed.

Well, I must make this letter catch the "Conte di Savoia". I have given 200 feet of film to a New York fellow who is going home –it is <u>undeveloped</u>. Further, the pictures were taken, as you can understand, in a tremendous hurry. The Paris Eastman Kodak shop has two films of mine, I wrote and told them to send the films to you — war broke out and I had to leave Paris.

Love,

Phil

September 7, 1939

NORTH AMERICAN COLLEGE
VIA DELL' UMILTA 30

Dear Everybody,

Italy has a new Crown Prince, just born yesterday. All of which means that we have a holiday on Monday; the holiday was not granted by the University, the newspapers simply announced that there would be a holiday and that was all there was to it. The baby was born on the anniversary of the Pope's coronation and very few people understood what all the bell-ringing and firing was about; everyone thought it was simply for the Pope. But about five o'clock in the afternoon, the bells started to hammer away as though the end of the world was near. Unfortunately, the Prince was born at Naples, not in Rome; otherwise there would have been a real celebration. The trouble is that they have so many celebrations that even the birth of a future King causes only a slightly larger ripple.

One of our professors has been absent from class for about three weeks. The common opinion is that he has gone to Spain on business. (He is a Spaniard and was chaplain in the army during the summer.) There is currently a wild rumor that he is an officer in the rebel army. Sounds rather wild, doesn't it? The fact is that things like that have happened. All of these Europeans, priest and seminarians, have had a military course and are liable to call by the government. During the World War, a French Jesuit went over to West Point as instructor for the cadets who were to be sent to the Front in a short time, and he went in the uniform of a French general. Furthermore, he was often in Washington and attended social functions, dances, etc. That sounds wild too, but nobody denies it; and it certainly is generally accepted. Every once in a while, a couple of Spanish seminarians leave the Sem to go home and fight in Franco's army. They certainly go in for flag waving and fighting over here.

As I type this (Sunday morning), there is a great crowd up at the Royal Palace cheering for an appearance by the King. Every time they have a demonstration they gather first in front of the Greg University, which has a large square in front of it, and march up to the palace. What amuses me more than the crowd, is the conduct of the Jesuits and inmates of the Biblical Institute that faces the Greg. The population in that Biblical Institute is the rarest assortment that was ever culled from the eccentrics, drudges, and bookworms of the world. Some of them look as if they should never be allowed out without a caretaker. When a crowd gathers in front of their place, they stare as though they were the first humans they had ever seen.

Love,

Phil

September 8, 1939
Enclosure

NORTH AMERICAN COLLEGE
Via Dell' Umilta 30

I have just returned from the American Consul who delivered to me a cable signed with Cordell Hull's name. So the family rates the personal interest of Cordell Hull! ! ! Soon I shall probably be getting a mention in Roosevelt's foreign messages. (Many thanks to the kind, interested friend who was responsible for the cablegram sent in the name of Cordell Hull.)

Well, I am sorry if I caused you any anxiety. I thought that the airmail letter I sent from Paris would explain matters. I thought I made it clear that I was going to Switzerland and then to Italy — both neutral countries and both safer than even the U.S. In the first place, you are not to believe the scare headlines and stories (if there are any) about conditions in Italy. Italy is as tranquil and calm — to the great disgust and exasperation of shop-owners and hotel proprietors — as the basement of a church. The greatest proof that Italy has no intentions of entering the war, at least for some time, is the continuance of the operations of the Italian Steamship Line. Furthermore, Italy is not like other countries (as the U.S., etc.), where propaganda by a chain of newspapers, or by a group of bankers, can arouse popular opinion to enter a war. The newspapers here print nothing except what the government wishes, and since the beginning of the war <u>there has been absolutely no mention of the Berlin-Rome axis</u> — Mussolini has no intention (at least for some time to come) of sharing the same fate with Germany. [1] Everyone feels that a new diplomatic approach is being arranged by Italy to get back into the good graces of France and England. The Italian newspapers stress the peace proposals of Mussolini and emphatically declare that Italy wants peace.

Even though the Italian steamers stop running it doesn't mean that the international situation is alarming; it only means that insurance rates have gone up too high.

Now, in regard to the attitude of the College, the Rector has said that if there is any imminent danger of Italy's entering the war we shall go home immediately. Of course, the Embassy keeps the Rector informed of everything, and I know from my talk with the Consul General that the Embassy will insist on our going home if things get threatening — they do not insist on our going home now and leave the decision up to the Rector. [2] Furthermore, I saw all their secret information reports (of a commercial nature) about the situation, and believe me they know what's going on. The food, lighting, etc. at the College is positively unchanged by the situation; the Vice Rector even brought over a new Ford for the use of the faculty.

It is true that Archbishop Spellman of New York called home his men, but in so doing, he left it up to them, and they decided to go just to show that they were obedient to even his slightest wish; none of them wished to go or saw any necessity for going. Even the English College is still here in Rome. The Pope has issued orders to maintain everything in the colleges and seminaries just as though nothing were happening.

In the event that we should be forced to go home, the Rector can provide the money and then collect later from either the individual, or his bishop. There is positively no difficulty about any eventuality.

Comments: Enclosure of September 8, 1939

(1)   Hitler had sent a message to Mussolini stating that Germany did not need the assistance of Italy in its campaign against Poland. The news of this assurance caused an electrifying reaction in Italy. There were celebrations all over Italy, and in the villages there were wine festivals with real Italian gusto. If anyone had any doubt about the abhorrence of Italy for war, they certainly would have had the doubts resolved.

(2)   In the College, we agreed very much with the decision of the Rector to stay in Rome until the war would involve Italy.

September 9, 1939

NORTH AMERICAN COLLEGE
Via Dell' Umilta 30

Dear Everybody,

Well, the embargo has been lifted, and the neutrality bill passed — and still we are here. So it looks as though we are set for a full year. [1]

Our class received diaconate last Sunday. It seems like a Presbyterian or Protestant term to be called a deacon; Deacon Hannan, some stuff. As usual, the ceremony was very long, another case of starting out in the middle of the night and getting no breakfast until noon. We are the last college in Rome to be ordained. The English and Germans have already been ordained priests; incidentally, did I tell you that the English and Germans were ordained together. A very edifying and encouraging sight. The Church tolerates no division, or scrapping, no matter what the governments do. During the summer, the English College had invited the Germans to come over for a day visit; the Germans appreciated it very much. It is amazing how casual one gets to seeing all these various nationalities (who are supposed to be at war with each other) mixing together. There is absolutely no friction between groups at the Greg — except that almost all frown on the natives, or other nationalities, who don't believe in soap and water.

This year is the first year in a long time that there will be no visitors at the ordination ceremony. I am going to try to have pictures taken of the ceremony, just to show you what it's like in our chapel. There will be some difficulty in securing enough light, but there are a couple of fellows around who like to meddle with that sort of thing, so I'll ask them to see what they can do.

I suppose that it is impossible to get a passport to come over. It may interest you to know that I had an opportunity of singing a Solemn Mass on Sunday after ordination in our College chapel; we shall be ordained on a Friday. One of the newly ordained priests sings a Solemn Mass in the chapel on the following Sunday. The priest is not selected; it goes in seniority, and I wasn't far from the top. Unless one's folks are over, it is not good business to accept the offer because it is better to get accustomed to saying Mass before tackling a Solemn Mass — especially for me, because of my operatic voice. Furthermore, I had made arrangements to say my second Mass (which occurs on Sunday) on the tomb of St. Peter, so I passed up the chance to sing the Solemn Mass. If I had sung the Mass, I think it would have been worth making a sound recording of it for home consumption.

In your last letter, you told me to expect another list of names for blessings. I must put in the order soon for the printing of them, but I'll get a sufficient number to take care of any eventuality. And that reminds me, that getting ordained is expensive business; blessings, holy cards, candy, fee for the dispensation for getting ordained before completing fourth year of theology, first Mass breakfasts, etc. No wonder the city of Rome lives on the ecclesiastical business.

Love,

Phil

Comments: Letter of September 9, 1939

(1)   The embargo act had applied to travel by Americans to certain European countries, and the neutrality bill declared that the U.S. was neutral in regard to the war in Europe, which meant that the U.S. from a legal viewpoint was not an ally of either group in Europe — the Berlin-Rome Axis or the Allies (France, England, etc.) These were very important developments for us because Italy now had no reason to ask us to leave, and the U.S. had no reason to recall us.

September 26, 1939

NORTH AMERICAN COLLEGE
Via Dell' Umilta 30

Dear Everybody,

The Rector has gone on a short vacation to Sicily, proving that everything is quiet. Mussolini gave a speech a few days ago that definitely settled any fears that Italy would get into the war in the near future. He ended by telling the Italian people to calm down and take his orders "in silence." Very good advice. As a nation, I think the Italians are the greatest bunch of gripers and belly-achers in the world. A whole flood of rumors and talk started to get around recently, because Mussolini had not made any great speeches (if you ask me, one of the curses in Europe recently has been the wholesale talking of government heads); one rumor had it that he had been shot, another that he was sick, another that he had fought a duel, another that he was retiring, etc. When the Italians start to talk and gripe they don't mean anything by it; it's just a habit.

The passage of this bill repealing the present Neutrality Bill interests us very much. One of the clauses in the new bill is supposed to order all Americans in Europe to come home. If that bill is passed much before December 8, it will mean that I shall not be ordained in Rome. Even though Italy is not at war, I am afraid that the government might give us the traveling order. The steamship rates, by the way, have gone up enormously — another reason why I'd like to stay until a little bit of calm and system is restored. Passage home now on the Rex or Conte di Savoia, or any of the boats of the Italian Line costs about $280!!!!! Before the war broke out, with the aid of a clerical discount, I could have gone home on either the Cunard or United States Line for $95. Furthermore, the Italian Line demands dollars from American passengers; they won't take lire. The Italian liners should make a pretty penny out of this war.

Now I can begin to reminisce about my trip and tell you about some of the people I met. The strangest and most interesting case was an Austrian woman traveling into Hungary. She spoke perfect English but wouldn't open her mouth until she had gotten safely across the German-Hungarian border, then she really opened up. Among other things, he told us that the taxes in Germany now amount to between thirty and forty percent of a person's salary. They were that high before the war began; what must they be now. Although she had two very large bags, she actually didn't have enough money to hire a porter (Germans are allowed to carry out only 10 Marks, about two or three dollars). What griped her most was that she had to give an account of what she intended to do on her trip (she was going to visit relatives), how long she was going to stay, etc. She was a very well-educated woman, spoke five languages, and wanted to go to the U.S. to teach, but she couldn't get very far with only 10 Marks.

We met another German in Switzerland who was in a fine "picklement." He lived in Paris, worked for the Paris office of the National Cash Register Company. He hated Nazism and didn't want to go back to Germany (he had been summoned for military service), but he wasn't a French citizen and couldn't become one, and further the French authorities didn't want the National Cash Register Co. giving work to Germans instead of Frenchmen.

In Italy, we ran into a real hysterical case. It was the day after war had been declared, and we were riding in third class to Rome. A worn-out Italian asked to see the paper after I put it down. I gave it to him; and after he had read it for about five minutes, he suddenly put his head in his hands and bawled at a terrific clip. After about a half an hour of this he temporarily controlled himself long enough to show us the clipping that had knocked him out — Italian refugees from French Tunis going into Italian Libya were forced to get off the train and walk to Libya. His father, brothers, wife and children were among the refugees, and he was certain that all would die, a preposterous idea. It took everybody in the compartment about half an hour to quiet him (what finally did the trick was the gift of a piece of chicken from a family sitting next to him; of course, it was Friday). In about fifteen minutes he was sound asleep.

On the train ride from Budapest to Paris I met a very strange fellow. He was an Englishman; we met at Strassbourg where the train stopped for four hours. Both of us wanted out to see the cathedral, and he took holy water and knelt in front of the Blessed Sacrament just as I did. After we had seen the cathedral, we sat down at a nearby sidewalk café, and he began to tell me what he had seen in Danzig, Poland, Rumania, etc. Finally, he started to tell me about the distinctive wines and liquors in those countries, and the rapturous way in which he described them led me to believe that he was a professional in such matters. Finally, I said, "Pardon me for inquiring, but are you a representative for a distilling company?"

"Oh no, I am an Episcopalian minister."

Well, blow me down. He was wearing brown shoes, light gray pants, a deep blue shirt. It finally developed that he was a pastor for a congregation in Barrington, Rhode Island, U.S.A. He had been "imported" from Oxford by these high-toned New Englanders. What an importation they had on their hands! I talked with him for about three hours on the train and found that he, although he believed in the existence of God, he didn't believe that it could be proved. I hope his congregation is not too particular about the brand of theology it gets thrown at it.

Love,

Phil

October 3, 1939

NORTH AMERICAN COLLEGE
Via Dell' Umilta 30

Dear Everybody,

Probably before this letter arrives a classmate of mine, Charlie Noll, will have arrived in Washington carrying a developed film and an undeveloped film. [1]

We had a lecture a few days ago from a priest who was editor of a magazine against Communism and Nazism. He is an amazing man and is very well informed. The picture he drew of conditions in the part of Poland taken over by Russia was terrible. As a matter of fact, I was speaking to a number of Ruthenian seminarians (they come from Ukrania, the eastern part of Poland that was taken over by Russia), and they said that everything seems lost for the Church. [2] The only safeguard is that those Eastern people have tremendous memories and are used to suffering — they never forget their national aspirations and are so accustomed to being beaten that they take it as a matter of course. I asked these Ukrainians if they had ever had a separate and independent nation (they were the largest minority group in Poland), and they answered very blithely, "Oh sure. Before the fifteenth century we were independent."!!!!! Four hundred years is just like five minutes to those people; they speak of a couple of centuries as though it were only a week. We in America have no conception of the mentality of these people. They are capable of untold suffering and never seem to be permanently beaten.

I expect to say one of my first Masses at St. Peter's and another at the church of St. Philip Neri (where one can say Mass in the room of St. Philip). I also hope to get down to Salerno, near Naples, to say Mass in the cathedral there where they have the body of St. Matthew. The cathedral is about 1200 years old. I also intend to dig up some stuff on the history of the remains of St. Matthew — how they happened to get there — and send it to Monsignor Buckey. All this depends on the trend of international events.

Love,

Phil

Comments: Letter of October 3, 1939

(1)   Charlie Noll was recalled by his frightened Bishop.

(2)   There are many sad stories about the conquest of Poland by the Nazis, and one of the most unusual was told by a group of Americans of Polish descent who were studying in a seminary in Eastern Poland. As soon as the invasion of Poland started, they tried to leave Poland but could not obtain any train tickets so they decided to buy a wagon and a team of horses from a farmer. The farmer was very unwilling to sell. Finally, he said that if one of the group was willing to marry his daughter, he would sell the team and the wagon. Whereupon they promised to return after the war, if it was possible, and one of them would marry the daughter. The deal was made; they bought the team and wagon and finally made their way out of Poland.

October 4, 1939

NORTH AMERICAN COLLEGE
Via Dell' Umilta 30

Dear Everybody,

Our short "bum run" to Assisi for the feast of St. Francis came off very nicely. We started from the College at about 5:25 A.M., had to climb the wall (the gate was closed), and, believe it or not, I distinguished myself by dashing down and stopping the tram just as it was leaving the station. Incidentally, I almost had to choke the conductor to make him wait for the rest of the fellows. We stopped at the American Convent in Assisi, saw a bit of the town, and went to Midnight Mass! I don't know why they have a Midnight Mass before his feast, except that St. Francis was the originator of the Christmas crib. We came home and ate the pious girls out of house and home.

On the morning of the third day I took a bus ride to Perugia, a neighboring town. The chief attraction (although Perugia is a very lovely little town) was the bus ride. It was fair day in Assisi and the narrow road was crowded with peasants going to the fair and hauling their goods for sale. The pay-off came when we met a woman driving a big, white pig; the pig was haltered and she managed it pretty well, but she couldn't get the pig fully off the road. She could drag his head off the road, but the pig insisted on putting his big behind squarely in front of the bus. By this time the thirty-five Italians in the bus were all participating in various ways in the removal of the pig. The solution came when the conductor, with a magnificent burst of Italian abuse and profanity, scared the pig off the road.

Perugia is an old town perched on a large hill. The mental attitude of Perugia can be gathered from this conversation I had with a native:

"Where is the old city hall?"

"There is no old city hall."

"Well, the guide book says that there is."

"No, the book is wrong."

"Well, is there any city hall?"

"Sure, the modern one they use today."

"How old is the modern city hall?"

"About six hundred years old."

I visited the museum connected with the cathedral and saw some old Mass books of the eighth century with the ancient musical notes. Good thing for the congregation that I won't be forced to sing from something like that. They had only a one-line staff instead of the present five line staff, and the notes went up and down the page like fly specks.

After talking it over with some of the priests in the house, it seems better to wait a while before buying a chalice. I'll be in a better position to know what is best after I have used a couple of styles.

The rumor goes around that Italy is going to give out ration cards — all of which won't hurt the College. As a matter of fact, after the food is rationed, we'll probably get more and better food than we are getting under the present system. [1] This business of rationing food will cause much inconvenience to restaurants and hotels, to say nothing of the storekeepers. This Europe is getting into a mess. Speaking of food reminds me of the fellow at the college who took out an empty laundry bag one day and came back with a live goose! He killed it and ate it himself. It takes an extraordinary man to think of something original around here.

After having practiced some of the ceremonies of the Mass, I am beginning to find out just how many gestures some of the old priests leave out. At any rate, I hope to avoid the mistake of a priest who was here last year — he did everything too fastidiously and never could say Mass in less than 50 minutes. I can't imagine what they did with him in a parish.

Everything is as quiet as a deserted church in our section of Europe. Now that a war is actually on and the Italians see what it means, there is positively no war sentiment expressed at all.

Love,
Phil

Comments: Letter of October 4, 1939

(1)   As the supply of food worsened in Italy owing to the embargo on supplies to Italy by England at Gibraltar and the Suez Canal, we sought to secure food during our daily walks at restaurants or coffee bars. The food at the College was the normal diet of Italians, and the meat was definitely below par. For instance, Europeans were accustomed to eating horsemeat, but we Americans found it difficult to digest (especially if the horse meat was old and tough).

October 15, 1939

NORTH AMERICAN COLLEGE
Via Dell' Umilta 30

Dear Everybody,

Soon, I hope to get a good series of pictures on Rome — I'll fix that up nicely. If you only knew how difficult it was this year to travel and to get pictures at the same time, always keeping a jump ahead of the war, you wouldn't be surprised at the pictures.

The Italian soldiers have had their pay increased from 2 cents a day to 5 cents!!! In granting the increased wage, the authorities said that they realized the high duties of the soldiers and the demands of their families!! When the next peace treaty is signed I hope Italy gets plenty; they are so poor that it hurts.

This part of Europe seems to be settling down for a long wait. This war will certainly upset plans for ordination. Nothing has been decided yet, but it is definitely established that the Gregorian University will open this year.

Love,

Phil

October 18, 1939

NORTH AMERICAN COLLEGE
Via Dell' Umilta 30

Dear Rob and Mary,

Much obliged for the letter. In regard to Father Harry, I have little information. After tracking and tracing him up and down the backwaters of the Mid-West (through the efforts of others) I ended with this classical piece of precise information: He is somewhere in Kansas, probably teaching at a college. The last time he was heard from he was (take a deep breath and hold on to something firm) coaching athletics. A four-year tenure in the North American is apparently supposed to equip one for doing anything from tying the shoes of the fat pastor to showing healthy young animals how to tackle other healthy young animals. Our course is based on a literal interpretation of St. Paul's exhortation to his disciples "Be all things to all men." I shall locate his exact whereabouts when I get to Rome and get his address from the office. The executive staff at present consists of one sinus-stricken Monsignor who has been on the verge of leaving for fourteen years — just like weekend guests.

We went to Castelgandolfo to see the papal gardens, to inspect his dairy and to test his apples and grapes. We approved of everything. The former owner of the papal gardens is supposed to have awakened one morning and found that his villa and grounds had been given by the government to the Holy Father. The Papal coat of arms is worked out elaborately with shrubs and plants in the garden. I wrote and told the family about it, so . . . . .

Best of luck with the new home. I'll write later when there is something to say — when we get to Rome. Retreat starts very shortly.

Love,

Phil

October 21, 1939

Dear Everybody,

We have just finished our customary retreat at the beginning of the school year, which explains the notable lapse of time between this and my last letter. About the chalice, I certainly see Dad's point about the sentiment of having some of Cleary's silver in the chalice, (1) and I also see the wisdom of saving some dollars. (Another consideration for having it made over here is this: I can arrange it so that the Pope will use it to say Mass if I have it with me here.

Last Sunday, I was subdeacon at a Solemn High Mass at Marino, a little town near our villa. We take turns being subdeacons at the various churches in the neighboring little towns. But don't think that these little towns are small fry; the church to which I went had a bishop for pastor! ! ! The bishop was simply an honorary bishop, he had no see; the parish is very old and was very important (some centuries ago), so they give them a bishop for pastor. Furthermore, they had a number of canons. All that sounds impressive, as it should. But the ceremonies and the condition of the church are a fright. The floor of the church is dirty; the rugs are worn and dirty; the altar boys are ragamuffins. (The altar boys also form the choir, and as soon as they get into the sanctuary they scram like a bunch of wild geese; the singing, by the way, is just incredible — the organist uses no music and the choir boys, whose ages are from six to eleven, just try to use their memories. Their version of the Latin is really unforgettable.) I made out very easily, no reason why I shouldn't have, because the only thing they demand is that you stay in the sanctuary. They complimented me afterwards but that means nothing because they compliment each other — and only the Lord knows how little they deserve it. The high point came when, after the ceremony just as I was about to leave, I noticed the bishop giving what I thought was a special blessing or benediction, to a little boy who apparently

354

had his head bandaged. I asked about the affair and found that I was watching a confirmation (all this was in the sacristy); they roll off a confirmation just on demand.

Marino is a well-known little town, famous for two things — the annual wine festival and its anti-clerical sentiment. I have seen the former but have had no experience with the latter. I have also seen the way they make their wine; they do it in the approved old fashion way of having the grapes crushed by a couple of barefoot men. When the men get tired of walking on the grapes, they come out and walk around the dirty streets a while and then go back into the wine press — all of which explains the distinctive flavor of Marino wine.

If Monsignor Buckey could have seen the way they conduct Sunday High Mass at this church (it has the dignity of a cathedral), he would have had to go on another trip to the Holy Land. He could have "hissed" for an hour at the altar boys without producing even the turning of a head.

I forgot to mention that the invitations generally sent out over here are really not invitations — they are blessings with the short announcement at the bottom, Philip Hannan ordained priest, December 8. The prevalent custom here is to wait until ordination day and bless the announcement, and send it. The blessing is not florid or over-done; it is simply, "May the Blessing of Almighty God descend upon you in the name of the Father, etc., Do you think it is necessary to have plain invitations made for those on the mailing list who are not Catholics? Personally, I don't think so; the blessing won't harm them. The point is, a good one too, that it is better to send a blessing from Rome than an invitation — since everyone knows that they can't come anyway. Unless I hear otherwise from you, I'll have the ordinary blessing type made with the plain announcement at the bottom, Philip Hannan ordained priest....

Congratulations on the new car; the Hannans are really looking up.

Love,

Phil

Comments: Letter of October 21, 1939

(1)   The Cleary's were old and close friends of the family. They were collateral descendants of the first Cardinal in the United States,

Cardinal John McCloskey of New York, and had inherited a considerable amount of jewelry including a large diamond, which Cardinal McCloskey had given to a niece as a wedding present. She had married a Southerner, and the Cardinal was afraid that they would be left penniless by the Civil War. I was given the diamond which is on my chalice and which I still use today.

October 31, 1939

NORTH AMERICAN COLLEGE
Via Dell' Umilta 30

Dear Everybody,

At last they have repealed the embargo. As yet I don't know what effect it will have on American travel to Italy; there is just one thing that I would like to mention — the cost of travel will be so high that I shall not expect to see you and won't be disappointed if you don't make it. The cost of travel has been doubled by the increase in insurance rates. I don't know if you were aware of that.

In the event that you do come over, I can see to it (I am quite sure) that someone will meet you in Naples. [1] Father Dick Hiester or someone else could go down to meet you. And if you come please bring in some good candy and American cigarettes; the custom at the college is to pass out cigarettes and candy after ordination as the fellows come in to receive blessings.

On the feast of Christ the King there was a consecration of twelve missionary bishops by the Pope in St. Peter's. I had a good ticket and landed myself opposite the main altar. Furthermore, I had smuggled in the movie camera. As the Pope was carried out he came within twelve or fifteen feet of me; instead of kneeling for his blessing I crouched and kept pumping away at him. As you know, it is forbidden to carry a camera into St. Peter's, especially to take a movie of the Pope. With the combined excitement of grabbing illegal pictures and dodging the Swiss Guards, I was having a time of it. It is a weird feeling to be running a movie camera just behind a burly Swiss Guard, especially when his spear is so long and sharp. Another distinct heart-stopper is to sight one of the guards through the camera and take pictures of him while he is staring daggers at you. It wouldn't be difficult to dodge only the Swiss Guards, but there are also the Papal Gendarmes, the Noble Guards, the Palatine Guards, etc.; they spread everywhere, just like the rash. But the big factor in my favor was that everyone stares at the Pope as he passes — that is everybody except me. After the consecration, the bishops walked around the basilica giving their blessing to the people, and they were in the biggest fub and fog I have ever seen. One bishop just held up his hand as though he were a politician giving a blow to the constituents. They were real missionary bishops. One came on borrowed clothes; he was an American (two of the bishops consecrated were Americans). The only thing his own was his handkerchief.

The ceremony was magnificent. Pius XII is very easy to manage during ceremonies, and sings well. He was in the choir in his Seminary days. The twelve bishops celebrated Mass with the Pope — I heard thirteen Masses at the same time.

Love,

Phil

Comments: Letter of October 31, 1939

(1)   My parents were hoping to come to Rome for my ordination, and the situation kept changing every week. Meanwhile, the value of American cigarettes and candy was increasing almost daily.

November 12, 1939

NORTH AMERICAN COLLEGE
Via Dell' Umilta 30

Dear Everybody,

Well, this morning the Rector gave eight of us the call to priesthood, to be ordained the eighth of December. The rest of the class will be ordained in March, an awkward and embarrassing arrangement. But I know that this good news would have some disagreeable aftermath — one hour later we heard over the radio that Russia had marched in against Poland. A lovely situation, anything can come of this, but no matter what happens we shall be taken care of. No cause to worry. The American ambassador in Italy has not even sent the notices of warning to American residents (they always do that whenever a serious situation arises).

What really precipitated this latest crisis was the prophecy of the Rector. On every occasion, he expresses some pontifical opinion that immediately causes the opposite to happen. [1] This is our Rector's record as a prophet:

> The day he came as Rector he boasted about the healthy climate of Rome and stated that he had never been sick a day when he was here as a student; two days later he became very ill and spent three weeks on the flat of his back.
>
> The first day of the villa season he said that it never rains in or around Rome during the months of July and August; that afternoon there was a cloudburst.
>
> Last year during the famous September crisis he predicted that nothing would happen and that Germany dare not move; Germany took over Czechoslovakia.
>
> This morning, when he gave us our call, he observed that the international situation was settling and that there was no danger of the war spreading; twenty minutes later it was announced that Russia had marched in on Poland. [2]

The Vice Rector recently assumed the mantle of the soothsayer (when he was in the U.S.) and achieved the same success as the Rector. At a testimonial dinner given him, he said that all the war scares were manufactured by the U.S. newspaper men and that Europe was calm; further, he announced that the new college would be begun soon. Two days after he landed in Europe war was declared, and the North American College is not now in a position to build even a dog kennel. From all this, you can see that both the Rector and Vice Rector would make excellent newspaper editors.

The thrill that I received on being called to priesthood was certainly dampened by the state of Europe at the present time. Frankly, I don't know what your attitude is on trying to come to Rome; I think it is possible from the physical viewpoint (the Italian Line is still running), but I don't know whether the U.S. would grant a passport. It all goes to prove that there is no sense to these d - - n wars. Incidentally, the Church stands to suffer extremely heavily in this war — Catholic Poland will be crushed, Nazi Germany with Communistic Russia and Japan, will certainly be a grim set-up against the Church.

Which reminds me of the story going the rounds that the Pope was supposed to deliver the first encyclical of his career on the occasion of the scheduled Worker's Youth Congress in Rome for September. The Congress was called off. Everyone expected a very strong encyclical, just as Pius XI would undoubtedly have had some definite thoughts on the international situation. It is rather well confirmed that Pius XII tried to call a peace conference through his Apostolic legates and nuntios, but things had gone too far.

Before it fades away into the dim past, I must tell you about Budapest. Well, the city was formerly two cities located on either side of the Danube, Buda and Pest; they were joined by bridges only about a century ago. Buda is the part that has the fortress and the range of hills crowned by the Royal Palace and the Coronation Church. At the base of the hill, on which is built the Palace, is a lovely bridge, illuminated at night, across the Danube. At night the city is like a picture from a fairy tale. The heights of Buda, crowned by a succession of governmental buildings, glow like a magical city suspended between the sky and the dark swirling current of the Danube. The illuminated bridge, like a pearly necklace on the swarthy bosom of the river, connects Buda with Pest, the lively part of the city. The half-Eastern Parliament building stretches along the Pest bank of the Danube. The hotels and stores, as well as the commercial part of the city, are located in Pest. Budapest has no great boulevards as Paris, but it has a long avenue along the river (the Pest bank) and on this avenue are situated the famous cafes and hotels. There must be about a mile and a half of outdoor cafes and hotels along this avenue. There is where one hears the famous Hungarian stringed orchestras; the <u>Blue Danube</u> played by a stringed orchestra is really inspiring. The music in Hungary is very distinctive; it has a thousand moods and fancies. There are a number of gypsy orchestras and to hear one of them for an evening is like living a whole life in a few hours. Their instruments are different from those used in modern orchestras and have a more delicate sweetness.

We arrived in Budapest in time for the feast of St. Stephen, the patron saint of Hungary, celebrated on Sunday the twentieth of September. There is a very colorful procession to the Coronation Church before the High Mass at ten o'clock, and after the Mass there is another procession. As you can see, the procession is the main attraction, and it would be the main attraction of the day even if there were a million other affairs. The whole life of Hungary is represented in the parade: the army, the government, the Church, the peasants, all organizations. I think the army started or headed the procession, marching along in their very curious "drag step." This "drag step" is the oddest caper in creation; the trick is to drag your foot during the first motion of the step and then to slap it on the ground in completing the step. When a whole company does it in quick time, it looks like the St. Vitus dance. After the army came swarms of organizations all tricked out its special uniforms, and behind them were the usual flocks of nuns. Then came the peasant groups, each section and village in its own peculiar outfit. At a distance, all of them look as though they had gotten gummed up in a theater-costumer's dressing room. Each peasant must wear the equivalent of about five normal outfits — a whole gross of petticoats, two or three skirts, a couple of jackets, a shawl, or bonnet, as large as a sail. They say that these costumes are handed down from mother to daughter, etc. That's only half the story. The mother must hand down hers to her daughter who has also made one of her own, then her daughter hands down both to her daughter. After a few generations of handing down like that, you finally achieve what they have today — one person wearing all the costumes of twenty generations at the same time. The men weren't neglected in the process either. Some of them wear long, white, pleated skirts, and others wear velvet pants; but all of them look silly. The women look very colorful and charming; the men look as though they had gotten themselves into a mess and haven't yet found any way out of it. The whole conglomeration makes a maelstrom of color. I took pictures of it in color, so you can see for yourselves.

Even the peasant costumes were forgotten, when the government corps came along escorted by various detachments of guards. The government delegation was preceded by a magnificently outfitted detachment of cavalry — followed immediately by four street cleaners!!! These Hungarians don't miss a trick. The government delegation was headed by Admiral Horthy, Regent of Hungary, walking with head bared. He is a very distinguished looking man. His ministers walked behind him, and flanking them were officers in Hussar uniforms — black boots, embroidered velvet coats and pants, huge fur capes, giant plumed hats. There was also a section of the Royal Hungarian Life Guards, scarlet uniforms, fur capes, steel helmets, long spears. The relic of St. Stephen was carried by four priests; behind the relic walked the Cardinal Primate of Hungary in his full pontificals. There was enough color in the procession to last a person for a year.

In the afternoon, I went to see the peasant dances in the city theater. There was much whirling and stomping with a sort of ponderous gracefulness. What was really astonishing, was the ability of the girls to balance something on their heads while dancing. One group (this was a wine festival dance) came out and danced balancing wine bottles on their heads. About a half hour later another group came out (in a harvest festival dance) balancing baskets with fruit on their heads.

On Sunday evening, there were fireworks. The highlight of the affair was a map of Hungary in lights showing how much territory they claim from Rumania and Jugoslavia. [3] One gets a very vivid insight into the problems of the Balkans on such an occasion. Each little nation is very distinctive and nationalistic, claiming every inch of its territory, and since there are so many frontiers it is inevitable that there be endless quarrels.

In the course of my three-day stay in Budapest I saw everything. The great hall of the Royal Palace decorated in yellow and white marble and illuminated with great chandeliers is the most tasteful of its kind I have seen — far prettier than the Hall of Mirrors at Versailles. Sightseeing in the Parliament with a Hungarian-speaking guide was the most unique experience; the only two words of English he knew were "cherry brandy" — for some yet unknown reason they sold little souvenir flasks of liquor in the foyer of the Parliament Building. The Hungarian language, Magyar, is very musical and almost impossible to learn; as far as I could make out, it has no connection with anything I have studied. The word for corn on the cob is *kukuruz;* the word for beer is *sherezeu* (it's pronounced like that, I have forgotten the spelling.)

From Budapest, I went directly to Paris, passing through the tip of Germany the day that it was announced that they had concluded a pact with

Russia — which almost bowled over the simple Germans who had always been taught that the Russian Communists were their greatest enemies.

To tell you the truth, I can't get very interested in writing because I shall be home within a year to tell you all about it.

Marty Killeen is also being ordained in December. We were the dark horses, neither of us having been prefects (apparently one of the recommendations for being ordained early, but both of us had good marks). I am very sorry that the whole class is not being ordained in December because of the possibility of being sent home before the rest are ordained in March. About eleven will be ordained in December, and about 16 or 17 will be ordained in March.

Latest flash: all Italy is agreed that Italy will not enter the war for some time.

Love,

Phil

Comments: Letter of November 12, 1939

(1)   All of the bishops and priests were trying to reduce the danger of war by denying its imminence. Monsignor Fulton Sheen, for instance, announced on his return from Europe that there would be no war "because the people will not permit it." Of course, the people were being manipulated by the dictators.

(2)   The action of Russia in taking the eastern part of Poland was a crushing blow to the Polish nation and to the Church. By this action, Poland no longer existed.

(3)   In the Versailles Treaty after World War I, the Allies dismembered the Austro-Hungarian Empire, making Hungary a separate country but also taking a large part of its territory, Transylvania, and giving it to Romania. To this day, the Hungarians in Transylvania strongly wish to be returned to Hungary, and are considered by the rest of Romania as a very divisive group.

November 16, 1939

NORTH AMERICAN COLLEGE
Via Dell' Umilta 30

Dear Everybody,

Perhaps before this letter reaches you, Italy and Hungary shall have formed a sort of commercial union; the rumor around Rome is that Italy is going to take the lead in the Balkans — a very good plan to keep Russia from spreading all over that section. Yesterday, word got around that Mussolini was to speak from the Palazzo Venezia about the situation. He spoke only a few sentences and said nothing startling, but Rome was certainly steamed up about a possible close alliance with Hungary. All of which proves that Italy has no intention of going to war.

This morning there was a Solemn Requiem Mass for all the departed alumni. I was the subdeacon; everything went well, and nobody fainted even when I sang the epistle. Of course, I didn't cause any riotous applause, but I got through it with tolerable success. I can say this anyway — I was the least nervous person in the ceremony.

Last night was the occasion of the annual "Mission Meeting"; once a year the organization that collects money for the missions has its meeting to elect officers and perform the business of the year. Every year a near riot is caused. For the past three years, an attempt has been made to impeach the president and to amend the constitution — and every year the attempt is defeated, but not without a great deal of snorting. What slightly complicates the situation is the little custom of having everyone vote both for and against a measure; the president will say, "All those in favor of the motion say 'I'." Everybody yells, "I". And when he says, "Everybody opposed to the motion say 'No'," everybody yells "No". You can see why not too much business is done at a meeting. Another slightly irregular procedure is that for electing officers. Nominations are opened, and a number of candidates are put up; then the president, or secretary, will make their own nomination — then the nominations are closed. No matter if everyone votes against the nominee of the president and the secretary, he always manages to win by a very large majority. Some few are beginning to suspect the president of dirty work.

So far, I haven't heard anything about our new Washington cathedral. How does the Monsignor like his new dignity? Has the Archbishop taken it over yet? I still don't know for certain whether I belong to Baltimore or to Washington — not that it makes much difference; the Archbishop will send his men wherever he wishes anyway. [1]

Marty Killeen and I will have, I think, our first Mass breakfasts together. After the first three Masses to which we are allowed to invite a few fellows from the college, we eat breakfast outside the college. Since the Rector has allowed only a couple to go out with each priest, we thought it better to team up with somebody in order to form a good-sized breakfast party — of course, single-handed, I could form a whole party when it comes to eating. By the way, since I suppose the family would like to give Marty some sort of present, I can buy one and sign your name.

I must get out and fix up blessings, holy cards, etc.

Love,

Phil

Comments: Letter of November 16, 1939

(1)   Washington, D.C., was made an Archdiocese in 1939, and Archbishop Curley was the Archbishop of both Archdioceses, the separation of the Archdioceses to occur after the death of Archbishop Curley. As expected, the creation of the new Archdiocese did not change the governance of the Archdioceses as a single unit.

November 23, 1939

NORTH AMERICAN COLLEGE
Via Dell' Umilta 30

Dear Everybody,

I postponed writing this letter until I had heard from you about coming over; I had hardly expected that the U.S. would give you a passport — although I met a businessman at the American Embassy who had just come from the U.S. The only compelling reason for a trip to Europe, as far as the State Department is concerned, seems to be for making money. Too bad; however, the validity of my first Masses will not be hindered by your absence.

During the past week I received a very nice, though short and terse, note from the Archbishop; the usual "congratulation" note. But no matter how short a note he writes it always bears his unmistakable stamp, i.e., in speaking about Washington he said, "I have never been more busy in my life, and the addition of Washington, which is just as much an Archdiocese as is New York or Boston ...." [1] As I told Father Stricker, the Archbishop shouldn't bother to sign his letters.

Monsignor Buckey sent me a pleasant, very scrawly letter; his handwriting is far better than I had expected from a man of his years. He asked me to get him some pictures of the tomb of St. Matthew in the cathedral at Salerno. I think I can manage it in the course of the year. Father Stricker sent me a fine check for an ordination present; he seems to be doing quite a bit of diocesan work — matrimonial board, etc.

Now for a bit of the ridiculous. On Thanksgiving Day, some of us went to the tea at the American Embassy villa. All the busybodies, fakes, stuffed shirts, quacks in the American colony were there. I had a very pleasant time rifling the food and drinks — trying to get back some of the tax money. The funniest incident of the afternoon was when I met the Associated Press agent, who happens to be a Washingtonian. He was feeling more than a little illuminated and his wife, who is from Charleston, was even more unsteady. When he found out that I was from Washington, there was no end to his sociability — they wanted to take me down to Albrecht's, the German beer place to which I took Mom and Bill on their first afternoon in Rome, remember?

This morning I was deacon at a Solemn High Mass in the church of Saint Mary on Broad Street (Santa Maria in Via Lata) — I was the smoothest minister at the ceremony, and that is certainly no compliment. It was terrific. The little church has six canons; it occupies the site where St. Paul was supposed to have been in prison. The church occupies a part of the famous Doria Palace (old Doria was a great Genoese admiral who commanded part of the forces that beat the Turks in the battle of Lepanto) and has some exquisite marble work in it. We had a congregation of two persons. Thank God that the next ceremony in which I participate I shall be the minister.

We go on retreat on Thursday or Friday evening — December 1. Actually, the first Mass I say will be on December the eighth — the Mass during the ordination is said by the ordaining bishop and all the newly ordained priests. On December 9, I'll say Mass over the tomb of St. Philip Neri; on December 10 on the tomb of St. Peter, and on December 11 in the catacombs of Saint Priscilla, in a very famous old chapel there about thirty feet underground, where one can still see the paintings on the walls dating back to the end of the first century. I'll remember the family in all of them, especially in the first. I am especially anxious to say Mass in the catacombs and in the old church of Saint Clement — perhaps Dad and Mom remember it (where the old Irish Dominican showed us around the underground churches). The great reason for being ordained early in Rome is to give us the opportunity to say Mass in the shrines. (2)

Love,

Phil

Comments: Letter of November 23, 1939

(1)   The note from Archbishop Curley referred to the action of the Holy See in making Washington, D.C., an Archdiocese separate from Baltimore, but remaining under the jurisdiction of Archbishop Curley, who thus became the Archbishop of two Archdioceses. Washington became a separately functioning Archdiocese only after the death of Archbishop Curley, and Archbishop Patrick A. O'Boyle became the first Archbishop of the separated Archdiocese.

(2)   The ordinations in Rome did not have any of the complicated arrangements usually attendant on ordinations in the U.S. I was very pleased that we were free to focus completely on the spiritual nature of priestly ordination without any serious distractions — except the war. Fortunately for us, the "phony war" of the first year of the war, in which there was no great action after the invasion of Poland, allowed us to carry on life as usual at the College.

I was deeply thrilled to have the opportunity to celebrate

my first three Masses in such wonderful shrines as those I chose. I was particularly moved by the opportunity to celebrate Mass in the Catacombs of Priscilla in the famous Greek Chapel (so called because all the inscriptions are in the Greek language) in which the oldest fresco of the Mass is on the ceiling.

December 10, 1939

NORTH AMERICAN COLLEGE
Via Dell' Umilta 30

Dear Everybody,

December the eighth was a tremendous day, *Deo gratias*. There is a warm, rich feeling that comes with ordination that can't be described because it does not come from the hands of man. The priesthood, like every masterpiece, returns to the individual just as much as he brings to it; it has a wealth that can't be exhausted, a depth that can't be measured. For myself, I didn't experience any highly emotional, wildly exhilarating feeling that comes and goes like the wind — just an abiding realization of a deep and lasting power. I can't tell you how much I appreciated the generosity that made possible my marvelous opportunities in Europe, culminating in ordination on the feast of the Immaculate Conception. [1]

The ceremony lasted only two hours, from seven to nine. Then I had the usual movie pictures taken of me, and then I made a phonograph record, which I'll send home to you. By this time the fellows in the college were going around the rooms to get the blessings of the newly ordained priests, so there was work to be done. [2] The fellows in my diocese had done a wonderful job on my room — I shouldn't have recognized it if they hadn't put my name on it. To add more excitement and business to an already over-filled morning, everybody filed out to go up and get the blessing of the Pope at St. Mary Major. Again, the miracle of the present age was being re-enacted. The Pope drove from the Vatican to St. Mary's (a distance of about two miles) in an open car and despite the immense numbers of enemies to religion in the world, without any sort of guard or accompaniment. The result was that it took him about two and a half hours to make the trip; the people just poured out in front of the car and stopped it. What is even more amazing is that there is never even a suggestion of mobbing the Pope; he has such tremendous dignity and his person is so sacred that there is never any pushing or pulling at him — but that doesn't mean that they don't wreck the car demanding his blessing.

I said my first Mass at the tomb of St. Philip Neri. Everything went very well; I discovered that luckily I don't get nervous at all. Father Dick Hiester was the assistant priest, and he told me that I was colder than a cucumber (he was certainly right — these unheated Italian churches certainly refrigerate you). This morning, I said Mass on the tomb of St. Peter; I deeply regretted that you couldn't have been here for that. I had to wait for a bishop to say Mass — no matter how long reservations have been made, a bishop takes precedence if he just walks in and wishes to say Mass. For both my Masses, I have had a very enthusiastic congregation; the Italians certainly whip out the responses for all the prayers they know. And when they know that a newly ordained priest is celebrating Mass, they all pile up to Communion (I hope they had all been fasting). Tomorrow morning, I shall say Mass in the catacombs, my favorite spot in Rome. I forgot to say that, of course, my intention for all three Masses is the family and relatives. There are so many shrines in Rome that it will take all year to say Mass at the places which have a particular claim on our devotion.

The number of telegrams I received was marvelous; thanks to all. I hope shortly to get down to answering most of them — only Father Stricker knows how much is to be done in Rome around this time. The Archbishop was splendid, sent me congratulations and his blessing. As far as I am concerned, he is the tops. Even my old classmates at Basselin sent me and Marty cables.

Love and priestly blessing,

Phil

Comments: Letter of December 10, 1939

(1)   In retrospect, I think there was a distinct advantage in being ordained in Rome with the war as a backdrop and conscious of the fact that the war itself was a commentary on the spiritual needs of the world. There was also an advantage in the fact that there was no

preoccupation about such mundane accessories as arrangements for a reception, concern about relatives, etc. The focus of ordination in Rome was the spiritual grace and priestly power, as well as responsibility in being "another Christ." Another notable advantage was the presence of the great shrines of our faith, constant reminders of our supernatural identity. I have never regretted being ordained in Rome during the war.

(2)   After ordination, the newly ordained priests went to their rooms to give a blessing to the other students and friends who also received candy and an American cigarette (strictly rationed). Seminarian friends from other colleges were welcome including the German seminarians. They approached diffidently and uncomfortably, always saying, "We apologize for this war. We are very sorry that our country caused it, and we regret that because of this war your parents and friends could not come here to Rome for your ordination."

December 18, 1939

NORTH AMERICAN COLLEGE
Via Dell' Umilta 30

Dear Everybody,

This has been the luckiest week I have spent in Rome; first of all the packages came, and I assure you that they were enjoyed as no other ever were (I'll explain why later), and then I won a fifteen percent reduction on a chalice at our annual mission lottery.

About the packages. For some time they have been threatening to cut down on the sugar supply in Italy, and at last they have announced that it will begin on the first of February. That means no more cakes or sweets in Italy. Just after news of that had been received, I got the package with two fruit cakes and candy in it. You can understand how much it was appreciated. Then like a gift from heaven, the next package came the next day — with the layer cake and fruitcake in it. The layer cake, despite the fact that it was six weeks old, was in very good shape. The heavy icing had preserved it very well, added to the fact that there must have been much butter and eggs used in making it. The layer cake almost caused a riot, the first one that had been received in good shape from the U.S. A million thanks for the packages. About forty fellows also told me to send their thanks and regards.

Don't get worried about this business of rationing sugar, etc. in Italy. There is no food shortage whatsoever in Italy (you know positively that I'll leave if things get bad). Italy must be making a huge amount of money on this war by this little method: the people are not allowed to have coffee and a number of articles that are not absolutely necessary, but that doesn't mean that the government doesn't have any of those articles — it only means that the government is selling them to the countries that are at war and are willing to pay a good price. A fellow from Naples told us that every day they are sending stuff to England, and they must be sending stuff to Germany too. Everybody is losing except Italy. Nice arrangement. No matter what the newspapers say, Italy is very quiet.

For the past few weeks a priest from Germany who speaks English has been telling us about conditions there. He insists that Germany has a tremendous amount of war stuff stored up and that they are not in want at all. Strangely enough, the quietest section in Germany, he says, is the section just beyond the front because the people have a tremendous confidence in the Siegfried Line. They are convinced that it can't be taken and are not worried; the people that have a bad case of nerves are those who live in the important cities and fear air attacks. His guess is that a huge offensive will be launched this spring; the Germans are not content to sit tight like the French and English because although they are not in want and have things well controlled, they know that they must break through some time. In some places they are developing the usual case of war nerves, especially the older people who remember the awful times following the World War.

In case my next letter doesn't arrive in time, Dad and Mary can be assured that I'll say Mass for them on their birthdays.

Many thanks for the packages.

Love,

Phil

Comments: Letter of December 18, 1939

(1)   The German priest revealed how badly misinformed were the German people relying on the strength of the Nazi war machine. The Germans exhausted their supplies for war and food for their people long before the war ended. In Berlin and other places in Germany, we saw at the end of the war just how little they had, and many of their soldiers said that, in the last weeks of the war, they had practically nothing to eat and their military equipment was in bad shape. I saw a very revealing hand scrawled sign on a pile of rubble in Berlin saying, "This is why he (Hitler) needed five years" referring to the boast of Hitler that he needed only five years to make Germany the wonder nation of the world. In German, the sign read, "Dafur brauchte er funf Jahren."

Christmas, 1939

NORTH AMERICAN COLLEGE
VIA DELL' UMILTA 30

Dear Everybody,

In my hurried last letter, I neglected to tell you all the details leading up to ordination.

For our retreat, we went to the Jesuit headquarters in Rome, and had an Irish Jesuit for the retreat master. The building is an endless affair, scattering in about six directions, apparently designed by the bricklayer. Each room had a radiator that could have been used for a chair, or a hat-rack, or anything other than a heater — sometimes, there was a very faint suggestion of heat in them, just enough to awaken hopes. The food was the real Italian article, everything swimming in oil. Occasionally, we had potatoes that were, as usual, covered with oil. We were there for seven days and every dinner and supper boasted a dessert of specked apples. When we saw the apples roll in for the fourteenth consecutive time, we were ready to quit. It was interesting to see just how they live, interesting but not enjoyable. At the end of the retreat, the Irish Jesuit asked us to write down a few suggestions or impressions about the retreat. The first thing I told him was that the food effectively destroyed any possible inclination I may have had to join the Jesuits.

The retreat was good, but a couple of incidents turned up that were not exactly on the pious side. We all decided that we had to have a bath the day before ordination. On inquiry, we found that there was one bathtub in the building — luckily it was on the floor on which we were living. At first, they told us that there wasn't any hot water and that it couldn't be gotten; so, we told them that if the bathtub had been installed with faucets marked "hot" and "cold", they must have some sort of hot water system — even though they never had used it. At last they promised to heat the water. But when the day for taking the bath arrived, we found that their idea of heating water is just to take the chill off. The only conclusion we could come to was that the tub had never been used. Another thing that disturbed the holy atmosphere of the retreat was the "boner" of one of the fellows. We used to practice the Mass before tea-time (tea is served in the middle of the afternoon because supper is at eight); this fellow came down to tea with some of the vestments on. He only noticed it when the maniple (the vestment worn on the arm) started to get into his plate. There was precious little silence kept for the next five minutes.

On December the eighth, I made a phonograph record; it has already been mailed. There is only one caution to be given — the needles are in the package and are to be placed in the machine so that they give the least friction (you'll understand when you see the shape of the needles — they are curved).

I said my first Requiem Mass at St. Gregory's yesterday. It gave me a tremendous thrill — even though I did have to battle ants on the altar. As a matter of fact one got into the chalice and eventually found his way down my throat.

The change of 'one day not being a priest' and the 'next day being a priest' is so great that it takes quite a time to sink in. Occasionally at the altar the thought pops up, how in the world did you get here? The prospect of saying Mass in the morning changes everything very radically; the whole day seems controlled by it. Even the fellows who used to be good sleepers, get up even before the bell rings.

There are some very interesting and sad stories about the French priests, students and professors who were called into the army. In France everyone receives military training, and everyone is subject to military call in case of a war. Many of the professors and all the students were recalled from Rome. One former professor was in the air force, and he has been shot down already. By a curious trick of fate, some of the former students are in command of their former professors. The priests who are called into active service prefer to be privates, so we were told, so that they can occasionally administer the last sacraments on the battlefield; if they were officers they couldn't stop to give the sacraments. This war is certainly going to seriously cripple the Church in France. Some priests have even been put in the spy service; the reason is that men with a vow of chastity are not an easy prey of women spies of the enemy. So far, Germany hasn't called up any Seminarians, probably because they haven't mobilized yet. If you ask me, the Church in America is in a very enviable position, at least in its relations with the government.

Another rumor going around is that the Italian schools will close in the latter part of March.

Love,
Phil

P.S. Merry Christmas to all; my Christmas card this year will be the three Masses I'll celebrate on that day for the family.

December 26, 1939

NORTH AMERICAN COLLEGE
VIA DELL' UMILTA 30

Dear Everybody,

I decided to get back to the use of the boat service, because it is almost as fast as the airmail. By the way, the Italian postal service is becoming a riot; they announced in the newspapers that they had "real mountains" of mail at Naples, but that it was still unsorted. However, to relieve the crush, they were going to add five mail sorters!! That's their idea of quick service.

Needless to say, no Christmas mail reached the College — even though the boats have been in port for about a week.

It is really amazing to watch the importance and esteem of the Pope growing daily. The recent visit of the King of Italy to the Pope, and the return visit of the Pope to the King, have made a tremendous impression on the people. Thank God that the Church has a real genius in the chair of St. Peter.

Many thanks for the cablegram (thanks to Tom and also to Bill and Jane). This Christmas was the best I have ever spent in Europe, all because I could say Mass. I celebrated my three Masses in the church of St. Mary Major where the Crib is preserved and where the feast is officially celebrated. [1] I said two of my three Masses on the altar of the shrine in which the relic of the Crib is kept. I had made reservations for saying Mass there some time ago, being assured that I could start at six in the morning, the hour that the church is opened. Being properly over-zealous, I got up at five in the morning (having gone to bed at two in the morning after Midnight Mass), rooted Henry Cosgrove out of bed to serve my Masses, and started out. We arrived at St. Mary's at about five thirty, or a trifle later, in the vain hope that the church would be open before the scheduled time. I should have known better. The church didn't open until 6:25!! By which time I was ready to commit murder instead of say Mass. It was extremely edifying there at the shrine, and Henry proved invaluable in looking after the things that the sleepy sacristan overlooked — such as unlocking the gate leading to the altar (for a time it looked as though I should be forced to negotiate a little hurdling in my vestments), lighting the candles and lights. I said two Masses there before my allotted time was up (naturally everybody in Rome is anxious to say Mass there), and the following priest came down to claim the altar. So Henry started out to locate another altar, leaving the congregation to make the responses during the latter part of my second Mass; they took up the job wholeheartedly, and when the men faltered the women went to bat. In fact, after a while I began to wonder who was saying the Mass. An Italian congregation divides itself into two well distinct groups — those who pay absolutely no attention and those who pay so much attention that they almost push the priest off the altar. One American priest over here told me of going to the altar to say Mass to find the altar step crowded with pious old women. They didn't move aside to allow him to pass, so he tapped one on the shoulder and said, "I am going to say Mass here." She came back with, "Me too." Soon Henry came back with the news that he had located an altar; so I completed my three Masses. Because of its associations with the Nativity, Mass at St. Mary's on Christmas is just about enthralling, that is if you get there early enough in the morning to beat the crowd; otherwise it amounts to a football game. After Mass, we beat it over to a restaurant and fed our faces in a very wholehearted American fashion. All in all it was a very heart-warming Christmas. On Christmas night, we had an entertainment consisting of three one-act plays, the second one being devoted, as usual, to a devastating attack on the faculty.

The first one of my Christmas Masses was said for John, because of his birthday. I didn't say Mass for him on his birthday, because I said Mass at a Roman parish church, and one is supposed to say it for the congregation. And therein lies another story. I said the nine o'clock Mass on December 24 at the parish of San Quirico, a little church near the Roman forum. There were a number of Communions and Benediction after the Mass. It was my first job at doing parish work, great stuff — I won't be fully satisfied until I have preached in Italian and also heard confessions. But to get back to the Mass. The pastor is a very good-natured old man who lets the parish run him; he has to give the altar boys candy to keep them tolerably quiet. During the Mass, he led the prayers (they recite some of the prayers with the priest celebrating Mass) and then began a short sermon — but as soon as he began to speak, it seemed to me that everybody also began. But that was nothing compared to the singing; unlike St. Matthew's where they almost burst a piston trying to stir up a few timid squeaks from the congregation, this congregation needed a silencer to keep it down to a mild roar. Needless to say, I couldn't distinguish the tune or the words.

Did I tell you that I have said Mass at the shrine of the Holy Cross — right behind the altar is the case containing a very large portion of the Cross (the section with the inscription on it, and the inscription is easily visible); in the same case, they also have one of the nails and two of the thorns besides a relic (a finger, I believe) of St. Thomas the Apostle.

A few weeks ago Arnold Lunn, the English lecturer, gave us a very interesting talk. He had just returned from a long trip in the Balkans and painted a very dismal picture. [2] He had a number of good cracks, such as, "They say that England owes America millions of gold sovereigns and that

America has never collected any — well, you got one sovereign, through Wally Simpson," and "We English contend that we have never been beaten. The Revolutionary War in America was a fight between two British armies and the army farthest from its base was beaten."

Many thanks for the much-appreciated cables; they made an already perfect Christmas more perfect.

Happy New Year to all.

Love,

Phil

Comments: Letter of December 26, 1939

(1)   The opportunity I had of saying Mass on the altar of the crib in St. Mary Major on Christmas, demonstrates what a privilege it was to be ordained in Rome during the war. Today, with the increase of the number of visitors and other factors, there would be no chance of getting permission to say three Masses in St. Mary Major. I took particular delight in saying Mass for my brother, John, born on December 24 and for the other members of the family on their birthdays.

I was very eager to celebrate Mass at all the great shrines in Rome especially Santa Croce in Gerusalemme — Holy Cross of Jerusalem.

(2)   The lecture by Arnold Lunn, famous in his day, about the situation in the Balkans shows how Rome became the center of information about every nation in Europe, and also how the war was a factor in every aspect of life in Europe.

Jubilant crowd watching "white smoke" announcing election of new Pope.

Crowd awaiting Benediction by newly elected Pius XII in piazza of St. Peter's, Sunday after election.

Illumination of St. Peter's for Canonization

Placing of Tiara on Pope Pius XII, March 12th, 1939

Group at Coronation of Pope Pius XII

First benediction of Pope Pius XII, March 2nd, 1939

First blessing of Pope Pius XII after Coronation, March 2ⁿᵈ, 1939

First Mass in St. Peter's by Pope Pius XII

Ordination group, December 8th, 1939.

Ordination group, December 8th, 1939. Phil Hannan third from left in back row.

After Ordination with Seminarians of the Baltimore Diocese.

Giving a Blessing to a fellow student.

Walked up the Matterhorn en route from Paris to Rome, August, 1939.

Snowfall on Rome, December 30, 1939.

1940

January 2, 1940

NORTH AMERICAN COLLEGE
Via Dell' Umilta 30

Dear Everybody,

I celebrated the New Year by helping out in a parish that has 40,000 parishioners. The outskirts of Rome have few churches, though there are about 350 churches in Rome. Two fellows from the College go to Saint Joseph's (the church with the 40,000 parishioners) every Sunday and holy day of obligation to say Mass and help distribute Communion. The parish church is not nearly so large as St. Matthew's, so you can imagine just what sort of a general jamboree they have there on Sunday. A couple of children made their first Communion, and they were put in the sanctuary during Mass; their parents and near relatives were also allowed to kneel in the sanctuary. It was the first time I had seen women in the sanctuary (except for nuptial Masses) in my life; that would be promptly condemned if it happened in the U.S. but it's alright in Rome. I was surprised to find that they give sermons on Sundays in some of the parishes, but they don't give sermons at regular times during the Mass – they come out about once an hour and start it up regardless of what part of the Mass is going on. I was near the end of my Mass when the priest came out to preach, so I tried to say the prayers at the end of Mass (the Hail Mary's etc.) very quietly. No use. The congregation bellowed them out as though they were at a hog-calling contest. Did that embarrass the speaker giving the sermon? Not at all — he just raised his voice to a roar and proceeded to out-shout everyone.

For the first time within the memory of the Romans, there was a six-inch fall of snow. It snowed on the night of the thirtieth of December. Next morning a number of us went over to St. Peter's to get pictures of the dome in its cover of snow (very little snow had remained on the dome; it had blown off) and on our way back, just at the great square in front of St. Peter's we had a snowball battle with the populace. There were only about a dozen of us, and there must have been over two hundred Romans against us. We enjoyed a very friendly fight. Of course, the natives have only good will when it comes to throwing things; they can use their feet well but not their hands — and that's how we could easily take care of about 200 hundred of them. I was particularly pleased to take care of one fat-faced Italian priest, or seminarian, who was helping his fellow citizens; he threw three snowballs in my general direction, so I waited until he stooped down for snow. I managed to deposit a huge lump right on his moon face – and that was the end of his battling for the day. The affair ended as all such things do — the local police came along and indicated that it might be better for us to limit our activity to sightseeing. Everything was very pleasant; I had waited for four years to unlimber my arm at something useful like that. In the middle of the fight, a cameraman came along and got pictures of the affair and a picture appeared in the newspaper the next day, but it was so indistinct that we didn't receive any disagreeable notoriety. A very scandalous and very enjoyable morning. Whenever it snows, the Romans act like two-year-old kids; everything is like a big holiday.

The inevitable snowman was also made. Of course, it was modeled on the Rector – it had a bishop's miter, cross, ring and sash. The Rector had no objections to that, but if the snowball throwing keeps up around the college there won't be a sound window left. Four were broken on the first day. Unfortunately, the snow came during the holidays; otherwise we should have received a day off.

I sang my first Solemn Mass on the last day of 1939. And although I had short notice to get ready for it, I was a surprise to all the fellows in my class – who had expected the worst. The quality of the tone could have been improved, but I didn't go off key once. The only natural gift I have that redeems my many faults is my ability to keep cool. If I make any mistakes, I can't blame it on nervousness. With a good choir, a Solemn Mass is extremely impressive for the celebrant; there is so much added significance. I watched a Mass said in the Eastern rite a few days ago and was almost appalled by the amount of singing and ceremonies the celebrant must learn; they chant, or sing, during the whole Mass — which lasts for a solid hour.

Happy New Year to everybody, even though this may not reach you before June.

Love,

Phil

Comments: Letter of January 2, 1940

(1)   The Mass schedule on Sundays in St. Joseph's Church conformed to the very large number of parishioners. There were three Masses in progress at the same time — one at the main altar, another on one side altar and a third on another side altar. The Masses began about fifteen minutes apart, and thus, the parishioners arriving at various times could simply find the Mass that was just beginning, to attend for themselves. The pulpit for the sermon was located almost in the middle of the church, thus enabling the preacher to be heard by almost everyone in the church. Although this system violated every sense of decorum we have, it did not interfere with the piety of the people. They were reverent and followed the Mass that they selected very easily.

(2)   The snow battle in the piazza of St. Peter was a huge lark. We had a great time and fortunately the police in Rome were very patient and forebearing. There were no hurt feelings, and at the end of the battle we all laughed, and shook hands wishing everyone a Happy New Year – *Felice Capodanno.*

January 8, 1940

NORTH AMERICAN COLLEGE
Via Dell' Umilta 30

Dear Everybody,

The American College at Louvain in Belgium has been closed; a few of the fellows came down here, but most were sent back to the U.S. It was only a precautionary measure. Again, they have started to give out ration cards in Italy. The system is this: everyone gets a card by which he can buy a certain amount a day; if the person goes on a trip or moves out of Rome, he must take his card with him; otherwise, he won't be able to buy food. So far, they have only given out the cards — they haven't rationed food and don't intend to. It makes absolutely no difference to us. Other than that, there is absolutely no change in the very peaceful condition of Italy. We haven't had any coffee in Italy for some time now — it can be shipped in by friends in other countries, but the duty on it is terrific (a dollar a pound is the duty). The government is making a pretty penny on the rich who can afford to pay the duty; those who can't must allow the government to confiscate any coffee that is sent to them — they allow it, but they certainly squawk about it. Italians love to complain and shoot off at the mouth anyway, and they are given plenty of opportunity now. The package you sent me has not arrived yet; no cause for worry, everything is late. I have been very lucky with duty on packages. The other package I received from you this year cost just ten cents. They haven't any definite system here, and it just depends on your luck.

There is very little news around and what is more amazing, no wild rumors. Before the war started there was a fresh story every minute and miles of intrigue and counter-plots reported in the newspapers. But once war began and the grim business of war or keeping out of war started, all wild talking stopped immediately. It seems that only the American newspapers are allowed to fight everybody's war in their columns; over here everything is kept in step.

On Little Christmas, the Epiphany, all the members of the Deacon Class went to wait on tables at the Home for the Aged, run by the Little Sisters of the Poor. The College also furnished the entertainment — an orchestra and choir. Some stuff. There are four refectories there, and the one in which I served was for the old ladies. Things went along smoothly and quietly until the orchestra started to play a couple of the Italian songs; when they played a very popular song called "Giovenezza" the old girls got up and waved and applauded — they can't yell much, all played out. Some organization. As each one was served, she tried to make a speech that usually ended in very expressive head wagging and hand waving. Finally, the Rector of the College came around and gave to each old man a cigar, and to each old lady a little bag of candy. A great day. My idea of living saints is embodied in the members of the Sisters who run those places; the old people are childish, and they have to watch them, and wait on them as though they were infants.

Love,

Phil

Comments: Letter of January 8, 1940

(1)   Belgium feared from the outset of the war that it would be invaded, learning from its experience from World War I. Unfortunately, they were correct in their assumption, and in May they were invaded. The American College in Louvain acted very wisely in allowing their students to leave before the *blitzkrieg* by Germany overran their country.

(2)   Everyone realized in Italy that rationing was inevitable, and so there was no unexpected complaining. The laughable aspect of the rationing was that the government had tried to develop a conviction that coffee was not really an Italian drink, and that it was foreign to the Italian taste! I don't know what genius got this idea, but no Italian was convinced of it.

January 28, 1940

NORTH AMERICAN COLLEGE
Via Dell' Umilta 30

Dear Everybody,

I got a big belt out of the little Christmas party attended by Monsignor Buckey. We all voted (I told a few of the fellows about it) that Mom's first idea of giving the Monsignor a nice shiny nickel was the best. The last impression I have of Monsignor Buckey was his wandering around the farm on the day of Mary's wedding clutching a big glass of beer and worrying about how he could refill it. I think that despite the fact that the old Monsignor is very well liked in the parish, he is not sufficiently appreciated — compared to some of the parish priests I have seen over here he stands out like a mountain in the middle of a prairie. And speaking about the American clergy, reminds me of what a priest from Germany told us, "What Germany needs is a whole set of democratic American bishops to get down and meet the people."

Actually, I think that the Germans expect their bishops to be far above them and removed from them — they like to be bossed and regimented. Enough of preaching.

Just to show you that Italy has not changed a bit, even during the war, let me tell you about their latest notice. You know that it snowed during the last part of December – the first good snowfall in about ten years, and the largest snowfall in the memory of the present generation (it was about five inches of snow). The snow melted and disappeared before January 2. Then, just exactly three weeks later, the government posted a notice that there was a city law to the effect that every property owner had to clean the snow off the front of his property under penalty of a heavy fine. That's being either about three weeks late or about thirty years early.

Despite any news to the contrary, Italy has not started to ration food. They have limited the sale of white sugar. As Father Stricker remarked in a letter, "Italy must have nit the years of plenty. In my time they didn't have anything to ration." I am convinced that Italy is shipping out foodstuff to the warring nations and making a nice little pile. Occasionally, some government official makes a rousing speech to the effect that Italy must be prepared to wield the sword at any time, but everyone knows that that's just to keep them from going to sleep (which they have started to do.)

A few days ago, I wrote to the Archbishop telling him that if he wished me to study after this year, that I was willing. [1] He told us when he was over here last May that he thought it was a good idea, and that we could do it if we wished – but that was before the war started, so I am leaving it up to him. Actually, there is positively no danger in being in Italy now, or even if a war started because it would be easy enough to get out. But I did tell him, or rather ask him, to allow me to come home this summer. Even if he does wish me to study longer, he always allows the fellows to come home in the summer. I have begun inquiries about boat accommodations and find that it won't cost as much as I had expected. The diocese pays for the tickets. Another thing I have been investigating, without much luck so far, is some way to get over to the Holy Land before July. Perhaps the best way will be to go by railroad to Constantinople and then by boat, or perhaps by railroad again, to Palestine. Of course, there are boats always going to the Holy Land, but they are very expensive, and I'd see more of the Balkans if I went by railroad through southeastern Europe. Well, we shall see.

Love,

Phil

Comments: Letter of January 28, 1940

(1)   My idea of continued studies was very unrealistic. I was interested in studying church history, with a special emphasis on the early years of the Church. I was convinced that there was real catechetical value in developing more knowledge about the catacombs. The remark of Archbishop Curley about post-graduate studies was priceless, "Don't get sick over here (Italy) from graduate studies. It's more useful to have a live donkey than a dead Ph.D."

February 7, 1940

NORTH AMERICAN COLLEGE
VIA DELL' UMILTA 30

Dear Everybody,

Just came back from a trip to Milan — we have a three day holiday before Lent, carnival days. We were scheduled to go to Siena, but decided it was better to go to Milan (I hope the Rector doesn't object; he'll never know that we changed our minds unless someone else tells him). It was the best "bum run" I have yet had. We went up to Milan on Sunday, the fourth; I said Mass at ten minutes to five!! It was the chance of a lifetime: there was a 70% reduction on the railroad, there was an opera on at the famous *La Scala,* and we had a chance to say Mass on the tomb of St. Charles Borromeo in the cathedral. And, we certainly took advantage of it. Milan is about as far from Rome as Hartford is from Washington, and the train fare was not four dollars (round trip).

To start from the beginning. We left Rome at seven o'clock in the morning. We got into snow when we reached Bologna, and about four o'clock we pulled into Milan — just in time to hop a cab and beat it to the opera in time for the last two acts of *La Boheme*. *La Scala* is not very ornate on the outside but inside it is very lovely. There are six balconies, but only the two highest have rows of seats; all the rest have boxes or little sections. All the walls are done in red damask but the ceiling is gold and cream. It is much like the inside of the Paris opera house. There is just one enormous chandelier in the opera house in the top of which is the little cabin for the spot light — a very neat arrangement.

But the decoration is nothing compared to the really superb scenery. The Italians have a natural flare for the theatrical, and they do it beautifully, richness without extravagance and ornateness without gaudiness. There is just one thing in which they lack smoothness – the handling of the spotlight. The acoustics of the opera house are marvelous, giving the effect of having the singers about ten feet away.

There was an opera again that evening, so we came back for it, a new one called *Ghirlino*. It was a sort of child's fantasy, but was very pleasing. One of the most popular numbers was a children's chorus that was executed about as perfectly as possible. The costumes were exquisite — which reminds me that for Mary and Mom the chief attraction would have been the orchestra section which looked like a congress of stylists. And being Italians, they took delight in showing off their clothes. There is no self-effacement or furtiveness with Italians when they are decked out to impress the world.

During the opera, one of the fellows in our group met an opera singer he had met on the boat coming over. This fellow is an Italian American born in Boston and married to a very charming Irish girl. He has been scheduled to sing at *LaScala* three times, his name has been on the program three times, and he has never put a foot on the stage — can't get the permit he needs from the government. He invited us out to his apartment, and we had a very pleasant evening. This would probably interest Bill; this fellow never sang a note, didn't know he could sing, until he was seventeen; then he sang in a choir and got on the Keith circuit, then sang on the radio; he was sorry that he had ever walked into a choir loft, because it prevents the building up of a good range; I asked him is a fellow around thirty was too old to have his voice trained, and he laughed — he cited one opera star who didn't start until he was forty, and he himself is about thirty-five; he believes that voice training is the whole business, and told me frankly that even I have a better voice than Tito Schipa (considered the best opera artist in Italy), but Schipa has been magnificently trained. Don't think that I am the least bit interested in developing my voice; however, I thought maybe Bill would be interested to learn what the opera stars think about voice culture and the importance of training. These fellows work incredibly hard at their business; when we arrived at this fellow's apartment he was listening on the radio to an opera, following it in his book and marking down how the singer was doing this phrase or that passage.

We also learned from him about some of the latest taxes. He rents an apartment, and believe it or not he even pays tax on the air space!! He pays a tax on the furniture – which was very cheap and scarce – another tax on the piano, a tax on the radio and a general tax on the apartment. Only a rich man can afford to have a pool, or billiard table, in his home because one must pay three taxes on that. He said that when he left the States he, like everybody else, was complaining about the high taxes, but now......[1]

On Monday morning, I went to the cathedral and said Mass in the crypt under the main altar, on the tomb of St. Charles. The cathedral in the morning, with the sunlight streaming through those huge glass windows, makes a tremendous impression. Too bad I wasn't ordained when we were there before. On the next morning, I went to the church of St. Ambrose where they have the bodies of three saints just over the altar; the bodies are in glass casements.

Love,

Phil

Comments: Letter of February 7, 1940

(1)   The enormous taxes in Italy were a major preoccupation of the people, especially the businessmen, and this diverted their attention from the war. Many actually believed that Italy would never be involved in the war and that Mussolini would arrange to have Italy receive some of the bounty of war with no price paid by Italy.

February 15, 1940

NORTH AMERICAN COLLEGE
Via Dell' Umilta 30

Dear Everybody,

This winter is the worst I have spent in Rome. Today, it is very cold; yesterday, it was like spring. The weather is as unpredictable as the natives, or maybe the natives have an effect on the weather. At any rate, the poor Italians are having a terrific time this year — grumbling about the government, afraid to death of war, annoyed by the weather, fearing more taxes. The latest tax is a two percent sales tax on everything; the proceeds from this are to defray the expenses for the projected World's Fair to be held in Rome in 1942. [1] I can't for the life of me figure out how they expect to get people to their Fair, unless they make Germany, France and England agree to an armistice. So far, the government has disregarded the war entirely; actually they are digging subways for Rome — but somehow I can't believe that they are serious about this business, because they can't deny the fact that the war is at their northern frontier.

Did I tell you that I said Mass recently (on the feast of St. Ignatius of Antioch whose body is buried beneath the main altar) in the Church of St. Clement — do you remember the very old church that has two churches beneath it, and is in the hands of Irish Dominicans? The main altar there is what they call a papal altar, it is so arranged that the celebrant says Mass facing the people instead of having his back to them.

I am having plans for a chalice drawn; I have been experimenting with a number of types to find out which pleases me most. When I have things all set, I'll send you a picture, or a drawing of it.

Happy birthday to Dad, if my next letter doesn't arrive in time. I'll say Mass that day for him.

Love,

Phil

Comments: Letter of February 15, 1940

(1)   Incredibly the government not only planned a World's Fair for 1942 but began the preliminary work on some of the sites. In fact, a new section at the outskirts of Rome was to be developed, and today that section is called EUR.

February 20, 1940

NORTH AMERICAN COLLEGE
Via Dell' Umilta 30

Dear Everybody,

You must pardon me for not having written recently — the other fellows in our class are being ordained, and they must learn the Mass, etc.

Your last letter made me laugh for a week — the stuff about Italy's closing the schools at Easter time to save coal bills. That story is as silly as saying that we in Washington close the schools in summer to save money on the coal bill. Another thing was that you thought we would be sent home if there were no coal supply to heat the college. If that were true, I should have been in Washington, D.C., about December 1 of 1936.

Sumner Welles received a cordial reception in Naples, but the representative to the Vatican, Myron Taylor, was left in the cold. (1) Two of the members of our faculty went down to welcome him. Incidentally, they rode down in a car and got in a wreck. The Taylors are said to be very nice people; they also seem to be typical, rich Americans. Although they have a villa in Florence and a car up there, they didn't bother to bring the car down from Florence — they just brought one over from the U.S., a little Rolls Royce.

Myron Taylor is scheduled to come to the College soon, so we shall see him at close range.

Love,

Phil

Comments: Letter of February 20, 1940

(1)   Sumner Welles was the Under Secretary of State and apparently was on a mission to see if he could enlist the help of the Vatican in making a deal with Italy and possibly with Germany to stop the war. Although unofficial, the purpose had some notable significance because the representative of the President to the Vatican, Myron Taylor, was involved in it as was also the Ambassador of the U.S. to Italy. Obviously, the effort did not achieve anything.

March 6, 1940

NORTH AMERICAN COLLEGE
Via Dell' Umilta 30

Dear Everybody,

The Days of the Giants have returned to the College. A reception was held for the President's personal representative to the Pope, Myron Taylor. [1] I like especially the way they decorate the College for such events; since it is impossible to dress up our refectory that looks more like a shooting gallery than a place to eat, they haul in practically a whole forest of shrubbery and hide everything. When they have succeeded in concealing perfectly the identity of the place, they begin to add the nice touches. The final touch is to haul in miles of red carpet to cover the stone floor. By this time, all the fellows are sitting around trying to figure out how long we will have bad food to pay for this extravagance. They bear it all in silence, until the heat is turned on to impress the visitors, then the real ranting begins. The final explosion occurs when good food is brought into the refectory for the guests. Everything went off very smoothly. Myron Taylor gave the fellows a very short talk, wishing us success. As usual a number of important personages turned out for the occasion; the Cardinal Secretary of State and four other Cardinals were present, the American Ambassador to Italy, a number of other ambassadors, etc. — and, of course, the usual number of hangers on who come because they have nothing to do.

One unusual incident did occur. The reception was scheduled for Sunday afternoon; Saturday afternoon old Cardinal Tedeschini came to the College all dressed up in his finest. He met an old servant who told him his mistake, so the Cardinal beat it out the door. When he came back on Sunday the fellows gave him a hand, and someone said, "Welcome back!" The old Cardinal turned redder than his robes, but took the joke well.

Another thing happened in connection with the reception that is worth mentioning (if I haven't told you of it before). Our Vice Rector and Spiritual Director motored down to Naples to meet Myron Taylor, but on the way down the Vice Rector hit one of those typical Italian carts and splattered it all over the province of Naples. The driver was not even scratched, but that didn't prevent him from screaming that he was killed. It soon developed that the driver of the cart did not own the cart or the horse, so presently along came the owner of the horse to file suit for damages and the owner of the cart did the same. In a few hours, when the good word had spread around the countryside, a whole crowd of Italians was trying to dig up damage suits against the rich American priests.

The Italian government has developed a new wrinkle that has had an effect upon our schedule. In a new economy measure designed to save coal, they have decreed that no gas can be used until seven o'clock in the morning — thus shoving our breakfast back about half an hour. The breakfast food has also been changed a little; some genius has devised a new type of drink — different from coffee and different from chocolate, and for that matter, different from anything I have ever tasted. The first morning that it was served, a number of fellows went in to see the servant whose job it is to make the breakfast drink, and they found him being assisted or tutored by a woman sent by the company that sells the stuff. She admitted that they had gotten the recipe mixed up but promised to do a better job the next morning. It did improve the next morning, so everyone is temporarily pleased.

Tomorrow there will be ordinations in the College again. One of the chief advantages in being ordained in March is supposed to be the fine weather — of which there isn't any at the present time. The weather has been consistently stinky this winter.

As the spring comes on, there seems to be growing in Italy a feeling of security; there are no war jitters at the present time. I am personally convinced that nothing will happen to hasten our sailing about July. As the Italians say, "We can't fight against Germany, and we can't fight with her." And they could also add, "We don't want to fight anyway." I find it almost incredible to believe that my four years in Europe are about finished; and it is even more incredible to realize just how much the world has changed in that four years. When I came to Rome, as perhaps you remember, the French franc was worth fifteen to a dollar, the Italian lira was worth about eleven to a dollar. Today the franc is about forty to a dollar and the lira is quoted around twenty-one — which sums up pretty well just what has happened to the governments of Europe. Whatever ideas I had about the value of European money before I came here, the last two years have changed them completely. Another observation that has impressed itself on me is the complete unreliability of newspaper predictions. When I came over, the war in Spain was on, and every newspaper in America was predicting that it would lead to a new World War, and that Spain and Italy would be against France. Spain's war ended and was laid neatly to rest before the present war began, and Spain has shown no more interest in helping Germany than Ireland has. The general conclusion I have drawn is that the weather report is the most reliable and factual item in a newspaper.

What a country this is! — two fine spring days, rain, a night of snow, then sunshine.

Love,
Phil

Comments: Letter of March 6, 1940

(1)   Although Myron Taylor never had the rank of an ambassador (he was the personal representative of President Roosevelt to the Vatican), he was accorded a great deal of respect by the Vatican and the Americans in Rome. It was never explained why Myron Taylor gave us a special dinner in our college; but whatever the reason, it was a great success for us. The presence of so many distinguished Cardinals showed the importance attached to it by the Vatican.

March 8, 1940

NORTH AMERICAN COLLEGE
Via Dell' Umilta 30

Dear Everybody,

Some time ago I told you that the Archbishop had offered to allow us to stay over for graduate study if we wished. Two months ago I wrote to him and asked to be sent back to Europe this September. He sent his reply quickly — we need all available priests in the archdiocese. Apparently many vacancies have occurred during the year. The will of the Archbishop is the will of God for me, so there is no room for regrets. I like very much the prospect of finally going to work, but I should also like to do some further studying.

Frankly, I had half expected the Archbishop to refuse because of the war, but apparently that didn't affect his decision. He realizes as well as anyone in Europe that Italy will not enter the war unless it wishes to, and there are no real indications now that they so wish.

Monsignor Fitzgerald, the Spiritual Director at the College, told me a good story about the recent reception for Myron Taylor. Prince Barberini, the head of one of the most distinguished noble families in Rome, came to the reception decked out handsomely and with his mustache nicely trimmed up. The Barberini family has a tremendous palace in Rome (close to the Majestic Hotel) that contains something like a thousand or more rooms. The first thing Prince Barberini said to the Rector was, "Has Mr. Taylor chosen a residence yet?"

"I don't think so," said the Rector.

"Well, tell him I have an excellent apartment for rent." The only thing these old princely families have is real estate.

Apparently the Myron Taylors are having a tough time in Rome. They went to the swankiest hotel in Rome, the Excelsior, to find that the hotel is not heated (the large hotels in Rome don't have enough guests to fill the basement); they asked that a fire be built in the fireplace in the room, but they got the chimney deranged so that it smoked them out.

Mrs. Taylor has had such a bad cold that she hasn't been able to attend any of the receptions, and according to Mr. Taylor the only possible business they have in Rome is to attend receptions. You can gather from that, that the diplomatic career of Myron Taylor is not a howling success so far.

I have started to say Masses for the repose of the soul of Willie Ryan. I was glad that you told me about the anniversary of Aunt Mollie and Grandpa — my memory for such things is no good. Four years has certainly made a difference in the various families.

Before I leave I certainly must make a shopping tour to Florence. I have a number of orders for plaques to be filled, so I think I'll go back to that shop across the Ponte Vecchio where we bought so much stuff in other years. That fellow is the best packer and shipper I have met in Italy. After that, I had better see some steamship line and make arrangements for chartering a freighter, or fleet of freighters, to cart back the stuff. Those plaques weigh like anvils.

Love,

Phil

March 12, 1940

NORTH AMERICAN COLLEGE
Via Dell' Umilta 30

Dear Everybody,

Myron Taylor presented the College with the best banquet that has been seen in that dilapidated picture-gallery that we use for a refectory. All the kitchen help were given the day off, and the staff of the Hotel Excelsior (the best in Rome) took over; the two-inch thick cups and plates of the College were replaced by an elegant service and waiters in tails flipped out the tastiest dinner we have had in Rome, washed down by Orvieto and Castel Bracciano wine; there were three glasses for every plate, and only one glass was for water. The courses were interrupted by community singing. Evidently, Myron Taylor likes singing with his meals; first he wanted to bring special entertainment during the meal but the Rector talked him out of that, so he insisted that the fellows sing. That was only an excuse for him to sing (not a solo, but along with everybody else). It was peculiar to see a bunch of clerics (a Cardinal, a Bishop, and the Rector of the Gregorian University were among the guests) rolling off such numbers as My Wild Irish Rose, Clementine, Way Down Upon The Swanee River, etc., but nobody seemed to mind. The climax of the evening (if it wasn't the smooth wine) was a movie supplied by the American Ambassador, who was also a guest, <u>Pinnocchio</u>. Myron Taylor attended Cornell, so the choir sang the Cornell song — which put a big beam all over Taylor's ample face. Taylor gave us a short little speech, very religious in tone, explaining his mission to the Holy Father. The highlight of the evening, I thought, was the sight of the Rector of the Gregorian (who was seated next to Taylor) trying to sing Clementine and the other sentimental stuff; he resembles very closely Father Coleman Nevils, former President of Georgetown, and I must congratulate him on his success in appearing at ease in a difficult position.

The papers at home must be kicking up some sensational stuff; five of our fellows have been recalled recently. Don't believe anything you read about the possibility of Italy's entrance into the war. Some of the fellows will stop by Washington; I gave a couple of undeveloped films to one of them, (Father Showalter), to give you. Did you receive any films from the Kodak Company of either Paris or Lucerne? I left some in Paris to be developed, the war chased me out of France, then they sent them to Lucerne, but I had left Switzerland before they arrived. The last I heard was that they would forward them to my address in Washington.

Recently, I drew a hundred dollar check, then a fifty to take advantage of a very extraordinary rate of exchange that the bank was offering for a short time; they needed American money for commerce and gave about thirty lira to a dollar. My chalice will thus cost me considerably less than a hundred dollars.

This should reach home before Mother's Day; I'll say Mass for Mom.

Another canonization is scheduled for the end of this week. If there is an illumination at night, we shall be allowed out to see it. It will at least be something to think about other than the war. Rome is certainly bare of tourists this year.

Love,

Phil

April 3, 1940

NORTH AMERICAN COLLEGE
Via Dell' Umilta 30

Dear Everybody,

It's about time for me to tell you about Easter. Holy Week in Rome this year was not nearly so international as it has been in other years; I don't remember seeing any Americans, or any foreigners, except a few Swiss. [1] The great change this year was that the Cardinal whom we watched perform the ceremonies last year in St. Peter's, was not there because he is now Pope; I remember distinctly how excited a delegation of French people became when they saw the very dignified Cardinal Pacelli carrying out the ceremony of washing the main altar at St. Peter's.

Well, Holy Thursday I decided to see what sort of repository they have in the Vatican, so I battled, along with about ten million people, to get into the Pauline Chapel. The Pope himself carries the Blessed Sacrament from the Sistine Chapel to the Pauline Chapel on Holy Thursday, and places it in the repository. They have the whole altar decorated in candles — no color at all except the uniforms of the Swiss Guards who are on duty. They do a magnificent job of grouping the candles. The thing to do in the afternoon is to listen to one of the big choirs (either at St. Peter's where the Sistine is holding forth, or at St. Mary Major, or at St. John Lateran) sing Tenebrae in the afternoon. There are three famous choir directors in Rome and each one shows off his best on Holy Week; most of them use their own compositions and seem capable of strangling even the burliest bass if he goes off. No organ is used so the voices come into clearer relief.

Good Friday is my favorite. The most important thing to do is to go up the Holy Stairs, near St. John Lateran, on one's knees; the wear on the knees is nothing compared to the frazzling of the nerves from all the pushing and struggling. I can stand all the jostling that even an overweight Italian woman is capable of doling out, but what gets me rattled is the wave of kissing that comes over the people (mostly women) when they venerate the crucifix at the top of the Holy Stairs. They get what seems to be a special type of stranglehold on the crucifix and proceed to kiss every inch of it at least twice; and all this is going on while hundreds of people wait to do the same thing. That isn't all. If some over-devout and under-intelligent person sees something that is supposed to be venerable and plants a devout kiss on it, at least twenty others will try to do the same thing. Perhaps Mom remembers that the Holy Stairs are covered with wooden planks, and that halfway up there are a couple of glass openings in the woods so that one can see the surface of the Holy Stairs. Somebody got the absurd idea that those glass openings marked some special spot on the Holy Stairs; the first thing I knew somebody started to kiss the glass, then everybody tried to push over and kiss the glass. Which reminds me of an even sillier incident. At the foot of the Holy Stairs, there is a statue (life-size) of Christ being betrayed by the kiss of Judas. Kissing statues is the specialty of the Italians; so as they pass by this statue, they kiss the foot of Christ — but imagine our surprise when one of our fellows saw some of the befuddled pious kiss the foot of Judas. The ceremony of the burial of Christ in the Greek church is very impressive, even though, one can't understand what they are singing.

Holy Saturday afternoon is the big afternoon for the priests, for then we go out to bless houses. Each fellow is assigned a section of Rome (a very small section, because everyone wants everything blessed). Besides that, I was given the job of blessing the rooms in the College; most of the fellows were in bed, because I went around during siesta time. A generous sprinkling of water wasn't enough even to rouse some of them. When I ran across a card game in one room, I blessed the whole thing, including the cards. The Italians are very eager to have every room in their home, or apartment, blessed. They usually line up the kids and ask to have them blessed, especially the bad ones. Even though many of them don't go to Mass, they certainly are respectful to the priest when he comes in their home; and all have some offering to make. Lord help you if you unknowingly pass by a door without going in. Stores, coffee shops (with all the patrons still sipping coffee), garages, etc. get their blessing too.

On Easter morning, I said Mass at six o'clock on the main altar of the Church of St. Marcellus, a very famous little place near the college. I got over to St. Peter's in time to see the Mass celebrated by the Pope, and to get some good movie films in color of him blessing the crowd after the Mass. Then, in the afternoon, I started out for Sicily, stopping off at Salerno. (2) More about that when I write next.

Love,

Phil

Comments: Letter of April 3, 1940

(1)   The major ceremonies of Holy Week were carried out with no nervousness about a possible involvement of Italy in the war. The Italians were so eager to think that they would not be in a war that they gladly assumed that they would not be involved.

(2)   The reference to Salerno and Sicily refers to the fact that I had a very serious case of rheumatic fever, and received no medicine for it from our house doctor except to "drink some warm wine." I went to the hospital, conducted by Irish Sisters who were splendid, and the doctor prescribed only that I have no salt, or other condiments, in my meals. The pain was excessive and my whole body was affected, even to the point where my eyes could not tolerate any light; the only light permitted was a candle behind a shade. The climax came one night when I could feel the pain stabbing at my heart. I prayed with all the fervor I could muster. In an hour, the pain began to ease around my heart, and I was confident that my system had beaten the disease.

    The lack of food hampered my recovery, so I asked my friend, Henry Cosgrove, to smuggle some bananas into my room, an easy task while wearing a house cassock. The window was left half open, and during the night I would eat a couple of bananas and throw the peels out the window. In a short time, I felt much better and, against orders, would arise and walk around the bed. Eventually, I told the doctor that I felt very strong, and wished to be allowed to get out of the bed. He refused, saying that I did not realize how weak I was, and that if I attempted to stand up, I would collapse. He even called in a supervising nurse (a Sister) to order me to stay in bed. I insisted on getting up, stood up easily and walked around the room (which I had been doing for a week at night). The doctor said in amazement, "It's a miracle." I showed no awareness of being in the presence of a miracle, and the doctor gave me a lecture saying that I was an unworthy priest, because I did not acknowledge the miracle I had been granted.

That afternoon, as I was packing up to leave the hospital, a furious gardener came up to the nurse and said, "I have been picking up banana peels for some time, and I think that they have come from this room." The sister asked me, "Do you know anything about this?" "Not a thing," I responded and left hurriedly.

I returned to the college, and the Rector allowed me to make plans to go to Taormina in Sicily to recuperate.

April 28, 1940

NORTH AMERICAN COLLEGE
Via Dell' Umilta 30

Dear Everybody,

In her last letter, Mom said something about not receiving a letter according to the usual schedule. Well, the reason is a very peculiar one, in fact almost ridiculous; the truth of the matter (I didn't wish to worry you, but if you were to hear it from another source you might have gotten more worried) is that I had a touch of rheumatism for a couple of weeks. A very simple matter, but somehow the ailment affected my eyes, and I couldn't see to write or type. By the great goodness of God, I recovered in a very short time; as a matter of fact, I was only in bed for a couple of weeks. The greatest reason why I recovered so fast was that I was about the most impatient patient Rome has ever seen; ordinations were scheduled for the seventh of March and I was determined that I was going to assist at the first Masses of three fellows — actually, I didn't make it, but my stubbornness made for a rapid recovery. You can't imagine what a bull-headed, contrary, determined, nerve-frazzling patient I was. My sickness was very comforting in one regard: I found that I have an exceptionally strong heart (which was the real reason why I shook off that old man's disease in such a short time), and the doctor told me that I had as strong a constitution as he had ever seen. You won't believe this, but it's the gospel truth — I gained four pounds during my stay in bed! My eyes were affected because I had used them so much, and they were the only part of my body that was tired. Now my eyes are stronger than ever because of the rest I gave them; as for the rest of my well-padded frame, it is just as comfortable and well as a big over-stuffed chair. To put the finishing touches on my recovery I went down to Sicily with two other fellows (Henry Cosgrove and a fellow from the West named Kelley) and basked in the sunshine at a place called Taormina. You can see that I thoroughly enjoyed my ailment.

Taormina is on the coast of Sicily, built on a high cliff overlooking the sea with a snow-capped volcano in the background, Mount Etna. Taormina boasts that it is the only resort in the world in which a person can go skiing in the morning and swimming in the afternoon. I didn't care to do either. The scenery is lovely, and I tried to squeeze some idea of it into some feet of film. I also went to visit Palermo and found that it was great as I thought it would be. Monreale was built by the Normans, so was Mont Saint Michel; both are exactly opposite, and both are great masterpieces. The only thing common to both is that they are built on a height, presumably to flaunt them more easily before the world. One represents the strictly formal and logical aspiration of the northern mind towards God; the other shows a person basking in the rich sunshine of Sicily and thanking God for it. I said Mass in Monreale. The royal chapel in Palermo is even more beautiful and richer than Monreale, but everything else in Sicily, built less than a thousand years ago, is certainly nothing to boast about.

I forgot to tell you that in going down to Sicily, we stopped off at Salerno, and I said Mass on the tomb of Saint Matthew; of course, I offered it up for the family and for the new niece, and I also remembered Monsignor Buckey. We didn't stay in Salerno any longer than we could help. Coming back, we stopped over at Capri to break up the long trip back from Sicily. I have decided that it doesn't pay to keep well.

Speaking of saying Mass, I had a real experience in the large Jesuit church in Naples. I said Mass at the main altar, a huge pile of marble work that looks to me like the display counter for a crockery store. I had just finished the prayers at the foot of the altar, and had started up the steps, when I saw a big cat climbing around the tabernacle! Not having touched even beer, I decided that I wasn't dreaming, so I called for the sacristan who very nonchalantly chased the cat off the tabernacle. A few more such experiences and I'll be ready for anything the Archdiocese of Baltimore has to offer.

I just received Dad's letter from Indianapolis with a very fine check enclosed, much obliged. I had a big laugh out of the fact that he and Tom could go from Indiana to Chicago in three hours — the train I took from Taormina to Palermo took seven hours to cover about 160 miles!! But they do have a nice little trick for avoiding inconvenience in crossing from the island of Sicily to the mainland of Italy; the whole train is run onto the ferry, so we actually crossed the sea in a train.

At Taormina, we were amazed to find that they had just had a storm of ashes from Mount Etna; they were sweeping ashes off the street when we arrived. Another thing that we found surprising was that we were asked if we were Jewish or Aryan. They seem to be having an anti-Jewish program in Sicily; imagine a Jew with a name like Cosgrove, or Kelley, or Hannan. The war has just about ruined resorts like Taormina that depend almost entirely on English and German visitors. Only one large hotel was open, and all the large stores were shut. The American Express and Cook's haven't been open in six months. Money down here is about as scarce as hen's teeth.

There is no reason to believe that we shall come home sooner than usual, that is about the middle of July. The schools in Italy are still open and their closing would not be an indication of anything. The Italians still hope that Sumner Welles can effect some sort of reconciliation — let's hope so, but how?

Love,

Phil

May 2, 1940
Ascension Day

NORTH AMERICAN COLLEGE
Via Dell' Umilta 30

Dear Everybody,

Just time enough, I hope, to get a short note into the mail. The priests of the College had a special audience with the Pope a few days ago; it was marvelous. We were taken to the room immediately next to his private study, and he came in to see us. He whipped out of his study as though he had just popped up from his work. We all knelt, and he immediately began a little talk in English, the main thought of which was:

"Dearly beloved sons, you are going back to America, which we love so much (I remember that phrase distinctly), to labor as selfless priests for the Church; it is with this thought that we give you the Apostolic Benediction and for all those whom you include in your intention." (I included all of you.)

Then he went around the room allowing all of us to kiss his ring. At the end of that ,he took the Rector with him into his private study, and we left in a daze. Any reports about his ill health are very much unfounded. He was even more impressive this time than when we were received after Archbishop Curley's visit. The Pope's command of English is amazing; I think he prepared the little speech he gave, but even at that, he is a wonder. We all came away feeling that the climax of our four–year stay had been reached.

We attended the canonization ceremony today of the foundress of the Good Shepherd nuns and of Gemma Galgani, an Italian. I was in a very good position, because I tagged along with the fellows from the Capranica College (from which the Pope comes) and landed near the tomb of St. Peter. The illumination at night was postponed, because it rained yesterday and filled the oil cups with water; when they dry they'll have the illumination.

Soon I should start to make preparations for my first Solemn Mass at St. Matthew's. As a courtesy, I'll ask Monsignor Buckey to make all the arrangements, indicating that I should like to have Father Stricker and one of the other assistants as deacon and subdeacon. Unfortunately, I can't give any definite date because I don't know definitely when we are going home. Rumors are getting thicker over here about war (which I don't believe until it happens); and in the event that war does come, then we shall go home much quicker than I had anticipated. More of our fellows have been recalled by their nervous bishops, probably because the American newspapers are just about firing the first gun for Italy.

I am hard pressed for time these days, because of the amount of studying that has piled up, so don't think that I am sick, if you only get short notes for the next few weeks. I may try to have my examinations moved up to the end of May. In that case I shall be very busy. However, I'll write shortly to Monsignor Buckey.

Love,

Phil

May 10, 1940

NORTH AMERICAN COLLEGE
Via Dell' Umilta 30

Dear Everybody,

On Denny's birthday I said Mass for him in the catacombs of St. Sebastian; I had gone out there especially to see the inscriptions they have on the walls proving that St. Peter and St. Paul were buried there for a time. In case of a war, those catacombs would make an excellent bomb shelter; some of the passages of the catacombs are between seventy and ninety feet deep.

Rome is getting to be a very interesting place. You can just imagine how the rumors are flying around. They say (I just heard about this today, so I have no way of checking up on it yet) that the semi-official paper of the Church the <u>Osservatore Romano</u> will not be allowed to be sold in Italy. It will be possible to get it, if one goes over to the Vatican, but it won't be allowed to be sold in the newsstands. Recently the articles in the <u>Osservatore</u> have been so impartial and true that everybody has begun to subscribe to it, with the natural result that a bit of tension has grown up. A Fascist newspaper has carried some very bitter articles against the <u>Osservatore Romano</u> accusing it of being "a foreign newspaper printed in Italy." A lot of the other stuff they have to say about it is lurid; they even went so far as to accuse it of being "pro-Communistic, pro-Jewish, pro-Massonic." Of course, the English and French are taking a beating too in the newspapers. I heard that two English students were dumped in the hoosegow because they tore down some propaganda against the

English. I don't believe that story.

Of course, I should be making plans for my first Solemn Mass, but what can I do? Normally I should arrive in the U.S. about the first week in August; but now that Belgium and Holland have been invaded, there is no use trying to predict anything. There can be no question that the people in Italy would certainly hate to go to war, but I don't think that their wishes will be the deciding factor. The Pope is making a tremendous effort to do what he can to preserve peace. The Crown Prince had an audience with the Pope just about a week ago, and when the Pope visited a large Dominican Church in Rome (Santa Maria Sopra Minerva), he made a tremendous appeal for peace. He climbed the pulpit of the church and gave a rousing talk; the people in the church gave him an ovation that would still be going on if he hadn't stilled it. The Pope delivers his talks with an abundance of gestures. The occasion that took him over to the church was the crowning of St. Catherine of Siena as patron of Italy. I took some pictures of him as he passed in his car; whenever he goes out on formal occasions, he always keeps the top rolled back so that the people can see him. You can imagine what a hand he gets.

The ninth of May is a big Italian holiday, Army Day, and everyone was expecting an important statement — but nothing happened except the usual parade. Don't get nervous about us; our safe passage home is guaranteed.

Love,

Phil

May 26, 1940

NORTH AMERICAN COLLEGE
Via Dell' Umilta 30

Dear Everybody,

I hope that you have learned by now that we are scheduled to sail on June 1 aboard the S.S. Manhattan; it will probably arrive in New York on the ninth of June, unless held up by the British censors in Gibraltar.

Despite much loose talk, everything here is safe and no difficulty is anticipated in embarking. I have not been able to get all the plaques you asked for because we have not been given permission to travel in Italy; the whole college is supposed to stay in Rome until we grab the boat train. However, I have collected quite a raft of stuff, as you'll see.

Please make arrangements for the first Solemn Mass on the Sunday following the first of June – which will be the sixteenth of June. I wrote to Monsignor Buckey asking him to make arrangements, but I did not give the date of my arrival. Please tell him when I shall arrive in Washington. Tell you everything when I see you – must get this off in ten minutes, because we were just told that the air service has been resumed. Please explain why I can't write to Monsignor Buckey, telling him about the date of the first Solemn Mass on June 16.

See you later.

Love,

Phil

Comments: Letter of May 26, 1940

Practically the whole College embarked on the S.S. Manhattan, sailing from Genoa. The students, priests and seminarians slept in the main ballroom which was converted into a dormitory. The boat was completely filled with passengers. The Manhattan was tailed by a German submarine during the entire distance of the voyage, leaving us only as we entered the coastal waters of the U.S. The laws of naval warfare would have allowed the sub to seize the ship if the U.S. declared war on Germany. The passengers were not worried and the only displeasure was voiced by some passengers, "It's uncomfortable to have so many priests and seminarians on the boat, but maybe it's good insurance for safety."

As the ship passed the Statue of Liberty in the harbor of New York, all the refugees knelt on the deck in prayer, and tearfully thanked God for their deliverance and the protection of the United States.

I prayed with them, an enormous flood of thanksgiving welling up inside me for the incredible gifts that the Lord had bestowed on me – the blessings of my stay and studies in Rome, the burgeoning realization of the freedom and opportunities afforded by it through Divine Providence and the culmination of these gifts in the ineffable privilege of the priesthood of Jesus Christ. What a gift! I had the feeling that I had been given a four-year retreat in preparation for the priesthood, and now I was to begin my priestly ministry . . . . . .

"*Introibo ad altare Dei.*" ("I will go to the altar of God" — the prayer said by the priest at the beginning of Mass.)

I was also convinced that, some day, the United States would be drawn into the war; and I, who had seen some of the terrible sources of the war, would some day, by the grace of God, serve as a chaplain for our troops, preferably in combat where chaplains were needed the most.

First Solemn Mass in Washington D.C., St. Matthew's Parish (later Cathedral).

First Solemn Mass in Washington D.C., St. Matthew's Parish (later Cathedral).

Back home, family portrait; Dad, Mom and Mary in center; Back row (right to left) Jerry, Bill, Father Phil, John; Front row (right to left) Frank, Tom, Denny.

Ambassador Philips of U.S. to Italy, Amb. Kennedy of U.S. to England, and Bishop Ralph Hayes, Rector of College, on left of Amb. Kennedy.

416

Rob Mahoney (husband of Mary), Father Phil's sister Mary, and Mom.

Greeting by Pope John Paul II in front of St. Peter's, Rome.

A Catholic Chaplain in Combat Boots
An incredible story of heroism and saintly selflessness

Fr. Emil Kapaun, assigned to the 8th regiment of the 1st Cavalry Division during the Korean War, took care not only of his own men, but of all the U.S. and U.N. troops who had been taken prisoner in the infamous Camp Five.

Archbishop Philip M. Hannan, former Chaplain of the 82nd Airborne in WWII brings this astounding story to the screen for the first time ever. From inside the cauldron of battle horror, the compelling account of Fr. Kapaun's incredible heroism and saintly selflessness is documented by the courageous men who fought alongside this "Doughboy Chaplain."

Fr. Kapaun died a heroic death as a prisoner of war in Korea, May 23rd, 1951. His enormous, passionate devotion to God and to his country will forever be an inspiration to all soldiers who must fight against tremendous odds to preserve the freedom of the world.

Documentary written and produced by: Archbishop Philip M. Hannan, Former Chaplain of the 82nd Airborne in WWII.

Length: Approximately One Hour
Format: VHS
No Commercials

TO ORDER:

Focus Worldwide Network
106 Metairie Lawn Drive
Metairie, LA 70001
(504) 840 – 9898
Hours of Operation: M-F 8:00 a.m. –5:00 p.m. (Central Time)

ONLY $20.00!
Includes s/h

www.focusvideos.com

419

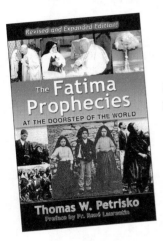